John Gutzon de la Mothe Borglum
1867-1941

Six Wars At a Time

The Life and Times of Gutzon Borglum
Sculptor of Mount Rushmore

by
**Howard Shaff and
Audrey Karl Shaff**

**with a Foreword by
Mary Ellis Borglum Vhay**

Published by
The Center for Western Studies
Augustana College, Sioux Falls, South Dakota

In cooperation with
Permelia Publishing
Darien, Connecticut
1985

Library of Congress Catalog Number 85-070296

ISBN 0-931170-27-3 Hardcover
ISBN 0-931170-26-5 Paper

First Edition March 1985
Second Printing May 1986
Third Printing September 1990

The Center for Western Studies
Augustana College, Box 727
Sioux Falls, South Dakota 57197

Permelia Publishing
Box 2254
Darien, Connecticut 06820

Fenske Printing Inc.
Rapid City, SD 57701

*Dedicated to the members of
Gutzon Borglum's crews who
have become our friends*

Contents

Authors' Note

We first saw Mount Rushmore in 1977 when, like so many others, we visited the monument on our way to Yellowstone National Park. At that time we did not intend to write this biography, but we were thrilled by the carving. So many questions had occurred that when we returned to our Connecticut home we tried to learn more about the man and his work and became swept up in the idea of writing this book.

In the course of our research we have spent endless hours in many places and have tried, to the best of our ability, to be as accurate and honest as possible. We hope this biography will not be the final word on Gutzon Borglum, but that others will explore and deal with the questions that remain unanswered.

We had some deep concerns in the handling of such issues as Gutzon's anti-Semitism and his involvement with the Ku Klux Klan. Writing about those subjects in the 1980's, we found it extremely difficult to convey that, while it was no less wrong during Gutzon's lifetime, anti-Semitism today is a far worse evil than it was before the Nazis showed the world where prejudice can lead when taken to the ultimate. We also felt a strong obligation to make sure our readers understand that the socially acceptable Klansmen of the 1920's were not the same radical, racial fanatics who exist today in the splintered organizations that carry the banner of the KKK.

In all situations we tried to present Gutzon Borglum as we saw him. In his contacts with others we tried to present the situation primarily from his point of view. But the biography must speak for itself, and you, the reader, must be the judge. We hope you enjoy meeting this most remarkable man.

Keystone, South Dakota   Howard Shaff
October 15, 1984   Audrey Karl Shaff

Acknowledgements

So many people have helped us that it is difficult to name them all. The fear of leaving someone out is very real, but we must try because we do feel a deep sense of gratitude.

First, there are the men of Rushmore, the hardrock miners who worked with Gutzon Borglum on the mountain and shared their stories with us. Second, there are the members of the family: Mary Ellis Vhay, Gutzon's daughter, became a friend and speaks for herself in the introduction; Monica Davies, Solon's daughter, was a tremendous source, who continued to help even when our views on issues did not agree; and there are other relatives who shared memories and family stories.

Then there are the librarians at the Library of Congress, the Stamford, Darien and Pequot libraries in Connecticut, the University of Illinois, Emory University, the University of Nevada, the University of South Dakota, the Newberry Library at the University of Chicago, Dakota Wesleyan University, Black Hills State College, and Augustana College. We received help from the historical societies of Newark, Los Angeles, New York City, Stamford, Atlanta, and Pierre, the staff of the Los Angeles County Clerk's office and their counterparts in Chicago and from our many friends in Omaha, Los Angeles, San Francisco, Atlanta, Rapid City, Mitchell, Sioux Falls, Vermillion, Chicago, Salt Lake City, Reno, San Antonio, Longview, Ingram, Washington, Boston and New York.

Richard Jensen and the staff of the Historical Department of the Church of the Latter-Day Saints shared research material with us, and we are extremely grateful that Richard was willing to share his insights.

We owe a special thanks to Dr. Duane Pankratz of Freeman, South Dakota, founder of the Rushmore-Borglum Story and our good friend. Without his support and encouragement this book might not have been possible.

And finally, to Dr. Sven Froiland, Director of the Center for Western Studies, at Augustana College, Sioux Falls, South Dakota, for becoming a part of this project and to our editor, Harry Thompson, for making coherent sentences out of what were at times rambling thoughts and in every way making this biography a better book.

We thank you all.

The Center For Western Studies

The Center for Western Studies is a cultural museum and a study and research agency of Augustana College, Sioux Falls, South Dakota, concerned principally with South Dakota and the adjoining states, the Prairie Plains, and with certain aspects of the Great Plains and the Trans-Mississippi West.

The Center serves as a resource for teachers, research scholars, students and the general public, through which studies, research projects and related activities are initiated and conducted, and by which assistance can be provided awareness of the multifaceted culture of this area, with special emphasis on Dakota (Sioux) Indian Culture.

The Center was founded in the conviction that this region possesses a unique and important heritage which should not be lost or forgotten. Consequently, the Center for Western Studies seeks to provide services to assist researchers in their study of the region, to promote a public consciousness of the importance of preserving cultural and historical resources, to collect published and unpublished materials, art and artifacts, important to the understanding of the region, and to undertake and sponsor projects, to sponsor conferences and provide permanent displays and shows which reflect the art and culture of the West, particularly the Sioux.

The Center maintains an archives and possesses one of the finest collections available of books relating to all aspects of the American West. The Center continually seeks to expand its collections in order to provide maximum assistance to interested scholars, students at all levels, and the general public. The collections include excellent representative Sioux Indian art, bead and quill work, Western art consisting of original oils, water colors, bronzes, photographs, and steel engravings.

Foreword

The ensuing biography has been painstakingly researched and documented. It is the factual story of an extraordinary man.

This introduction is based on my memory of the same man from my viewpoint. From any angle, he was a remarkable person. His family were immigrants from Denmark seeking religious freedom in America. Possibly that seeking for freedom was in his veins, as his life was spent seeking new challenges in an effort to better and beautify the world.

As time goes, we were not together very long. I came late in his life and he died early in mine. Mother gave me to him for a birthday present.

He was not a tall man; his shoulders were broad, his build stocky. I remember he always wore a hat, out of doors, to cover his baldness. His bigness and presence came from within, generated by an energy that was inexhaustible. His mind was overflowing with ideas to better whatever was at hand, with a scope that covered the world from sculpture to political planning, aviation, flood control to horse racing. He believed so strongly in his concepts that he was frustrated and amazed if they did not reach fruition. His doctrine was simple and straight forward — good would overcome evil. Considering that much of his life was a crusade against mediocrity and stupidity, it is hard to understand how he met his personal disappointment while keeping such optimism for the future.

He gave my brother and me the priceless gift of a childhood free of restriction, other than the restrictions imposed upon us by our own mental and physical ability. He acquired a trout stream in Connecticut, close to New York, surrounded by 500 acres, calling it Borgland. It gave us such confidence and feeling of place, we were not overwhelmed by the following nomadic period of our lives.

The loss of Stone Mountain Memorial was a turning point in all our lives. He couldn't go back to his old habitats; he needed to be separated from New York. His friend, the Governor of North Carolina, gave him a studio in which to work and there he lived for almost a year.

For my father it was a time to "Stoop and rebuild with worn out tools . . . if you can force your heart and nerve and sinew . . . to serve your turn long after they are gone." For my mother, a test of devotion and inspiration for my father to lean upon. Soon he was off to meet new challenges, to carry his precious family, and we were always very precious to him, to a fuller life. Borgland was never again the hub of our existence although we returned again and again. My mother lived there after my father's death.

As a family, we relied heavily upon each other for emotional support. That reliance never changed through the years. Long after both Mother and Father had died, my brother and I gave each other the same unstinting devotion.

The Rushmore years were the most difficult for my father. From the onset, the mountain work was besieged by money problems. He was subject to severe headaches, his heart was weakening, and the long years of working in wet clay activated arthritis. There was still so much he was planning to do. The continuing disputes at Rushmore became more involved as the spider web of government bureaucracy became more restrictive.

When my mother was hospitalized with pneumonia, he was childlike in his fear of losing his beloved "Mary."

His optimism faltered as problems increased to a point that his creative ability was put in question by petty officials.

His letters to me are among my treasured possessions. I would like to quote one I received when affairs at Rushmore were at their most critical point:

My dear baby Girl,
Your letter — birthday just received. I don't know why my letter should make tears — except of hope and confidence, and I guess that's tearful on the gay side. Life has been one long struggle for a morrow that never came beyond just a hint of what it might be, if it wanted to be nice. I haven't any interest in heroics except they represent the best we can do. It's a little hard not to put off being our best because it requires a little something more than average and it requires purpose and so few people have any purpose that involves more than a day's interest. Life is a kind of campaign. It means plans, purpose, resolution and maybe fight; and people have no idea what strength comes to one's soul and spirit through a good fight. Fighting has always meant physical combat, which is all wrong; nothing comes of that but blood and bruises. I mean the fight of propagating plans that extend through several weeks — several years — then if you've built a road for your Spiritual engine let it round itself into a life. Life is a drifting thing caught in passion, calm, disease or death unless organized to one's abilities; and our abilities create our hunger and our need for action. These conditions

are hard to understand, hard to administer but that must not be an excuse for not trying to find, direct and master them as soon as possible. Put that underfoot and you are well shod; the very ground under you becomes yours.

Since writing the above, the sky has cleared a little — I'm not worrying. Theodore Roosevelt once said to me "I can lick the world with one friend and God on my side."

My love to you always, my baby.

Dad

He did win that fight. Congress and the president supported him by lifting onerous red tape and rewarding his flagging optimism with a new contract to complete the four heads he had created.

To me, both Gutzon and Mary were exceptional people, perfectly mated. They shared a complicated life with vigor and humor. They met triumph and disaster with equal grace. They gave me so much, including the will to succeed and the strength to cope. I can only thank them for the privilege of being part of the great adventure both he and she made of living.

Mary Ellis Borglum Vhay
August 27, 1984

Prologue

John Gutzon de la Mothe Borglum had spent sixty years preparing for this moment. His dream of creating "a monument as large and as grand as America herself" was about to become a reality. He raised his jackhammer and rested the four-pointed chisel solidly on the rock called Rushmore. Despite his age, he felt young and strong as he took a deep breath and drove the vibrating steel into the granite. He wiped his forehead on his sleeve. Moving his feet along the vertical surface of the rock he braced himself against the leather harness that held him securely in the bosun's seat and then paused to change bits before drilling the next hole. As he did, he looked down at the crowd hundreds of feet below.

From where the spectators gathered, Borglum seemed little more than a human fly darting across the granite wall on a spiderweb strand of steel. Even to the jaded he was quite a sight. Watching a man work in such a precarious position was a thrill and they applauded with enthusiasm. The crowd was large, especially for the sparsely populated Black Hills of South Dakota. Many had come simply to see a show on a beautiful summer day. Others came to catch a glimpse of President Calvin Coolidge. They sensed that history was being made and wanted to be a part of it. Some were skeptical. They thought the whole idea of carving a mountain was absurd and that Borglum was just another fancy eastern dude who had come to fleece them. There was some opposition from a small, vocal group outraged by the idea of men tampering with the natural beauty of the Black Hills, the Paha Sapa, the mystic holy land of the once-mighty Sioux. Many others were counting the tourist dollars that were sure to come their way, but most of the crowd were simply pleased with the beautiful day, the festivities and the project.

At the foot of Mount Rushmore, state and local officials shared the speaker's platform with the president. Smiling, they tried to get into position to be photographed with "Silent Cal," but the president ignored them. He was too busy with the children lined up in front of the platform waiting solemnly to shake his hand. Cal was wearing his usual

1

single-breasted suit of sturdy New England tweed, but for the occasion he had added cowboy boots and a huge ten gallon hat, which kept falling over his eyes. It was difficult to tell what was in the president's mind. The day before he had made his famous "I do not choose to run for president in 1928" statement. Most political observers found it hard to believe he meant what he said, even though Coolidge rarely joked about anything.

The president had seemed bored and ill at ease until Borglum appeared at the top of the mountain. Then Coolidge became totally absorbed. He settled into his seat, hiked up his pants leg to reveal the fancy tooling on his boot, folded his arms across his chest and watched the descending figure so intently that at times he seemed to be holding his breath.

Borglum drilled the second hole, then moved on to drill two more. When he finished, the four master points for the gigantic portrait of George Washington were set in the ageless granite. The carving of Mount Rushmore had officially begun. The date was August 10, 1927.

Joining the official party on the speaker's platform, Borglum shook hands with the president and waved his hat to the cheering crowd. He accepted Coolidge's congratulations and presented the president with the jackhammer bit used to drill the first hole. He gave the second bit to South Dakota Senator Peter Norbeck, the driving force behind the project and the third to the man who thought up the idea of a Black Hills carving, Doane Robinson, South Dakota State Historian. The fourth bit he kept for himself.

August 10, 1927, was both a beginning and an end. It was the culmination of a journey that began in Denmark in 1839 with the birth of Jens Moeller Haugaard Borglum, father of Gutzon Borglum.[1] Jens was a Mormon convert who had come to the United States in 1864 and had settled in a primitive village in Idaho. In 1866 he took his wife's sister as his second wife, and in 1867 she gave birth to John Gutzon de la Mothe Borglum.

Even as a child, Gutzon possessed a facile mind. He was strong-willed and opinionated. The only truth in his eyes was what he believed, and even that was subject to change at any time. Throughout his life Gutzon considered only his own point of view valid, and he never quite understood why others did not accept that fact without question. He was disliked by some, loved by others and admired by almost everyone who knew him. Supreme Court Justice Felix Frankfurter, his friend, often spoke of Gutzon's wit and fervor and told stories about the Borglum

2

ability to hold an audience spellbound. He knew Gutzon was a self-proclaimed anti-Semite but saw his prejudice more as a facet of a complex personality than as a fatal flaw. Like so many of Borglum's friends, he was willing to accept the man on his own terms, especially in sensitive, social areas where Gutzon's actions did not necessarily match his words. Recalling their early days. Frankfurter wrote, "Gutzon was for war, all sorts of war, six wars at a time."[2] Frankfurter made it clear that he would not have had his friend be any other way.

Gutzon attempted to write his autobiography many times. The attempts have survived in bits and pieces, which, unfortunately, have no coherence beyond the title, *The One Man War*.[3] The title was chosen long before the first word was written, and it is as much of a personal statement as the book itself would have been. It was Borglum's way of recognizing that, if life were stripped of all pretense and complication, reduced to a single factor, that factor would be conflict. So many of his battles were the result of his own actions that it is difficult not to conclude that in some instances he created problems because he thrived on controversy.

In his journal, Borglum summed up his early years by writing, "I marvel at my nature, strange and complex as it is. I, who at ten ran from mother and father rather than submit to oppression, fought against trammels of all sorts, ran away again at 14, again at 16 and 18, all through my teens continued to fight. Married early in my twenties and from then on made forebearance a business. . . ."[4]

This is a dramatic, but fair, assessment of how he saw himself. It also provides an insight into the complex relationship he shared with his father, while giving no hint of the fantasy world he wove about his mother. The woman referred to as "mother" was actually his Aunt Ida, the first wife. His real mother, Christina, left the family when he was four. Her departure had a traumatic effect on Borglum's life, though he rarely admitted that even to himself.

As he grew older and became a public figure, Gutzon also became a vocal critic of public policy, and he gave advice to everyone — those who would listen and those who would not. His insights, particularly his predictions about the future, bordered on the clairvoyant, but usually his manner prevented his advice from being taken seriously. He was often so caustic in his attacks that few could see beyond the sting of his words, unless he wanted them to.

Borglum, an intelligent and charming man, could, if he so desired, talk anyone into anything. His physical presence attracted people, particularly women, and he seldom walked into a room without being noticed. Forty years after his death, his daughter, Mary Ellis, said, "all the women loved daddy."[5] Borglum loved to box, fence, fish, hunt and ride horses. He loved a joke and a good cigar and could tell a story with the best. But he also had a perverse side that often made him reject the very people who were trying most to help him.

He frequently railed against the financiers and bankers who were his patrons and advisors. "Parasites," he called them.[6] He saw them as a non-productive class and wondered why any society would allow them to exist. He said they sapped a society's lifeblood and vitality to serve their own greedy needs. All bankers were bad, as far as Borglum was concerned, but the worst were the Jewish bankers of New York with their European heritage, Wall Street connections and insatiable capacity for evil.

Borglum believed what he preached and carried his message wherever he went. He seemed to be in an endless fight, declaring a truce only when a commission was at stake or a personal relationship took him beyond the issue. Most of the men who were his enemies in theory were his friends in practice. They were the people he went to when he needed to borrow money or obtain support for a project. They bought his art, defended him, gave him advice and entertained him at their estates. Jacob Schiff, Bernard Baruch, Paul Warburg, Samuel Colt and Eugene Meyer were just a few of the Jewish businessmen who were his friends and patrons.

Eugene Meyer's experience was typical. In 1907 he purchased Borglum's magnificent marble portrait of Lincoln and presented it to Congress. A few years later he lent Borglum the money to buy his Connecticut estate with the understanding that he would receive monthly payments on the note. When Meyer had not received a payment for seven years, he became impatient and wrote a strong letter demanding a settlement of the debt. As a result, a new note was signed at a higher rate of interest and the two became bitter enemies. They exchanged harsh letters for the next twenty years as Meyer tried, unsuccessfully, to collect what was owed him.[7]

Meyer's dunning letters continued until Borglum's death. Then, after the estate was probated and the sad story of Mary Borglum's affairs became known to her friends, a committee was formed to help her. The committee contacted Meyer to ask what could be done, and he answered, "Now that he's no longer around to falsely accuse everyone and hurt the feelings of anyone who tries to help him I'm sure we can come to terms."[8] Meyer was not angry at Borglum. He was hurt, and he proved

4

that by forgiving forty years of accumulated interest and settling for the principal.

With Sam Colt there was a similar problem; only in his case he was the one who died. When Borglum needed money in 1915, he gave Colt three of his marble statues as collateral for a loan. In the twenties Borglum decided he wanted to reclaim his works, but the executor of the Colt estate refused to acknowledge his claim. No records existed to prove that the transaction had been anything but an outright sale, and the executor would not accept Borglum's word. He was furious. He wrote an angry letter denouncing people "who make nothing but money . . . contribute nothing to society . . . take the soul of an artist and give him only dollars in return."[9]

Until he was well into his thirties, Gutzon was a private person, who shared only his art with the public. It was not until his first marriage ended and he had settled in New York City that he became interested in politics, aviation and world affairs. But once his name appeared in print, he became a crusader looking for a cause, as this statement by Borglum indicates:

My monumental work occupies but a small part of my time. America is in such a formative state that it is impossible for one so temperamental as I am to sit silently by and see commercialism and self interest corrupt good taste. So I find myself, too often and too much for my comfort, in the very midst of quarrels that seem only remotely connected with art. I am obliged to write and to speak a great deal, and I hope that out of it all I may be no less a man and a human being, and if that be so, so much better an artist.[10]

Life, as Gutzon lived it, was a struggle full of complications. His dream of creating a memorial to the South on the granite of Stone Mountain in Georgia came apart because he could not resist becoming involved with the Ku Klux Klan. Instead of staying within the boundaries his art provided, he tried to reach beyond and mold the Klan into an effective political force.

The image of the hooded Klansman is a familiar one. Since the early thirties he has been seen as a bigot out of step with his times. By then the KKK had become a fringe group so few in number that it was not taken seriously, but that was not the case in the early twenties.

In 1922, when Gutzon's friend D. C. Stephenson was installed as the Grand Dragon of the Northern Realm, 200,000 robed and hooded Klansmen gathered in Kokomo, Indiana, to witness the ceremony.[11] For Stephenson it was to be the first step in a journey that would lead him

5

to the White House, with Gutzon acting as one of his most trusted advisors. Their plan was to organize the KKK into an agrarian party, by-pass the big city bankers, and win on their own terms.[12] They might have succeeded had it not been for other KKK leaders who were equally ambitious, very corrupt and strongly opposed to Stephenson.

As an artist concerned with the creation of his monument on Stone Mountain, Gutzon should have sensed the inherent danger and stayed clear of Klan involvement, but he could not. He gambled and lost, and the result was the destruction of his work.

The only positive result of the Stone Mountain fiasco was the lesson learned by Gutzon and the South Dakotans involved in the Mount Rushmore project. Despite their many disputes, one or the other always backed off before a point of no return was reached.

Paradoxes and contradictions were a part of Gutzon's nature. He fought with Woodrow Wilson and accused the president of covering up the billion dollar aircraft scandal during World War One. Yet he later accepted a commission from the Polish government and created a memorial in Wilson's honor. When Hitler began persecuting the Jews in the manner Gutzon had been advocating for years, he was outraged. Gutzon told the press that no civilized society can stand idly by and allow such barbaric laws to be practiced, and no one thought it odd that his sense of humanity proved stronger than his prejudice.

Once he had declared himself, he became outspoken in his criticism of the Nazis, and because he was so flamboyant newsmen reported everything he said. Hitler heard Gutzon's words, but did not respond until his storm troopers overran Poland in 1939. He then called a press conference and announced the he had ordered the Wilson Memorial destroyed. "The Third Reich," Hitler stormed, "can not tolerate such poor art. The artist made the head too big, the legs too short, the . . . ."[13]

When Gutzon started carving mountains, first in Georgia and then in South Dakota, he believed America's millionaires would fight for the honor of financing his projects. He could not see how they could resist, but as with so many other aspects of his life this was just another example of his inability to separate his own viewpoint from the facts. He promised to raise large sums so often that it became a constant source of irritation to the committees that were trying to work with him and almost destroyed his credibility.

Three years after he had been run out of Georgia by a posse, Gutzon was still enthusiastic. He told a friend connected with the Georgia monument that if the committee brought him back to complete the work he could raise five million dollars in thirty days.[14] This was an incredible statement to make at a time when the work at Mount Rushmore was stalled for lack of funds. Even Senator Norbeck, the project's strongest supporter, was discouraged. "Gutzon," he wrote, "the fact that neither you nor I have been able to raise a dime for the past year is making everyone doubt us. We are beginning to look like fools,"[15] Still, Gutzon refused to believe those with money would not see the grandeur of the plans forming in his mind, and he continued to make promises that could not be kept.

Gutzon was truly a product of his times. Born in a log cabin on America's frontier, he transcended his humble beginnings and lack of education, and became the archetypical American. Without question he left his mark. Future generations, for thousands of years, will know him if only because of the portraits on the mountain.

Gutzon was proud of his roots. He said in 1912, "I am convinced," "that whatever is good in my art came from my mother and the old Danish race to which she belonged, but whatever gives my art strength, which makes it prevail here, comes from the courage imparted by the west."[16]

But who was "mother?" She was woman. She was love, gentleness, patience, even if she were only an image in his mind. Father was another matter. Gutzon's relationship with his father was his first war, and the doctor was a tough opponent. He taught Gutzon and his other children to be fiercely independent. He taught them to be proud of who they were. He instilled a yearning for knowledge and introduced them to the philosophers. Jens Borglum was stubborn and intelligent. He did what he thought was right and adhered to his principles. He often chose the hard road and paid the consequences for his acts. He endured the ridicule of his family and countrymen when he became a Mormon and accepted the Church's scorn when he decided it was time to move on, and he never stopped searching for the mystical truth. He began that search when he became disenchanted with the state religion in Denmark and joined the Church of the Latter-Day Saints at the age of seventeen. His father's search for truth formed the bedrock of the character of Gutzon Borglum.

Dr. James M. Borglum,
father of Gutzon Borglum

Ida Michelson Borglum,
first wife of Dr. James Borglum

Christina Michelson Borglum,
wife of Dr. James Borglum, sister
of Ida, mother of Gutzon and
Solon.

8

1
The New Jerusalem

The first Borglum to fall under the spell of the Mormon missionaries in Denmark was Maren, Jens Borglum's sister.[1] She was converted, baptized and then all but disowned by her angry parents, but that did not prevent her from bringing the message to her brother. A year later Jens became an eager convert, and he set his sights on the promise of life in the "New Jerusalem." He left his position as a carpenter's apprentice to become a missionary among his people. He had been chosen primarily because of his willingness to accept hardships.

With no income and no future other than the hope provided by his new faith, he walked from village to village preaching the gospel, despite the constant physical danger. Mormon missionaries were often harassed by angry mobs and threatened with arrest by officials who saw them as a threat to the established order. To support himself Jens sold LDS tracts and depended on the charity of those who looked to him for spiritual guidance. It was a meager existence at best. He slept more in fields and barns than he did in beds, but he was young, strong and healthy and willing to put up with anything.

Jens was looking to the time when the test of his faith would be behind him and he would be called to "Joseph's Land," the New Jerusalem by the great salt sea in America. There, he thought, he would take his rightful place, serve the people and rise to new challenges.

The future seemed bright for Jens Borglum. At the very beginning his talents were recognized. He had been made a deacon after five months and a priest in less than a year. He was given more and more responsibility as he rose through the ranks. He prepared many for the journey, but for some inexplicable reason his call did not come. Jens became deeply disappointed as he watched others, seemingly less worthy, start on their journey, but he continued to serve, convincing himself that the wait was a test of faith.

When his call finally came it was anti-climactic and Jens knew that better than anyone. He was not being called to a bright new future in America or even to a place in the Church. His call was a matter of political expedience. Denmark and Germany were at war over the provinces of Schleswig and Holstien, and the Danes were losing. Rather than have their young men drafted into the Danish army, the Mormons decided to bring them to America. Jens was one of those who received hurried orders to leave.

Despite the high offices he had held, Jens was not given even a lowly position during the journey. It was almost as if the Church were saying, "We are paying our debt to you by bringing you to America, but do not expect anything beyond that."

The message was not lost on Jens, but he had little choice. The moment he had been converted he had, for all practical purposes, given up his Danish citizenship and become a citizen of the New Jerusalem. For men like him there was no turning back, especially when the only other choice was fighting an unpopular war on the losing side.

On April 3, 1864, Jens left Copenhagen for the English coast with several hundred others. Three days later, after a dreadful trip across the North Sea and a long train ride through Germany, they reached Liverpool. Three weeks later, on April 26, they assembled on the dock alongside the *Monarch of the Sea*, an old sailing vessel that was barely adequate for the nine hundred Saints waiting to board. Before boarding they were divided into groups of one hundred, and then these groups were divided into groups of ten, who went up the gangplank together to sign the manifest and receive a quarters assignment.

As was the custom, families were settled in the large center section, bachelors in the rear hold and single females in the front compartments. With the right mix this worked fine, and when it did not there was a simple solution. The leaders created as many new families as were needed by ordering the engaged couples, who were waiting to wed in Salt Lake City, to marry in a mass ceremony and by pairing enough others to eliminate the crowding. That was the way Jens Borglum and Ida Mikklesen (later changed to Michelson) were married. They had known each other for several years. Ida's brother, Christian, a missionary with Jens, had often brought him home, but there is nothing to indicate that Jens and Ida were more than casual friends before they were married on the night of April 27, 1864.

The next morning the ship was towed down the North Channel and out into the open sea. Thirty-four days later, after a journey plagued by rough seas, they landed in New York. To celebrate, Jens changed his name to James, and Ida's ten year old brother, Lave, who was with them became Johnnie. As with most Mormons they were quickly passed through immigration at Castle Gardens and sent on their way.

They travelled as a group by river boats and trains until they reached the frontier at the town of Wyoming, Nebraska, several weeks later. The New Jerusalem was still 1100 miles away, but in Wyoming, Nebraska, for the first time since they left their homeland, they were on their own. The Church had brought them that far. To get to "Joseph's Land" from the camp, they had to make their own arrangements. The only way to reach Salt Lake was by joining one of the freight-carrying wagon trains and walking alongside the ox-drawn carts, but that was expensive and James and Ida had no money.

They were forced to borrow $168 from the Church's Perpetual Emigrating Fund and then wait for space on the first wagon train that would take them. The walk, which took ten weeks, is described in the journal of a fourteen-year-old woman who walked with them:

> The first of the country was the rolling plains of Nebraska which were covered with . . . buffalo grass. The road was crude, just a rutty, dusty, winding, seemingly endless pair of ruts through which those before us had labored. . . . When we reached the Platte the prospects of fording the river were appalling. . . . Those who went first usually had the chance to dry their clothes properly and the agony of fear was not so long-lived. . . . In the first ford the entire oxen and the wagon were lost. The driver barely escaped with his life . . . sudden rainstorms often fell on the weary travellers, drenching them and turning the road into a sea of mud that was sticky as glue. . . . It was grueling work to get through. Every morning the travelers rose early, women to prepare breakfast, wash dishes, pack for the march, while the men yoked the oxen . . . every spiral of smoke away from the camp, every sound, every cloud of dust meant a potential enemy — the Indians or a possibile buffalo stampede. At night . . . a few miles more westward, we gathered around the campfire for . . . services and songs before climbing wearily into makeshift beds. . . .[2]

On September 15 they reached Salt Lake City with little more than their youth, spirit and determination. Ida and James were allowed to remain with the empty wagons, which were left in the town square, while James searched for work and living quarters. James took any work that was available. He was employed as a carpenter on the Tabernacle and other buildings in the rapidly growing city. He worked in one of Brigham Young's knitting mills during the winter of 1865, probably because it was too cold to build.

A few weeks after their arrival (and after James had earned some money), they found two small rooms and set up housekeeping. In March 1865, Ida gave birth to their first son, Miller, the first Borglum to be born in America. In November, after a terrible journey during which their ship almost sank in a storm, their wagon train was attacked by Indians and the whole party was almost trapped by an early snow in the mountains, Maren and her husband reached Salt Lake City. They were accompanied by Ida's younger sister, Christina. All three moved in with James and Ida until they could find other quarters.

Seventeen days later Christina, James and Ida went to the Endowment House, where they were united in marriage "for time and eternity." Shortly afterwards, the Church offered James a chance to take his family north to help start a new settlement. It meant going into the wilderness as a pioneer, but it also meant there might be a bright future if the venture were successful.

Feeling it was worth the chance, the Borglums went to the Bear Lake Stake, in Ovid, Idaho. James built a crude, two-room log cabin and tried to become a farmer in a rugged land. He had plenty of timber for fuel and construction and fertile soil for his crop, but the settlement was so far north that it was almost impossible to make anything grow. They could not produce a decent crop in the short season and found it equally difficult to endure the long, bitter winters.

Confrontations with American Indians also caused trouble for the settlers. The Mormons did not fight Indians unless their lives were threatened. Brigham Young had decided, when he first brought his people to the territory, that it would be wiser to feed them than fight a constant battle, but Indians were not always inclined to accept Mormon charity. The problem was not serious in the more established communities, but in the outlying settlements it was a cause for concern.

Log Cabin at Bear Lake Stake, Ovid, Idaho, in which Gutzon was born.

In 1866 the settlers in the Bear Lake Stake were forced to spend much of the winter inside the log fort they had built for protection. In that same year their crops were destroyed by grasshoppers and an early frost. It soon became obvious to James that there was no future for him in Bear Lake Stake, but he could not leave. Both his wives were pregnant; there were no prospects of work elsewhere and no money to spend looking. Until his situation improved, James's only choice was to continue to take what he could from his land.

On March 17, 1867, Christina gave birth to a son, John Gutzon de la Mothe Borglum. A month later Ida gave birth to her second boy, Auguste. The two-room cabin was rapidly becoming too small for the growing family, and life was becoming harder and harder. Under these adverse conditions, tempers were becoming short, as one Borglum biographer observed:

> In this wholly new relationship [polygamy], whose emotional pressures could not possibly have been foreseen, there developed an incompatibility between the sisters which was not conducive to happiness and domestic peace.[3]

When James learned that work was available with the railroad in Ogden, Utah, he felt he had found at least a temporary solution to his problems. Leaving Ida and her brother, Johnnie, in Ovid with her sons, he took Christina and Gutzon to Ogden. For Gutzon, it was the beginning of a lifetime of moving, of shifting from city to city, sometimes staying years, but never really sinking roots. Most of his moves as an adult were for good reasons. There were mountains to carve and commissions that demanded his presence, but there were times when he seemed to be pushed by the restless spirit he inherited from James.

James was the sort of man who sensed the existence of something beyond himself. From the moment he became disillusioned with the Mormon teachings until his death many years later, he never stopped searching. At different periods in his life he was a Protestant, a Mormon, a Catholic and a Theosophist.

Gutzon followed a similar path, seeking his answers in his art, politics and civic involvement. Neither father nor son ever found what he sought, but the need to continue to search had much to do with shaping Gutzon's character.

The move to Ogden worked out well. The railroad was approaching Utah from east and west. Crews were being hired to lay track. Warehouses and shops were being built, stores were opening and speculators were flocking to the area in the hope of striking it rich, but the Mormons had everything under control.

Brigham Young had waited too long and planned too carefully to have his plans upset by outsiders. His campaign to bring the railroad to Mormon territory had begun in 1854, when he wrote Senator Stephen Douglas:

> Friend Douglas . . . What are you going to do about a railroad to the Pacific? . . . You need not be sly in expressing your views. . . . For rest assured that whatever route the road takes it will be in the very best interests of Utah and precisely where we had rather had it.[4]

There seems no doubt that Young, even at that early date, knew that the railroad would help solve his problem if the territory attracted too few or too many people.

With work and good wages, James was able to buy a small plot of land and a house in Ogden for himself, Christina and Gutzon. With Ida and the others in Ovid, family life became calmer and he may have given some thought to living that way, with a family in each place, but he was still unhappy. His disappointment with the Church, primarily because of his lack of an official position, continued to plague him.

He wanted to leave but could not. He, Ida and Christina had walked to the Mormon territory as tough, young pioneers. They were all still young and tough, but with three small sons and both women pregnant again they could hardly walk back the thousand miles. Like so many others who had become disenchanted with the LDS, James knew the railroad was his only hope.

Preparing for the railroad's arrival, James settled his affairs in Ovid and moved Ida and the children to Ogden. Once again they were all together in a hectic household, but events were moving so rapidly they had little time to dwell on their situation.

In May, when Gutzon was two, the golden spike was driven into place at Promontory Point, Utah, and the dream of a transcontinental railroad was a reality. In December Christina gave birth to her second son, Solon Hannibal Borglum, and six months later Ida's third son, Arnold, was born. Now the Borglums were free to leave. James sold his holdings in Ogden and bought railroad tickets for Omaha. It was an exciting, but sad, time for James. He was abandoning a belief to which he had given total devotion for more than twelve years. He was not certain he was doing right for himself, his family or the Church, but he believed he was doing the only thing possible under the circumstances.

14

The Borglums chose Omaha because Ida and Christina had family there. They knew they would need help. Polygamy would not be condoned in Omaha, or any city outside the Mormon territory, and was a criminal offense under federal law. They had no idea of how they would deal with the situation. Still they boarded the train and took themselves beyond the influence and protection of the Church.

This was truly the beginning of their immigration. For the first time since their conversion, their lives were completely in their own hands. They were on the move with no agents to make arrangements, no group to travel with, no elders or bishops to tell them what to do. After twelve years such freedom was both exhilarating and frightening.

2

Omaha

Omaha in the winter of 1870 was a bustling, thriving metropolis. It had passed beyond the frontier-town stage with the coming of the railroad. The merchants had quickly established themselves as the civic leaders, but they could not stop a large group of adventurers, fortune-seekers and hangers-on from making the city their home.

There is no record of how the Borglums survived or what work James found to support the family for the first few months while he searched for something on which he could build a future. His chance came when he met a homeopathic physician named H. H. Sisson. Dr. Sisson, a Civil War veteran, befriended James and suggested he think about becoming a doctor. The idea inspired James. He seized the opportunity feeling he had found his true vocation. Homeopathic medicine was a way of ministering to people. That was what he longed to do, but before he could think about taking a medical school entrance examination there was much he had to learn. Dr. Sisson helped him study, lent him textbooks and probably money, and prepared James for the Missouri Medical College in St. Louis.

At thirty James had finally found his vocation and he was thrilled, but that did not relieve his concern about his family and their dangerous situation. The national outcry against polygamy was reaching a fever pitch. The press and politicians were damning the disgrace and demanding action. Federal marshals with warrants issued by federal judges were invading even Mormon territory and giving polygamists a choice: renounce their plural marriage or go to jail.

Despite the danger, the Borglums tried to stay together. When the United States census was taken in the summer of 1870, they were all living in the same household. To avoid prosecution they registered Christina as Christina Michelson, a domestic. Gutzon and Solon were listed as her sons with no mention of who their father was. The other children were listed as Borglums, and James and Ida as husband and wife. The fact that they had to resort to such an elaborate subterfuge made it obvious they could not remain together much longer.

The break came when James was ready to begin his medical studies in St. Louis in 1871. He took Ida, her newborn daughter and the five boys with him. Christina stayed behind. Barely out of her teens, Christina had to make a life for herself.

The decision to leave Gutzon and Solon with James and Ida was the only logical choice, but that did not make it any less difficult. Gutzon was old enough to know he was losing his mother and he was devastated. He became an angry, rebellious child who remained angry for most of his adult life. Recalling this event Gutzon wrote:

> Not many years after Solon was born she left us. I was five. She turned to me as she lay ill. There were tears in her eyes and she was trembling as she took my hand . . . and she told me to take care of little Solon . . . I never forgot it, but I wondered why. I thought she was going to stay with us. She and father had always been with us. I could not understand. . . .[1]

The implication is that his mother died, though the words are ambiguous enough to allow for other interpretations. Combined with some of Gutzon's other writings, this account becomes a story of a little boy left alone in a cruel world. Gutzon expressed these feelings many years after his mother had left. They reflect the fact that even as an adult he could not accept her leaving him and making another life without him. As a result, in almost every account of Gutzon's life, Christina is shrouded in mystery from the time she left the family.

Christina was gone, but James and Ida knew where she was and what was happening to her. Whether Gutzon, Solon, or the other children also knew is hard to say. All of them, with the exception of Gutzon, respected James's wishes and did not speak about their past. When Gutzon did, his stories were fanciful and were not necessarily reliable. They came as much from his vivid imagination as from his memory. There is a strong possibility that he knew or thought he knew where she was and that he became a chronic runaway trying to rejoin her. Christina was certainly the subject of Gutzon's childhood fantasies and later a central theme in his philosophical sculptures.

Christina left Omaha and moved to Chicago shortly after James and the family went to St. Louis. She married a man named Harry Wilson, had three more children and eventually moved to Los Angeles. There are strong indications in her sketchy history that she was widowed before she went west. Los Angeles County records contain information about her children, but nothing about her husband. Evidence also suggests that, shortly after Christina moved to Los Angeles, James spent several months there with her and then decided to bring out the whole family, perhaps so they could all be together again.

The facts are difficult to establish because the oldest children were sworn to secrecy by James, and none of the Borglums ever spoke about their Mormon past. The four children born after Christina departed grew up knowing her as Aunt Tina, their mother's younger sister. They might never have learned the truth if Gutzon and Solon had not become so famous that the world wanted to know about them. In 1900, when Solon's work was acclaimed at the Paris Exposition, he wrote home asking James what he should tell reporters. His father's answer was simple and direct: ". . . the world . . . does not need to become acquainted with the particulars of our life. It is not their business and they don't care. . . ."[2]

The Borglum brothers: Miller, the oldest, is in the center; Gutzon is to his right, with Auguste, Francis and Solon in the front (left to right).

19

But they did care, not only about Solon and Gutzon, but also about Auguste, the brother who earned a fine reputation as a musician. So the questions were asked and when they could not be ignored, wild stories, designed to hide the facts and confuse the issue, were fabricated by members of the family, none of whom were more adroit at telling tales than Gutzon. In one of the notes he wrote and put aside for the day he would find time to write his autobiography, he gave this description of his father:

> James de la Mothe Borglum at 23 a Latin and Greek scholar in his last year as a medical student. He took passage with his sweetheart . . . they were married in London . . . . The honeymooners lingered a day or two in New York . . . . The team boss had died. James . . . an able doctor and popular with the people was chosen to converse with some visiting Indians. One of them asked to examine Borglum's pistol and shot himself . . . . The Chief blamed the white spokesman. . . .[3]

In the same note Gutzon mentions his mother, but not by name:

> By the time I was seven I knew what it meant not to have a mother of my own. I didn't want to stay around things that reminded me of her anymore. So I ran away. . . .[4]

His mother had died, and when his father remarried, a cruel stepmother took her place. Sometimes the first wife was named Christina and sometimes Ida. The only consistent fact was that the stepmother was responsible for his being an unhappy, brooding child. Gutzon told this or a similar story so often that it appears he was trying more to convince himself than anyone else.

James graduated from medical school as a homeopathic physician in 1874 and returned to Omaha to open an office. A few months later he exchanged practices with Dr. W. J. Earhart of Fremont, Nebraska. Fremont was a much smaller town, closer to the frontier and more to James's liking.

In one of his journals, Gutzon tells a story about Dr. Earhart that provides another insight into the way his childhood fantasies and memories were intertwined. In a third-person account of his family's arrival in Fremont, Gutzon wrote:

> . . . reached the little frontier outpost of two streets and a couple of hundred people on the Oregon Trail and there father began his career as a doctor and surgeon . . . the young father took the office of a Dr. Earhart,

a dandy sort of gentleman who seems to have been more of a beau brum-
mel than a physician and quite out of place in the prairie town. . . . He
was giving up his position to return east, having lost his wife. He seems
to have come from England; then it was discovered the wife died under
strange circumstances; inquiry was made; the body exhumed; examined;
poison found in great quantity. Dr. Earhart arrested . . . found guilty and
sentenced to be hung. The morning of the execution he was found dead.
He had poisoned himself. . . .[5]

Dr. Earhart was never arrested for any crime. He switched practices between Omaha and Fremont, much as James did, until he tired
of the west and returned to his home in Philadelphia. The story could
be dismissed as a product of Gutzon's imagination if not for the fact
that in 1877 a Fremont doctor had been tried and convicted of murdering
his wife and had committed suicide the morning he was to be hanged.
Even though Gutzon had the wrong doctor, his memories cannot be
easily dismissed. Making allowance for the passage of time, his stories
must be granted some validity and the picture of an unhappy young
rebel living a bittersweet childhood believed, at least to a degree.

When asked by a reporter about his earliest memories, Gutzon
answered:

The first thing I remember was a Sioux Indian's face pressed closely against
the window of our main room. I was sitting at my grandmother's knee,
who had been telling me some Norse stories and I have never been able
to disentangle the Vikings of Denmark from the Sioux Indians. I do not
know how old I was but I hid in her clothing.[6]

The only grandmother Gutzon could have known was Christina's
mother. Most of the Michelsons had converted to Mormonism, and the
mother had followed her daughters to America and then settled in
Omaha. The recollection seems like a Bear Lake story because, by the
time they had reached Omaha, Gutzon would have been too old for
such a tale. Yet there was no grandmother in Idaho. The story could
have been told to impress the reporter, or it could have been a com-
bination of childhood memories that Gutzon wanted to believe. Gutzon's next memory was the traumatic departure of Christina, a hazy
recollection of St. Louis and moving back to Omaha "after they left
the great city by the great river."[7]

All the characteristics that were so strong in Gutzon the man are
apparent in these childhood recollections: courage, rebellion, the stubborn need to be right, the vivid imagination and the ability to dramatize
both romantically and tragically. Of these early years he wrote:

21

Of course I remember little or nothing about my first five or six years. They seem, as I recall them, a dreamland with terrible mountains, great rivers and lakes; terrible clashing of elements and into all this are woven all the old folklore of Denmark which I eagerly gathered at my mother's knee.[8]

Gutzon saw himself as "a very direct human being, happily freed in spirit and soul, pagan and Christian, at once law abiding and lawless, fearless and alone, recognizing life as an inalienable gift to one's self to use to better immediate and world conditions."[9]

As a boy Gutzon lived in a world of fantasy that blossomed when he discovered his artistic talents and had an outlet for his restless, wandering imagination. He wrote often about his haunting ambitions and dreams, as in this account:

One was to return to Denmark and become a builder of ships . . . or to enter the Danish navy . . . the other was to return to Indian country and there do as all white people did . . . hide, ride, hunt and kill the "enemies" of my race. . . . Father would not consent to my going to Denmark . . . and there live with my uncle . . . nor becoming a naval architect . . . nor killing off the whole Sioux tribe . . . my next ambition was to go to West Point . . . that was worse and although my father's position gave him the option to send a son to West Point he was a pacifist. I was told that was another boy's madness. . . .[10]

After Christina had gone, Gutzon's childhood stories usually concern only two people, him and his father. There is hardly a mention of other children, not even Solon, except in oblique references to Gutzon's being the "favorite" son. There is some mention of his stepmother, but primarily the stories center on the relationship and adventures shared by father and son.

The town of Fremont was a dusty frontier stop for those heading west. Cattle drives ended there, and the town had a reputation for being a place where those who were running from the law would not be bothered. There were frequent gunfights and many hangings. As one of the few doctors in the area James was kept very busy. He attended to the needs of the townfolks, the ranchers and cowboys, as well as the Indians on the reservation. As part of his daily routine he delivered babies in crude, makeshift shelters, set bones on the open prairie, probed for bullets without asking questions, stitched cuts after vicious barroom brawls and took care of the sick in bunkhouses and jails.

He was the typical frontier doctor. He had no hours or days off. Emergencies occurred at all hours, but mostly, it seemed, in the middle of the night. When a rider came galloping into the yard yelling for the doctor, James went for his emergency bag while one of his boys hitched the horse to the buggy and waited in the yard. Then man and boy headed into a night often so black and impenetrable that they had to give the horse his head and trust he would guide the buggy away from deep ruts, mudholes and ditches.

On clear nights the black sky filled with more stars than a boy's mind could comprehend. Such nights created an intimacy that James's reticence prevented at other times. When the mood was right James would talk about his life and his search for truth and meaning. He would fill his son with stories about the Greeks, the patriarchs of the Old Testament and the promise of the New. He told him what it meant to be a man, a Dane and a Borglum. James spoke about their family and the rich heritage that could be traced back to the fifteenth century. He told of the bestowing of the heraldic "de la Mothe" by a grateful king who had been saved from death by his squire and how that squire then established the family name. Years later each of James's sons remembered the nights on the prairie as very special times that were theirs alone. Gutzon, as well as each of his brothers recalled, "I was my father's favorite assistant."[11] Gutzon vividly recounted what usually waited for them at the end of the ride:

> Half of father's practice was repairing gunshot wounds, the other half delivering babies . . . being the sturdiest of the six children (actually there were nine, but three were girls) he [Gutzon] helped his father, travelled with him, aided him as nurse and general companion. . . .[12]

The wildness of the frontier attracted Gutzon as a boy and remained a source of inspiration throughout his life. Recalling one of the times he ran away from home, Gutzon wrote:

> Two terrible wolves followed me for six miles. I could not have been over eight. They came so close I touched the nose of one to tell him to keep further back and no effort was made to attack me. . . . This explains my utter confidence in the goodness of wild horses, wild animals, wild Indians and wild men. I have invaded their haunts since I was seven and I have never failed in being protected and safe. . . .[13]

Horses were a passion all his life. Gutzon claimed he bought his first pony from an Indian for fifty cents. "I have never been thrown from a horse," he boasted; "and I gentled all my ponies bought from the Indian herds. . . ."[14]

The Borglum children received little formal schooling, especially in the early years as James moved about establishing his practice. Gutzon probably received some education in St. Louis, but no record of his attendance exists. His first recorded classes were at a Catholic boarding school in St. Mary's, Kansas, that he and his brother Auguste attended when Gutzon was twelve. Being sent to St. Mary's was most fortunate for Gutzon. In his notes he wrote:

> I began drawing things and copying pictures, and I was told about great artists. At the school from drawing of maps and caricaturing of the teachers . . . my interest grew into serious study, such as I could get in school, of the Italian artists of the Renaissance. At the Jesuit College in Kansas my first attention was called to the seriousness of an artist's life. . . .[15]

When asked about Gutzon's schooling, however, Auguste recalled:

> I do remember that he was constantly drawing or sketching in the spare moments and frequently in his study hours when he was supposed to be studying his lessons . . . the teachers showed considerable opposition toward Gutzon in his tendency to follow his inborn talent . . . an attitude that persisted until we left for summer vacation. . . .[16]

Auguste also remembered that on their way home for that summer vacation Gutzon displayed one of the characteristics that became so pronounced in later years:

> Gutzon went into this art store and bought paints and drawing materials because he said he wouldn't be able to buy them at home. He spent so much we didn't have money enough left for our fare, but the conductor let us ride anyway.[17]

Gutzon might have been sent to St. Mary's to discourage him from running away, but because Auguste was also sent the possibility exists that James was trying to introduce his son to their new religion. James had never taken his Mormonism lightly. Even after he left the Church and graduated from medical school he thought about his commitment. A short time after he began his practice he offered his services to the Church as a teacher and physician, but President John Taylor would not accept his offer. In his letter to James he said:

> The knowledge of physiology may be very well in its place, but lectures on the subject without the principles of the Gospel, I am afraid, would

24

not be productive of good; for we are taught that faith is one of the principal operations through the power of God in the healing of disease. Were you a good LDS, and full in faith, I should say come. . . .[18]

James was not "a good LDS" and that was the last known contact he had with the Church. A short time later he took his family to St. Patrick's Church in Fremont and had them all baptized in the Catholic faith.[19] The children, with the exception of Gutzon and Solon, were again listed as the children of James and Ida. Gutzon and Solon were listed as the children of James and Christina, with no explanation of their relationship.

Auguste and Gutzon returned to St. Mary's for one more term while the other Borglum children attended the Omaha high school that became Creighton University. The following year Gutzon took some classes at Creighton and, as far as the records show, that ended his formal education.[20]

3
California

Gutzon was seventeen when the family arrived in Los Angeles, a growing, bustling community of almost 80,000 people. The city was enjoying one of its periodic real estate booms as it made the transition from a winter resort for the wealthy to the most important commercial center on the west coast.

An aspiring artist could not have picked a better time to arrive, though the art field was not as filled with opportunity as the newspapers suggested. Many of the paintings being sold to the wealthy patrons, who were building new homes in the city, were poor imitations of the European masters or mass-produced commercial work. American buyers seemed to prefer imported products. A conflict was developing locally that would eventually involve Gutzon, but not until he earned some recognition.

Gutzon had made his decision at fourteen, when he discovered his talent, but that was a teenager's choice, which could have been discarded with age, especially since his father considered art a foolish career for a man and tried his best to discourage Gutzon. James's opposition to Gutzon's decision may have deterred some, but it only increased Gutzon's determination.

In practical terms the only effect it had was to force Gutzon to take a job, though food and shelter were not of immediate concern. James had rented a house large enough for the whole family and for a doctor's office. In a short time he established a fine practice and earned enough money to deal in real estate. He willingly provided for his children, but he expected the older ones to work.

Gutzon's first job was that of an apprentice to a master engraver in a lithography firm. It was hard, tedious work, but he learned a great deal about engraving in the six months he was there and that made the effort worthwhile. When he decided he was not being paid enough he left and took a position with a crew of fresco painters. It was a fine job for an aspiring artist, though the work was monotonous because of the constant repeating of patterns. "In a short time," Gutzon wrote, "I was the best in the shop and was assigned only the most difficult jobs."[1]

But when he once again demanded more money and was refused, he quit. James was furious with him, probably because he saw too much of himself in his headstrong son. Arguing vehemently, James tried to talk him into returning to the job, but Gutzon adamantly refused.

At eighteen he knew what he wanted out of life and was determined to achieve it. He had been fighting with his father for so many years that it is doubtful he really listened to his arguments. All he knew was that people were living the type of life he desired. He was meeting them. They seemed to have neither the talent nor the ambition that he had, and many, including Lisa Putnam, a painter who wanted to take him under her wing, were willingly accepting him. He continued to live at home and argue with James, but when Lisa offered to teach him and share her studio he gladly accepted her offer.

Two of Gutzon's friends from those early days remembered the studio. Both wrote about it with fondness, though they seem to be recalling two different artists; neither one seemed aware that it was Lisa's studio and that Gutzon was simply sharing her space. Bob Davies, who was the same age as Gutzon, worked in a shop below the studio. Davies wrote:

> His walls were the most fascinating thing in my life. They were hung with pictures of stagecoaches and horses leaping in every direction. These things were painted in oils and I thought they were the finest things in California.[2]

Charles Lummis, an older and more critical friend, expressed similar admiration for the studio:

> It was nine years ago this writer found a green, serious lad belaboring canvas in a bare room. . . . He had no money and not many friends. The paintings he was at had many shortcomings and showed his lack of education. Yet there was in them a creative breadth that promised to make him heard. . . .[3]

Others apparently shared this opinion since Gutzon's early paintings sold well enough to make local critics aware of him. The *Los Angeles Times* reviewed his work in September 1887:

> A new young artist is coming to light here of whom it is safe to predict that the city will someday be proud. There is such a wilderness of dabblers here, and such a dearth of real artists, that the discovery of one of the latter . . . is to be hailed with genuine delight . . . the young man

without money, or adequate training has been struggling along by the bitterest self-denial . . . the young man's name is J. G. Borglum and he has a studio with Mrs. L. Jaynes Putnam [Lisa] . . . Mr. Borglum hopes to study this fall in New York. . . .[4]

The picture that emerges is of a young man with a single-minded desire to succeed, but that is only partially true because Gutzon was a complex individual. He expected to succeed, and others assumed that he would. He was charismatic, charming and intense. People were attracted to him even when he was still just a youth from the prairie and not quite sure where he was heading, but knowing he was in a hurry to get there.

In later years Gutzon made his early struggles appear harsher, possibly because he felt that made his achievement seem greater or because he felt it was expected. With his wry sense of humor and flair for the dramatic he could always be counted on to provide the struggling artist-in-the-garret image that made such good copy. Unfortunately, by doing so he often obscured the traits that made him so unusual. If he had actually been the obsessed, one-dimensional person of his own accounts he would not have attracted critics, friends, patrons and a woman as worldly as Lisa Jaynes Putnam.

Still life signed "Johnnie Borglum," c. 1885.

29

Lisa, a still-life painter and teacher, was several years older than Gutzon. In 1887 she was at the height of her career. Born in New England, she had studied art and music in the East and established her reputation as an artist before marrying and moving to Wisconsin. When her marriage ended in divorce she moved to San Francisco, where she studied with William Keith, the most famous American landscape painter of his day. In 1884 she moved to Los Angeles and opened the studio she later shared with Gutzon. Nearing forty, Lisa was a forceful, talented, and self-confident woman. When she wanted something she went after it, and that evidently included Gutzon. She recognized his innate talent and that intangible quality that marks a person for greatness.

There was also a strong physical attraction. From their initial meeting to their final separation twenty years later, they were seldom apart. In one of his recollections, John Hart, Jr., the son of one of Lisa's good friends, recalled his first meeting with Gutzon:

> My father and mother brought us to . . . California. . . . I remember walking with my mother along the hills to visit her girlhood friend, Lizzie Jaynes, who was living on Temple Street . . . painting and giving lessons in art. She was recognized as an artist of great merit. . . . Soon after we settled in Sierra Madre she came to visit us, and before long she brought a pupil, then known as Johnnie Borglum. . . . He was many years younger than she . . . in fact he was just a rough Nebraska boy, sturdy, energetic and interesting . . . in a short time . . . he outdistanced his teacher in their art and she began to speak of him as a universal genius. . . .[5]

When the San Francisco Art Association offered Lisa a teaching position in 1888, she accepted. It not only meant she could once again study with Keith, but could also provide a good opportunity for Gutzon. He had been talking about going to New York to study, but he changed his mind and went with Lisa to San Francisco.

By then James and Ida had tired of the hectic life in Los Angeles. James traded a parcel of land he had acquired in Pasadena for a Nebraska ranch. He sold his other holdings and, taking all the younger children with them, moved back to Omaha. Solon and Arnold went with them to take over the ranch, Miller took a job with the railroad and Gutzon remained with Lisa.

Years later, divorced from Lisa and writing about his decision to study at the Art Association, Gutzon, just as his father had done with Christina, did not acknowledge the role that Lisa had played in his life. He had made a new life with his second wife and always believed that

Roses by Lisa Putnam Borglum

she was his true mate. As a result, when he spoke about his early achievements he made it appear that he had been driven primarily by inner forces:

> As I became acquainted with the fine arts I soon became aware that the landscape painter could not paint or draw a horse, cattle or sheep, that the cow painter could not paint a landscape that carried the mood of nature, as a matter of creative production equal to the cow painter. . . . I made up my mind that I should master each of the subjects and began at once. . . . I drew and painted . . . dogs, cattle, portraits. . . .[6]

In San Francisco Gutzon began a new, more intense phase of his career. The Art Association was small, but it had an excellent staff and reputation. About sixty students attended classes, which met above a public market. Isobel Field, one of Gutzon's fellow students, remembered it all as a great adventure:

> The stairs up from the street led directly into the long, wide room with a high ceiling bright and sunny, owing to a huge skylight. Eight or ten plaster casts . . . were arranged at intervals, replicas of the Greek ones in the Louvre . . . Venus De Milo, the Discus Thrower, Apollo . . . all on pedestals, each surrounded by a small group of students with easels . . . busily at work. . . .[7]

Another student, Emily Carr, remembered the old school with much less enthusiasm, however. She wrote that the Art Association:

> . . . was up over the old Pine Street Market, a squalid district . . . from the dismal street you climbed a dirty stairs . . . at the top sat a long-bearded curator tugging and tugging at his whiskers as if they operated his brain . . . the curator said . . . "You come along." . . . We passed through a big room hung with oriental rugs and dust . . . the art school lay beyond, but this was the only way in . . . the school had been a great hall once. The center was lit by a skylight. One corner was boarded up — on the door was printed, "life class — keep out." The whole place smelt of rats. Decaying vegetables lay on tables . . . still-life studies . . . long rows of students stood at easels drawing. . . . I was given a lapboard and a chunk of bread . . . a very dirty janitor was hacking up a huge crusty loaf; all the students were scrambling for pieces . . . I took my place in a long row. On one side was a sweet-faced girl . . . on the other a dirty old man with a tobacco-stained beard. . . .[8]

There is one more story in Isobel's memoirs that is worth repeating because, true or not, it reflects the degree of Western sophistication to which the students were exposed. The plaster casts were replicas of the Louvre masterpieces. They were a gift to the citizens of San Francisco from the citizens of Paris. "It was said," Isobel wrote, "that when they unpacked the boxes and found the Venus De Milo to be without arms, the city sued Wells Fargo and was awarded damages."[9]

In all his notes and recollections of San Francisco, Gutzon never mentioned anything about Lisa, his social life, or the physical aspects of the school. He seemed to remember only his desire to learn and the encouragement he received from his instructors. He gave William Keith so much credit for his development that one would assume he was a favored student, though he could not have been. Keith was an eccentric who refused to allow males in his classes. Sometimes, when he was particularly fond of a female student, he would allow her to bring a guest to his studio.

Lisa must have brought Gutzon's work to Keith's attention, and he must have seen enough potential to allow Gutzon to come to his studio. With Keith's accepting him, Lisa's telling everyone he was a genius and his own unlimited faith in himself, Gutzon took it for granted that he would be famous before he was thirty. It may have seemed like an idle boast to many, but not to Lisa. She shared his dream, nurtured it and did all she could to make it a reality. Her interest was deeply personal. Soon after they met she gladly made him the most important part of her life. Gutzon had to have been flattered and impressed. Receiving attention from a worldly, talented woman like Lisa was a wonderful experience for the young artist.

Had Lisa not recognized his genius and not been more interested in his career than her own, Gutzon might not have thought he was in love, but she did and he reacted accordingly. Perhaps part of the attraction was that Lisa was the same age as Christina. If she did represent his returning mother, Gutzon was certainly not aware of it, but the possibility cannot be easily dismissed, even though to him they were simply a man and woman of similar interests and in love.

After several months in San Francisco, Gutzon returned to Los Angeles while Lisa remained behind to finish her contract. He reopened their studio on Fort Street and began a large painting of a stagecoach drawn by six horses careening down a steep mountain road. This painting, one of several he created with a similar theme, is now in the collection of the Joslyn Museum in Omaha, Nebraska. Considered one of Gutzon's finest works, *Staging Over the Sierra Madre Mountains in California* earned a number of favorable reviews and brought Gutzon's work to the attention of a woman who would become his most influential friend, Jessie Benton Fremont.

Like so many other women, Mrs. Fremont sensed something in Gutzon that set him apart from other men. Women were always his most ardent supporters. Time after time his friendships with men became wars, but the women who befriended him always remained loyal. Gutzon did not seem to be going out of his way to charm women, but he still managed to earn their undying support and loyalty.

Mrs. Fremont brought her husband, General John Charles Fremont, the famous Indian fighter and explorer, to Gutzon's studio to have his portrait painted. Gutzon was hard at work on the portrait of the old man when Bob Davies began dropping by the studio again. Davies was impressed as he later recalled:

> I saw the painting from the first touch of the brush. Fremont always came in on the arm of his wife who seemed the one person he wanted to please. She brought with her a military coat adorned with gold fringe and epaulets, a garment the great Indian fighter wore with dignity . . . it was a good picture . . . day after day it assumed more life and grandeur. . . .[10]

Mrs. Fremont quickly recognized the uniqueness of Gutzon's talent and decided to involve herself in his career. She had grown up in wealth and power and knew how to use both to her advantage. Her father, Senator Benton of Missouri, was the primary backer of Lewis and Clark and had fought all his life to settle the Western territories. Senator Benton conducted much of the nation's business from his St. Louis home, and Jessie, his only child, was always at his side. Despite the customs of his day, which decreed that women should be seen but not heard, the senator often sought Jessie's advice.

After her husband's career was established Mrs. Fremont began exerting her influence. Through the years she helped struggling artists, writers and politicians. For anyone with ambition the friendship of Jessie Fremont was a valuable asset.

Gutzon was working on the General's portrait when Lisa Putnam returned from San Francisco. She had come back because she wanted to be with Gutzon. Her presence bolstered his spirits and her faith in him gave him a stronger sense of purpose and dignity.

On September 15, 1889, Gutzon, twenty-two, and Lisa, forty, were married. After the reception, the newlyweds left Los Angeles for a long honeymoon, which took them along the coast. They stopped to paint, sketch and walk on the beaches until they reached San Francisco, where they stayed awhile to visit friends.

When they returned to their studio, the *Los Angeles Times* announced that they were home:

> Mr. and Mrs. Borglum have returned from their bridal tour and are again in their pleasant studio. Their brushes have not been idle while they were rehearsing the old, old story, the beauty of which seems to have lent inspiration to their efforts.[11]

The long article described the work that had been done and particularly praised one of Gutzon's paintings, *Solitude*. The painting depicts a coastal scene with a dark sky, pounding surf and a solitary "gnarled and scraggy cypress with its funeral drapings of grey-green moss."

The honeymoon over, the Borglums settled into a routine. Lisa took over the teaching of their students leaving Gutzon free to paint. Favorable publicity from the Fremont painting had brought in other commissions, and he was becoming a figure in the art community.

Despite his youth, other artists looked to Gutzon for leadership. In one of his first involvements with a community activity, he helped form the Los Angeles Art Club, and at the first meeting, which was held at the Borglum studio, he was elected vice-president. Although Henry Merrit, an older Los Angeles artist, was elected president, Gutzon was the motivating force behind the club's establishment. This became obvious a short time later when he and Lisa decided to spend some time in Europe and the club temporarily disbanded.

The decision to study in Europe was a major step for Gutzon and required a change in his thinking. He had no faith in the dead influences of old ideas, but he had begun to recognize the importance of studying the masters and learning their techniques. Lisa encouraged him primarily because she knew that once they left Los Angeles she would be able to introduce him to other cultures thus expanding his vision. Lisa was beginning to believe that the horizons of Los Angeles were too limiting for all she planned for Gutzon.

They discussed a European trip with Mrs. Fremont, and when she gave her blessings they quickly settled their affairs and prepared to leave. They left Los Angeles toward the end of 1890 with over fifty paintings they hoped to sell along the way and letters of introduction to Mrs. Fremont's friends in Chicago, New York, Paris and elsewhere.

4

Paris

As the train pulled into the Omaha station, the Borglums were lined up on the platform waiting for Gutzon and his bride. They were looking forward to seeing Gutzon for the first time in two years. They assumed he would look older, but they were not prepared for the confident, well-dressed man who stepped off the train with his rolled-up canvases and fashionable wife.

Gutzon was dark complexioned and his thick hair was just beginning to recede. He was a muscular and sturdy man who carried himself well and appeared tall, though he was not quite five foot ten. But a physical description does not convey the sense of his attraction. What set him apart, even at an early age, was his presence. Gutzon Borglum projected the image of a man who was going somewhere.

Even Solon was there. He had come in from the ranch to be with his brother. Ida had dressed all the younger children in their finest outfits in an obvious attempt to impress Lisa. Everyone was thrilled and Gutzon and his wife were welcomed happily. For the time being, at least, all the animosities and endless arguments of the past seemed to be forgotten.

Gutzon was pleased with the reception and welcomed the chance to spend time with his brothers and sisters. He was particularly happy to see Solon, and Solon was even happier to see him. As soon as he could pull Gutzon away from the others he took him to James's basement, where he had set up a special exhibit.

During the long winter on the ranch Solon had discovered a talent. He lived in a cabin that was practically buried in snow for most of the winter and had filled the endless hours drawing. He sketched horses, cattle in the snowdrifts, the bunkhouse, the cowboys taking care of chores and everything else that caught his eye. The drawings were primitive and crude, but undeniably magnificent.

Unaware that Solon had any thoughts about art, Gutzon was overwhelmed and he reacted with his characteristic enthusiasm. "Why, Solon," he exclaimed, "you should be an artist."[1] It was the right thing to say at the right time. If Solon had not been sure before that moment, he was certain then. Within a very short time he gave up ranching, moved back into his father's home and began to study with a local artist. Gutzon's influence on Solon should not be underestimated. He wanted Solon to be successful and enjoy all that life had to offer. Gutzon felt good about himself and he wanted his brother to feel the same way.

Gutzon had achieved a degree of fame, certainly by Omaha's standards, and his visit was treated as a big event. The city's leading art collector, W. W. Linninger, had opened his gallery for an exhibit of the paintings the Borglums had brought with them, and all of Omaha's social elite turned out for the opening, which was front page news in the local papers:

> Mr. and Mrs. J. G. Borglum . . . have been receiving a most enthusiastic ovation . . . their pictures were placed on exhibition at the Linninger Art Gallery. . . . Mr. Borglum is an artist who thinks and feels for himself, and who will be guided by that inner voice. Europe will not spoil him. He will not return to this country to paint French peasant girls and Swiss lakes. . . . Mr. Borglum has originality enough and independence enough to be trusted to think his own thoughts and paint his own pictures . . . when he returns . . . Mr. Linninger will have reason to congratulate himself on his perspicacity which led him to see in this young man the talent, which rightly directed, will certainly bring him extraordinary success.[2]

Lisa was also praised by the critic, but in a more subdued manner, probably because she preferred it that way. "Mrs. Borglum's work," the article said, "is in still-life and her studies of California grapes excel anything in that line that has been seen in Omaha."[3]

The praise was wonderful, especially since the Omaha articles were quoted in the Los Angeles papers, but what was really important was that Linninger purchased most of their paintings. That meant they could go to Europe with little concern about money.

In Paris Gutzon and Lisa took a studio at 65 Boulevard Arago. Settling down to a domestic life, they filled their days with a leisurely routine of informal study, painting and sightseeing. They spent evenings in the cafés on the Left Bank and in the studios of the Frenchmen who were changing the concepts of the art world.

To keep in touch with all his friends in Los Angeles, Gutzon wrote periodic letters, which were printed in the Los Angeles Times. In his first letter he briefly described his new home and lifestyle:

38

Located on the pleasant Boulevard Arago. . . . We have all the comforts our student life desires. . . . The public conveyances are uncomfortable. slow and primitive. I bought on my arrival in Paris a new style of tricycle with four wheels, so we can see Paris, or even Europe with our new conveyance.[4]

Gutzon liked France and the French people, but he found much about their art that displeased him. Because he considered himself unique, he did not want to be associated with a movement or school that would classify his work. He believed an artist was an individual or he was nothing. That was why he found little in any of the schools of art that impressed him. As far as he was concerned an artist was destroyed the moment a label was put on his work. So although he was enjoying himself as a painter he felt he was wasting his time. In another open letter home he wrote:

Men and women had better never left their native land, but evolved their ideas as best they could, sincerely and naturally. . . . In France there exists a sort of contempt for feeling and sentiment, and the story-telling quality in pictures . . . here artifice pervades everything, nature, animals and people all seem to be playing the part of somebody else.[5]

He may not have had much respect for the established painters, but he did enjoy the circle in which they travelled. He and Lisa had arrived as the new salon was being formed. Artists, inspired by the work of men like Rodin and Dalou, were challenging the old salon and everyone was choosing sides. This made for good arguments, and Gutzon was pleased to join in on the side of the new just as he had in Los Angeles.

As much as he disliked the French painters he delighted in the French sculptors:

The ability to represent form is what has placed them so high in sculpture. They have reached a point not far behind the best antiques, if not equal to them . . . the sculpture exhibit at both salons is very fine . . . sculpture by its very nature, is less affected by the fashions and mannerisms of the day. Paris . . . is the home of the greatest living sculptors. . . .[6]

The old salon appreciated the Borglums more than Gutzon and Lisa appreciated them. The old salon accepted paintings by both while the new exhibited Gutzon's first publicly displayed sculpture. *Death Of the Chief* is a small bronze depicting an Indian pony bending over the body of a dead chief, a particularly moving Western theme. Gutzon's claim to being a Western sculptor was based on this type of work, though once he became involved with other themes he rarely returned to the Western concept.

Gutzon was pleased to be showing in both salons and he shared his pleasure in an open letter to the *Times*:

> I send you a photo of my piece of sculpture. It has a splendid success having been placed in the row of honor. . . . My wife's picture, a . . . portrait of our large Danish boarhound, has also been well spoken of. . . . I do not know when we will return, but that we will as soon as possible there is no question. . . .[7]

The Danish boarhound that Borglum mentioned in the letter was a twenty-fifth birthday present from Lisa. There were two at the pet store. When Gutzon could not choose between them she bought both. The Borglums added another pair later, and when they returned to America they brought all four dogs.

With Lisa guiding him Gutzon was making great strides. The French salons were exhibiting his work. His paintings were being bought by American visitors referred by Mrs. Fremont, and he was receiving good critical reviews. Leland Stanford, the railroad magnate who had become Governor of California, placed an order for three large paintings, which Gutzon was to deliver after the Borglums returned to California.

Lisa believed, more and more, that Gutzon would be famous before he was thirty, and she was doing everything possible to make it happen. She had planned the trip to France because she believed that was where he should be at that stage of his career. No matter what he thought about the trip, the time was not being wasted. He made good use of what he learned in later years. He spoke often about many aspects of his life in Europe, but as the years passed the experience that really impressed him was his meeting Rodin. Gutzon always acknowledged the strong influence Rodin had on his art and philosophy:

> France taught me respect for the sincere effort of other men, courage in my effort, and that originality lay in being true to yourself. . . . "French art" is not the art which proclaimed France to be the art mistress of the modern world . . . but Rodin. . . .[8]

Gutzon had admired the work of Michelangelo from the moment he was exposed to the world of art in boarding school, but Michelangelo was dead while Rodin was alive and working. Gutzon had been in

Rodin's studio. He had watched Rodin work and had spoken with him about art. He felt that Rodin had caused sculpture to take on a new form.

After two years in Paris the Borglums were ready to move on. Lisa had been asked to exhibit at the Spanish International Exposition of 1892 and had accepted. The idea of going to Spain pleased Gutzon. He welcomed the opportunity to travel and used his time in Spain to good advantage. He developed an interest in Spanish architecture and spent much time inspecting the old missions. He also tried his hand at woodcarving and painted a number of portraits. Years later he described the painting that he considered his best work while in Spain:

> It is a portrait of a Catholic priest, Don Tomas . . . the canon in charge of the great cathedral in Toledo. A remarkable little man . . . extremely fond of bullfights. He and I attended them constantly. I first started painting him smoking a cigarette, but when he saw it he threw the cigarette away, saying it was undignified for a priest. . . .[9]

The bullfights attracted Gutzon as an artist, but not as a sportsman. He went as often as possible to sketch the action, even though, as his brother Auguste said, "It made him sick to watch them."[10] While he was in Spain, Gutzon also studied and prepared sketches for a huge mural depicting the Noche Triste, the historic battle between the Aztecs and the invading troops of Cortez fought in Mexico City in 1519.

Lisa and Gutzon returned to the United States after several months in Spain. They were accompanied by two servants and the four Danish boarhounds. Enroute to California they stopped in Omaha for another visit with the Borglums. It was again a joyous occasion, as Auguste remembered:

> Gutzon had previously warned . . . that he was bringing home five Great Danes. He, of course, was the fifth! The sensation the dogs made, as they all came bounding off the train in Omaha, was tremendous. It was . . . to be repeated at every stop along the line to Santa Anita, where their startling arrival was reported in the local papers.[11]

Gutzon seemed to be prospering beyond imagination. Awed by the spectacle, his family tried, without success, to find traces of their rough, intense Gutzon in the polished, wordly man who laughed with them. In all accounts Gutzon appears to have been putting on airs and doing his best to impress his family, but it was in good-natured fun, and they enjoyed themselves immensely.

Again Solon was waiting to show Gutzon his new works. He had studied with J. Laurie Wallace, a disciple of Thomas Eakins, and had developed rapidly. Gutzon looked at the sketches and drawings and shook his head in wonder. He was delighted with all that he saw.

The two brothers spent as much time together as they could—talking about Paris, art and the future. Most of the time, as their discussions ranged over a variety of subjects, Gutzon was the "master" and Solon the "pupil," who listened and learned. Unfortunately for their future relationship, Gutzon could never put that image out of his mind. Even after Solon was a recognized sculptor, Gutzon continued to think of him as "little Solon" and his pupil.

But that occurred later in their careers. In Omaha, together as men instead of boys, they were delighted with each other, and they spoke about how wonderful it would be if they could work together. Enthusiastic as always, Gutzon invited Solon to join him in California as soon as he and Lisa were settled.

Lisa was not consulted. The idea of asking his wife for permission to invite his brother never occurred to Gutzon, which meant that he did not see her role as she perceived it. Lisa saw herself as Gutzon's teacher and manager, as well as his wife. She was directing his career in all its aspects and fought against any distractions and anyone who could disrupt her plans. She had continued her own career after their marriage, but she had added another one, and that career was Gutzon.

To serve her purpose, she tried not to be a public person, preferring to place Gutzon in the limelight. He joined the art societies and received most of the commissions, but usually when they were interviewed she did the talking and she spoke about him.

A bond developing between her husband and his rough cowboy brother, just as Gutzon was acquiring polish, had to be perceived by Lisa as a threat. Gutzon was still her pupil. She could not allow him to reverse the roles and become Solon's teacher, but she was not aware that Gutzon had that in mind. Had she known, she certainly would have stopped the relationship before it had started.

5
Sierra Madre

When Lisa and Gutzon reached Los Angeles, they took their dogs, servants and baggage and went to the Sierra Madre home of Lisa's friends from Wisconsin. The Harts were pleased to see them and somehow managed to find room for them.

Sierra Madre was a sleepy little village of adobe buildings, ranches and small farms nestled in the foothills of the mountains. It was a beautiful, almost perfect setting for an artist, and both decided it was where they would like to live. A few weeks after they moved in with the Harts they bought a parcel of land from John Hart, Sr., and built a studio.

The Borglums named their new home El Rosario. It was a small adobe building with a room that served as studio and living quarters, a small room for the servants and a large run for the dogs.

Gutzon was thrilled to be back in California, where he could enjoy the outdoors. In Paris he had missed camping, fishing and the open spaces he had known all his life. In California he took every opportunity to visit the woods. Shortly after their return, he sent a note to a friend who expected to meet him in Yosemite:

> I could not make the trip I planned alone, yet I must make sketches of redwoods, and at once, so with my wife started . . . for Santa Cruz mountains and there have painted and drawn trees and stage roads for the past ten days . . . my stage pictures will very soon be so they can be seen . . . these are the ones I am painting to the order of the late Senator Stanford. . . .[1]

Gutzon was very busy. He had the Stanford commission for three large paintings and a number of lesser commissions. He was also working on the Noche Triste mural in an effort to have it ready in time to exhibit at the 1893 Columbian Exposition in Chicago, and he was hoping to find time to get back into sculpture while the ideas that had formed in Europe were still fresh in his mind.

43

He was hard at work on the mural and the Stanford paintings when Solon showed up at El Rosario. Gutzon was overjoyed because his brother had come to study with him. If all went well, they would someday do great things together. Despite his heavy workload he would find time to teach Solon, just as Lisa had taught him. Then, after Solon matured as an artist, he could take his place, if not at Gutzon's side, at least close behind him. Had anyone told Gutzon that Lisa would be offended by this dream or by Solon's presence in their home, he would have been shocked. When she did make her feelings known, he was hurt more than Solon.

The brothers should not have been surprised. Lisa lived in a carefully constructed world. All her energies were committed to Gutzon and his career. She had no need for another pupil, and if she had it would not have been a student as undisciplined as she felt Solon was. She had made her plans carefully, and she did not want any intrusions or changes, particularly in Gutzon's view of their roles or his attitude toward her. Seeing how close the brothers were had to make her jealous. Solon and Gutzon shared memories she was not a part of and could never understand.

Aside from that, she had no desire to share her husband with anyone and certainly not with a footloose bachelor who might put ideas in his head. She was content with their lives and prepared to battle anyone who threatened to disrupt the delicate balance of their relationship. The difference in their ages caused problems enough. That not only would they never have children, but that Gutzon would, in effect, always be her child, had to be dealt with constantly. Their marriage lacked many things from Gutzon's standpoint, and she tried to compensate by emphasizing his career.

These tensions made Solon her enemy and caused her to attack him with uncharacteristic rudeness. The woman whose good nature made Gutzon comment on his wedding day, "I have just married the kindest woman in the world," became an angry shrew whenever she confronted Solon or anyone else she felt could divert Gutzon's attention.[2]

El Rosario was not large, for it was designed for a working couple who did not plan to enlarge their family. Lisa said there was no room for Solon. She could not send him away because she did not want to risk an outright confrontation with Gutzon, but she did make Solon so uncomfortable that he left. First she insisted he sleep outside on the patio. Then she demanded that he feed the dogs and clean the kennel to earn his keep. Neither the sleeping outdoors nor the work was a hardship for a hardy Nebraska cowboy like Solon. He had lived out on the range winter and summer, but being treated as a hired hand in his brother's home hurt him deeply.

Solon was an introverted man, proud and sensitive. Gutzon's invitation, encouragement and praise had triggered something in him, and he thought of little else as he prepared to join his brother. He naturally assumed that Lisa would welcome him. Suddenly facing a rude and angry woman was more than he could bear. He stayed a short time and then left without a word.

Solon's leaving made Gutzon realize how little he controlled his own affairs. There seems little doubt that Lisa's rude treatment of Solon was the beginning of the end of their marriage. Gutzon remained with her for several more years, but in an ever-worsening situation. After Gutzon saw a different Lisa, one he did not admire, his attitude began to change. This change was not an abrupt, but rather a gradual erosion of his feelings. When Solon left, Gutzon was hurt and angry, but he had little time for reflection.

With the deadline for the 1893 exposition rapidly approaching, Gutzon was concentrating on the mural. It had been started as soon as they moved into El Rosario. Charles Lummis described the work in his magazine, *The Land of Sunshine*:

> A heroic painting of the most romantic episode in all the history of the Americas, the "Noche Triste". . . . This great picture of that gray causeway of Mexico, with the soldiers of Cortez floundering across the gap beset by the Aztec wolves, is not yet finished, but it stands far enough . . . may properly be termed great. . . . Mr. Borglum has not only the grasp, but the seriousness of large art. . . .[3]

When it was too late to finish the painting for the exposition, Gutzon put the mural aside and concentrated on his next priority, the Stanford commission.

Gutzon was adapting to a satisfying if not exciting lifestyle. In his letters and sporadic entries in his journal, there is little mention of Lisa during this period, possibly because she was trying to make him feel he was in control after the fiasco with Solon. She must have sensed her hold was weakening, and she had to have been concerned.

Gutzon's career seemed to be advancing just as they planned. Mrs. Fremont was taking an active interest in his affairs and she agreed to sit for a portrait. Her biographer described one of the sessions:

> In 1894 young Borglum was sitting in the cottage . . . at work on the bust of Jessie Fremont. Her small granddaughter Juliet was visiting at the time,

45

and Jessie was much amused at the child's concern as to how grandmother's "head" would look after being wrapped all night in a wet cloth. . . . When Borglum finished the bust Mrs. Fremont . . . and her family declared themselves well pleased, for the young sculptor had caught the warmth of her. . . .[4]

When Gutzon renewed his interest in the art association he was surprised to learn his rebel group had become the old salon in the few years he had been away. He became active, but a few months later, when a dispute arose over an exhibit, Gutzon and many of his friends pulled out to form a new association, The Society of Fine Arts. This caused a great deal of bitterness in Los Angeles art circles, and the controversy received much attention in the *Los Angeles Times*. The paper reported that the old association was "less broad" and had fewer artists. The article praised the new society's "great sincerity, untainted by affection" and promoted its exhibits. Eventually the rift was healed, and most artists, including Gutzon, showed work in the exhibits of both organizations.

Gutzon's interests seemed unlimited. He was convinced that in his studies of old mission buildings in Spain he had acquired an expertise that, combined with his artistic talent, made him the ultimate authority. He fought bitterly against those who believed conservation meant restoration, or who insisted on creating facsimiles and calling them originals. Most of his fighting was within the organization created by Charles Lummis to restore the sixteenth-century mission at San Juan Capistrano.

Gutzon joined Lummis' group when its members began to organize after their having worked together informally for a number of years. This put Gutzon in close contact with Lummis, who saw himself more as Gutzon's benefactor than friend. He felt he was helping Gutzon and, as he was to point out later, thought he was furthering Gutzon's career.

Lummis printed several of Gutzon's articles on art in his magazine, had him design a new masthead and used several of his illustrations. Gutzon enjoyed writing, particularly about art. In later years he expanded his interests and wrote about many subjects and involved himself in politics and public affairs, but during his California days he centered his ability and energy on his art. When he did write about other subjects, he wrote about such topics as the association or the mission group. What Gutzon wanted most at that stage of his development was acceptance and recognition. His sights were still set on being famous by the time he was thirty.

Gradually, the relationship between Lummis and Gutzon soured until it became a bitter feud. Starting with a minor disagreement over

Unfinished poster for San Juan Capistrano. c. 1894.

the masthead, it became a war when the San Juan Capistrano group formed its organization and elected Lummis president. Gutzon had expected the position to be his, and when he was not even appointed to the board of directors he was furious. A debate over the conservation-restoration question had been going on long before Gutzon joined them, but he quickly became the leader of the conservationists, though not without creating anger, which was reflected in the election.

Gutzon took the rebuff personally and blamed Lummis. In an angry, intemperate letter he gave vent to his frustration:

> This closes connection with you. . . . I regret now that I began the revival of interest in the missions. . . . You make yourself President and dish up the rest of the club to suit your plans . . . You attempt to add insult to what you of course meant as injury when you wrote "your intelligent interest we will recognize officially in some other way." . . . Lummis you stooped to a depth I believed you were incapable of . . . . If your actions had not shown you were conscious of the underhandedness of the work you were indulging in I should have dropped you without further reference to the matter . . . . I could not permit my name to remain on the rolls of an organization you are the head of . . . .[5]

Offended, but wanting to appear the gracious victor with the maturity to exercise restraint, Lummis answered:

> . . . genius is privileged to do inscrutable things and think inconceivable thoughts. . . . If you presume I was self-seeking I must pity both your perceptions and your rules of conduct . . . I cannot share your fears . . . since luckily no person alive monopolizes all the intelligence or all the heart extant. . . .[6]

A week later Gutzon tried to get in the last word. "Mr. Lummis, adios," he wrote, "create and pervert this matter as suits your fancy. I have erred in believing reasoning with you possible."[7] But Lummis would not be outdone:

> You mistake your place in the controversy. It is I, not you, who have the "adios" to say . . . I could not expect to be made an exception among the long list of those who have been similarly rewarded for befriending you . . . your record in this seems to be consistent. . . .[8]

Disconcerting as the argument with Lummis was, Gutzon's problem with the estate of Governor Stanford was of far greater consequence. Stanford had died before Gutzon could complete the commission. When he attempted to deliver the paintings to Mrs. Stanford she refused them and would not pay the $10,000 still due. Gutzon tried to settle the matter with her attorneys, but they rejected his claim without countering and told him, "Mrs. Stanford cannot see how she can do otherwise. . . ."[9] It was such a nebulous response that Gutzon had no recourse but to sue.

The judge ruled that since the contract was oral and Stanford was no longer there to pass judgment Mrs. Stanford was not liable for an agreement she had not made herself. It was a bitter blow for Gutzon, one that went beyond the money. With his work selling well he knew he would not have trouble finding a buyer for the work. What had been hurt was his pride. No artist likes to have his work rejected or his integrity questioned, and for a man of Gutzon's temperament it was particularly distressing.

He began to feel that California was not the place for him, and with that thought came a host of negative feelings. He tried to offset the sense of being personally and emotionally disconcerted by telling his friends that he was thinking only in terms of his career. The problem was not him, but the American attitude toward art and artists. He said he felt America was simply too young as a nation to appreciate the arts. He returned to this thought often in his career, especially when he was seeking large sums for his monumental sculptures. It was why he could never understand how financiers could reduce art to a matter of dollars and cents or how a millionaire could pass up the opportunity to be connected with one of his projects. This viewpoint often caused Gutzon serious problems.

Gutzon's negative feelings were so intense that it should have been simple to leave, but it was not. Lisa liked California and wanted to stay there. Her attitude had to be considered, though Gutzon was not sure they could reconcile their differences. Then the final blow came: someone poisoned the Danish hounds. Gutzon had gone to feed them one morning and found all four dead. It was a terrible shock to Gutzon, Lisa and many of her friends. Mrs. Fremont wrote:

> It will not comfort you two for your lost companions. . . . There is a widespread feeling for your beautiful dogs, even I, shut off as I am, get its echo.[10]

Now both Lisa and Gutzon knew they had to move on. Lisa could no longer fight his decision without risking having him go without her. Gutzon's mind was set; the only question was where to go. They had enjoyed France and Spain, but they did not think they could earn a living in either country.

They had to choose a place where they could settle, establish a reputation and earn a living. Mrs. Fremont urged them to consider England. She knew the British well and had many friends in the royal court who could help them. Gutzon decided to follow Mrs. Fremont's advice. They would move to London.

6
London

The year was 1896 and Gutzon was nearing twenty-nine. He was leaving the United States, for the second time, with a gnawing sense of frustration and returning to Europe. Part of his feeling was based on the troubles in California, part was his growing dissatisfaction with his marriage, and the rest was a nagging doubt. He was fast approaching his goal of being famous before thirty, but hitting the goal seemed less attainable than it had a few years before and he did not know what he could do to change his situation.

They travelled east just as they had before. Gallery exhibits were arranged in Omaha, Chicago and New York, and again enough paintings were sold to tide them over until they were settled. Social stops were made along the way, thanks to Mrs. Fremont. She had written letters of introduction to a dozen wealthy people, including Teddy Roosevelt, who was then New York's Police Commissioner. For the most part these were courtesy calls, which provided future contacts.

Reaching London after several weeks of travel, they took a studio in the Kensington section, then introduced themselves, by means of the letters written by Mrs. Fremont, to members of Britain's high society. These contacts brought some immediate commissions that kept Gutzon busy, but they were not as financially rewarding as he had anticipated. Painting portraits to earn a living was not artistically inspiring and did little to help Gutzon's flagging spirits.

Finally, as their money began to run out, Lisa tried to pressure him into returning to California, but he refused. Gutzon was discouraged, but adamant. Hoping Mrs. Fremont might be able to influence Lisa, Gutzon wrote and told her his troubles. Mrs. Fremont's answer was to the point:

> If you come back from London I shall be sorry and disappointed in you. English people demand stability and there is to be no talk of even preferring someplace else. . . . You cannot recast a national mould and England is set to its "slow and sure.". . . I do not blame Mrs. Borglum's American

impatience, but stay where the money is. . . . Take this kindly because it is the result of great interest in your career. . . .[1]

Gutzon did take heart from Mrs. Fremont's letter and Lisa backed down. Deciding to try something new he sought work as an illustrator and asked a friend, Hal Dane, to write letters of introduction for him to the editors of some of the leading magazines. Dane refused and told Gutzon, "let them know you are a member of a good artistic society. That is your best introduction."[2] He was referring to the French salons Gutzon had been admitted to, and was pointing out that Gutzon's timidity was uncharacteristic. It was a vote of confidence and it worked. Gutzon sought and received a number of assignments from magazines and contracts to illustrate two books.

Lisa and Gutzon had been in London almost a year when Solon arrived. He was on his way to study in Paris and had stopped to visit. The two had probably not seen each other, or been in contact, since the fiasco in Sierra Madre, but the bond between them was too strong to keep them apart for long. This time Solon was planning to stay only overnight, but the reception from Lisa was no warmer than it had been in California. She refused to allow Solon to sleep in the studio even for that short a time.

Both brothers ignored her rudeness — Gutzon because he was embarrassed and Solon to spare his brother. If James had not written scolding Solon because he had wasted money on a room when he could have slept on the floor in Gutzon's studio, no one would have known, but James inquired and Solon responded.

James had asked Solon because he did not share the same kind of closeness with Gutzon. James and Gutzon loved each other, but theirs was a carefully contrived relationship. It had thrived on anger for many years and then developed into a polite cessation of hostilities after Gutzon's marriage. What appeared to James as phenomenal success gave Gutzon stature, but it also created a formal attitude which Lisa encouraged. A feeling existed that Gutzon had achieved success despite James, not because of him, and James was more aware of this than anyone. It had been impossible for James to think of any man, let alone a son of his, wanting to paint pictures for a livelihood. He enjoyed art, but it was not something a man did to earn his living.

James' attitude made Gutzon's success seem more remarkable, but it created a barrier between father and son. When the couple had stopped in Omaha on their way to Paris in 1899, bringing all the trappings of wealth and culture, they were greeted as celebrities. For James this was almost incomprehensible.

He may have wished he could be closer to Gutzon, but the choice was no longer his. Lisa wanted her husband to be independent of his family. Gutzon accepted this partly because he was still angry and felt James and Ida were responsible for his losing Christina.

Solon's relationship with his father was quite different. Too young to remember his mother, he grew up loving Ida and James as his parents. When he decided to become an artist, Gutzon had already proved that a man could earn his living that way, and James had a better attitude. Not only did he not object, but he took great pride in his sons and helped Solon all he could.

According to members of Solon's family, Solon made an agreement with Gutzon while he was in London. To avoid competing with each other, Gutzon would remain "Borglum the painter" and Solon would become "Borglum the sculptor." Solon's family further claims that Solon sealed the bargain by leaving his paints and brushes in London.[3]

Gutzon never mentioned any agreement with Solon in his letters or journals. When he started his career in Los Angeles, and again when he was in Paris, he said that sculpture was a truer medium for an artist than painting. He became a painter because it provided a better market for newcomers, but he told Bob Davies and others that he would turn to sculpture when the time was right. Lisa never agreed with him about this. She considered painting the higher form of art. She may have been the one who made an agreement with Solon, thinking she was getting him out of their way.

After Solon left, Lisa once again began to talk about returning to Sierra Madre. Because she was tired and discouraged she threatened to go alone, probably because she could not believe that in a showdown Gutzon would not relent or follow her soon after she was gone.

When Gutzon and Lisa reached an impasse, she took a number of Gutzon's paintings and left for California. On the way she stopped in Chicago and arranged for a number of exhibits, which were very well received. She and Gutzon may have been temporarily separated, but she was still taking care of his affairs. After interviewing Lisa in Chicago, a reporter wrote:

> . . . at the present Mr. Borglum is in Europe where he is meeting with deserved success and recognition . . . one of Mr. Borglum's pictures was bought as a wedding present for the Princess Maude and he was especially honord by Queen Victoria who asked to see his paintings and sent him a letter. . . . These are slight indications of the brilliant future awaiting this talented artist. For, although Mr. Borglum has accomplished so much he is barely thirty, and has his future before him. . . .[4]

Another reporter, touching on one of Gutzon's inner struggles without realizing it, tried to explain why Gutzon signed his work in so many different ways:

> The work of John Gutzon . . . A Collection of Paintings by John Gutzon (M. Borglum). . . . What strikes one at first in the signature is that the last name of the artist is enclosed in parenthesis. He formerly signed his name as John Gutzon M. Borglum, but a brother who is a sculptor also uses the name Borglum, a fact that has led Mr. Borglum, who desires to preserve his originality, to take the first part of his name as his signature. The M. Borglum being retained only until the public becomes accustomed to his new name. . . .[5]

The explanation was Lisa's, not Gutzon's, it is obvious she considered Solon the sculptor. As far as the use of the various names was concerned, the explanation sounded logical, but it did not explain why Gutzon had used different combinations long before Solon thought about becoming an artist. "Johnnie Borglum," "J. Mothe:" the name changes were part of Gutzon's search for an artistic identity. When he finally became a sculptor he became Gutzon Borglum and never used another name.

Lisa's assumption that Gutzon would not remain in London without her was a delusion. He was unhappier with his marriage than with his career, though it often was difficult to separate the two. Gutzon did feel oppressed by the British who, as Mrs. Fremont had said, "kindle slowly." Despite Lisa's glowing reports in her interviews, the British did not grant Gutzon real recognition, but he had to stay until he achieved his goals or found something better. To do otherwise would have meant admitting failure.

He was thirty and not yet famous, at least not by his own standards. He was in his prime, but he was losing faith in the future and brooding over the marriage that he felt was a major part of his problem. Having passed her fiftieth birthday, Lisa was in a different stage of life. She no longer sought worlds to conquer; she wanted to settle down to what Gutzon saw as a sedentary life.

Their differences could not be easily reconciled. When Gutzon felt overwhelmed by them, he focused his frustration on their not having children because that could be dealt with. This feeling had not existed at the start, when both knew their relationship would be childless. It was fine then because, in essence, Gutzon was the child of their marriage. Lisa's energy focused on his needs, but after a time her constant attention became irksome.

Gutzon felt the need to take control of his life. When he did he found her difficult to deal with, and rather than face the real issues he dwelt on the sadness of their not having children. Gutzon's London journal is filled with variations on this theme:

Oh god, how my body would like to keep pace with my soul — stamp and rant as it does. And my poor brain is a killing pen where the tenderest emotions of son, man and parent appear, smiling sadly, are dissected and torn to bits. . . . Why should I yield or wish to yield my very soul for a child, I have no place for a child, see few children, yet the parent in me fairly weeps at times. . . .[6]

Gutzon's London journal is a peculiar document. There are melodramatic passages and pages filled with expressions of self-pity, followed by others that convey a sudden sense of determination, yet the overall effect is of Gutzon's wry sense of humor. This is especially apparent in his short, cryptic messages: "Full days," he wrote, "full of cares, headaches and heartaches."[7]

When the journal was started, Lisa was still in California demanding that he join her and threatening never to return to London. He may secretly have hoped she meant what she said, but Gutzon was not yet ready to admit that even to himself:

My new life leaves me alone as it will for some years at least. . . . I feel ripe and ready for this struggle of my life. I am in perfect health, my mind was never more alive to the possibilities in art. . . . Mrs. Borglum will rebel against staying in California — I am greatly troubled over any pain I may give her. . . . I may yet get back to the wild interest that made all work play — effort an intoxicant — and life so delightful. . . .[8]

Throughout the journal he made pledges and wrote sermons for himself:

Up with every taste of life that heals and builds and warms the strife and makes man keen and sound of mind — soul complete and whole — but down with every flesh's desire that shackles — and hold him in mire. . . . Love and work are two gifts that are really worth living for — for godsakes — or better for your own sake keep the hands busy or the mind will overcrowd and become morbid. . . .[9]

Gutzon felt a need for friends, and at times he seemed to dwell on his physical desires:

I have made one, perhaps two great friendships. Some have found strong attachments for me, but it is worthwhile noting those personal, bodily attractions?[10]

Keeping a record of these attractions was apparently worthwhile, because he continued to write about them, as in this note: "Oh what a day this has been. Climax, pain and terrible possibilities have arisen through a friendship. . . ." When Gutzon was feeling good about himself, or his work, the mood was reflected in his journal:

> I have smoked and allowed myself other indulgences . . . my nature . . . has too long been restrained by an over "austere control" . . . there is little harm in the vices — it becomes purely a question of their judicious use. . . ."[11]

His moods varied widely, and he often wrote about his disappointment in himself:

> How indifferently I take this half wish to keep some record of my thoughts. The question of "what use" destroys so much in me that I must rigidly fight the feeling. . . .[12]

The journal provides good insights into Borglum's psyche, but it should not be taken too literally. It was his self-expressive outlet, and he was often swept up in his own dramatic flair for making life seem more tragic than it actually was. Even he recognized this trait, as in this passage:

> This curious life ever eventful and ever full of pain and struggle yet my bitterest struggles have been with myself. . . . I have so questioned every act — thought and emotions that I begin to wonder is it best? I am much inclined to think not. . . . I am sure it holds me back from much I should do as feeling as a child. I must watch this and in the future analysis discover where analysis should and should not be applied.[13]

Gutzon was living a bachelor's life. He was travelling in unfamiliar circles and facing adult situations without Lisa's guiding influence. Spending weekends on the estates of his wealthy patrons, painting portraits, enjoying the polo matches and joining in the hunts, he was drifting in and out of relationships with people, like Madame Helen Bricka, the woman who brought his work to the attention of Queen Victoria and arranged the private showing.

Gutzon's allusions to his passionate friendships and his dwelling on the "parent in me" lead to various speculations, centering primarily on *Phyllis*. The question is who modelled for *Phyllis*, a white marble bust of a young girl of perhaps four or five Gutzon carved in London? Why did Gutzon seem to treasure the statue and take it with him from

Interior of London studio at St. John's Wood.

home to home? Why did it occupy a place of honor in the center of the dining room table? And why, when he was photographed in his studio with his nieces and nephews, did he place *Phyllis* on a pedestal in the center of the group?

The Borglum children remember the statue as a decoration and insist that their father never placed any significance on it. None of Gutzon's writings mention the statue, not is there any mention anyplace else, except in a story printed in a university student newspaper in 1948.[14] The author, Howard Pierce, had been Gutzon's chauffeur at Mount Rushmore in 1939. He writes about the talks they had on the drive to the mountain and claims that the "old man" told him Phyllis was his daughter, who had been born in London.

Passion, love, abstinence and indulgence were the over-riding themes in Borglum's life at this time, as these passages from his London journal indicate:

> Yes . . . I've felt the thrust. The first shivering pierce of love, but quickly I bade it be gone — and killed the impulse before it could soar aloof my reason — and something in me died.[15]

> Love is friendship in ecstasy, passion but the senses in riot. Virtue, that is virtue by abstinence, is dangerously near vice. . . . What is virtue, but a pretty name for economy? Is it virtuous to live the life of a celibate?[16]

During this period Gutzon continued to work in the Kensington studio. He was painting and illustrating for a living and working on statues and other paintings for himself. He was busy, but was not satisfied with his work or progress. At times he blamed the problem on the inadequacies of the studio and gave thought to moving. He even considered sharing a new studio with a friend:

> A short half hour with Brangwyn [British painter Frank Brangwyn]. I do enjoy him. He rings like true metal — he is an artist. We talked about taking Leighton's studio, but he agreed with me that it was too farceful . . . for really earnest working artists.[17]

There were ups and downs, but overall Gutzon was becoming increasingly depressed:

> '97, sad, hard year it has been, troubled and eventful to the brim . . . everything hangs back and only at what seems like rare moments do I grasp the work and accomplish anything, then for days gloom and mediocrity seize me and I feel a dabbler, an experimenter, an unformed and unpracticed student.[18]

Toward the end of 1897 Lisa realized that Gutzon would not follow her, and she returned to London to try to save their marriage. Before leaving the states she borrowed $5,000 from a cousin in Seattle to lease a large studio and home in the St. John's Wood section of London. It was a move born of desperation. The extensive repairs and remodeling put them heavily in debt and made what was already a difficult financial and personal situation worse.

They called their new home Harlestone Villa. It was a large, beautiful building with spacious gardens. They had chosen it in the hope that it would snap Gutzon out of his depression, and for a while it seemed to accomplish its purpose. The Midland Railroad Company, planning a new hotel in Leeds, had commissioned Gutzon to paint the lobby murals. The contract was sufficient to cover their debts and to make him feel that he was right in staying in England:

> The work is for a purpose. That is not against it . . . I am as pleased as a child to feel free to fancy and form my fancies. It is . . . the first order of the kind I have ever enjoyed — yes, the first of any consequence — it is epoch making in my life. It's the turning point not only in my fortunes but my art — liberation in every way. My experience, my years of bounding labor, oppression, financial embarrassment. . . .[19]

But even having a commission he finally was enjoying, as he had not done for several years, could not help his relationship with Lisa. Gutzon was finding it more and more difficult to live with her:

> If I was not naturally a happy nature, not forgetting philosophically, what a hell my existence would be. . . . I have been in this room practically all day alone — save Lisa . . . tomorrow will repeat today . . . and all tomorrows promise the same. . . . I know I have warm . . . friends who love me. All of whom want to come and see me and why don't they more often? Plainly and truly they feel a want of spontaneous welcome. . . . How long will this continue? . . . It's destroying my life. Society I do not want. How I hate so many of its leaders, the typical ones, cold, flippant, immoral in everything — and she is a fair sample of society and her personality and conversation is as poor.[20]

He would hit bottom and bounce right back. Regardless of the circumstances Gutzon could not stay depressed for any length of time, even when he tried. A few days after he wrote his bitter complaint about Lisa and how "it's destroying my life," he wrote:

> A Monday in July . . . happy day, happy in many ways . . . . The composition of my panels . . . but partly conceived and will be drawn duly.

59

Apaches Pursued, early 1900's bronze.

I am delighted with my own fancy in the arrangements of my figures and the life and nature—I can now practically weave into these works. . . . I know I feel for the first time consciously an artist—how I have prayed for it and I am not disappointed. Oh, if it will only give me back some of my young life that seems dead in me. Literally seems killed. How little I knew I was throwing myself away—the me in me—my soul's soul . . . .[21]

Despite his black moods, Gutzon was not as out of touch with life as he thought. He could still laugh and make jokes. When it was time to deliver the panels to the Leeds hotel in 1899, he took them there and then dropped a note to his brother Auguste in Paris:

The panels are O.K. and all are delighted—the only thing they complain of is that they are too good . . . . I took a run over to Liverpool Tuesday and had quite a lark about town—went to the great floating docks. Dined sumptuously—boozed, got locked up and generally had a good and respectable time. Came back the same evening . . . .[22]

Another year had passed. Gutzon was pleased with the reception his panels had received and was, temporarily at least, able to pay his bills. Feeling better about himself and probably to defy Lisa, he decided to try his hand at sculpture again. He took a theme from his boyhood — three Indians on the backs of wild horses — and turned out a beautiful work that he called *Apaches Pursued*.

There was a boundless energy in Gutzon that required passionate causes. He became intensely interested, for example, in the struggle between the Boers and the British Empire. In a letter to Auguste he observed: "Well, if the Boers fight as they have struggled diplomatically England will have the worst case of dysentery she has had in a century."[23] When the war did come Gutzon filled his studio with maps and charts and closely followed every battle, partly for himself and partly because he was illustrating the battlefront reports for several British newspapers.

Gutzon gained recognition slowly until he was accepted in the Royal Society of British Artists. The honor made him one of the few artists to belong to prestigious societies in three countries, and it also brought him new commissions.

Lisa did not approve of Gutzon's friends, but she did not mind the society people, whom Gutzon described as "cold, flippant, immoral in everything," and the Borglums entertained them regularly. The parties made it apparent that the initial renovations of the villa had not been adequate and they were forced to do further work, which once again put them heavily in debt. Suddenly their new home became a problem. The more they attempted to repair the more they discovered that needed repairing. The continual renovations were costly, especially when added to the expense of entertaining in the grand manner. They had created a social trap from which it was difficult to escape once they started to travel in a circle that expected them to entertain.

In London Gutzon had become friends with Joseph Duncan, Isadora Duncan's father. Joseph had left his family when he was charged with bank fraud shortly before Isadora was born. By the time he was cleared of the charges, Isadora's mother had divorced him. He eventually moved to London and started a new family. As an expatriate, he travelled in the same society as Gutzon and they became friends. When Joseph was offered a job in San Francisco, he booked passage for himself, his wife and daughter on the *Mohegan*. All three were lost when the ship went down at sea.

More than a year after her father's death, Isadora went to London. Many assumed that she had made the trip to collect her father's insurance, but that was not true. There was no insurance. Isadora went

Boer Soldier Returning From War, bronze, 1898.

to London hoping to find work. When she was unable to get theater bookings for her unusual style of dance, she began performing in drawing rooms and studios during the fall and winter of 1899. She was not dancing for a fee, but relying on the generosity of her host and the hope that someone important would be there to discover her.

One of the drawing rooms she danced in was at Harlestone Villa. Because Gutzon had been close to Joseph Duncan, Auguste assumed she had come to Gutzon's because he was Joseph's friend. Auguste's story was told to the other members of the Borglum family and became a part of the Borglum lore. Calling it Isadora's debut, of course, enhanced the story:

> . . . the debut of Isadora Duncan was arranged. The studio at St. John's Wood . . . made a suitable and picturesque background for such an event . . . there was an intermission during which the brother [Isadora's] spoke of the dance . . . . His discourse was too long . . . . Gutzon noticed he was tiring his audience, he called to me to open the side door for air, in the hope of shutting off this too lengthy talk. Finally Isadora danced out into the garden, sort of floating away, like a nymph, scantily-clad and coquettish — the illusionness of the foliage adding to the charm of the movements — of Isadora Duncan.[24]

There is no evidence that Gutzon befriended Isadora, or saw her again after she danced for his guests, though in later years he enjoyed telling reporters that the great Duncan had made her debut at his villa.

Gutzon's position in the world seemed set as 1899 drew to a close. He was a society portrait painter of exceptional talent. He was reviewed regularly, and his works were well received whenever he ventured beyond the portrait. Despite his unhappy domestic situation, he seemed to have managed to achieve a fragile peace within himself. He was not famous as he had expected to be, but there was always the future and the hope that his fortunes would change.

Plans were being made for the Paris Exposition of 1900, the great celebration to welcome the twentieth century, but Gutzon was not involved. Had he wanted to exhibit in Paris, there seems no question that he could have. His membership in the Royal Society and in both of the prestigious French salons would have made him welcome, but for some reason he decided not to participate.

The Borglums were, however, well represented. Solon was exhibiting and Gutzon was pleased. He was so proud, in fact, that despite his financial difficulties he invited James, Ida and two of his sisters and offered to pay their way from Omaha to Paris. They eagerly accepted this kind gesture. Everyone in the family was expecting a grand show, but none was prepared for the magnitude of Solon's triumph, Gutzon least of all.

The year before the Exposition, Solon had married Emma Vignal, the daughter of a Paris minister. Emma was an educated woman and as adventurous as her husband. Shortly after their wedding they went across the ocean and halfway across America to honeymoon on the Crow Creek Reservation in South Dakota. After four months there they carefully packed the dozens of small clay sketches Solon had created and returned to Paris, where Solon turned the small models into powerful works of art. His life-size scenes of the American West captivated the French. He became an overnight sensation known to the public and critics as "the sculptor of the West."

Gutzon could not have prepared himself for this reception. He wandered from statue to statue wondering how Solon could have come so far in such a short time. How had Solon managed to become a sculptor with the courage and freedom to create truly original work while he was painting portraits? There were only questions with no answers, all of them rooted in the fact that the nature of his dream was the intangible quality Solon had turned into reality. For Gutzon the experience became a crisis. "I feel like a dabbler," Gutzon had earlier written in his journal, "an experimenter, an uninformed and unpractical student."[25] At the time, this was more a self-indulgent reflection than a serious statement, but having viewed Solon's work Gutzon was haunted by this image of himself.

After the exposition Gutzon returned to London to resume work, but found concentration difficult. His journal is filled with accounts of his languishing in the garden while the city hustled by on the other side of the hedge. Gutzon knew he could no longer remain in London, but he would not consider returning to Sierra Madre. He did not know what to do until he received an offer from a Paris foundry that wanted to cast limited editions of *Apache Pursued* and the *Boer Soldier*, another of his London works.

The foundry's offer made up their minds for them. The Paris trip took on the aspect of a holiday as they packed, knowing they would not return to London, though they were not saying that to anyone at the time. Gutzon and Lisa knew that moving offered no real solution, but they were going to try because the only alternative was to end their marriage. Lisa did not want another divorce, and Gutzon had not yet mustered the courage to admit that he did.

7
After London

The final entry in Gutzon's London journal is dated April 27, 1901:

> Eleven years ago, lacking six months, I came to this court 65 Boulevard Arago. I am here again and as by magic without thought, without premeditation, without even a defined wish I have come back and installed near my own quarters. This is the last I shall note.[1]

They were back in Paris and most things were just as they had left them, including their old apartment. Solon and Emma had moved on to New York, which was just as well as far as Lisa was concerned. Emma knew how Lisa felt about Solon and probably how poorly she had treated him. She was not the kind of woman who hid her feelings, and all her life she blamed Gutzon for allowing his brother to be mistreated. Years later, when she returned to Paris to visit her parents, Emma instructed Solon not to take their son to visit Gutzon. "I want him to grow up like you, not him," she declared.[2]

Auguste was in Paris continuing his studies and planning to marry Emma's sister, Lucy. Lucy shared Emma's feelings about Lisa and Gutzon, and Auguste, who loved both his brothers, felt he was in the middle of a situation he could not control. Gutzon felt the same way, but Lisa's attitude had become part of his perspective. It affected his relationship with many of his friends and his family and prevented him from seeing Auguste as much as he would have liked, but there seemed little he could do.

Why Lisa did not soften her attitude is difficult to understand. Alienating Gutzon's brothers did not serve her purpose in going to Paris. She was hoping that a holiday, coupled with the opportunity to earn enough money to pay their debts, would change Gutzon's feelings about their marriage.

Arrangements were made for limited castings of the *Boer Soldier* and *Apaches Pursued*. But before the first royalty check was received, the deal went sour because the foundry began selling unauthorized castings. Gutzon was forced to go to court to stop the foundry from casting, and another dream was gone.

The Paris holiday was not turning out as they had hoped. The problems between them were too serious to be solved by a change in scenery. The difference in their ages had become pronounced with the years. Lisa was no longer an asset as far as his career was concerned. Gutzon certainly did not need a teacher any longer, and he felt she was meddling in his affairs, preventing him from achieving his potential. It seemed only a matter of time before they would be forced to go their separate ways.

For Gutzon the moment came when the Midland Railroad offered him another contract: more murals for a new hotel in Manchester. After completing the Leeds panels Gutzon had written Auguste saying, "the only thing wrong with them is that they are too good."[3] William Towle, the man in charge of the railroad company, agreed. He offered Gutzon the second contract and gave him a sizeable advance even though he did not need delivery for at least two years.

With the money and a major commission in the works Gutzon was suddenly at a crossroads. He either had to seize the moment and make his break or admit to himself that he never would. He could not continue to live as he had been living and remain the man he thought himself to be. The money gave him his chance, and he decided to make the most of the opportunity.

In later years, just as James had tried to hide his Mormon past and his two wives, Gutzon felt compelled to change his own history. In most of his accounts he dismissed his marriage to Lisa as a passing episode in his life, which was of little consequence and best forgotten. When he could, he made believe she had never existed. When he could not, he relegated her to a minor role.

Ironically, when Gutzon was Lisa's student their relationship had meaning. When Gutzon matured he began to feel oppressed by her constant attention. Their marriage might have had a chance even then if she had been able to change with him, but Lisa could not. While he sought worlds to conquer she began longing for a peaceful existence. Such differences could not be reconciled, especially when the two were incompatible in other ways. Gutzon wrote in his journal, "Is it virtuous to live the life of a celibate? . . . Oh! It hurts like some man's voice in pain who thought love had placed above some warring witch, some hell-born bitch who'd turn him under heel."[4] There are enough of these entries to make it obvious that Gutzon felt a lack of warmth, sex and affection and blamed Lisa for their absence.

Why did they stay together so long? From Lisa's standpoint, she preferred to be Gutzon's wife despite their difficulties. She felt that if she stayed with him long enough he would eventually begin to want the same things she did. Having had her own way with him for so long, she could not accept his rebellion as permanent. Gutzon's reasons were more complicated. He felt gratitude, loyalty, and a sense of dependence he did not like to acknowledge — he felt responsible. He had made his choice and felt obligated to live by it. He had blamed James for abandoning Christina, and that made it even more difficult for him to do the same to Lisa. There was an unwillingness to act, a nagging doubt, that prevented him from making an irrevocable decision, and probably a morbid satisfaction in living a tragic existence. A tragic life might have appealed to his strong sense of the melodramatic. He saw himself as a maligned, suffering hero. "I am as Dryfuss on his little island encased in chains . . . and for why, I know not," he wrote in his journal.[5]

The last years with Lisa were the ultimate example of his inability to admit he had made a mistake. Stubbornness was a trait he acknowledged, but never understood:

> Today I was brought face to face with a curious characteristic . . . . I had left the house bicycling when I noticed the tire needed pumping. I could not turn back however . . . . I mounted and rode. Every depression gave me a nasty jar. I soon became conscious of this stubbornness in my nature. Still I could not turn back . . . this trait carried me from California to Paris — in spite of every sort of opposition and want. Not once, but several times . . . .[6]

It also kept him bound to Lisa longer than he should have been, but it could not keep him that way forever. He knew his career was stagnating despite the contract for the murals. He did not fit the European concept of an artist, but did not know where he fit. What he did know was that his roots were in America. Every time he became upset he thought romantically about Europe, but, as he explained, it never worked:

> I had fled to Europe in considerable disgust over Americans following dead European traditions. I left to spend the rest of my days in Europe as Abby did, as Sargeant had, as Shannon had done. The delight of being an artist and living the artist's life was one thing, but the delight of living in a country where an artist was respected, admired, and given the first place according to his abilities among the citizens of the state was reward that any man

of talent sought. But the call of the wild had been studied somehow, in some way, and born in the West, I turned back to America with an extenuating thought and excuse to myself that "I would only be there for a short time, I would return to Europe." Suffice to say I never returned to live.[7]

There are many stories about Gutzon's return to America. His family believed the trip was made at the suggestion of the railroad people who wanted him to return to the states to study mural painting and decorating in outstanding American hotels. This seems highly unlikely. The contract had been awarded because Midland was pleased with the Leeds panels. Gutzon had painted them in the traditional manner using such classic themes as King Arthur and scenes from Shakespeare. The second set of panels was to be an extension of the same concept. Gutzon, of course, did not need to study American techniques, or anything else, for that sort of assignment. His own explanation of his departure is more dramatic:

> I was talking to a young English officer in a restaurant; he had been summoned to India . . . . Immediately after he departed, I was standing on the Rue De Rivoli . . . a French cabby asked if I wanted a cab, and without further reflection, I told him I did. I had a small bag with me, six or seven hundred dollars in my pocket, but without further thought I said . . . "Gadinor, you have just 30 minutes to catch the train to Cherbourg." He kept turning to me every square or two and would tell me it was a long way and he was afraid we would not make it.
> "You'll make it all right and when you do there will be a big *pour boire*." Every block or two I had to increase my tip . . . I caught the train. I had to cuss . . . the man selling the ticket . . . either did not understand or pretended not to, so I cussed him in three or four languages, and pretended to call the police. I ordered passage for New York, reservations on the boat, caught onto the train just as it was moving out . . . . That is about all the thinking, and all the preparations that were made for my return to America after eleven years abroad.[8]

The story brings to mind the fanciful episodes that James recounted of his leading wagon trains across the prairie and facing hostile Indians with his trusty six-shooter, and is just about as factual. Gutzon wanted to believe his story, and, as happened so often in his life, he convinced himself and then expected everyone to believe him.

He boarded the *Rynndam*, which stopped in Rotterdam before making the ocean crossing. Among the passengers who were picked up in Rotterdam was a bright energetic young woman of twenty-three named Mary Montgomery. She was returning to the United States after earning her Ph.D. in Sanskrit and other ancient languages at the University of Berlin. She had been born in Turkey, the daughter of American missionaires, and had spent most of her life in Europe. Her parents died when she was a teenager, and she and her two older brothers were left on their own.

After graduation from Radcliffe College she returned to Europe to complete her studies. Her letters written toward the end of her stay in Berlin express concern about the direction her life would take because she had no strong ambition. Mary delayed making a decision until it was made for her. The wife of her brother George, a minister in New Haven, Connecticut, had died during childbirth. George asked Mary to come home to care for his infant son.

The moment Mary and Gutzon met aboard ship they were attracted to each other. He was a vigorous man, handsome, intense and knowledgeable about a wide variety of subjects. He had a polish acquired during his years in Paris and London, the flair of an artist and suppressed desire to enjoy himself. Suddenly, in Mary's presence, he was no longer a student, but his own master.

The contrast between Mary and Lisa was too obvious for him to ignore. Lisa was past middle age and looking forward to retirement. Mary was blossoming and reaching for the future. Lisa's physical attractiveness had vanished years before, while Mary was just becoming a woman. That he was running from Lisa and not at all certain the separation would be permanent made Mary all the more appealing.

8
Gutzon Borglum

November 1901: America was entering the new century filled with hope for the future. Vestiges of the bitterness of the Civil War still lingered, but most people were tired of the struggle and looking forward to a period of reconciliation.

The industrialization of America brought about a new aristocracy: Hearst and MacKay in gold, silver, telephone cables and newspapers; the Lehmans in banking; Belmont with his railroads; Frick and Carnegie in steel; the Rockefellers in tin, zinc and whatever else they could force from the earth; and dozens of others all led by the house of Morgan, the most powerful of them all. They were amassing fortunes that staggered the imagination and with their newly acquired wealth were building estates that rivaled the castles of the feudal lords of the Middle Ages. They became the Robber Barons, plundering and raping Europe with their dollars and taking treasures from French villas and Egyptian tombs with equal vigor. They had been led to believe that only the early European masters produced real art. As a result, they fought each other for the right to pay outrageously high prices for masterpieces as well as mediocre works. Their audacity was new to the world. Entire castles were dismantled and brought to the United States, numbered stone by stone. Hearst filled warehouses with his acquisitions, while Morgan spent millions on single buying sprees.

Selling "respectability" became one of the most flourishing businesses in the world. The wealthy judged each other on the basis of which dealer or agent accepted them as a client. Some, such as Frick, recognized quality and limited themselves to purchases of true value, but most bought quantity with an undiscerning eye. In such a market it was impossible to prevent forgeries, and much of what was bought was fake.

When the craze for European art was at its height, the wealthy did commission American artists to paint portraits, and some did buy American paintings that caught their fancy, but not on the scale with which they sought the works of European masters. This European bias was one of the reasons Gutzon had soured on California. The signs of change, however, were there, and hope ran high in the art community that a new era was on the way. Many felt that it was a good time to be an artist and to be in America.

The *Rynndam* was towed up the Hudson River and nudged into a berth on the west side of Manhattan Island. It was just north of the dock where James landed in 1864 and Christina a year later. Gutzon stood at the rail with Mary at his side and looked down at the crowd on the wharf. There were baggage handlers, draymen, steerers, cabbies, longshoremen, seamen, vendors, and the curious — all mingling with those who were meeting friends and relatives.

After saying a temporary goodbye to Mary, Gutzon was on his own. He walked east to Broadway, enjoying the sights and the excitement of coming home after his long absence, and found his way to the Marlborough Hotel where he took a room and settled in. His first order of business was to re-establish the contacts he had made through Mrs. Fremont and others whom he had met while living in London. Gutzon had kept up on the news in the art community. He recognized the signs of change as well as anyone, but he also knew that, as of the moment, nothing had changed. It was difficult for an American artist to survive, unless he could live on minor commissions, which paid little. The only alternative was to break into the flourishing monumental sculpture business or find work in the studio of one of the sculptors. Lorado Taft, Daniel Chester French, Augustus Saint-Gaudens, John Quincy Adams Ward and a few others were creating the bulk of the major commissions, while fine young artists, like Solon, were forced to take whatever work they could find.

It was a discouraging situation for most sculptors. A few years after Gutzon returned to the states, two of his friends, who were unable to bear the strain and disappointment, committed suicide. In an interview following Charles Harvey's suicide, a reporter asked him who was to blame, and Gutzon answered:

> . . . the five or six men who are in power . . . look here, I suppose three hundred million have been spent for works of art in this country. They are imported things. They come from the palaces, the tombs and the churches of Europe. Now if just five percent of that had been spent in producing the very best art we could do in this country, there would be no Harvey tragedies . . . .[1]

"And what's the cure?" he was asked.

"The cure is to be yourself. Fall down if you must, but get up and go on again."

It was advice Gutzon had given himself often. He was then thirty-four and ready to "get up and go on." If the only lucrative market was in monumental sculpture, he would become a monumental sculptor.

The market for monumental sculpture was not the result of any one factor, but it was as much the result of America's collective sense of guilt as anything else. America's frontiers had vanished in an orgy of cruelty and barbarism. The Indians and their buffalo had been slaughtered or driven from their land. Despite the bravado of the army and the politicians in Washington, the blaring headlines that cheered the "victories" and the rationalizations, few thinking people were proud of what America had done. Then, before the Indians were destroyed or relegated to reservations, the Civil War broke out and Americans killed Americans for four long years. The bloody battles of Shiloh, Gettysburg, and Atlanta all left the nation reeling. When the war was over Americans were different people. They had proven themselves capable of brutality beyond imagining and could not be proud of what they had done.

At the turn of the century, government, on every level, joined with private organizations to pay tribute to war heroes. It was a mania rooted in the hope that by erecting monuments the pain, the grief and the guilt would somehow go away, and all that would remain would be the glory. Heroic-sized statues on towering pedestals became the order of the day. They seemed to defy the world to deny the greatness of America's founders, political leaders and the men who fought the battles. With the government in Washington leading the way, the nation was trying to use its new-made wealth to bind its wounds.

In this way history set the stage for Gutzon's return and gave him his opportunity. If circumstances had been different, he might have stayed a few weeks and then drifted back to Europe, but they were not. He had been swept up in the competition for sculptural commissions and the excitement and challenge he felt in New York. New York was a tough arena, but exhilarating for a fighter, and Gutzon was a fighter. Everything he had done before led him to New York and prepared him for the great changes in his life and artistic medium. Washington set the pace in terms of monumental sculpture commissions, but New York was the hub. Its spirit captivated Gutzon and he rose to the challenge. Once he committed himself, he never doubted that he had made the right move.

Desdemona, painted for the home of Phillip Rollins in New York City, c. 1903.

Gutzon's account to the contrary, his trip to America was not an impetuous, spur-of-the-moment decision. Gutzon had arrived with several paintings and bronzes. Less than three weeks later, his works were being exhibited in Boston. Again he received good reviews:

I Have Piped was created by Gutzon in his New York studio, but only portions were cast in bronze.

de la Mothe is a great symbolist . . . behind all his artistic creation, whether in painting or sculpture, is his depth of intellectual power, a genius that might have made itself great in literature had he chosen that medium of expression. . . . Mr. De La Mothe Borglum is making a flying [meaning "hurried," in the days before the airplane] trip to this country. He will visit Chicago and Omaha . . . and later Washington and New York and he expects to again be in Paris in six weeks.[2]

There is no record of Gutzon's making the Chicago, Omaha or Washington visits, and it is doubtful that he did. He had found too much to do in New York. The Midland murals were not due for some time, but he had to begin the layouts, had to find a place to work and had to devise a strategy for winning some of the lucrative commissions he was hearing so much about. Reflecting on his experience at this time, Gutzon wrote:

. . . overwhelmed with work in New York, wined and dined by old friends, I ignored the lack of centuries of accumulated beauty and art, and accepted the rudeness and unfinished condition of things in terms of strength and youth, and went to work with a vigor. Commissions were poured upon me and I was asked to join in a competition for a monument to be erected for General Grant.[3]

The Grant monument was the thing. It was an exciting competition for a Washington, D.C., memorial to Ulysses S. Grant. The final contract would pay $250,000, one of the largest commissions ever offered and an opportunity no artist could resist.

Gutzon rented an old barn behind a row of Manhattan brownstones on East 38th Street, just west of Third Avenue, turned it into a makeshift studio and began working on his Grant entry. He was suddenly swept up in the work. His mind began filling with themes for philosophical sculpture, and he began work on a statue of a beautiful young woman with a satyr at her feet, which eventually became his *I Have Piped.*

His social calendar was as full as his work schedule. He had met many members of New York society through Mrs. Fremont, and most were eager to renew the friendship. He became a welcomed guest at dinner parties, where he met the patrons and architects who controlled the lucrative contracts and commissions. Some, like architect George L. Heins, of the prestigious firm of Heins & LaFarge, became not only clients but good friends. Heins and Gutzon shared a love for the outdoors and often went on fishing and camping trips.

Mary had become very important to Gutzon. She had gone on to her brother George's home in Connecticut, where Gutzon was a regular caller. He became friends enough with George to borrow money from him, which he started repaying by painting George's portrait. The painting was never finished because, according to George's son, Gutzon was able to repay the money and stopped working on the portrait.

During his Boston show, Gutzon met Francis Allen, a Boston architect. Allen asked him to submit plans and a bid for a frieze for a new Vassar College Library he was building. Gutzon designed a massive panel 150 feet long, submitted his drawings and then asked George if Mary could work for him when he was awarded the commission. When George realized that Gutzon wanted Mary to pose in what he, a minister, considered an immodest costume, he refused permission, but that did not affect their friendship.

Lisa was still a presence in Gutzon's life. Their London creditors sent her polite notes acknowledging small payments and making veiled threats about not wanting to sue. She did her best to placate them and waited, hoping Gutzon would come to his senses. Gutzon had been writing her about the pressures of his work and making lame excuses for not returning, but it was obvious their life together had ended.

Gutzon's entry for the Grant competition was displayed early in March 1902. It was an elaborate work, magnificent in both design and execution, though still in model form. Describing his work Gutzon said, "The thought in my monument was that Grant was a product of the rebellion, and rose out of the battle."[4]

It was a heroic statue and Gutzon's pride in his effort is understandable. The 190-foot frieze depicted, on one side, the "debate" that led to the conflict, on the other, a scene from the "war," and in the center, beneath the figures of Grant and two of his aides on horseback, was the "peace-maker . . . not surrenderer." Gutzon described the scene as ". . . fathers meeting their wives, cannon abandoned for the plow . . . Grant and Lee in the center demonstrating signs of friendship . . . ."[5]

It was a grand concept and worthy of serious attention. Gutzon had entered his model knowing it was good, but the work was never officially exhibited. When the thirty-one final entries were placed on display in a Washington gallery, Gutzon's model had been disqualified.

His work had received critical acclaim from the *Washington Evening Star* and other newspapers, but the committee had declared his work ineligible. The official reason was never made public, but Gutzon charged that the committee had not believed he had done his own work:

. . . Mr. St. Gaudens said there was no one in America who could do the work. I learned he believed the sketch had been made — as so much of American sculpture is — by foreigners employed in American studios.[6]

Even if it were true, this would not have been a reason to disqualify an entry. Models were entered from as far away as Rome, and joint efforts were common and perfectly acceptable. It would seem more likely that the reason for the rejection was the art establishment's desire to put Gutzon in his place. As far as they were concerned, there already was a "Borglum the sculptor" (Solon) in the field, and they saw no need for another. The Grant committee must have assumed that after the rejection, Gutzon would quietly pack his bags and return to Europe.

Anyone believing that did not know Gutzon. The rejection made him more, not less, determined. He realized that if he wanted to be a monumental sculptor he would have to fight everyone in the field, including Solon, and that was what he wanted to be.

The only way the brothers could have avoided competing would have been by working together as a team, but Gutzon's strong personality made that impossible. This was unfortunate for Solon because, talent aside, he could never approach a committee or a potential patron with the same sureness or aggressiveness as Gutzon could. Both brothers went after the same commissions, along with many other sculptors, and this caused misunderstandings and some bitterness. Because Gutzon usually emerged the victor, the bitterness was stronger in Solon's family, as this comment by one member indicates:

> . . . if Gutzon could have been less ruthless in fulfilling his ambitions, set bounds that did not exclude Solon — or fellow artists for that matter — this story [Solon's] from the very beginning would be different. One feels that neither man ever reached the full stature of his creative potential . . . the dream of two brothers collaborating . . . was more idealistic than realistic. In the torment of his own making the truth may be that Gutzon killed his own dream.[7]

Gutzon was deeply hurt by the Grant affair, but he learned much from the experience. He made sure the rejection did not pass without public notice and used the publicity to good advantage. He told the press there were only two men in America capable of modeling the horses on his rejected model or on the one submitted by H. M. Shrady, the eventual winner: Solon was one, and he was the other. He further claimed that Solon had made not only Shrady's horses but also the horses for the second and third place winners, and the charges were never denied by any of the men he named. The injustice of little-known artists

Gutzon and friends at large oak table he built for New York studio. Marble bust of *Phyllis* is in the center.

forced to work for famous sculptors became a cause, and Gutzon publicly vowed never to enter a competition again.

By the time the furor that this opposition had created died away, Gutzon was an established member of the New York artistic community. Overnight he had become "Borglum the sculptor," which was just what the establishment had tried to prevent. Obviously, his new-found popularity, though unavoidable, was at Solon's expense. Gutzon would have had to give up his career, or both would have had to change their basic natures. Inevitably, and unfortunately, members of the family were drawn into the dispute. Auguste summed up the family's distress many years later:

> The interior emanations of an individual are things that can not be analyzed by a third person, who to blame or who to forgive—I loved them both, Gutzon and Solon; I had many things to be grateful for from both. It made me very sad.[8]

Several months after Mary returned, her brother remarried and she was free to move to New York to join Gutzon and pursue her career. She opened a literary agency, took assignments as a free-lance editor and became Gutzon's studio manager and companion, but the situation between him and Lisa was still very much the same. She was in Europe waiting for him to rejoin her, and he seemed incapable of making her face reality.

The pressure became too much for Gutzon. On September 1, 1902, Gutzon was stricken by a high fever and suffered a nervous breakdown. He was rushed to the hospital while word was sent to his father in Omaha. James came as quickly as possible, but there was little he could do, even as a doctor. He waited, along with Solon, Mary and many of Gutzon's friends. For days Gutzon drifted in and out of delirium; then the fever broke and the danger passed.

By the end of October, Gutzon was well enough to travel to Omaha with James. Ida recorded their arrival in her diary: "October 19 . . . Gutzon improving rapidly . . . Gutzon was 35 and 6 months when he had that awful brain fever."[9]

While Gutzon was recuperating, Mary took charge of the studio. She handled the daily business, answered mail and met often with George Heins to discuss Gutzon's plans for remodeling the old barn he was using as a studio. She contacted Daniel Chester French to ask if Gutzon could exhibit at the annual National Sculpture Society show. Knowing Gutzon by reputation, French told Mary the Society would be pleased to grant him membership, but he would have to go through the formality of submitting his work to a jury. This further alienated Gutzon, who had publicly vowed never to do what French was asking, and reinforced his feelings about the establishment.

In Omaha, where Ida could fuss over him, Gutzon recovered his strength quickly. Much of his childhood bitterness disappeared during his visit. After his stay in Omaha he began exchanging letters with Ida, and he often expressed a genuine affection for her.

A thinner, balder, but fit and determined Gutzon returned to New York just before Christmas. His new relationship with James and Ida and the renewed closeness with his brothers and sisters, who showed great concern while he was ill, added to his sense of well-being.

He seemed to feel he had earned a new place in the family, and for the rest of his life he assumed the role of "big brother." At one time or another all the younger members came to New York to spend some time with Gutzon. When Francis, the youngest of the boys, graduated from medical school he brought his family to the city so he could take postgraduate courses. His daughter remembered the trip:

Father, mother, my brother . . . and I lived on Gutzon's bounty. Gutzon urged father to come — so my mother told me — we lived there for some months in a big house in New Rochelle and later in an apartment in New York. It must have cost him a pretty penny. My parents had no money. This was just one example of Gutzon's incredible generosity to his brothers and sisters . . . .[10]

But the most important part of his return to New York was being reunited with Mary. They had not been apart for long, but the separation tested their relationship and proved, at least to their satisfaction, that their love was genuine.

9
New York

As 1902 came to an end, Gutzon began preparing for the new year. His mind was filled with ideas for statues and pending commissions. He was working on the Midland murals, and with delivery due that summer, he had to make them a top priority. He was thinking about a statue of wildly charging horses, which eventually became his famous *Mares of Diomedes*. Originally intended as a Western scene from his childhood, it depicted an Indian clinging to the back of a wild horse with other horses madly following. To help the flow of the statue he removed the Indian's clothing. When a friend saw the work, he said it reminded him of Hercules and the mythical flesh-eating mares of King Diomedes. Gutzon liked the imagery and changed his theme without changing the statue. Whether the *Mares* is Western or mythological, its power is undeniable. When the work was put on public display, one critic wrote:

> . . . chose this story because it gave opportunity to express that intimate knowledge of and sympathy with the horse for which he is noted. Eight magnificent creatures are represented in "vehement and diverse action." Hercules, a masterly molded figure, lies stretched full length on the furiously galloping leader, while the wild, unreasoning, plunging, biting herd dashes along the steep declivity in mad pursuit. The portrayal is extraordinarily striking and spirited. While the steeds are frenzied, tumultuous . . . each is wrought out with that realism, tempered with the dignity and nobility of the ideal, of which this sculptor is the master.[1]

The large bronze was purchased by James Stillman, a wealthy friend of Gutzon's, and presented to the New York Metropolitan Museum of Art. It was acclaimed as the first work by a New York artist to be totally conceived and created within the city and put on permanent display without leaving his hometown.

As his reputation grew and he made more friends, Gutzon began to receive important commissions. He created a series of gargoyles for the Class of '79 dormitory at Princeton University. There was little money

Segment of the *Mares of Diomedes*, the first major work produced by Gutzon in his New York studio.

in the gargoyle contract, but Gutzon accepted the work, feeling it would lead to more lucrative commissions and because the concept fascinated him.

Originally, gargoyles were created for a purpose. They were molded in the artist's conception of evil spirits in the hope that they would attract kindred spirits, those who were flying about and might enter the building and bother the good folks inside. Gargoyles also served a more practical purpose, as waterspouts. As the belief in evil spirits diminished, gargoyles sometimes assumed a modern twist as depicted by Gutzon's gargoyle with a camera.

The busier Gutzon became the busier he wanted to be. He used his sketches of John Ruskin, which he had drawn in London, as a basis for a marble, full-figure portrait of the aged writer sitting with a lap robe covering his knees. This work also was purchased for and added to the collection of the Metropolitan.

The lessons he learned as a portrait painter were serving as the basis for Gutzon's sculpture. Whenever possible he worked life-sized or better. In later years he talked about his search for an art form "as large and as grand as America herself," but in the beginning he worked large because he found it most comfortable. It was only as his sculptural philosophy evolved that size became a statement almost as important as the subject. Usually he thought in terms of the larger size, but there were such exceptions as the small figure of Nero, which he created in 1904. He commented on his *Nero* in an article for the *New York American-Examiner*. His article was titled "How Your Face Betrays You:"

> Just as I fashion features in clay, so a man, by his thought process playing upon his facial muscles, assumes a countenance fitting the nature of his soul. . . . Take my Nero, for example, in moulding the mouth of Nero I used my observation of men of his type. His mouth is full and loose; its thickness expresses sensuality and grossness. He had little upper lip — in fact, according to historians, his lower lip closed over his upper. His mouth was unquestionably of his own creation; its fullness and looseness were consciously molded by a mind which reveled in gross things . . . . More eloquent than any characteristic, however, is the human face. It expresses goodness; it reveals evil; it also shows cunning, selfishness, just as clearly as generosity and honesty . . . .[2]

With all the work, Gutzon was earning a great deal of money, but he could not keep out of debt. The studio remodeling had been costly, and the maintenance was high because the work required a number of assistants. Travelling in the social circles he had cultivated was expensive, but it was a necessary part of his professional life. Years later, Mary explained:

> We were always in financial difficulties due to Gutzon's optimism, his generosity and the large sums involved. He would get a large commission and at once sit down with the sponsors to see how much could be done with the money, usually resulting in his making little or nothing after all expenses were paid, and in the meantime, knowing he was to receive a large sum eventually, he would loan or give money to some friends or buy some beautiful or rare thing . . . .[3]

They were in such dire straits in the summer of 1903 that, according to Mary, when it was time to take the Midland panels to England, they had to "pass the hat" in the studio to raise money for Gutzon's ticket. His assistants may have chipped in, but the bulk of the money came from Mary's brother. As soon as he boarded the *Oceanic*, Gutzon sent George a wire thanking him for the loan.

Gutzon delivered the murals, used part of the proceeds to settle with his London creditors and returned to New York as soon as he could. The studio and Mary were becoming the focal points of life, and he did not want to be away from either one. The studio became a meeting place for Gutzon and Mary's many friends. They were an extremely popular couple. Located only a few city blocks south of Grand Central Station, the studio became a popular place where people dropped in. There was always a crowd of celebrities mingling with studio assistants and students, reporters looking for stories, writers, politicians, prizefighters and performers from nearby Broadway. Describing these studio days, Mary wrote:

> To enter one first passed through a green door opening on 38th Street; next along an old driveway, flanked now by a strip of green grass and a border of red geraniums; then through another door to a small anteroom, beyond which was the great workroom . . . . On the street door was a forbidding sign, "By Appointment Only." People respect that sign on the door of a professional man; but an artist, they think, is different; he will not mind if anyone dropped in to loaf a while . . . and because he loved people and knew they had come from a distance he would not let them be turned away.[4]

Gutzon had finally achieved the artistic maturity that had eluded him for so long. In England he had been little more than a talented portrait painter plying his trade. With the exception of his deep concern over the Boer War, he had shown little interest in matters that did not affect his career. His lack of involvement with outside interests could have been due to the restraining influence of Lisa or to the natural timidity of an expatriate who does not feel at home. But in New York he found himself and quickly became an outspoken critic of policies that displeased him, whether in politics, civic affairs or the various clubs he joined.

Gutzon, in fact, became so involved so quickly that many of his friends became concerned that he would be distracted. When he was criticized for spending too much time on matters not pertaining to his art, he replied, "My friends think I should be eternally astride a ton of clay. They do not realize that that would not make for better art, but only for a lop-sided artist."[5]

Gutzon acted like a man in a hurry. He had felt suppressed for so long that he wanted to seize life and all it had to offer. He moved with a speed that often disturbed others. Soon after he was accepted as a member of the National Sculpture Society, he became involved in a controversy. Feeling the Society's rules were archaic he began a campaign to change them. Suddenly he found himself in a fight with the established members led by the acknowledged dean of American sculptors, John Quincy Adams Ward. It was a nasty fight, and before it was over the two had become enemies. Gutzon felt compelled to resign. In Solon's biography, which was written by his son-in-law, Mervyn Davies, there is another version of this incident:

> Membership of the National Sculpture Society was a very brief affair. Gutzon was notified of his election in December (1903); a month later his name was in the headlines: "Gutzon Borglum calls NSP a disgrace," and in April he resigned. The official version had it that Gutzon Borglum resigned after being called a liar by a member at the council meeting. The argument centered on who was Borglum the sculptor. Gutzon charged the society's respected president, J. Q. A. Ward, with "insult and slander" and some of the members with "brutality." Being of a personal nature it was decided to strike the incident from the record. Solon, by then a council member, was asked to persuade his brother to change his mind. He failed and the resignation stuck. It was another incident that drove Gutzon out on his own, making him feel he could not function within the system.[6]

This was the type of argument that earned Gutzon his reputation for being a tough, independent thinker. He was considered by friends and enemies alike a man who would give a good account of himself in a fight and a man who could not be dictated to by anyone.

From his London patrons and Mrs. Fremont, Gutzon had learned how to cultivate friendships with people of influence, and he used that knowledge to good advantage. He had met Teddy Roosevelt when he was still one of New York's police commissioners. When Roosevelt became President of the United States, Gutzon visited him in the White House and renewed their friendship. Through Roosevelt, and several others, he soon became a popular member of Washington society and a frequent commuter on the New York to Washington railroad.

He would often work most of the day, leave for Washington late in the afternoon and spend the night in the smoker car debating with anyone who would sit up with him. When the train reached Washington, early in the morning, he would go to the house of a friend, sleep a few hours and then spend the day attending to business. In the evening he would attend a party or an important dinner, then catch the late train for New York and be back in his studio in the morning.

People welcomed Gutzon because they enjoyed his company. He was exciting. He possessed unbounded energy and all the attributes of a good actor. He had stage presence, enjoyed the limelight and displayed an uncanny sense for the dramatic.

Felix Frankfurter had been a part of the Washington scene from the turn of the century. His first government job was in the Roosevelt administration shortly after he graduated from law school. He and his roommates welcomed Gutzon to their Washington bachelor quarters, which was known as the "House of Truth." In his memoirs, Frankfurter wrote:

> A great friend of mine in those days whom I saw a great deal of was Gutzon Borglum . . . . He was one of those artists who had delightful incapacities for running government, but knew exactly how to do it . . . . He was a gifted user of language, both by speech and on paper. He was eloquent . . . . It was all clear, black and white, passionate, uncompromising. He was a great admirer of T.R. Gutzon was for war, for all sorts of war, six wars at a time. People weren't wrong; they were crooked. People didn't disagree with him; they cheated him.[7]

Gutzon's fields of interest expanded with his confidence. The Wright Brothers and their flying machine triggered his imagination and became a source of endless fascination. He experimented with wing flaps, propellers and aerodynamic models of a remarkably advanced design, and filled his studio with prototypes until visitors began making comparisons to the studios of da Vinci. In 1908, when the Wrights demonstrated the military potential of their aircraft, Gutzon was at Ft. Meyer as one of three official timekeepers.

He found that he loved organizations. He joined the Metropolitan Club in Washington, the Salmagundi in New York, a dramatic club and a number of fishing and riding organizations. He became a Mason in the Howard Lodge No. 35 F. & A.M. in New York and rose through the ranks until he served as Worshipful Master for two years.

Gutzon was still asking Lisa for a divorce. She seemed reconciled to their separation but refused to consider freeing him. She had finally decided to leave Paris and move back to California, and she still seemed to have an unrealistic hope that something would save their marriage. Gutzon was upset by her attitude, but there seemed little he could do about the situation.

Gutzon and Solon, who were seeing each other despite Emma's objections, were still competing for commissions. There simply was no way they could avoid it. They were in a competitive business, and the man who did not believe he could produce better work than anyone else had no place in the market. Those who doubted their own ability, or were too timid to push themselves, were the ones who were forced to work for others. Gutzon was as aggressive as the best of them and at times appeared ruthless, especially where Solon was concerned. Most of the members of monument committees were civic or business leaders with little knowledge of art. Few knew that there was one "Borglum the sculptor," let alone two. Solon's friends felt that Gutzon took advantage of the situation, never missing a chance to talk about the days when Solon was his pupil. He had no compunction about giving the impression that he was the first "Borglum the sculptor" and often did. When he was interviewed by a reporter planning to write about "Borglum the sculptor," Gutzon told him:

> The confusion exists since my brother has come into the field. It is natural enough having studied with me and following as he does the same kind of work I gave my attention to when in the West. . . . He is younger and while the noise and the stir I have made have been a financial help to him it has great disadvantages, and following in the kind of Western work I did has made it further difficult . . . .[8]

When the controversy finally became too much for Solon, he left New York and moved to a small farm he purchased in the Silvermine section of Norwalk, Connecticut. Essentially a private person, Solon decided he could not continue to compete for the limelight nor keep his mind solely on the end results regardless of the consequences, as Gutzon could.

Gutzon could, with a single-minded sense of purpose, do whatever he felt had to be done. He saw himself as the best sculptor and acted accordingly, which caused most of Solon's friends to see an evil motive in Gutzon's actions whenever the brothers competed. It also caused many others, who might have stayed neutral, to choose sides and do what they could to help Solon because Gutzon seemed so much the aggressor.

That is what seems to have happened at the St. Louis Exposition of 1904, the magnificent fair honoring Lewis and Clark. The list of official sculptors, those who were given specific assignments, includes almost every artist of the period, with the exception of Gutzon, who is noticeable by his absence. Gutzon did exhibit two models of his, *Mares of Diomedes* and the bronze *Boer Soldier*, which won a gold medal, but these were works he chose to exhibit and not part of the official presentation.

Gutzon's work was in demand. That he was no longer a member of the National Sculpture Society did not affect his ability to obtain contracts. Many committees were reacting to his sense of independence, and many seemed intrigued by his refusal to enter competitions. He also received a great deal of repeat work. He seldom had a dissatisfied client because once he accepted a commission he gave no thought to how much the statue would cost or how much he would make on the job. If he had to spend the face value of the contract and more, he did so. He simply knew no other way to work. As a result, clients, such as George Heins, brought him as much work as possible. Heins was working on the massive Cathedral of St. John the Divine, in upper Manhattan. After almost ten years, the Belmont Chapel section of the structure was ready for sculpting, and Heins recommended Gutzon.

Gutzon was offered a contract and accepted, though there were so many statues involved that it seemed like a lifetime job. This commission set the stage for one of Gutzon and Solon's worst misunderstandings. Mervyn Davies, Solon's biographer, provides this view of the controversy:

> . . . illumination of how he succeeded in capturing this extraordinary contract, getting it away at least from Solon, is supplied by the following. One day, soon after the close of the St. Louis Fair, at a meeting in the vestry . . . The Rector . . . Huntington . . . Chairman of the sculpture committee of the new church, said to his parishioner, Mrs. David McIlwaine, Solon and Emma's intimate friend from Paris days, "We are going to give some work to your sculptor." He had a long talk with Mr. Borglum, he said, in the course of which he mentioned the St. Louis group and Emma's receptions, to which he had been invited by the McIlwaines, but which he had been unable to attend. It was not until after the meeting . . . on the way home it occurred to her it was strange this particular piece of good news had not been given to her by Solon himself, or Emma. Her first reaction was to be vexed with her friends. But the thought dawned: was it Solon to whom the Rector talked or Gutzon? She rushed over to her friends to learn the truth. When her suspicion was verified that it was Gutzon . . . it was too late; the contract . . . had already been given to Gutzon.[9]

There is no doubt that the conversation between Mrs. McIlwaine and Dr. Huntington took place, but the conclusion that he was referring to Solon is not necessarily borne out by the facts. If the hiring of the sculptor had been the duty of Dr. Huntington and his committee, the premise might have been valid, but the committee hired only the architects Heins & LaFarge. They hired the stonecutters, and the stonecutters hired the sculptor. The committee's responsibility was to approve or reject the statues after models were submitted.

A few years later, when Gutzon was deeply involved in the actual work, a dispute arose over another matter and the committee issued the following statement:

> . . . as to the conditions under which the services of Mr. Borglum have been engaged. He has been employed, not by the cathedral authorities, but by the contractors for the stone work . . . .[10]

Based on that statement and the fact that Gutzon was not only a close friend of George Heins, but also had done work for him prior to the awarding of the cathedral contract, it would seem that if anyone was confused about for which Borglum the contract was intended, it was Dr. Huntington. Hearing the name Borglum, and probably now knowing there were two, he made the association with Mrs. McIlwaine's friend and incorrectly assumed it was Solon. No one knows how much of this Solon and Emma knew, but once again they felt Gutzon had taken a commission meant for them.

The contract for the cathedral was a major commission. There were ten heroic-sized stone carvings and one bronze. In addition there were thirty smaller figures for the St. Savior's Chapel and twenty for the St. Columbia Chapel, plus a number of others — more than seventy-five statues all together.

When Gutzon had completed his first models, Dr. Huntington and his committee visited the studio. They were satisfied artistically, but Dr. Huntington had questions about the archangels Gabriel and Michael. He felt the female features of Gutzon's archangels did not fit the male image of angels. The reports of Gutzon's reaction varied. Rupert Hughes wrote:

> He did not pause to defend his statues by referring to the countless women angels of ecclesiastical art; he showed an almost superhuman superiority to the temptation of theological argument. He simply took a sledgehammer and knocked them to pieces.[11]

Mary wrote:

> Gutzon wasn't much concerned with the sex of angels. . . . It was a simple matter to remove the offending face and model one with sterner features. Gutzon kept the original face, had it cast in silver and used the photograph

91

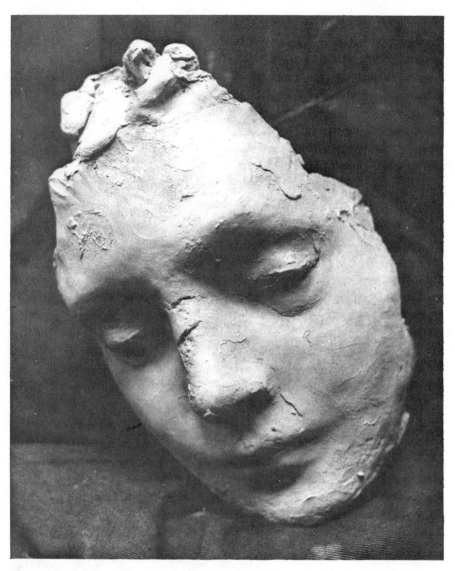

The mask of the *Angel of Annunciation*, which was the center of the controversy over the sex of angels.

for a Christmas card. . . . Everything was sweetness and light until a reporter noticed that Gabriel's countenance had quit being pretty and was now a little hard . . . .[12]

That reporter saw a good story, and once the newspapers took the lead they had a field day. Gutzon seemed to enjoy the furor and gave enough interviews himself to keep the story alive. In one he asked a reporter, ". . . if God sent an angel to the Virgin Mary to tell her she was pregnant, would he send a male or a female?" But Mary took the matter more seriously. She felt "it put upon the sculptor a stigma, a mark of an evil temper, which he carried to the end of his life . . . ."

The story finally died of its own volition and the work went on. No one had been hurt or offended by the argument. Gutzon's reputation as an irascible fighter grew. Some of the newspapers pinned a "bad temper" label on him, but that only made him more of a celebrity.

For the next few years, work on the statues proceeded routinely; then, suddenly, Gutzon's work on the cathedral project was news again. This time he was angered by the quality of the stonecutter's work and the changes that were being made in his models. In a letter to Heins & Lafarge in 1907 Gutzon complained:

This work is assuming such proportions, and the character of it deteriorating rather than improving, that some radical change in the methods of reproducing my work must be adopted if the work is to continue . . . the assurance . . . that the work would eventually be done as I wished . . . have led me into allowing a great deal of work to be placed that can not be accepted . . . the great blunder has been in not carving this work within reach of the sculptor.[13]

Gutzon expected immediate action, but nothing happened because his friend George Heins was seriously ill and his partner did not think the stonecutting was any of Gutzon's business. Finally, after waiting a month, Gutzon took the matter to Dr. Huntington:

It is more than a month since I sent a lengthy report to Heins & LaFarge on the character of the carving of the sculpture at the cathedral, and my protest against it . . . . I am thoroughly convinced the architects and contractor not only are not prepared to support me in this work, but are opposed . . . there is nothing further for me to do . . . but ask for a hearing . . . before the full committee . . . .[14]

Gutzon's letters forced the issue, and an agreement was reached that gave him control over the quality of the stonecutting. Much of the work he objected to was ordered re-cut, and a shop was set up on the cathedral grounds so that he could supervise the work.

The final word on the cathedral sculpture came several years later, in 1925, when attempts were made to discredit Gutzon by reviving the story of the destroyed angels. Dr. Huntington was asked for details of his "trouble with Borglum." His answer was short and to the point:

> Angels still stand serene in their places where Borglum put them. We never had any trouble with the sculptor.[15]

10
Six Wars At a Time

Gutzon was no longer painting. After the Midland murals he had switched to sculpture. He was trying to concentrate on his numerous commissions, but he also created other statues that seemed to work their way into stone because of an inner need. *Nero* had been one of these philosophical works and the *Mares of Diomedes* another, but the most important was a group of female figures. This concept started with a London painting titled *I Have Piped* and became a series of marble figures after he settled in New York.

The idea probably began forming the moment his mother, Christina, left, and it remained in his mind, dormant at times, but still there, until he was able to give it form. It is possible that Gutzon had to wait for someone like Mary to come into his life to give him what he was not getting from his relationship with Lisa. For him Mary represented love and family — all that the relationship between a man and a woman should be. Her influence on his philosophical works was as profound as Christina's.

As each statue was finished and put on public display, it aroused a variety of emotions, particularly within Gutzon's family. When Ida saw a photograph of *The Female Atlas*, she was overwhelmed. Somehow the statue made her feel that it was intended for her. She felt vindicated and wrote Gutzon to say:

> Arnold has brought me yesterday a clipping of Mother, the Burden Bearer. I can not quite express my feelings, because it is so great — the woman Atlas represents the burden, and also the great love of Motherhood. Take it as it is. I thank you more than I can tell you.[1]

Most were able to identify with the *Atlas* and others in the series, such as *Motherhood* and *Womanhood*, but the statue Gutzon called *Conception* aroused controversy and puzzled many. In discussing the statue Gutzon said, "I have depicted such a mouth in the head of the woman, with eyes closed, who embodies the thought of inspiration. . . ."[2]

Gutzon in New York studio with model of *Conception*.

Mary, who could never understand how anyone could criticize anything Gutzon did or question his motives, wrote:

> In those days in New York, before Gutzon became involved in many big public memorials, he had more time to express his creative fantasies or "pipedreams" in marble. A larger than lifesized nude figure of a woman . . . caused some stir and was considered too daring in certain circles. To him it represented the holiness of creation . . . and was created in the same reverent, humble spirit. . . .[3]

Mary was everything to Gutzon, but Lisa was still his wife. She stood between the two, even though she was 3,000 miles away in California. Lisa seemed reconciled to the fact that he would not return to her, but she still refused to give him a divorce.

If it were possible, he would have bought his freedom, but as usual he was spending more than he was earning and his creditors were draining his resources. Yet Gutzon was not concerned. "You're right," he wrote a friend, "I have been extravagant. I wanted to spent $5,000 on my family this year and they managed to make it $11,000."[4]

Most of his debts, however, could not be shrugged off that easily. A serious situation, with threatened lawsuits, was developing with a cousin of Lisa's who had lent them the money to lease the St. John's Wood studio in London. Now that Gutzon and Lisa were no longer together, he was demanding payment. Gutzon, no longer able to ignore the threatening letters, wrote Lisa's cousin to plead his case:

> Dear Wallie . . . I acknowledge all of the notes and shall meet them at the earliest possible dates . . . . You probably know that we have separated since I left London. I have given her everything there was to give . . . household property . . . deed for our home in Sierra Madre . . . . The home was mortgaged but I offered to take steps to clear that . . . which she refused. Still, I hope a settlement of such nature will be effected . . . that this intolerable, unnatural relationship cease, and that she divorce me . . . . When Lizzie went to California, she took everything with her . . . . I have nothing but my work. I am tired, tired and old. Ever since I was married at twenty-two I have tried to live an older age and forgone my youth . . . . You need only transfer a few of your own longings for home and children and the rest, to know what bitterness there can be to have life with every effort empty and be without them.[5]

Gutzon may have felt that his personal life was "empty" because matters were seemingly beyond his control, but he certainly could not feel that way about his artistic life. As a sculptor he was establishing himself rapidly and in a way no one had ever done before. He was successfully spending more and more of his time in Washington seeking commissions, much to the chagrin of the other sculptors he was competing with.

Washington's leading hostess, Mrs. Wadsworth, was a friend who could and did open doors. She arranged dinner parties in his honor and made sure he sat next to the "right" people. In many ways Mrs. Wadsworth filled the void that had been left when Mrs. Fremont passed away.

When Gutzon was invited to join Mrs. Wadsworth and her society friends on their annual trek by horseback through West Virginia, he hesitated because he did not want to be away from Mary, but he could not refuse and remain in Mrs. Wadsworth's good graces. He went along, enjoyed the scenery as much as he could and wrote Mary nightly: ". . . it's glorious — and I'm thinking ever of you — and planning for us and you know what that means."[6] A few days later he wrote:

> I fill every hour with thoughts of you . . . . I'm not tired of my trip but I'm tired, I'm lonely and I don't enjoy anything without you enjoying it with me.[7]

As the days with Mrs. Wadsworth passed, his loneliness and boredom increased, as did his longing for Mary:

> . . . a poor white trash town . . . in the mountains of West Virginia . . . . You must send wires telling me it is imperative that I return. I'm so lonely for you and wish it was you I was travelling with . . . . I'm surprised at how far from everything we are. The people simple as their animals and about as interesting.[8]

As always Mary followed instructions and wrote Gutzon a long letter explaining why he was needed at the studio, which she ended by saying:

> What a wonderful thing love makes of the world and life . . . the first creator and it seems to create old things anew and make them wholly fresh and virginal.[9]

Gutzon's friendship with Teddy Roosevelt provided easy access to the White House, and Gutzon used it to good advantage. Once he understood how Washington functioned, Gutzon began thinking about the possibilities of obtaining an official position, knowing it would give him a tremendous advantage.

The power base, in terms of monumental sculpture, was still in New York, but most of the financing came from Washington. After his bitter confrontation with Augustus Saint-Gaudens, John Quincy Adams Ward and the others, Gutzon realized he could not break into their ranks on his own terms. He adopted the image, therefore, of the "rebel." He turned their attacks on him to his own advantage while finding ways to secure his position.

He started by telling his influential Washington friends that he would like to become the Capitol Building's "Artist-Sculptor-in-Chief."[10] The position existed only in Gutzon's mind, but he felt it was needed. In a letter to one of his friends, he said that if he were appointed he would oversee the placing of all statues and approve the design for all artwork. He would see to it that there were no more "obelisks that could just as easily be a monument to Cleopatra" as to Washington. He said there would be no more statues of the "Father of Our Country" in Roman togas, such as the one Congress purchased from Horatio Greenough.

Gutzon wanted to complete the frieze in the Capitol Building Rotunda, but he was just one of many who shared that dream. The original work had stopped in 1888, leaving a section blank. The original design had been painted in, but it had been compressed and there was a thirty-foot gap. Committees had been meeting for almost thirty years in an attempt to choose an artist and a concept to fill the space, but they were unable to agree on either. Gutzon saw himself as the man for the job, but like the other artists, he was unable to convince the committee members. Not until 1950 did Congress finally pass a bill authorizing Allyn Cox to complete the work.

Gutzon seldom stepped lightly, no matter what the issue or who was involved. It was his fight with the establishment that prompted him to criticize Augustus Saint-Gaudens in a magazine article written shortly after Saint-Gaudens' death in 1907. Gutzon must have known that his article would raise a furor:

> With the passing of Saint-Gaudens the standard of good work was taken from us . . . he was not a great technician . . . . But he had something that made the whole world better because it was made. He gave us . . . one or two . . . great statues, then he dropped to the architect's standards . . . . Saint-Gaudens' sense of refinement led him to conventions, and lack of imagination to a repetition of those conventions . . . it is natural that his following should catch his spirit, acquire his style . . . and we have a pseudo-classic school for which dull mediocrity is without a rival in the whole field of art . . . . We have many good men — good for nothing. New York is filled with honest men, pusillanimous cowards, "sidesteppers" who dodge every opportunity . . . .[11]

Gutzon and an assistant in New York studio working on Sheridan Monument.

Clearly Gutzon was not one of the "sidesteppers." He seemed determined to take on the world with one article, and, as expected, the outcry was long and loud. Referring to it later, Mary wrote:

This sincere analysis of another man's work did incalculable harm to the sculptor's [Gutzon's] position in New York art circles when newspaper headlines announced: "Borglum attacks Saint-Gaudens." Quickly the controversy became nationwide and partisans joined with more zeal than discretion.[12]

As with all such arguments, the controversy eventually dissipated, but the bitterness remained and flared whenever another incident arose to remind those involved. Usually, where Gutzon was concerned, those offended did not have to wait long. Of all the commissions he was award-ed, none upset the art community more than the contract to create the General Sheridan statue in Washington, D.C.

Sheridan was one of the North's most celebrated Civil War heroes, who had risen from captain to major-general on the battle field. The story of his rallying his men in a skirmish with Jeb Stuart thrilled every Northerner. It was said that Sheridan's troops were fleeing in panic when he rode into their midst and sent them back into battle shouting, "You'll sleep in your tents tonight or you'll sleep in hell!"

John Quincy Adams Ward had been struggling with the Sheridan commission for seven years with no success because the family did not think any of his models did justice to the general. When Gutzon took the contract away from Ward the art community was outraged. Had it been anyone else but Ward, the switch might have seemed like a shrewd bit of business, but because of the men involved, it was assum-ed Gutzon had acted vindictively and had misused his social position.

Ward was deep in his seventies and reaping the rewards of a long and distinguished career. He was president of the National Sculpture Society and the acknowledged leader of the art community. In 1904, when Gutzon had joined the society, fought bitterly with the rules com-mittee and resigned, he sent his letter of resignation to Ward. In his letter Gutzon tried to give the impression that he was not upset and did not blame Ward for his troubles, but few in the society were convinced.

When Gutzon took the Sheridan commission away a few years later, Ward's supporters assumed he had simply been waiting for his chance to get even. Ward's supporters claimed that Gutzon's good friend Mrs. Wadsworth had arranged a dinner party, invited Mrs. Sheridan and seated her alongside Gutzon. During dinner, Gutzon convinced Mrs. Sheridan that he was the only sculptor who could create a statue wor-thy of her husband.

After waiting seven long years, Mrs. Sheridan did not need much convincing. She was discouraged with Ward's efforts and found Gut-zon's enthusiasm contagious. A few days after the party, she showed up in Gutzon's studio with her son, Lieutenant Phil Sheridan. Before Mrs. Sheridan and her son left to return to Washington, they had prom-ised Gutzon the commission.

Gutzon did not disappoint the Sheridans. He was exhilarated by the swirling controversy, and he produced a magnificent statue that was an exciting departure from the standard of the day. The public had come to expect that monuments would portray old warriors in stately positions, mounted on high pedestals, but Gutzon gave them something else.

Using the younger Sheridan as his model, Gutzon posed General Sheridan so that an observer could sense the battle and almost hear the General's famous rallying cry. Then, to heighten the effect, Gutzon installed the statue at ground level, creating an atmosphere of vitality. The Sheridan monument established Gutzon as one of America's foremost monumental sculptors. After it was put on public display, no committee with a commission to award could afford not to consider Gutzon Borglum.

11
"The Jewish Problem"

While she managed the studio and took care of Gutzon's affairs, Mary also pursued a career as a literary agent, worked as an editor on the *Encyclopedia Britannica* and helped Dr. Isidor Singer, a renowned Jewish scholar, with his massive *Jewish Encyclopedia*. Dr. Singer was older than Mary and Gutzon, but he became a close friend and introduced them to some of the day's most prominent Jewish leaders. Through Dr. Singer and others, Gutzon eventually became friends with men like Felix Frankfurter, Samuel Colt, Eugene Meyer, Paul Warburg, Bernard Baruch, Mortimer and Jacob Schiff and many more, with whom he often debated what he termed "the Jewish problem."

It is difficult to reason why Gutzon would risk insulting people he cared about and involve himself in an endless debate that could only alienate friends and patrons, but he did. There was nothing about him that could be termed moderate, neither in his actions nor his thoughts. He thrived on controversy, though he often went to great lengths to deny that fact. Gutzon was simply ruled by his emotions. He seldom weighed the consequences of his words, and he loved to debate. His Jewish friends, for the most part, laughed at his ideas, took him for what he was and were often his staunchest defenders.

Many of his friends ignored his diatribes. They seemed to realize that, as an artist with a restless soul, he needed to rid himself of a great deal of undisciplined thought and energy before he could create. They also knew that his views were often misunderstood or that he would speak in haste or anger and then turn around and defend the same people he attacked.

Gutzon reacted to most situations, whether minor or catastrophic, with such speed and vehemence that he often left others vaguely disconcerted. It was impossible for anyone who came in contact with him not to react emotionally, either positively or negatively.

The San Francisco earthquake of 1906 was devastating. By the time the tremors, fires and explosions had subsided, after three days, over seven hundred inhabitants were dead and five hundred city blocks were gone. There was no power, water or transportation, and there was a danger of epidemic. All that the survivors had to sustain themselves were their courage and determination to rebuild.

The whole nation rallied to their aid. Gutzon, Mary and some of their friends quickly put together an art exhibition and, less than two weeks after the quake, raised a substantial sum of money for the victims. Mary described one reaction to Gutzon's efforts:

> . . . some weeks later, a well-known painter said to the sculptor's friend, Sidney Smith, as they were sitting before the fire in the Balsam Lake Fishing Club, to which the sculptor also belonged, "I don't like that man Borglum." "Why?" Smith asked. "Oh, he's so dammed quick! We raised a fund to help the . . . fire sufferers, and he got it to California before we knew what was going on." This he did through his friend Jacob Schiff, of the Kuhn, Loeb and Company banking firm.[1]

Like it or not, that was the way Gutzon functioned, and, difficult as it may be to understand, men like Jacob Schiff were his friends. Why difficult to understand? Because Gutzon was an avowed anti-Semite, while Schiff and his brother Mortimer were leaders of the Jewish community. The Schiffs somehow managed to transcend Gutzon's public utterances, perhaps because they had grown accustomed to the public view of their faith and had learned not to take offense. Years later Gutzon and Mary's daughter, Mary Ellis, tried to explain this feeling:

> It wasn't the same in the teens and twenties. We loved and hated and disliked whomever we wished without it being a sign of moral turpitude.[2]

That may have been. It certainly was the attitude of Gutzon's Jewish friends, who seldom allowed what he said to disturb their friendship. Gutzon was obsessed with a belief that the international bankers, most of whom he believed were Jewish, were attempting to take over the world. He believed there were inherent characteristics, unique to the Jewish people, which made them greedy and anti-social with all but their own kind. He felt that, as a result, they had no rightful place in the family of man. In his paper "the Jewish Question," Gutzon wrote:

> Jews refuse to enter the mainstream of civilization, to become producing members of the world community. They do not share or create, but choose instead to clannishly hold onto their old ways and with mere money buy and sell the efforts of others.[3]

104

For several years, "the Jewish problem" was a preoccupation with him. Gutzon wrote long dissertations on the subject and shared them with Dr. Singer. The essays were usually greeted with Singer's characteristic good humor. His answers, when he took the time to answer, were more like a patient adult's reprimand to a child than a serious attempt to refute or debate. In a typical reply Dr. Singer wrote:

> "Dear friend Gutzon . . . reading what you write someone would think you were an anti-Semite, when in reality you are a philo-Semite."[4]

To this, Gutzon replied, "Dr. Singer . . . if you were not a bigger man than you are a Jew, I would throw bricks at you . . . ."[5] And then he proceeded to list all the stereotyped complaints, all the trite, simplistic beliefs of the demagogues that were so popular at the time.

It was more a game than anything else. The two men cared for each other and were on solid enough ground to be able to express themselves in vunerable areas. Their argument continued for several years, with Gutzon attacking in an unrelenting manner, but then he stopped because he suddenly realized his friend was growing tired and old. When he learned that Singer, who was almost seventy, did not have the means to retire, he switched his energies to a campaign to create a retirement fund for his friend.

Gutzon became Singer's champion. He drafted a letter citing all the reasons why the Jewish community had cause to be grateful to Dr. Singer and mailed it to every prominent member of that community. The letter started with a touch of Gutzon's wry sense of humor: "I realize that I am the last person you would expect to find heading a committee like this, however . . . ."[6]

It is not surprising that few even bothered to respond because Gutzon's public attacks were not the kind that would endear him to those he was attacking. The only responses came from the men who knew Dr. Singer personally. None came from those who knew him only by reputation. Typically, Gutzon took the reaction as a personal affront and further proof of Jewish greed.

Of course, what was greed in one person was need in another, But Gutzon was rarely able to make the distinction. His friend Samuel Colt, founder of the United States Rubber Company, was a wealthy Jewish industrialist and one of the group Gutzon accused of raping Europe with their dollars. That did not stop Gutzon from accepting a commission from Colt for a Lincoln bust or prevent him, a few years later when he needed money, from borrowing $10,000 from Colt and giving him

105

three marble statues from his *Motherhood* series as collateral. In fact, Gutzon saw the transaction as a way of helping Colt understand the better things in life.

A problem developed when Gutzon decided he had the money to redeem the statues. He claimed they were collateral, but he had no papers to prove he had not made an outright sale, and in the years that had passed he had never made a payment on the principal or the interest. The problem was further complicated by Colt's death. When the executors of the estate rejected Gutzon's claim, he was outraged. Once again he had been cheated. Knowing he would have no claim in court, Gutzon took his case to the newspapers and attacked the "robber barons who suck the creative life-blood of the artist and strip him of everything he had that is beautiful or of value." The statement could apply, of course, to Morgan, Hearst and dozens of others who were not. Jewish, but Gutzon refused to acknowledge that and took his attack one step further. It was not Colt the man who had taken what was rightfully Gutzon's but his avarice as a Jew. "Colt," he wrote in a letter to the executors, "epitomized the Jewish character, that greed was a part of his inborn nature, his heritage . . . ."[7]

The incident with Colt was not an isolated occurrence. Jacob Schiff was one of Gutzon's close Jewish friends. The Schiff home in New York was always open to Gutzon and Mary, and they spent many weekends at the Schiff estate on Long Island. Gutzon often turned to Schiff for advice, despite his knowing that Schiff was a member of what Gutzon called "that race the neither produced, nor contributed, but lived off the achievements of others."[8]

The Schiff family, like many other leading banking families, had come to America long before the massive immigration of the middle and late 1800's. When these immigrants started arriving by the thousands and then by the hundreds of thousands, the established Jewish community was not pleased. It did not feel a kinship with the new arrivals. Their strange dress, European customs and peculiar religious views were distasteful and threatening to American Jews. Those who had arrived prior to the great influx had been assimilated. Those who had established themselves in banking, manufacturing or retailing were an integral part of their communities, even if they were not fully accepted. These men were Jewish by birth, German or Russian by heritage and American by choice. For the most part they travelled in their own circle, accepted the jokes that belittled them and did not try to join the clubs or fraternities that excluded them. They ignored the whispers and, if they were in a position to do so, demanded at least a surface respect from the ever-widening group that was dependent on them. As American Jews, they lived and functioned in a carefully constructed world, part of their own making and part forced upon them.

As a result, the millions of European Jews were more upsetting to the established members of the Jewish community than they were to other segments of the population because their social order depended on their being assimilated and not being perceived as different. For the most part, they wished the problem created by the immigrants would simply go away. The crowded tenements, the sweatshops, the lack of even rudimentary sanitary facilities and the generally subhuman living conditions were alien to American concepts. The non-Jewish community could dismiss the problem as a matter for the Jews to handle, while the Jewish community could only try unsuccessfully to claim they had no connection with these strange creatures.

Fortunately, there also were men like Jacob Schiff, men who could recognize a social injustice and react to it. Schiff organized philanthropic societies to help the refugees. He joined with others and opened soup kitchens, fought for child labor laws, forced an indifferent city government to provide sanitary facilities and to institute housing codes. Schiff did everything within his power to "mainstream" the immigrants.

Mainstreaming was the most important and the most difficult task of all. It meant convincing parents that their children had to go to school and learn to speak English. It meant modifying habits and customs, giving up century-old fears and becoming a part of the New World. Those who had come seeking opportunity and a better life did overcome their fears, but those who had fled from persecution saw the reformers as being as much a threat to their beliefs as the Czar and the Cossacks had been. They had left their homeland because their lives were endangered. Once they were safe, all they wanted was to be left alone.

The Jewish philanthropic societies dealt with their fears while attending to their physical needs. Many people were involved in the effort. Most were following the example set by Jacob Schiff. When he died, a committee was formed to choose a way of honoring the man who represented the social conscience. They decided to erect a monument in the lower east side section of Manhattan and offered the commission to Schiff's good friend, Gutzon Borglum.

Flattered by the offer, Gutzon wrote to the committee:

I have never met a man who exemplified all the characteristics of George Washington as much as Jacob Schiff. He was one of the few men I have met who were able to rise above parochial interests and serve all mankind . . . .[9]

The letter went on to warn the committee that the monument must represent Schiff's ideals, that it should not be merely a tribute to the individual. It should be a symbol of all that is best in man. Then Gutzon wrote, "But as a Christian I must decline . . . ."

Gutzon found many opportunities to express his racial feelings, and he seldom allowed one to pass. He corresponded with many of the leading anti-Semites of his day and kept up his running debate with Singer and others.

He had studied the question and he knew he was right. Gutzon believed the Jew was a parasite and Judiasm a plague. This did not necessarily refer to his Jewish friends, but only to the race as a whole. Nor did his feelings about Jewish bankers being non-productive parasites prevent him from using Paul Warburg as a financial advisor, or Meyer, Colt and others as patrons.

Gutzon voiced his anti-Semitic views until Hitler came to power and began saying much the same thing. The difference was that Hitler could take the hypothetical and turn it into the actual — the death camps. He would try to exterminate the German Jews and then the Jewish people of the conquered nations. When he started to exterminate, most people and governments looked the other way. Only a few spoke out, and Gutzon was one of them.

He told reporters that "no civilized man could condone such barbaric acts." He attacked the Nazis with vehemence and voiced his opinions at every opportunity. In his press conferences he tried to goad Hitler into responding. He saw the Nazis as a threat to everything that was decent in mankind and he included all Nazi sympathizers in his attacks. Speaking about Charles Lindbergh, he said:

The boy who flew the Atlantic is not the boy who accepts a gold medal from an S.O.B. and right hand bower of the Hitler regime.[10]

Lindbergh's pro-Nazi stand was particularly distressing to Gutzon. In 1927, when the *Lone Eagle* conquered the Atlantic Ocean, Gutzon was as proud as an American could be. The Borglums were living in San Antonio when Gutzon came rushing home shouting with pleasure and waving the newspaper that announced the flight. He told his children of the significance of the accomplishment, but what his daughter remembered most were the tears in his eyes.

Despite the provocation, Hitler never responded to any of Gutzon's remarks. He remained silent until weeks after he had invaded Poland in 1939. Then he summoned reporters and announced to the world that he had ordered that Gutzon Borglum's statue of Woodrow Wilson (erected in Poznan, Poland, in 1931) be destroyed and a sign put in its place that read:

> The American sculptor made the legs too short, the body too long and the head too large. Such an artistic eyesore cannot continue to stand in the city.[11]

12
After Forty

New York, March 24, 1907, 11:45 P.M.:

> It is now ten hours before I was born forty years ago, and I resolve this coming year to earn $100,000 — to build new and necessary living quarters — arrange my domestic affairs so that a little of the cheer of living may come to me . . . I shall prosecute the cathedral work to a finish . . . fight only when necessary and for no one, but ever for principles.
>
> Gutzon Borglum
>
> This for next year — 1907 — in March to 1908.[1]

"Principles" took many forms. When he was asked to join the board of directors of the Metropolitan Park Association, a citizens' group concerned with maintaining and planning for Central Park and other recreational areas in New York City, he accepted and threw himself into the work.

Riverside Drive, the highway running alongside the Hudson River on the west side of Manhattan, was being extended. Gutzon, as part of his duties for the park association, inspected the work, found it to be sub-standard and became involved in an argument with the private contractor. When he brought his complaint to the city engineers and received no satisfaction, he hired an engineer, who confirmed Gutzon's worst suspicions. Gutzon then went to the mayor and threatened a lawsuit, which forced the city to do most of the work over again and complete it properly. Very quickly city officials knew there was a new man on the park association, who was there to protect the public's interest.

At the same time, the newspaper reporters, especially those who knew Gutzon, prepared for some headlines, and Gutzon did not make them wait long. Only a few weeks after the Riverside Drive argument was settled, he filed a taxpayer's suit to stop construction of a road through Central Park. Gutzon objected because the planned route would have destroyed over three hundred trees, and again he forced the city to back down.

These were the principles he fought for, and neither his principles not his methods endeared him to the mayor or his cronies. They felt Gutzon was attacking them personally and Mayor Gaynor was outraged. When Gutzon objected to the mayor's choice for park commissioner, he wrote Gaynor and released his letter to the press.

When the mayor did not respond, Gutzon wrote again, repeating his objection and requesting the appointment of an investigating committee. The mayor replied bluntly:

> Your favor of April 10th is at hand. I suppose you wrote it for newspaper publication and will therefore file it . . . . I think it would be just as well if you publish your letters without sending them to me.[2]

It was Gutzon's turn to be indignant. He wrote Mayor Gaynor:

> It is kinder to say that you are unacquainted with, rather than unmindful of the services I have rendered you through . . . the parks. May I be excused for even mentioning them? I am aware of my duties as a citizen, and I shall continue to oppose neglect of the city's property by incompetent and sinfully inefficient individuals.[3]

But the Mayor refused to be outdone, and he answered the very next day:

> . . . I desire to have no further communication with you whatever, as I doubt your veracity. I desire to work with all truthful and earnest people, but not with notoriety seekers. . . .[4]

The mayor was mistaken. Notoriety was not Gutzon's goal. The mayor, along with most of Gutzon's friends, could never understand why he constantly put himself in a position to be attacked because they could not understand his motivation, which Gutzon explained this way: "Art is life. Unless it is life, it isn't art. . . . You've got to get down into it. The long-haired artist isn't essentially an artist. He hasn't established his connection with life.[5]

Gutzon needed controversy to rid himself of energies that would have destroyed his art. He used his outside interests as a means of purging himself so he could be disciplined enough to pursue his concepts. But he was also motivated by the instincts of a zealous crusader. In an interview a few years before he died, he observed, "My life has been a one-man war from its beginning to date . . . . Dishonesty and incompetence give any straight shooting, square dealing man a battle every day . . . .[6]

There were advantages and disadvantages to being controversial. Gutzon was well aware of both, though he loved to make believe it was all a mystery. As he wrote to his friend Leon Dabo:

I'll try to follow your good press tip. I am a damn fool about such things — laugh you cuss — and it's so. I'm talked about because I think things . . . and say things, but I never pay any attention as to how it gets into the papers or out of it.[7]

Gutzon knew the risks. A number of committees refused to consider him because of the continual controversies, not only political but between the two Borglums. The group planning to honor General George Custer dropped both Borglums from its list. Gutzon knew that his refusal to enter competitions, even those in which his winning was assured, closed some doors, but he felt as many turned to him for the same reason. There was a force behind his argument that his work spoke for itself. Each statue took him a step closer to his goal, and the truly outstanding works, such as his significant marble portrait of Lincoln, set him apart.

Bronze casting of marble *Abraham Lincoln* in Capitol Building, Washington, D.C.

To be the Lincoln sculptor was the dream of every sculptor of Gutzon's time. Commissions for memorials honoring Lincoln were eagerly sought. There was something about the Civil War president that fascinated sculptors. All of them knew that a successful Lincoln would establish their reputation.

Gutzon's opportunity to join the Lincoln sculptors came in late 1907, but not as a result of a commission. He had acquired a block of Greek panatello marble, which had reached New York as ship's ballast. Something about the stone inspired him and made him certain there was a Lincoln in it. Writing about the discovery and his research for the project, he said:

> And so I found the storm center of Lincoln's face was about his right eye. He would peer at you . . . this right eye half closed; then would follow the receptive expression that was generally misread as bewilderment, hesitancy and indecision. The mirth center was also in the right eye. The eye always gives the first evidence of humor in a merry soul. But sadness changed this . . . he smiled very, very often with his mouth alone when his nature took no part in it. It was the saddest feature that he had, and yet about the right corner there always lingered a little memory of a smile . . .the left eye was open, noncommital, dreamy. The brow seemed ever to question, and all this side of the face seemed primitive, unfinished . . . . I believe he knew this and it explains why he managed so often to get the photographer to the right side of him. This right side was as cautious as Cassius . . . . The profile from the left was pure middle-west plainsman . . . . Briefly the right side of this wonderful face is the key to his life . . . . It guards his plans — watches the world, and shows no more of his light than his wisdom deems wise. The left side is immature, plain and not physically impressive.[8]

That was the image Gutzon was trying to free from the marble. He was not bothered about not having a commission for the work because he knew the Lincoln in his mind would find a market and have an impact on his career. He also had a wealthy patron who took an interest in the work and was willing to help. Eugene Meyer was another Jewish financier who became Gutzon's friend and backer. Meeting Gutzon was exciting for Meyer. He had grown bored with his banker friends and was searching for new interests.

When an art dealer recommended that Meyer purchase one of Gutzon's paintings, he did. He then went to the studio to meet Gutzon and became involved in the Lincoln carving. Meyer was a Lincoln buff who owned a large collection of Lincoln memorabilia, which he made available to Gutzon. He also told Gutzon that when the bust was completed he would like to purchase it as a gift to the federal government.

Gutzon told him that could not be done because the government did not accept gifts from private donors, but he was buoyed by the offer.

When the statue was finished, Gutzon prevailed upon President Roosevelt to display the work in the White House on Lincoln's birthday in 1908. The president was thrilled when he saw the statue, and he suggested that it belonged in Washington. Seizing his opportunity, Gutzon brought Meyer to the White House to repeat his offer. Roosevelt phoned some congressional friends, and at his suggestion a joint resolution was quickly passed allowing the government to accept the gift for permanent display in the rotunda of the Capitol Building.

During the six weeks of the carving, Bob Baillie was Gutzon's assistant. When the *Saturday Evening Post* ran an article discussing the Lincoln bust in 1947, Baillie wrote to the editor:

> I was at the time assisting Mr. Borglum . . . had it not been for the moving spirit of Eugene Meyer . . . this special head might not have been carved . . . when I rolled the block of marble into the studio Mr. Borglum was disappointed with the size, but as Mr. Meyer was anxious as well as Mr. Borglum to have a head of Lincoln in Gorham's window by Christmas . . . Mr. Borglum decided to carve the marble . . . . Mr. Borglum studied the clay and the marble and in a short time the clay had taken shape. He asked me to begin carving the marble without waiting for a plaster cast . . . by working 10 to 12 hours each day for five weeks the head of Lincoln was completed . . . . It was only because of the unfailing interest both morally and financially that Mr. Meyer gave, this particular head was created. To me at that time when monies were low it was a relief to know I would get paid.[9]

For Meyer this was an exciting adventure. His previous activities had limited him to New York, but Gutzon took him to the White House and introduced him to the president and a whole circle of friends in Washington. Meyer was fascinated by the way Gutzon approached people in power, and for many years, until they had a falling out over money, he was one of Gutzon's strongest supporters.

From the first showing of the bust, Gutzon became a recognized Lincoln sculptor. When Todd Lincoln saw the statue, he called it the most remarkable likeness of his father he had ever seen, and the critics were unanimous in their praise.

Along with the critical acclaim, Gutzon was awarded another much sought after commission. He was given a contract to create one of the major figures for the Pan American Building in Washington. The original idea was to use many sculptors, but as time went on the committee in charge decided that was an impractical idea. They gave Isadore Konti part of the commission and asked Solon to make a condor and an eagle to go over the main entrance, while they thought about the disposition of the balance of the project.

Solon assumed his preliminary assignment would lead to his being awarded the second major figure. In fact, a luncheon was scheduled for a ceremonial contract signing, but Solon was told, at the very last moment, that a mistake had been made and the contract was being given to Gutzon.

Solon's friends were convinced that once again Mrs. Wadsworth had used her influence to change a decision in Gutzon's favor. Whether the accusation was true or not, Solon had good reason to be suspicious. Director of the Budget John Barret and Gutzon were friends of each other and of Mrs. Wadsworth. In a letter to Gutzon, Barret wrote:

> . . . at Mrs. Wadsworth's reception, and at her fancy dress party the evening before, I spoke with her about you. She said she expected you over here . . . .[10]

With all the rumors flying about, Barret became concerned that he was being compromised. When he expressed this to Gutzon, Gutzon replied:

> I could not help but feel I should be serving you all by withdrawing completely . . . upon my return to New York I sent for my brother and explained the situation to him as it was at the time and he was very frank and generous so that all unpleasantness has been eliminated from that quarter.[11]

Solon accepted Gutzon's explanation. He would not force a confrontation with Gutzon even when he felt he was right. After they met, Solon wrote the Philadelphia architects in charge of the project:

> As the work in question was intended for my brother, Gutzon, I do not regret it . . . . My brother has informed me of the way you wish to adjust the matter . . . .[12]

Solon was left with the eagle and the condor. Konti was assigned one of the large bas-reliefs and Gutzon the other. The committee assumed that settled their problems, but they were wrong. As the models developed, it became obvious that Gutzon and Konti were not working on the same scale. Many letters were exchanged in an attempt to make Konti work larger or Gutzon smaller, but neither artist would consider changing his work. In answer to their plea to change his models, Gutzon wrote:

Your letter has just reached me and I must remind you that there has been no deviation from the contract on my part . . . . I have tried to persuade you from the beginning to see what I believe I have earned the right to call good sculpture and good art . . . . Your letter has served to remind me that this matter is not proceeding in good faith and that I must inform you that the work has been suspended . . . .[13]

Despite his pronouncement, Gutzon continued to work, and after the war of words ran its course, the matter was resolved by having both sculptors adjust their scale.

By 1908 the studio was beginning to resemble the studios of the European masters. Statues of every shape filled all the nooks and crannies. There were half a dozen assistants and students. Gutzon's horses, stabled behind the studio, were brought in and allowed to roam free in the work areas so Gutzon could study their movements. They were like house pets, and guests were often startled when the horses tried to find treats in their hand or pocket.

The National Aeronautical Society held weekly meetings at the studio, where Gutzon's models of wing flaps and strange looking flying machines hung from the ceiling. Mary recounts the visitors to the studio:

Here passed a succession of studio helpers . . . like apprentices in medieval times . . . secretaries, models, friends and acquaintances, some of them important figures in the life of the city and the nation. Among his earliest helpers was Marion Bell, daughter of the inventor of the telephone, and her friend . . . . It delighted the sculptor not only to make these society girls sweep the studio or mix clay . . . but to make them like it, as they did.[14]

Gutzon enjoyed working with young people. Perhaps he was reliving his San Francisco days with William Keith, remembering the veneration of the students who surrounded him, or perhaps, as Eugene Meyer's biographer claimed, "Borglum imagined himself a re-incarnation of Leonardo . . . ."[15] Whatever his reason, the young people he worked with considered themselves most fortunate, and those who, like Malvina Hoffman, went on to become famous, remained grateful.

His desire to be with students brought him to the Art Students' League in New York as an instructor, where Gutzon taught an evening class for the joy of teaching. At the end of the semester he took his $500 fee and divided it as prize money for his most promising students.

Gutzon also became the spokesman for the league in a fiasco that was started by Anthony Comstock, the self-appointed preserver of New York's morals. When Comstock led a police raid on the league office and had the bookkeeper arrested for ". . . giving away, showing, offering to give away and having in her possession an obscene and disgusting book," Gutzon went to her defense.[16] Miss Robinson, who had been the only person in the building at the time of the raid, had given Comstock the school's catalogue. Gutzon immediately called reporters to his studio and said:

> It is a d--- outrage the way this man Comstock goes around . . . . Comstock is the one who is lewd. He is the one who has directed attention to what was considered purity, and expressed in art . . . . Why does not Comstock go into medical colleges and arrest students for dissecting bodies? Why doesn't he go into the libraries and confiscate Rabelais and Balzac?[17]

Students from all over the world wrote to Gutzon and usually received an answer. His letters were filled with his views on art and his personal philosophy. Writing to a young man who was planning to study in London, Gutzon advised:

> . . . originality does not mean do *new subjects*; there are no *new subjects*. Little artists do strong things but the great men, Michelangelo, Rodin, etc., they do things I always seem to be thinking of, that is they do and understand, but with such power we feel it belongs to them, do you understand?[18]

Despite all the activity of his busy schedule Gutzon often grew restless. He tried to relieve the restlessness by taking long weekends for fishing and by becoming a regular commuter between New York and Washington. When he felt confined in the studio, he went to the stone yard at the Cathedral of St. John the Divine to check on the stone cutters. He was always eager for adventures or new commissions.

When his friend Phillip Mighels brought Sam Davis and Clarence Mackay to the studio, Gutzon eagerly accepted their proposition. They had come to see if he would be interested in creating a monument in honor of Clarence's father. John Mackay had been one of Nevada's most illustrious pioneers. He made his first fortune with the Comstock silver lode and then used the money to finance the first transatlantic cable and to establish a newspaper chain. Gutzon liked the idea of a new commission, but having to go to Nevada made it even more appealing. The West was still very much a part of him. He thought of himself as a Western artist and dreamed of cattle, horses and open spaces.

While Gutzon prepared for the journey, Sam Davis returned to Carson City, Nevada, to arrange for a site for the monument on the grounds of the Nevada Capitol Building. Everyone concerned had assumed the lawmakers would be honored, but they were not. Davis had not told them of the plan in advance, and the legislators suggested that the project be scaled down and that the statue be placed in an alcove in the library annex.

Gutzon arrived while the debate was still going on and he quickly rejected the library plan. He said he was going to produce an heroic-sized statue that could not be housed indoors. He went north and found a suitable site on the campus of the University of Nevada in Reno. The Mackay family was delighted, and they donated $50,000 to the university. The money was used to build a Stanford White School of Mines building, which provided a perfect background for the statue.

Gutzon remained in Nevada for about six weeks as the guest of the Davis family. He enjoyed the area so much that he told the Davis daughters, who were his riding companions, that he had been born in Nevada. He said his parents were passing through on their way to the forty-niners' gold field and had been forced to stop and camp because of his arrival.

There was no malice in the story. Gutzon was being treated as a celebrity. Wined and dined, he wanted to leave something with his hosts besides the small bronze statue he had brought as a house gift. He rewrote his history to please them, and they were pleased. When Sam Davis made the dedication speech, he mentioned how proud he was that Gutzon Borglum had been born at nearby Goose Lake, Nevada.

Gutzon returned to New York in high spirits. He had spent much time thinking about his personal life and had decided to settle his affairs with Lisa, as Mary recorded in this letter:

> . . . when he found he couldn't stand being married to an old woman any longer he sent a lawyer out to California to investigate and discovered she had been divorced before and their [Gutzon and Lisa's] marriage was illegal because of something being wrong with the divorce papers.[19]

After twenty-one years Gutzon was free. Lisa accepted her position and stopped trying to hold him. She remained in California painting and giving art lessons until her death in 1923. On occasion, Gutzon wrote her about different matters that concerned them both, but as the years passed the part she had played in his life faded from his memory and she was seldom, if ever, mentioned. When Gutzon wrote in his autobiography about his early days in California, he recalled Mrs. Fremont, the Spencer Smiths, William Keith and others, but never Lisa.

Mary and Gutzon on their wedding
day.

Mary and Gutzon

On May 20, 1909, Gutzon and Mary were married in a simple ceremony performed by her brother, George. The *New York Times* announced:

> . . . after the wedding breakfast Mr. and Mrs. Borglum left immediately for Canada where they will remain until the middle of June when Mr. Borglum will receive the Honorary Degree of Master of Arts from Princeton.[1]

The degree was Woodrow Wilson's way of thanking Gutzon for the gargoyles he had created for the Class of '79 dormitory on the Princeton campus. Wilson was especially pleased because he had been a member of the Class of '79.

Gutzon and Mary set up a wilderness camp by a remote Canadian lake where they could fish, hike and be alone until it was time to return home. Gutzon relaxed and enjoyed what was one of the rare, comparatively quiet periods in his career. He was not, at the time, involved in any bitter controversy and felt certain he was about to receive a major contract for a Lincoln monument. The Lincoln was so important, from his point of view, that he took time from their honeymoon to write Paul Warburg, his friend and financial advisor, to tell him the news:

> . . . there are to be two monuments in Cincinnati. At present there are to be two Lincolns there, one the Alms Memorial by yours truly and the Tafts by Barnard! The latter I am trying to defeat. I want the Tafts to convert their enthusiasm into a Columbus and leave Mrs. Alms with the original plan, and all of Cincinnati are with me in this. . . .[2]

Despite his certainty, Gutzon did not receive the Alms contract, and once again he reacted by blaming the establishment. He claimed he was a victim of the established artists and their corrupt "machine," which controlled the committees. That may have been true, at least partially, but Cincinnati was another of those situations in which he

Gargoyle used to decorate Princeton University dormitory, Class of '79.

was competing against Solon, and the committee did not want to become involved in a fight between brothers.

The committee had considered Gutzon carefully. They wrote to Princeton asking for the reasons he was being awarded an honorary degree and received an answer that reflected Wilson's respect for Gutzon:

> It is because of the extraordinary promise he has shown as a sculptor . . . his keen sympathy with American feelings . . . . Personally Mr. Borglum is a most attractive man, impressing one with his simplicity, energy and fine cleanness of imagination. His conceptions are entirely free of any touch

of decadence, triviality or ineptness . . . they are pervaded by what seems
to me a very noble simplicity.[3]

Despite the high praise, the committee decided against both Borglums.
Unable to change the situation, Gutzon decided to take another trip.
He, at least, had not had his fill of fishing or honeymooning, though
Mary may have. Writing in the third person about the first weeks of
her marriage, she remarked:

> . . . after receiving the degree in June they continued their honeymoon on
> the Gunnison River in Colorado. By that time Mrs. Borglum was certain
> that her life was going to be vastly different.[4]

Shortly after their return to New York in the fall of 1909, Gutzon
received word that his father had passed away. James died much as
he had lived — true to his stubborn nature to the very end. He had a
favorite horse which balked at pulling the doctor's buggy, but James
insisted on using him. He was hitching the horse to the buggy, preparing to start his rounds, when the horse bolted. James was dragged,
kicked, and severely injured, but he refused medical attention and insisted on making his rounds. A few days later he became violently ill
and died.

Ida, having been with James for almost fifty years, felt the loss most
keenly, but she was still the pioneer woman capable of walking a thousand miles. She refused to lose heart, as indicated in this letter to a cousin:

> . . . but it is still hard to get used to that poppa don't come home. It is
> so dreadful lonesome — of course the time had come. He has gone to prepare
> for us — and it is such a happy thought that we shall meet again.[5]

Gutzon assumed the role as head of the family. He kept in touch
with his brothers and sisters and helped them with money and advice.
He wrote to Ida often, and when she opened a tea room in Omaha he
helped her financially until she was able to support herself.

Gutzon returned from the funeral and began, almost at once, to
negotiate for the most important commission of his career. Following
the success of his Lincoln in Washington, D.C., and despite his not being awarded the Cincinnati Lincoln, he set his sights on the Lincoln
statue being considered for Newark, New Jersey. He knew that if he
could win the Newark commission he could establish his reputation as
one of the most important, if not the most important, monumental
sculptors of his day. His rivals knew this also, and all were seeking the

123

commission with equal vigor, but Gutzon seemed to have the best chance.

Amos Van Horn, a wealthy New Jersey manufacturer, had been a proud member of the Grand Army of the Republic, the Union Army in the Civil War. Before his death in 1908, Van Horn bequeathed $150,000 for memorials to Presidents Lincoln and Washington and another $100,000 for a war memorial. J. Massey Rhind had been commissioned to do the Washington, but Gutzon knew if he received the Lincoln contract he would be the most likely to receive the war memorial contract because of the magnificence of the Lincoln concept that was forming in his mind.

Ralph Lum, a Newark attorney and a good friend of Gutzon's, was executor of the Van Horn estate. Lum was leading the fight to secure the commission for Gutzon, but he was running into opposition from some members of the committee who objected to Gutzon's adamant refusal to enter a competition. Gutzon had written to members of another committee:

> Bidding for statues of such importance as a general, a president, or any great character in history was . . . impossible and incompatible with good work . . . . I think . . . it is impossible for men of position to take up work of the high character . . . by the competitive method.[6]

Lum finally managed to produce an invitation for Gutzon to prepare a model of his magnificent concept. Once the committee saw his *Seated Lincoln*, the contract was his. The committee was so pleased, in fact, that they decided that he would also eventually be awarded the contract for the war memorial. It was an unprecedented victory, and Gutzon knew he had to make the most of the opportunity.

In describing the theme of his *Lincoln*, Gutzon wrote:

> Lincoln often wandered into the Garden of Gethsemane and always alone . . . .[7]

He was referring to the president's habit of ending his day at the War Office reading the latest communiqués from the battlefield. When the news was bad, as it often was, he would wander out onto the White House lawn, where he would sit on a bench and try to gather his courage and strength. Gutzon went on to explain:

> It is this feeling of aloneness that I have not been able to overcome in myself, and that I have done all I could to emphasize. It is expressed in the whole

Jonathan Karl on the knee of the *Seated Lincoln*, Newark, New Jersey.

attitude of the man, as I have tried to render him. Another thing I've had
in mind: Run over the seated figures in history; go back, for instance,
to . . . the modern Rodin's *Thinker*. Rodin's . . . is not really a thinker but
something broader than that, a man, the product of physical development,
brooding over his nakedness. The Lincoln I have endeavored to portray
is not thinking about himself or about anything that will be of advantage
to himself. His mind is engrossed with the vast responsibilities that have
weighed him down. He alone realized their magnitude; he alone knew the
strength he must have to support them and hold himself erect.[8]

Gutzon submerged himself in Lincoln. He became much like a fighter preparing for a bout. He took advantage of Eugene Meyer's huge collection of Lincoln books and memorabilia and sought out other sources that could contribute insights. When he felt he was ready, he began developing his theme in small models and then began the full-sized statue.

As the work took form, he decided to have the figure cast as a single unit, rather than allow it to be cut apart as it would be in a conventional casting, because he felt welding would weaken the final work. This was a much more costly method, but he wanted the best, even though he had to pay the additional cost himself at a time when he was having his usual problems with creditors.

Handling family finances had become Mary's duty even before they were married, primarily because Gutzon had no patience with money matters and no inclination to budget. Their lifestyle made her task extremely difficult. It was further compounded by Gutzon's habit of signing contracts and then putting most of the money back into the work. The amount of the contract gave him the feeling that he had money, and he spent accordingly, but more often than not, it turned out to be an illusion.

For the *Seated Lincoln* he not only paid for the more expensive casting but also contributed several thousand dollars to prepare the site. Placement of the statue was critical to the result he hoped to achieve. When he did not feel that the site donated by Newark was at the proper level, Gutzon had it changed at his own expense.

Seated Lincoln was dedicated on Memorial Day, 1911, in a grand ceremony with Teddy Roosevelt as the keynote speaker. Roosevelt had been out of the White House for almost three years. There was much talk about his seeking re-election because he was no longer friends with President Taft, but Roosevelt had refused to commit himself.

On the morning of the dedication, he crossed the Hudson River by ferry and was met in Jersey City by Ralph Lum. The two men then rode to Newark in an open carriage along a road lined with cheering spectators. By the time they reached Newark, Lum claimed, Roosevelt had been so moved by the enthusiasm of the crowd that he declared he would seek the nomination. That was the beginning of what became the Bull Moose campaign of 1912.

In March 1910, Gutzon and Mary's first child was born prematurely and did not survive. Both were devastated, but because he had convinced himself for so long that his marriage to Lisa had floundered because they were unable to have children, Gutzon had a particularly

Studio at Borgland, North Stamford, Connecticut.

difficult time. The loss of the baby forced him to think about his lifestyle, and his zest for the fast-paced life in the city began to wane. They still planned to have a family, and they both felt a need to create an environment that would nurture children.

Connecticut seemed to them a good place to look. Solon had moved there in 1903 and found the country life much to his liking. The area in which he lived, the Silvermine section of Norwalk, was close enough to allow commuting to New York, which was important to Gutzon. In a short time, Gutzon and Mary found what they wanted in North Stamford, Connecticut.

By combining several parcels of land and a small farm, they created an estate that Gutzon named Borgland. Owning the property thrilled him, and he quickly became the old, enthusiastic Gutzon. In a letter to his financial advisor, Paul Warburg, Gutzon wrote:

> I want to tell you what I am going to do in the country. I have found a good place . . . where I can build a . . . studio and save two-thirds of my time, save about half of my money and increase my working capacity at least one half. Which means saving fifty percent of my money and adding fifty percent of my income. I have worried more than I can tell you about the terrible loss of time that New York entails on a man who gets as actively into things as I have, and yet there is no way out of it if one is to be successful. I know you do not entirely agree with me . . . in your security

you sit amongst the Gods, shift your shoulders, and move finances of a nation . . . work has been accumulating upon me in the last few months faster than I have been able to deliver it, and I have more than I have ever had in my life, but what's the use if you can't do it?[9]

To write "you do not entirely agree with me" was more than an understatement. Warburg had been pointing out the magnitude of the financial obligation Gutzon was assuming with the purchase of a large estate and was trying to determine how Gutzon planned to pay for the land, the renovation of the buildings and a new studio. Gutzon's answer — that he should not be concerned because the land was a good investment — did not satisfy Warburg. Gutzon also told him that he could sub-divide and sell building lots at a huge profit if the debt became too much of a burden. Gutzon further explained:

. . . of course I realize that no man can do what I have done — with no bonds or dividends to draw upon without paying dearly in worry in every way and I expect to have to keep on for some little time. . . .[10]

Gutzon did not see "worry" as a deterrent, but only as part of the price he would have to pay. He was making a strong effort to convince Warburg, hoping his friend would loan him the mortgage money. When Warburg continued to oppose the idea, Gutzon told him he would be willing to sell some of the art works in the studio:

I suggest this because I must go on with my work as I have been. I am not going to turn out less good work than I have — but better — I have raised heaven and "hell" my friends say to secure the privacy so I could work more hours each day and I almost have that . . . .[11]

Warburg still remained unconvinced. When he advised strongly against seeking a mortgage in a commercial bank, Gutzon took his advice and went to Eugene Meyer. Meyer lent him the $35,000 he needed to buy the land and an additional $5,000 to renovate the old farmhouse he planned to use as a family home. When the purchase was made public, the Stamford newspaper reacted to Gutzon's enthusiasm and agreed that the land could always be sold at a profit. Under the headline "Well Known Sculptor Buys Estate," the paper reported:

. . . that the incoming of Mr. Borglum . . . will give impetus to the value of the land in that section can not be doubted . . . . It will draw attention to the inviting character of the neighborhood and investors will find reasons for setting out their stakes there . . . .[12]

The building Mary and Gutzon had chosen for their home was only one of several on the property. It was a charming old farmhouse, but because of its poor condition, it had to be gutted and rebuilt before they could move in. They remained in New York until the first room was ready. When the second was completed, they expanded their living quarters and then waited for the third and the fourth.

Suddenly, after years of living a cosmopolitan life in Los Angeles, Paris, London and New York, Gutzon was a country squire. He owned land and was part of a rural community. Plans for the estate filled his mind and he began to design his new studio and stable. Thinking about all the projects — the studio, the stable, the re-routing of the road in front of the farmhouse, the creating of a pond by damning the Rippowan River, which ran in front of the studio site, and stocking it with trout — made him resent the time he had to spend away from the estate. In an effort to stay at home, he attempted to work in a temporary studio at Borgland, but the weather and lack of proper facilities made it too difficult. He was forced to commute to his studio in New York.

Interior of Borgland studio.

129

Acquiring land changed Gutzon in many ways. Despite the debt and the additional time he had to spend travelling to his New York studio, he was pleased. No matter what it meant in terms of inconvenience, having an estate was tangible proof that he was moving up in the world. Gutzon was able to convince himself that hardships were a test. In his own eyes he was a maverick and a romantic, a throwback, if not to Don Quixote, at least to one of the Knights of the Round Table. When asked about his home, Gutzon answered:

> You ask about my home? . . . . All my conscious days I build my home, the haven for a strange, vibrant, haunting, wistful inner-self . . . . Sometimes I've half awakened and thought I found this other self working over me, as a frantic mother with a half drowned child, in an effort to clear away the wreckage of battle and war daily heaped upon me. Just where this self stays, how it looks, I only half know. But I do know it visits me only when I'm alone — when I'm securely and safely free from the meddling outside world . . . it corners me and tricks me into private places where it can in safety breathe to me the truth and beauty and the greatness of life . . . . I build my soul a home! . . . It is the gate to the infinite, to my universe . . . . Here I live. Here I meet the world, win or lose my contests with it . . . here my sun and hope rise . . . . The world must be young or have rested long when God attempts to give men great souls. The womb of the universe must be young and virgin when gods are born . . . . There are corners in my home, which if I successfully enter, quickens moods of productivity I never feel elsewhere . . . our spirit is always waiting there, impotent — unless we're alone![13]

Borgland was more than a roof over his head, more than a simple piece of real estate. The property provided a place to renew his spirits. He looked at the granite boulders scattered on his land and saw the walls of his majestic new studio. He saw the heavily wooded sections as tranquil places to walk with Mary. Together they started a "nature book," and on their walks they searched the ground cover and filled the book with sketches of the wild flowers they discovered.

The Rippowan River, meandering across the estate, was a special source of pride and pleasure. Gutzon made a ford for his horses and built a footbridge for his guests. He built his dam to create a pond, which he stocked with trout from a nearby hatchery, but it was not one of his successful ventures. The young fish died of a mysterious ailment. Then someone, undoubtedly a disgruntled, downstream neighbor unhappy about losing his share of the river, blew up the dam and restored the river to its normal course.

Gutzon fishing for trout in Rippowan River, which flowed through Borgland.

Despite all his new activities and the amount of time he spent travelling, Gutzon's work did not suffer. He continued to produce as commissions came in at a record pace. He was working out the final details for Newark's War Memorial when he signed a contract with a committee from Dayton, Ohio, that wanted to erect a monument honoring the Wright Brothers. Gutzon was also working on his statue of Henry Ward Beecher for Plymouth Church in Brooklyn and a number of smaller projects for his friend Archer Huntington, who headed the Numismatic Society.

His acceptance by the committees awarding contracts did not bring Gutzon the acceptance of the group he disparagingly called "the establishment," and this often made him bitter and angry. When an interviewer asked him what he would do if he had $10,000,000, the reporter was able to turn his answer into a magazine article:

WHAT WOULD GUTZON BORGLUM DO IF SOMEONE SHOULD
GIVE HIM $10,000,000?
. . . the very suggestion brings with it visions of marble and bronze statuary flying through the air in irrecoverable fragments. One can see the second blowing up of the "Maine" — not the ship but the monumental eyesore at

Columbus Circle . . for Borglum is the big insurgent of the art world. He is the man who declared that most of New York's statuary is meaningless and bad . . . . Borglum hurled his bombs right into the most sacred inner precincts of our so-called world of art. He has listed its regents as "our organized mediocrity"and the "high priests of imitation." "Damm him utterly" has been their answering scream . . . .[14]

Most of the time Gutzon's running arguments with his fellow artists were wars of words that earned both sides some much needed publicity, but there were times when there were serious confrontations. When the Academy of Design, New York's prestigious society of architects, wanted to build a headquarters and exhibit hall in Bryant Park, a city-owned property, Gutzon opposed the idea. His opposition could not be taken lightly because he was a member of the Parks and Playground Association of New York, and the plan needed his support to succeed. Gutzon told the academy that if it would rid itself of its snobbish, exclusionary requirements, open its doors to young artists and truly serve the public he would support its plan. The condition was impossible to meet because the academy did not see itself the way Gutzon did, and after many exchanges the plan was dropped.

Gutzon's enemies were angry. They vowed to get even and did so at their first opportunity, which came a short time later. San Francisco was the host city for the 1915 Panama-Pacific Exposition, the work for which was begun in 1912. As with most World's Fairs, all the art work was assigned and supervised by a committee-appointed sculptor-in-chief. Gutzon wanted the appointment. He went to several friends, including Jacob Schiff, to ask for their support. They promised to help, but they ran into a great deal of opposition. A friend of Schiff's, A. F. Matthew wrote to tell Gutzon that the opposition statement came from his having opposed the placing of the new academy in New York's Central Park. Gutzon wrote back at once:

. . . of course I can answer all the points raised — could if they were well founded . . . . I am difficult to get along with if crookedness . . . and compromise arise . . . but as to my being cranky, inflexible, or lacking in elasticity or resourcefulness — that is bosh . . . . I'm called a glutton for work and a wasteful fool for the amount I generously give my patrons over and above the business agreements . . . . It very much amuses me about the architects . . . and the fear of me . . . . I have never had any personal trouble with any architect . . . . My fights are and have been against dead schools — not personalities. I have no row with individuals, but, of course, every constipate mentality looks upon new ideas as something that may stampede humanity . . . .[15]

It was, unfortunately, all rhetoric. There was nothing Gutzon could do to further his cause or prevent the committee from appointing New York sculptor Karl Bitter to the post. The announcement hurt and angered Gutzon. He felt compelled to continue to fight for a lost cause. He wrote to a member of the committee to express his feelings:

> . . . it would be as untrue and as insincere if I did not say to you this is one of the greatest disappointments to me. As an artist and a Westerner I had a great dream about the opportunity to my old state, and believed I might help bring and develop in her something genuine and beautiful and keep east of the mountains the dead, bored, professional art . . . . One of those fool dreams that can't come true! Somehow I don't seem to have realized it is not Californians who are building the fair . . . .[16]

Despite the disappointment, Gutzon still wanted to be a part of the exposition. He wrote to Bitter seeking a major commission, and when this was refused he became angry with Bitter:

> I think you will understand a simile better than a direct statement. Suppose your hometown in Germany were to undertake some huge sculptural work and by some scheme or other I was given the work and not you and then the great mass of that work I gave to unknown, untried and in many cases mediocre people and gave you some unimportant, and to you distasteful, subject . . . . I am an artist and I have an artist's pride in the purity, good taste and fitness of the art works to be made in his homeland and in his time . . . .[17]

Offended by Gutzon's letter, Bitter replied:

> . . . do not let envy get the better of you. Your "simile" presents me as an intruder who snapped from you what would in your opinion justly belong to you. It is true I was already grown up . . . when I arrived and became a citizen . . . . It imposes upon me particular duties which I wish to discharge by giving preference to the most talented of our young sculptors . . . opportunities are now given to Aiken, Beach, Calder, Manship, your youngest brother — Solon Borglum . . . that much in reply to your statement that "untried and mediocre people" are given the great mass of the work . . . .[18]

And that was where the matter rested. Gutzon refused the minor commission Bitter offered him and took no part in the exposition. He had purged himself with his angry letters, and then went on with his other work. As far as he was concerned, it was just another skirmish in his long, continuing battle with the establishment. As irritating as the affair had been, he knew it meant little when compared to the important matters of life: Mary was pregnant again.

14

James Lincoln Borglum

Gutzon was elated beyond his wildest imagination at the birth of James Lincoln Borglum on April 9, 1912. From the day the boy was able to travel, which in Gutzon's opinion was shortly after he learned to walk, he became his father's companion, almost his alter-ego and an ever-present part of his conscious thought. Lincoln learned about all-night train rides before his feet could touch the floor of the smoker cars and how to sleep in hotel beds before he was barely out of his crib. When Gutzon learned the plans for a Lincoln monument in London, he wrote and told the committee to ". . . remember Lincoln is one of mine!"[1] This was a reference to his success as a Lincoln sculptor, but it was also a joyful reminder that he had a son named Lincoln.

For the first weeks after the birth, Gutzon rarely left the baby's side. He hired and fired nurses and, by his hovering presence, disrupted the household beyond all reason. When Mary was well enough to take charge again, she chased him back to the studio and the vexing problems of their desperate financial situation. As Warburg had predicted, Borgland was proving to be an expensive luxury, but there was little they could do but continue to struggle and hope for the best.

With Borgland several miles from downtown Stamford, Gutzon found it difficult to get into town to buy supplies or catch the train for New York. Deciding to solve the problem for himself and his neighbors, he organized a bus company ". . . so the farm women might have a chance to come to town while their husbands are using the horses in the field."[2]

Mary recalled how Gutzon ". . . was very happy in the designing of bus bodies to be fitted over Reo truck chassis and in arranging a suitable pageant to celebrate the beginning of the service."[3] And they were both pleased with the prospect of earning money from the bus service to ease their financial burden, but it did not work out that way.

The bus business proved to be far more complicated than he had imagined. Gutzon found that he had to have a terminal at the railroad station. This meant he had to build a garage on railroad property with borrowed money, thus increasing his debts. When Gutzon could not meet the note the bank foreclosed, the bus company folded and Gutzon was deeper in trouble. Years later, when she was trying to hold off creditors in another financial crisis, Mary wrote:

> For the past six or seven years he has been paying the debts of a defunct bus company he helped organize . . . which any . . . businessman would have put into receivership . . . .[4]

As it turned out, however, the failure with the bus company was neither a major catastrophe nor typical of Gutzon's Borgland activities. It was just one of his periodic over-zealous business adventures that caused some worrisome moments. Most of what was done at Borgland was of a more productive nature.

When he built the studio, he hired a crew of Italian stonecutters, who camped in a wooded area near the building site. On Gutzon's instructions they dug up the pink granite boulders that lay half buried in the Borgland fields and then cut and set the blocks for the massive walls.

Gutzon designed what was to become a trademark of Borglum buildings, a giant fireplace that could accommodate eight to ten-foot logs. When the studio was almost complete, he invited the officers of both Connecticut and New York Masonic Grand Lodges to a gala dedication. In a letter to a friend, Gutzon wrote of his plans for the studio cornerstone:

> . . . I shall have a hole made in the stone, and such data and records as I can get showing the doings of the day will be put into a little copper box and placed in the stone . . . to further confound posterity.[5]

The studio was almost a mile from the main house and on the other side of the river. Gutzon planned it that way because he wanted to be able to ride his horse to work. He also thought he would have more privacy if the studio was away from the house, but it did not work out that way. Visitors who dropped in for an hour in New York became weekend guests in Connecticut, and the Borglums were seldom without house guests.

Gutzon's move to Connecticut did not prevent him from keeping his commitments in New York. He continued to serve on the Parks Board, remained an active member of his Masonic Lodge and the other clubs he had joined, and he continued to use the New York studio even after he shifted most major works to the new studio. It appeared that he was trying to enjoy the best of both worlds.

As he settled into his new life in Connecticut, he developed an interest in local politics. Mary wrote that he:

> . . . was promptly introduced to the famous Connecticut Town Meeting and was intensely interested because he had never heard anything like it. He came home . . . to write that he had just learned the part an individual could play, first in his hometown, next to his state and finally in his native land.[6]

Gutzon had been a Republican most of his life, but he had never been politically active. By 1912, however, it was difficult for a Republican not to become involved. The party was torn by dissension. The split had begun in 1908, when President Theodore Roosevelt decided to back Howard Taft as his successor. As a member of the Roosevelt cabinet, Taft, it was assumed, was committed to Roosevelt's "New Nationalism," but as it turned out he was not. As a loyal cabinet member, he had felt compelled to support presidential policy, but as president he felt no such compunctions.

The Roosevelt faction in the party, feeling betrayed, reacted by declaring that they would not support Taft for re-election. At this time talk began about Roosevelt's making a third party bid. Roosevelt was sympathetic, but he refused to consider campaigning outside the regular party and, at least publicly, would not encourage those who wanted to work in his behalf. The Progressives, as they began to be called, then tried to talk Roosevelt into endorsing another candidate. Their argument was a strong one. It seemed obvious that Woodrow Wilson would be the Democratic candidate, and it appeared that he would have no difficulty defeating Taft. The Progressives argued that if they, meaning the Republicans, were going to lose the White House, why not make their point with the Old Guard supporters of Taft? Roosevelt's anger eventually swayed him, and like an old war horse he decided to accept the challenge, but not as a third party candidate. He said he would fight for the party nomination at the Republican convention.

Gutzon's involvement started on the state level. After attending the town meeting. Gutzon became an outspoken critic of the entrenched politicians. He accused Stamford's Mayor Rowell of corruption and charged him with all sorts of infractions. Most of his claims were backed by the local papers, and many of the Progressives began to see Gutzon as a potential leader. When they asked him to join their group officially, he accepted. Gutzon was suddenly in a battle and getting his first real taste of politics as a politician, rather than as a petitioner seeking commissions. To him the cause of the Progressives seemed too just to be denied, and he prepared to fight.

When the Republican Convention rejected Roosevelt and renominated Taft, the bitterness in the Progressive ranks made a fight for control of the party inevitable. Roosevelt declared himself "fit as a Bull Moose" and entered the race on his own ticket. Rallying behind his old friend, Gutzon became a leader in the Connecticut Progressive Party and in so doing showed an amazing grasp of political in-fighting. At his initial meeting the regular organization tried to take control. They brought a large delegation, demanded to be seated and then offered a deal. They would vote for Roosevelt if Gutzon and his Progressives would allow the regulars to continue to control local politics and patronage.

Gutzon rejected the offer, but still managed to keep control of the stormy meeting, which lasted almost until morning. The next day the *Stamford Advocate* printed the story as page one news and quoted Gutzon as saying that, when he had refused the mayor's offer, Rowell had shouted, ". . . then it's a fight to the knife and the knife to the hilt in your heart."[7]

Although new to the rough and tumble of politics. Gutzon loved every moment of it as he threw himself into the campaign. On many afternoons she campaigned outside the gates of the Yale and Towne factory, and before long the workers, mostly Italian, Polish and Slavic immigrants, began to look for him at shift change because they enjoyed his rousing speeches. He arranged torchlight parades through downtown Stamford and delighted the crowds by exhibiting his pet donkey, Shamrock, with a paper-mâché elephant's head on his rump to illustrate how much difference there was between the two old parties.

These tactics won the crowds but earned him the enmity of the regular Republicans and the Citizen's League, which controlled the city. It became a common practice to read in the newspapers angry letters denouncing:

> The upstart sculptor who had not been able to achieve fame in his own calling and was trying to gain a little notoriety by attaching himself to the Roosevelt kite . . . .[8]

But there were a greater number of friendly letters supporting Gutzon and praising him for his efforts.

Roosevelt and Taft ran against each other, and Wilson won easily, with Roosevelt second and Taft a distant third. Roosevelt almost

The Wheeler Fountain in Bridgeport, Connecticut, where Lincoln Borglum was baptized.

won in Connecticut, and as a result the Progressives were established as an important political force. Roosevelt was defeated, but he had proven that the Republicans needed him and his Bull Moose Progressives if they hoped to regain the White House. Soon after the election, he thanked Gutzon:

> My Dear Borglum, In this great fight for elementary justice and decency . . . and for honesty everywhere, there are many men to whom I feel grateful . . . . You come high among these men; and in this very inadaquate but far from perfunctory manner, I wish to express my profound acknowledgement. [9]

With the election behind him, Gutzon returned to the studio and the work that waited for him. He was commissioned by the Wheeler family of Bridgeport, Connecticut, to create a monument honoring the founder of their family, one of the original partners in the Singer Sewing Machine Company. Gutzon decided to create the Wheeler Fountain, with drinking troughs for people, horses and dogs. It seemed a strange choice for an artist who was upset by the Washington Monument because "it could just as easily be a monument to Cleopatra," but the Wheeler family had left that up to Gutzon, and he wanted the fountain.

There is a strong possibility that Gutzon's decision was based, at least in part, on his newborn son. On the rim of the main bowl of the Wheeler Fountain he sculpted four infant faces, which serve as water spouts. All four are portraits of the infant Lincoln.

The monument was constructed in the center of converging Bridgeport streets. Gutzon built a board fence around the area to keep the curious away, and it was behind the privacy of that fence that Mary's brother, George, baptized his nephew in the fountain.

Knowing Gutzon would not enter a competition, many committees went through the formality of inviting him to do so, and then accepted his refusal and awarded him the contract. The committee formed to honor Governor Peter Altgeld of Illinois went through this procedure before choosing Gutzon. Altgeld, a controversial figure, was the governor who pardoned the men convicted of the Chicago Haymarket riots and bombing, which shocked the nation in 1886. A rally was held in an attempt to unionize Chicago workers, but it became a riot after a bomb exploding killing eleven people. With no clues leading to the person who planted the bomb, authorities arrested the union organizers, and the courts ruled that their efforts constituted inciting to riot and found all guilty as charged.

Altgeld Memorial, bronze, 1915, Chicago, Illinois.

Altgeld had not only defended those found guilty, but as soon as he could he pardoned them, knowing he was destroying his own career. It took many years before tempers cooled sufficiently for the truth to become known. When the truth was known, Altgeld became a symbol of a man willing to sacrifice himself for a just cause.

Gutzon wanted the contract, but refused to enter the competition. When two contests failed to produce a satisfactory concept, the committee was publicly ridiculed by the press, and Gutzon was awarded the commission.

The statue had been completed and its dedication was approaching when the Chicago Municipal Arts Commission criticized the work from both an artistic and a political standpoint. The commission said that the figures representing labor, which were kneeling at Altgeld's feet, were insulting and disturbing to the symmetry of the work.

As with most debates of this nature, only the complaining commissioners and Gutzon took the argument seriously. With Gutzon vigorously defending the work, the story remained news for several days and then ended abruptly when the mayor fired the entire commission and ordered the dedication to proceed as scheduled on Labor Day, 1915.

Gutzon continued to war with the establishment and at the same time tried to win the acceptance of his fellow artists. He joined efforts to form new societies, but because he saw himself only as a leader he invariably alientated others and ended up on the outside. In one such attempt, he helped form the Association of American Painters and Sculptors in New York. The purpose of the association was to provide exhibition space for new and unknown artists who were having difficulty being seen.

The association rented a New York armory, where each member was allotted a share of the space and the right to recommend the work of non-members. Under the rules, if an outsider failed to receive the endorsement of the jury, the sponsoring member could exhibit the rejected work in his own space. It was a revolutionary concept, which seemed simple enough to work, but somehow it failed.

Gutzon charged that works he had approved as head of the jury had not been hung, whereas some he had never seen were being displayed. He was particularly offended by Marcel Duchamp's *Nude Descending a Staircase*. In an article for *Lotus Magazine*, Gutzon charged:

There has been no modern art, except that all art is modern at the time of its production . . . nor is there any lead or force in the plastic asthetics which deserves place outside the comic cuts of the day, removed from the sacred niche where rests the honored movements of every age . . . . A mass of lines crossed upon an empty space interests the curious only because it is called what a child knows it is not — "A Woman Coming Down a Stairs" was a title applied to nothing and the lie becomes notorious. The lie succeeded, but what the drawing claimed did not exist.[10]

Following what had become a familiar pattern, Gutzon stood on principle, fought with factions inside the association and finally felt compelled to resign.

Despite the fact that they were usually on opposite sides of such arguments, the bond between Solon and Gutzon remained strong. Living as close as they did, they were able to visit often. Solon's biographer writes:

> . . . .Gutzon's large black Lincoln would travel the narrow dirt roads of Silvermine, up the steep Borglum hill and drive into Rocky Ranch . . . . Solon's children came to know their uncle and aunt . . . . No seeming resentment for what had occurred in the past prevented Solon from welcoming his brother into his house . . . . With twinkling eyes Gutzon and Solon laughed happily together . . . . Solon and Gutzon were dreaming again.[11]

The brothers were not only dreaming but also collaborating. Gutzon's friend Archer Huntington wanted to create a sculptural garden in the plaza fronting the American Geographical Society Building in Manhattan. He hired Solon and two other sculptors and put Gutzon in charge of the project. The themes for the major statues were heaven, earth, water and man. The plan was that each sculptor would create a concept for each of the figures; then they would meet and decide which man would be assigned to each theme.

The commission was apparently more important to Solon than it was to Gutzon. While Solon worked on a concept for the entire garden and the figure assigned to him, Gutzon did little to develop his own theme. He had learned, because of his busy schedule and the demands on his time, never to work faster than a client desired, and there was no pressure from Huntington.

The millionaire had been a friend and patron of Gutzon's for a long time. He knew he could get what he wanted, when he wanted and was willing to wait while whatever Gutzon had in his mind became a reality.

15

Stone Mountain — Ku Klux Klan

In 1915 John Temple Graves wrote an editorial in which he suggested that Stone Mountain, a huge granite prominence just east of Atlanta, would be a fitting site for a visible expression of the South's noble struggle for independence.

Graves' idea inspired a dynamic, elderly woman who had lost her husband in the Civil War. Helen C. Plane, President of the Atlanta chapter of the United Daughters of the Confederacy (UDC), was a woman of action.[1] As soon as she read Graves' editorial, her mind began to fill with practical ways to turn the idea into reality. She thought of some of the greatest sculptors of the day — Lorado Taft, Rodin and the South's favorite. Sir Moses Ezekiel — and discussed with Graves the possibility of contacting them.

Then, while he mulled over her idea, she went to her chapter of the UDC and with their approval formed the Stone Mountain Memorial Association. A memorial to Southern valor was still very much a nebulous idea, but with Mrs. Plane as its champion it was beginning to take form. Once she had her organization, she decided the next step was to find a sculptor. After much deliberation, she chose Gutzon, wrote to him and invited him to Atlanta.

Gutzon wrote back at once. Judging from his answer, it seems he thought he was just one of several sculptors being considered:

> I should be glad to go to Atlanta at the request of your organization . . . but could not do this as a chance competitor. The class of work I am producing and am called upon to do does not admit of the chance or caprice inseparable from competitive strife . . . . I would strongly advise you to assure yourselves of this; to find a sculptor who has the ability, the imagination, the courage, as well as the sympathy to place Lee in the unique position he holds among great men . . . I could go to Atlanta the early part of August . . . .[2]

Gutzon was obviously excited by the concept. His imagination seized upon the staggering possibilities. After ending his letter, he added:

145

Gutzon making preliminary sketches for Southern memorial at Stone Mountain.

P.S. Since dictating the above I have been thinking about a great idea — and the mountain to carve it on — I have a scheme I believe big and fitting for Lee and his cause.[3]

When Gutzon arrived in Atlanta, he was met at the train station by Mrs. Plane and the women of her UDC committee. Mrs. Plane was polite and cordial, but she would not shake his hand. He was a northerner and thus could be related to the man who fired the bullet that killed her husband.

The women took Gutzon to Stone Mountain and introduced him to his host, Sam Venable, head of the family that owned the mountain. Bubba Sam, as he was called by his family, was a bachelor and a Southern gentleman from the old school. He ran the Stone Mountain quarry, which had been started by his father and uncle, and remembered when the stone was cut by slaves. As a small boy he had been hidden in the barn where he watched, through a knothole, as Sherman's troops marched across his family's plantation to set up camp at the foot of Stone Mountain. He became a man in the days of Reconstruction and never forgot his Southern ways or what it meant to lose a war.

When his father passed away Sam took over the family business. When he deeded the side of the mountain to the Stone Mountain

Memorial Association, he did so for himself and his two sisters. Many years later it was one of the sisters, Mrs. Roper, who was at the heart of the claim by Solon's family that Stone Mountain was another commission Gutzon took knowing it was meant for his brother.

Solon had strong ties in the South. Mrs. Plane acknowledged this after the project was underway. When a reporter asked her why she had chosen Gutzon as her sculptor she answered:

> I knew a great deal about Gutzon Borglum's creations — also of the Gordon equestrian statue in our Capitol grounds, the work of his younger brother and pupil, and without consulting anyone I wrote to him early in the summer offering to pay his expenses to come here to study the possibilities of the mountain for our purpose.[4]

When Solon created the Gordon Monument in 1907, Mrs. Roper was a member of the Gordon committee. Solon had spent many weeks with her and her husband as their guest. During that time he made many friends. Once again, it seems, that unless these friends knew much about art they would not have known that Solon had a brother who was a sculptor. When Mrs. Plane spoke of "Borglum the sculptor," Solon's friends would have assumed Solon was the man to whom she was referring, and he was the one they expected.

Solon's daughter, Mrs. Monica Davies, recalling her family's plans to go to Atlanta to work with Uncle Gutzon, said, "Father kept saying he would go as soon as he finished his part of the commission . . . ."[5] The "commission" was the Audubon Garden for Archer Huntington. Gutzon did intend to include Solon in the Stone Mountain project, but in exactly what way is unclear. Mary recalled:

> When he was first asked to come to Stone Mountain he sent for Solon because he wanted him to be associated with the work . . . .[6]

Mary offered no explanation beyond that. The records suggest that Solon's contribution was limited to giving advice and helping to raise funds in the early stages. He apparently expected to do more, and probably would have, if circumstances beyond the control of everyone concerned had not intervened. Once again, what Solon thought was going to be an exciting project that would show the world what the Borglum brothers could accomplish became another bitter disappointment.

But that was later. On his first visit to Stone Mountain, Gutzon was exploring, trying to plumb the depth of the mountain and learn its secrets. He climbed the gentle back slope, tested the curves of the

Corabelle Venable presenting Stone Mountain deed to Mrs. Helen Plane of the United Daughters of the Confederacy.

steep face of the cliff and hiked the seven-and-a-half mile circumference at the base of the mountain. He visited the quarry and watched the workers cut the stone. He roamed through the ruins of the old slave quarters and slowly filled with a sense of the mountain's history and destiny.

At night, after dinner, Gutzon sat on the porch with Bubba Sam and watched the sunset turn the mountain lavender and rose, then deeper and deeper shades of gray and purple until he and Sam could no longer see the stone but only sense its presence. Then, in the darkness, Gutzon listened to Sam's stories about the war and how hard it had been to stand by helplessly while the old ways disappeared. Sam told him about the South's struggle to retain its pride and talked about what were, to him, the horrors of Reconstruction. Gutzon sat quietly and listened. An idea was forming, but it frightened him a bit because it was larger and grander than anything ever attempted. He had ended his first letter to Mrs. Plane by writing, "I have a scheme big and fitting for Lee and his cause," but that was only a vague and shapeless thought.[7] At the mountain the ideas were taking form.

After three days, Gutzon was ready to return to his home in Connecticut. He had met with the UDC committee and outlined his plan. The women had given him their approval, agreed to seek the backing of the national UDC at their next convention, and appointed Gutzon the official sculptor of Stone Mountain.

The project was official. There was an organization, a treasury of $2,500, a sculptor and a concept that would cost several millions. Gutzon's idea was spectacular, Lee and his army marching across the face of the granite cliff. He had no idea of how he would project the image onto the stone, how he would position his workers on the sheer cliff, or how he would remove the thousands of tons of rock that would have to come off the mountain to reveal the figures; he only knew he would find a way.

The staggering cost and the huge initial sum that were needed before the work could begin were of more immediate concern. Mrs. Plane and the women of the UDC were dedicated, but they were not experienced as fund-raisers, and much of their enthusiasm stemmed from Gutzon's optimism. While they thought about their problems, other factors were at work that would have a profound effect on the memorial, the most important of which was the rebirth of the Ku Klux Klan.

The twentieth-century KKK officially began on Thanksgiving evening, 1915, on a cold, windy, pitch-black night at Stone Mountain. Fifteen men, led by "Colonel" William Simmons, groped along the back slope and made their way to the top. Moving as quietly as possible, in deference to the solemn occasion, they slipped into bedsheet robes and pointed, hooded caps provided by Simmons, and formed a semi-circle in front of a crude stone altar on which lay an open bible and an unsheathed sword.

After Simmons led the men in prayer, he lit a huge cross, and the men pressed closer, standing shoulder to shoulder in the flickering firelight listening to Nate Forrest, grandson of the Klan's founder, Civil War hero General Nathan B. Forrest, administer the Klan oath. When the ceremony was completed, Simmons was the Grand Dragon of the reorganized Ku Klux Klan.

Once again the Klan was a part of American life — and a part of the Southern memorial. Sam Venable was one of the hooded figures, and his nephew, Jimmy, was another. Helen Plane, as a member of the fair sex whose "honor and chastity" the KKK was sworn to protect, could not attend the mountain ceremony, but she was certainly with the "boys" in spirit.

149

On December 17, 1915, just three weeks after Simmons burned that first cross, and four months after Gutzon's visit to Atlanta, Mrs. Plane wrote to Gutzon:

> "Birth of a Nation" [the Reconstruction movie that was playing to record crowds in the South] will give us a percentage of Monday's matinee . . . . I feel it is due to the KKK which saved us from Negro domination and carpetbag rule, that it be immortalized on Stone Mountain. Why not represent a small group of them in their nightly uniform approaching in the distance?[8]

Gutzon was not sure how he should respond. The KKK had not existed when he first went to Georgia. He needed time to assess the situation, but he did not want to risk offending Mrs. Plane, so he included a KKK altar in his plans for the memorial.

At the beginning, Gutzon put aside the technical problems and concentrated on raising funds. The mountain carving had quickly become a consuming passion with him. He committed not only all his time and energy, but all his resources as well. By the time his work on the carving ended, he had mortgaged everything he owned for the sake of the Southern memorial.

Because of the pressures of his many activities, Gutzon was commuting between Stone Mountain and his Connecticut home, with frequent stops in Washington, until January 1916, when he decided it was time for an official dedication at Stone Mountain and time to move his family to Georgia. Mary was expecting again, and she and Gutzon wanted the baby to be born in the shadow of what they hoped would be their greatest triumph.

Their daughter was born March 25, 1916, on Gutzon's forty-ninth birthday. Delighted, he wired friends saying he had just been given the finest birthday present any man had ever received. They named their daughter Mary Ellis, Mary after her mother and Ellis in honor of Mary's doctor, James Ellis, brother-in-law of Sam Venable.

For the first Stone Mountain ceremony, Gutzon wanted to drape a huge Confederate flag over the spot on the mountain where he would carve the portrait of General Lee. In the planning stage, it seemed a comparatively simple task, but before it was accomplished it presented the first of many serious challenges.

Stone Mountain has sharply curved sides. The mountain slopes about fifteen feet for every one hundred feet of drop. For as long as anyone could remember, a red line had been painted near the summit to warn of the danger. Despite this, many had gone too far and had either slid to their deaths or been forced to hang on for their life, while daring rescuers made their way down to them on ropes.

When Gutzon asked a crew of Venable's stonecutters to work their way down the slope to secure the flag, the men flatly refused. As far as they were concerned he was asking them to kill themselves. It was then that Gutzon realized the magnitude of his problems. If he could not get a crew to perform a seemingly simple task like securing the flag, he knew he would never convince men to spend days on the sheer mountain carving the rock.

Just at that moment Jesse Tucker appeared. A builder and jack-of-all-trades, Tucker had heard there was a problem on the mountain and came to see if he could help. After Gutzon explained the problem, Tucker edged himself past the red line and worked his way down the slope. Setting himself against the rock he hammered a metal anchor into the stone, then eased across and secured a second anchor. Taking heart from Tucker's example some of the men joined him and helped hang the huge flag. When Tucker returned to the top he had a new job: superintendent at Stone Mountain.

At the dedication ceremony on Saturday, May 16, 1916, several Georgia politicians made speeches, and Sam Venable presented the deed that gave the Stone Mountain Memorial Association twelve years to complete the carving. On the following Monday, construction began on the top of the monument. Gutzon had decided he wanted a work platform halfway down the slope and a set of steps to reach it from the top. Materials were hauled up the back slope by oxen as far as possible and then carried the rest of the way on the backs of Tucker's laborers.

Gutzon remained in Georgia just long enough to assure himself that Tucker had everything under control. Then he headed for Chicago to attend the 1916 Republican Convention.

Roosevelt, the Convention
and the Old Guard

Since the debilitating three-way race of 1912, the Republicans had been splintered. Wilson and the Democrats were firmly in control of the nation, but they were not having an easy time. The pressures on Wilson were increasing almost by the hour. The war in Europe was taking a frightening toll on men and machines. Old boundaries were rapidly disappearing in an orgy of destruction that threatened to engulf the entire world.

The French and British were trying to force the United States into the war as their ally, while the Germans were doing everything they could to keep the United States neutral. Spies and saboteurs from both sides were everywhere. They had infiltrated America's factories, ports and even some of America's government agencies. Sympathizers for both sides were active politically. With the 1916 election approaching, control of the White House became critical.

Wilson seemed certain to be re-nominated by acclamation and was an odds-on favorite for re-election. He had promised to keep the United States out of the fighting, but it seemed only a matter of time before he would be forced to commit troops.

The Republicans believed Wilson's policies were leading the United States into a catastrophic situation, but they were too divided to mount a united, earnest campaign. Gutzon felt so strongly about the danger to America that would result from Wilson's re-election that he finally rejoined the regular Republican Party. He still considered himself a Progressive, but he felt differences had to be put aside for the sake of the nation. In a long letter to Roosevelt, he declared:

> . . . the return of Woodrow Wilson . . . to a term of years sufficient to secure the complete moral and political degredation of the nation . . . . We have seen a Solomon sit and watch the quartering of little people, and drop to the lowest level in the hands of a party incapable and unwilling

153

to govern. We have seen our foreign policy laughed at by both the good and the bad of the world . . . no country is so small as not to be large enough to insult with impunity the American nation and every principle we stood for has been flung back in our faces until the list of national insults has become greater during the Wilson presidency . . . than during the rest of our national existence.[1]

The letter was written before Roosevelt had officially declared himself a candidate. The Progressives, with Gutzon very much in the lead, were urging him to be their candidate in the hope that they could then make a deal that would re-unite them with the regular party and give them a voice in establishing Republican policy. There was a strong feeling among the Progressives, admittedly based as much on emotion as logic, that Roosevelt was the only man who had a chance to defeat Wilson.

Many of the Old Guard Republicans agreed with that assessment, but they could not easily forgive or forget what they felt was Roosevelt's betrayal of Taft in 1912. There was no way they would take him back, even if it cost them the White House. Most of this Old Guard had declared for Henry Cabot Lodge, and they were determined to win the nomination for him if only to prove that they still controlled the party.

There were other delegates backing favorite sons. There were farm candidates led by Senator Bob La Follette. There were also a number of anti-war and pro-war faction candidates, and none of the splinter groups seemed willing to put aside their differences for the sake of party unity.

Gutzon realized early that the opposition to Roosevelt would be too strong to overcome, but he could not abandon his old friend. As long as Roosevelt did not take himself out of the race, Gutzon had to support him. Attempting to persuade Roosevelt not to run, however, Gutzon wrote:

You can be the next nominee for the presidency of the United States, if you wish, but it will be wrung from the covetous grip of powerful forces, and I would question the result that would follow or the precedent of such a conquest. However . . . I shall be in the field fighting for you until the polls close, in every way my power and ingenuity can devise. But I think that the poorer part of the play.[2]

This was an attempt to make Roosevelt withdraw in favor of a man Gutzon greatly admired, General Leonard Wood. He tried his best, on several occasions, to convince Roosevelt, but the president would not agree. Roosevelt expected the convention to deadlock and to be forced to turn to him.

Most political observers agreed that that could happen, but only if Roosevelt found a way to re-unite the Progressives and the party before the convention. The Old Guard was willing to discuss the possibility, and it was finally agreed that Roosevelt would be given a chance to win the nomination on the open floor in return for his promise to withdraw, in favor of Lodge, when it became apparent he had no chance. To make the deal feasible, both sides felt Roosevelt's floor leader had to be someone they trusted, and Gutzon was given the job.

Gutzon was fully aware of what was going on. He suspected the motives of those closest to Roosevelt, but he accepted the position because it gave him an opportunity to exert his influence. Besides, he reasoned, he had nothing to lose. He had no ulterior motive and wanted nothing for himself. Politically he was a true patriot, guided by his conscience and his beliefs. Gutzon also enjoyed the limelight and knew that his career would benefit from the publicity.

In agreeing to represent Roosevelt, Gutzon made one condition. He would lead the floor fight if Roosevelt agreed to switch to General Wood as soon as it became obvious he could not win. Roosevelt, however, had already made a similar arrangement with the Old Guard by agreeing to back Lodge.

Gutzon was aware of the Lodge deal, but he felt Lodge would not be acceptable to the Progressives and would therefore have no better chance of securing the nomination than Roosevelt. On the other hand, Roosevelt was so certain of winning that he would have made a dozen deals on the assumption he would never have to deliver.

Gutzon may have been idealistic, but he was not naive. He knew how to assess the chances of the various hopefuls as well as anyone, and the weaknesses of a Roosevelt candidacy was obvious to him. He knew that if Roosevelt did not come out strongly for someone early in the balloting he would lose his chance to affect the final outcome.

They had an agreement, and Gutzon intended to keep his end of the bargain, but as the convention approached he increased the pressure on Roosevelt. Others in Roosevelt's inner circle were doing the same, for different reasons, and this led to the circulating of all sorts of unfounded rumors. In April, a columnist claimed that Roosevelt had withdrawn in favor of General Wood. Gutzon immediately wired his congratulations:

You have said the first thing that has been said to make impossible the bitter struggle that might otherwise occur and endanger the success of the majority of the people in this country, who believe in their souls we cannot stand four more years such as we have passed through.[3]

When the report turned out to be false, Gutzon was dismayed, but no less determined. He still believed in Roosevelt and felt certain he would eventually do what had to be done.

The July convention was almost anticlimactic. Gutzon arrived in Chicago in high spirits, certain he had everything under control, when in fact backroom deals had been made and the issues settled in advance. The coalition of Progressives and Old Guard Republicans, joined by expedience but sharing no mutual trust, had already had a falling out. The sentiment for General Wood, never as strong with others as it was with Gutzon, had evaporated. Too many felt a military man would not have a chance against an incumbent running behind a banner proclaiming, "He kept us out of war!"

After the nominations and the early balloting, it appeared obvious that neither Lodge nor Roosevelt had a chance, and the nomination was up for grabs. Roosevelt was waiting for news in his Long Island home at Oyster Bay certain that destiny was about to touch him once more. Gutzon knew this would not happen. He telegraphed Roosevelt, pleading for an announcement backing Wood, but received no reply. He telephoned and spoke to Roosevelt, but received evasive, noncommital answers.

When ballot after ballot took them into the early hours of the morning, the convention began to lean toward the compromise candidacy of Charles Evans Hughes. At the last moment, in a desperate effort to save face, Roosevelt tried to swing his delegates to Lodge, but it was an empty gesture, which came too late.

Hughes was the candidate, and a weary, angry Gutzon returned home. He felt that Roosevelt had betrayed him, and he told Mary he felt as if he never wanted to speak to him again. When he settled down, however, Gutzon realized his friend was as much a victim as he was, and he joined him in supporting Hughes.

The convention changed Gutzon's political perspective. Having seen the professionals at close range, he realized he did not think or act as they did, and he committed himself to the true Progressives he had met at the convention. He became stronger in his feelings about the plight of the farmers and the need for land reform. He began to align himself with the Midwest agrarians and became one of the principal leaders of the North Dakota Non-Partisan League.

Gutzon's involvement on a national level did not prevent him from remaining active in local politics. When Roosevelt went to Connecticut to placate those whom Gutzon considered political bosses, he was offended and wrote Roosevelt to tell him so:

> I should be unfaithful, a quitter and a traitor to all I have . . . struggled for . . . should I fail to protest . . . your coming into this district under the patronage of . . . the Boss of Bridgeport . . . you are surrounded by men . . . leaders in the particular brand of political criminality you have for a quarter of a century . . . fought . . . four years ago I returned this congressional district to the . . . party . . . . You came not as a guest of the Progressive Republicans to strengthen clean politics we have suffered to secure, but as a guest of our enemy . . . . I am giving this letter to the . . . press.[4]

Roosevelt accepted Gutzon's attack with his usual good humor. When reporters asked him about Gutzon's comment, he dismissed the incident with a shrug, and remarked that Borglum just did not like some of his friends.

17
The War to End All Wars

Wilson was re-elected, but by a surprisingly narrow margin. He had campaigned as the man who had kept America out of the war, but no one expected America's neutrality to last. Too much was happening. Too many powers were exerting pressure. Every country involved in the fighting was trying to buy American products, while at the same time trying to sabotage the shipments heading for their enemies. By 1917 American national security was being hampered by espionage groups from France, Italy, Germany, Britain, Japan and a dozen emerging nations that hoped to win their independence when the fighting ended.

Ethnic groups that had been absorbed by the Austrian Empire — Illyrians, Ruthenians, Bohemians, Slovaks, Moravians, Silesians, Czechs and others — saw the war as a way to gain the freedom they had lost centuries before. All knew a German-Austrian victory would end their hopes while an Allied victory would at least give them a chance to establish their nations.

The wave of immigration that had peaked at the turn of the century had brought many of these Old World people to America, where they were assimilated. They thought of themselves as Americans, yet they still dreamed of an independent homeland for their countrymen. Backing the Allied war effort, they banded together to form such ethnic associations as the Bohemian National Alliance. These groups worked as independent units to counter German espionage and disrupt German efforts. At the same time, they tried to force America into the war and sought Wilson's recognition for their personal cause.

One of Gutzon's suppliers of granite, Emile Voska, an American of Czech ancestry, formed a unit that successfully penetrated the German embassy. With the information he gathered, Voska was able to stop many, but not all, of the German plots. The German network was too large and too well staffed by Americans who believed in the German cause to be stopped by one group. German spies worked the ports, railroads, factories and major trading centers in large numbers. Despite this, America still managed to produce and to supply the Allies.

When the Germans realized that they would not be able to stop the flow of American arms to their enemies, they increased their U-boat attacks on the open sea and declared an open season on all of America's ships. This provocation Wilson could not allow. On April 6, 1917, he asked Congress for a Declaration of War. The effect on America was sudden and dramatic. Within hours street corner orators were rallying the people on the home front, and army recruiting stations were besieged by men eager to enlist in the fight against the Hun. As for Gutzon, Mary wrote:

> . . . Promptly the sculptor volunteered for military service, or tried to, but by an odd and most unexpected whim of fortune . . . his desire to serve his country was turned into another channel . . . .[1]

The chain of events that led him to that "channel" started when Jesse Tucker, Gutzon's superintendent at Stone Mountain, joined the army, which stopped the work on the mountain. When Mary and the children left Georgia to return to Borgland, Gutzon remained just long enough to shut down the operation and say goodbye to his friends before starting for home. On the way he stopped in Cleveland to visit a friend, Lester Barlow. Barlow was an engineer who was working on some of the Stone Mountain problems. Both were extremely active politically, both thought the Wilson administration was weak, and both mistrusted the morality and dedication of the bankers and industrialists whom they felt thought only of profits. Both were concerned about rumors they had heard about the poor state of the country's aircraft production. They decided to investigate by inspecting plants in and near Dayton, Ohio.

Prior to the war, the United States had done little to develop fighting aircraft or build an air force. In 1908, with Gutzon present as official timekeeper, the Wright brothers had successfully demonstrated the military potential of their airship. Everyone was amazed by the machine, but in the next ten years the government spent less than $14,000,000 to develop that potential.

"When my brother and I built and flew the first man-carrying machine," Orville Wright said, "we thought we were introducing into the world an invention which would make further wars practically impossible."[2] The Wright brothers thought the world would be afraid to wage war because their machine would create such havoc, but few military men really shared their view. They saw the airplane as a minor weapon, useful only for directing artillery or as a fancy, meaningless machine to be used in dogfights against similar machines.

As a result, the United States entered the war with less than one hundred pilots and only a few dozen obsolete aircraft, which were not of combat quality. America soon realized that its military situation would have to be rectified if Europe were to be saved.

In July 1917, just three months after war was declared, Congress authorized $600,000,000 to finance the building of an air force. The money was to be used for aircraft development and production, the building of air fields and the training of personnel. By October the air force numbered 150,000 men, with 17,000 being trained as pilots. America seemed to be on its way to building a mighty flying force, but that did not happen. Control of the industry had fallen into the hands of greedy profiteers with political connections but no knowledge of production.

After his inspection tour, Gutzon took a train to Washington. The situation was so critical that he felt compelled to report directly to Wilson. What he had seen was treasonous. Despite the feelings of urgency, he was politely refused an interview at the White House. It was the first time any president had not welcomed Gutzon, but he understood that Wilson was too pressed by the demands of the war to see everyone who wanted an audience. When Wilson's secretary, Joe Tumulty, asked him to put his charges in writing, Gutzon did so and then went home.

He had scarcely reached Borgland when the White House phoned to suggest he take his complaint to the newly-formed Aeronautics Board, which had been set up to oversee the industry. Gutzon refused to do this because he knew the board could not be impartial. Edward Deeds, a member of the board, was the principal stockholder in one of the plants Gutzon had inspected. The other members of the board also had vested interests in the industry, as Gutzon acknowledged in his reply to Wilson's suggestion: "they are all auto people—that's the trouble."

Wilson was a proud, honest man concerned with, among other things, his place in history. He was disturbed by Gutzon's charges and gave serious thought to appointing a board of inquiry with Gutzon at the head. In a note to Tumulty he asked:

What did you find out about these matters that Mr. Borglum is so excited about? I think it is important to get to the root of this thing . . . . If Mr. Borglum has a grievance or a personal element in it, it is rather important that we should know.[3]

Tumulty made inquiries and concluded that Gutzon had no ulterior motives. He reported this to the president, and on January 2, 1918, Wilson wrote to Gutzon:

> Knowing the earnest and loyal purpose with which you have written me . . . I urge you to come at once to Washington, lay the whole matter frankly and fully before the secretary, and by your investigation discover the facts in this business. The Secretary of War [Newton Baker] . . . will be delighted to clothe you with full authority . . . every facility of inquiry will be placed at your disposal. . . . I would be most happy to have a report from you personally to me on any phase of the matter which remains in the slightest degree doubtful in your mind.[4]

This was a remarkable invitation from a wartime president to a member of the opposition party, and it set in motion one of the strangest chains of events in American history. Recounting his call to Washington long after the war, Gutzon claimed he had been appointed to this position so that he could not talk. The facts bore this out, and it worked for quite a while.

Gutzon went to Washington immediately, at his own expense, and began an investigation. He quickly discovered that Secretary Baker and the others assigned to aid in the investigation were antagonistic and were determined to do everything in their power to undermine his efforts.

Despite the hardships and the constant harassment by petty officials who tried to mislead and discourage him, Gutzon spent months learning the truth. When he was finished, he reported evidence of criminal fraud involving hundreds of millions of dollars, proof of political payoffs, which reached, if not to Wilson personally, at least into the White House, and a plot that connected Washington, London, Paris and Berlin in a conspiracy. Recounting the investigation, Gutzon wrote:

> . . . regarding Pro-Germanism of Wilson's administration . . . just look over the names and nationalities of the most important people at the most important checking points of our government, or that part of it that dealt directly with foreign matters, then check up Baker and Baruch and about a dozen others . . . . Had I lied about the War Department and praised it . . . I would not only have been a Major-General, but . . . would have probably replaced Mr. Colonel House or occupied some equally prominent position as court fool.[5]

Gutzon was understandably angry and bitter. He made many charges, but the most controversial of all was the plot he laid at the doorstep of a British munitions manufacturer, Sir Basil Zaharoff. The story seemed so bizarre that most of Gutzon's critics ridiculed or ignored the charges, but they could not ignore the fact that America spent over one billion dollars and failed to produce a single worthy fighting aircraft during the war.

In *The Wild Blue Yonder*, Emile Gavreau describes a cartel of French, British and German munitions manufacturers, aided by associates in Japan and the United States, who agreed to keep the German iron mines at the St. Mihiel salient free from attack. By agreeing to protect Germany's ability to mine iron and, therefore, to continue to produce arms, the Zaharoff-led cartel was able to prolong the war and thus sell more munitions. How long the situation would have continued is difficult to ascertain. Not until the United States was drawn into the conflict, however, was Germany's ability to produce hampered.

Zaharoff's cartel was not concerned only with immediate profit. Its members reasoned that no matter who won the war the German iron mines and munitions factories would be important in the economic recovery. There was also a strong feeling in the military, which was endorsed by the cartel, that, if an aircraft could sink a battleship that required thousands of tons of steel and man-hours to produce, all military strategy would become obsolete and all industry would be endangered. For the munitions and steel manufacturers, this would be far worse than a military loss by either side.

For this reason the cartel did everything it could to control the war effort, and it was successful until it ran into the fiercely determined American commander General John Pershing. When Pershing realized that his country could not, or would not, supply the aircraft he needed to end the war quickly, he forced the French and British to supply him by threatening to take the aircraft from them. He then used his air fleet to attack the St. Mihiel salient and Briery Basin, thus forcing Germany to surrender, but by then the United States treasury had been looted of over one billion dollars, and thousands of men had died needlessly on the battlefields.

Gutzon's own life was threatened while he was conducting his investigation. One attempt was made when someone shot at him while he sat with friends at a sidewalk cafe. He persisted, despite the danger and lack of cooperation, and completed his report, which he delivered to Wilson. In his cover letter he said:

I am placing in your hands today a report. . . . The statements, grave as they appear, are based upon a mass of information available to you . . . . What I suggest is . . . immediate seizure of the manufactories I

163

Gutzon Borglum with his children, Lincoln and Mary Ellis, by the Rippowan River which ran through their Stamford, Connecticut, estate.

believe that you might seize this whole bankrupt program . . . that would result in rebuilding, would give us time to correct the present ills and with men who desire it we can still deliver some fighting machines in Europe.[7]

With his work in Washington completed, Gutzon returned to Borgland to wait for the president's response. He was concerned, exhausted and completely unnerved by his experience. He had uncovered a scandal of such magnitude that he was not certain that the government could survive the repercussions. Yet he saw no way that Wilson could avoid taking action.

The president, however, did not share that view. For him it was not quite that simple. The need to straighten out the aircraft industry and to deal with the scandal of wartime profiteering was obvious, but how and when to proceed were entirely different matters. With troops at the front lines, the effect of a scandal of such proportion on morale and the nation's willingness to continue to back its leaders had to be considered. Wilson also had to face the hard truth that the men named in Gutzon's report were, for the most part, wealthy, influential members of his party. They were friends of long standing, and any accusations made against them would implicate, at least by inference, the president himself.

Wilson's solution was to do nothing for as long as he could. Meanwhile, Gutzon waited and fumed. When his patience finally gave out, after several weeks, he wrote to Wilson demanding action and received a response that is incomprehensible. Contrary to the clear mandate of his original invitation asking Gutzon to come to Washington to investigate, Wilson wrote:

> I am afraid that you have for some time been under a serious misapprehension . . . the investigation which you, of your own motion, undertook of the aircraft production . . . . I wrote . . . that . . . you were . . . at liberty to examine any evidence that was in our possession. I never at any time constituted you an official investigator . . . we have at no time regarded you as the official representative of the administration . . . . I hope you will be willing . . . and feel it is your duty to put at the disposal of those whom I have constituted official investigators all the evidence . . . in your possession.[8]

Wilson then appointed Charles Evans Hughes, the Republican he had defeated in the 1916 election, to head an investigation committee. He was hoping the appointment of Hughes might placate Gutzon and take the issue out of the realm of partisan politics. Gutzon, however, saw the naming of Hughes as just another attempt to cloud the issues and decided he could no longer remain silent. He turned all the Wilson letters over to the newspapers and waited for the storm he was certain would follow.

This decision to take the matter to the public was an agonizing one for Gutzon. His motives, from the beginning, were purely patriotic. When he began, he had no way of knowing what he would discover. He was not seeking to uncover a scandal, but only a way to correct whatever was wrong with the United States' aircraft industry. He realized after his investigation that he was dealing with powerful forces, which would stop at nothing to destroy his reputation if he went public, but Gutzon felt he had no other choice. Almost at once, reports appeared in the newspapers claiming that Gutzon had secret interests in aircraft plants and that he was trying to peddle his influence in Washington, but his enemies could not cloud the issues, not even with help from the White House.

When Wilson's letters to Gutzon were released, the administration charged that it was a political attack of no substance. It claimed that the letters dealt only with past history, the result of an honest attempt to build a huge industry too fast. The government predicted that it would be only a matter of weeks before thousands of aircraft would be at the front. Suddenly, railroad cars loaded with crates marked "Warplanes — Do Not Delay" were heading for the ports amid a great deal of fanfare. Not until long after the war was it revealed that most of the crates were empty.

The campaign against Gutzon intensified. The *New York Tribune* questioned his knowledge of business. Other newspapers and magazines rallied to Gutzon's defense, believing he had uncovered a conspiracy that had to be confronted. An editorial in the *North American Review* stated:

> Apparently the position of the president is about this: We wished at every point to assist you and to make possible for you to do what we urged you in our letter of January 2 to come at once and undertake, with full assurance that every facility of inquiry would be put at your disposal and that you would be clothed with full authority to get at the bottom of every situation. Now if you complain that we have not kept our promise in all this, the answer is you are not an official representative of the administration. Had we regarded you as an official representative, of course we would have furnished you with what you lack. But you can see that you are not an official representative of the administration. And there is the muddle of the Administration-Borglum controversy . . . .[9]

It all came to nothing. Investigation followed investigation for years. A few indictments were handed down, and some petty officials did go to jail, but eventually the public grew tired of the scandal, and it dropped from the news. Reflecting on the affair after Gutzon's death, Mary expressed their frustration this way:

> Until the day he died Gutzon could not think about the aircraft investigation without getting angry. He could not understand how they could not have taken action on his charges, when what he should have been wondering was how they allowed him to investigate in the first place.[10]

18
Czechoslovaks

The United States was engaged in a war being fought thousands of miles away on European battlefields. For most Americans, the war meant loved ones fighting in places with names they could not pronounce, marching bands, Liberty Bond rallies, and the lively tune to "How ya gonna keep 'em down on the farm after they've seen Paree?"

For Gutzon, the war was a time of intense and mixed emotions. With his findings in the aircraft investigation ignored and his motives distorted by enemies who labeled him an impeder of the war, Gutzon was determined to involve himself in the struggle.

Solon, after being rejected by the army because of his age, had gone to Europe as a volunteer with a YMCA unit that was very active in the front lines. Gutzon was very proud of his brother's determination, but could not see himself in such an anonymous role. He felt he had much to contribute on a higher level and longed for an official position. With the aircraft scandal hanging over the nation like a dark cloud, he expected personal vindication and a call at any time. In the meantime, he tried to return to his art career and to the problems created by the debts that had piled up while he was in Washington.

Wartime, Gutzon quickly discovered, was not a time for monumental sculpture. The committees had disbanded, and all efforts were going into fighting the war. He managed to keep the studio going with some private commissions and the models and plans that would be needed at Stone Mountain when they started up again. He also continued to work on the monumental orders that had been contracted before the war, the largest of which was the General Sheridan for Chicago.

Gutzon's friend, Ignace Paderewski, the Polish pianist turned statesman, was in America trying to win backing for the free Poland he hoped to form after the Allies won the war. Another revolutionary, Thomas Masaryk, and his Czechoslovaks were fighting in Russia as independent soldiers while many of their people were volunteering for the armies of France, Britain and the United States. Still others of their countrymen were deserting to the Allies from the Austrian army into which they had been drafted. To enlist or desert took a tremendous amount of courage. The Emperor of Austria had declared that all of the people descended from the ethnic groups that made up his empire were his subjects. He claimed their loyalty even if they were citizens of another country and ordered that they be hanged as traitors if captured in an enemy uniform. Despite this threat, the men still flocked to the armies of the Allies. These men were motivated by a rich heritage. No matter where they were born, they were raised with a dream of independence for the land of their ancestors. Each generation hoped to be a part of the struggle that would lead to the ultimate victory. The war gave them their first hope in over two hundred years.

There were many leaders, but Paderewski and Masaryk were the most important, and Masaryk was the most powerful. Masaryk was a dynamic, forceful, charismatic former professor who commanded universal respect and total loyalty from his followers. When the Wilson administration seemed sympathetic to his cause, Masaryk left the fighting in Russia and came to America to appeal for official recognition. To help bolster his argument, he set up the machinery for establishing an army of volunteers in America.

One of Gutzon's assistants at Borgland, a young Czech named Micka, had come to the United States to study art and had found a position with Gutzon. When the war broke out, he was forced to stay in America. He was in the studio while Gutzon was in Washington conducting the aircraft investigation. Homesick and worried about his family in Europe, he often confided in Mary and told her of his countrymen's dream of independence. Mary was able to converse in his native language, and it did not take long for his impassioned arguments to win her to his cause.

Micka spent many of his off hours in the Slovak community in Stamford. He joined the local chapter of the National Bohemian Alliance, which was headed by Rudolph Voska. Voska was Gutzon's tailor and, according to his daughter, a creditor of long standing. She said that whenever Gutzon was asked for money he would pay what he could and at the same time order a new suit to maintain his credit.

When the alliance was asked to locate a suitable site for a training base and camp for Masaryk's troops, Voska thought of Borgland and its hundreds of acres. He discussed the situation with Micka; when he learned that Mary was sympathetic he approached her, and an agreement was reached. Gutzon may not have even been aware of the situation until then. Mary Ellis, Gutzon and Mary's daughter, said,

Mary Ellis with Czechoslovakian volunteers at Borgland camp. The camp station wagon is a 1915 Ford.

"we always assumed the camp was mother's idea. She certainly did all the work."[1]

Plans for the camp were announced in the *Stamford Advocate* under such banner headlines as "Bohemians To Train in North Stamford." Other stories tried to reassure the neighbors by reporting that the men would not be armed, but still there were skeptics who wondered if Gutzon was training a private army. In preparation for the first contingent of 150 volunteers, a building at Borgland was converted into a hospital, material was purchased by the alliance so the men could build crude barracks, supplies were brought in and a huge striped tent was borrowed from the YMCA in Bridgeport, Connecticut.

The purpose of the camp was more political than military, though the trained soldiers were sent to Europe and did fight. Masaryk and his government-in-exile did not expect their small army to have a great impact in battle, but they believed that their presence would focus attention on their cause in a dramatic way. The Czechoslovaks realized that their only chance of achieving independence lay with a sympathetic United States willing to fight for Czechoslovakian independence at the peace table. Masaryk had no illusions about the future if the United States did not become involved in their cause. That is why he spent so much of his time in the United States forming a constitutional government and fighting for recognition. When he finally convinced Wilson that his cause was just and worth supporting, it was a wonderful moment for the Czechs.

According to Mary, Gutzon was in New York when the announcement was made that Wilson had officially recognized the Czech government-in-exile. There was no radio at the camp, but Gutzon telephoned and told her not to let the boys go to bed. When he arrived home he went to the barracks and personally broke the news and then joined in the night-long celebration. A huge bonfire was lit and the men danced, sang and shouted themselves hoarse.

Once Gutzon had committed himself to the Czech cause he became totally involved. He worked through the night of July 3, 1918, with Mary and their friend Eliot Norton revising the Czechoslovak Declaration of Independence. Norton later became United States Ambassador to Czechoslovakia, and he often referred to himself and the Borglums as the "Three Musketeers of the Czech movement." They had been asked by Masaryk's secretary to edit Masaryk's draft of the Declaration. Although he was married to a Brooklyn-born woman and spoke English well, Masaryk did not feel comfortable writing in English.

Gutzon also joined a select group that included former President Howard Taft and Henry Cabot Lodge in sponsoring a Victory Meeting For the Oppressed Nationalities of Central Europe in New York City's Carnegie Hall. Recalling the triumph of his friend Paderewski, Gutzon wrote:

> Paderewski spoke just before Masaryk . . . he began much as he plays, though I suppose few people thought of this . . . he touched historically on the suffering of his people . . . . I felt that I was listening to a great product of art, a gifted orator . . . one could have heard a pin drop . . . and then the audience rose in unrestrained homage. Finally, when the applause had subsided, Masaryk stepped to the front . . . . Silent, pale . . . he looked at Paderewski and then he spoke, "I know now what to say. I, too, have been carried away by the master speech of Poland's great leader and liberator." . . . Then it came to me. It is because he is a great artist that he can understand and know these things.[2]

Being close to so many of the men who were reshaping the world was an enriching experience for Gutzon, just as being with soldiers in the camp was an exciting one. Dealing with the officials of the alliance, however, was not nearly as satisfying or rewarding. Gutzon and Mary felt compelled to complain bitterly and often about the conditions in

170

Thomas Masaryk, Gutzon Borglum and George Luks during Masaryk's visit to the Borgland camp.

the camp, but little was done, because the leaders in New York knew the Borglums would not let the men suffer. When there was a shortage of blankets, and Gutzon could not get them from the alliance, he talked the Red Cross into donating a thousand blankets. When the camp was hit by a flu epidemic and four of the men died, Gutzon and Mary had to prevail upon the Stamford Burial Society because the Alliance had not made any other arrangements. It seemed to the Borglums that the officials cared not about the men, but only the political purpose of the camp. Even small matters concerned Gutzon and Mary. When they learned money was so short the men could not afford such extras as tobacco and ice cream, the Borglums spent their own money rather than allow the men to do without.

The Czech troops were, for the most part, devout Catholics, but the camp commander was an atheist and would not allow services even on the night before the men left for overseas. When Mary heard about the problem, she arranged for Father Kubechak, a priest from nearby

171

Yonkers, to share a pot-luck supper in the Borglum living room on Sunday nights, and invited the troops to share it with them.[3]

One of the best days in the camp was the Sunday Gutzon arranged a pageant and auction, which were attended by half the citizens of Stamford. The troops built a replica of a Moravian village with thatched-roof huts. Gutzon and his friend, artist George Luks, dressed as peasant artists and walked through the village displaying their poster "The Coming of the Czechs" to the "natives," citizens of Stamford decked out in native costumes. Suddenly soldiers appeared and arrested the artists. As they were leading the villagers away, shots were heard, and the men of the camp, dressed in the blue uniform of independent Czechoslovakia topped with Tam O'Shanter hats, came running down the hill shouting that peace had been declared.[4]

Mary Ellis Borglum was two at the time of the pageant. Her mother dressed her in a lovely velvet dress and moved her tiny rocking chair onto the stage so she could be near her father when he held the auction. Gutzon was holding up the poster and laughing as he tried to get someone in the audience to bid $500 for the work. He succeeded with Mrs. Havemeyer, a society friend from nearby Greenwich. Before she paid her money, Mrs. Havemeyer tried to tease Gutzon. "I'll give you $500 for her," she said, pointing to Mary Ellis. Gutzon's smile faded. "No," he said almost in a whisper, "she's not for sale." Everyone who knew Gutzon commented on his fine sense of humor. He could give and take a joke with the best, but not when it involved his children.

The affairs of the camp were big news in Stamford. From the day the first group arrived, the *Stamford Advocate* kept the town informed of the doings at the camp:

With one hundred or more of the Czechoslovaks at his heels, a night prowler, believed . . . to be a Teuton spy, fled for his life about ten last night through the woods at Borgland . . . . Yesterday a number of men from the camp came to Stamford without permission and during the day some of them obtained liquor and became quarrelsome . . . .[5]

. . . Our city is going to have a colossal bust of President Masaryk, cut out of an enormous red granite boulder which stands on an eminence above the camp . . . all the soldiers who pass through the camp are to take a hand in cutting the boulder to shape . . . . Standing at attention with American and French flags, and their own colors flying in the breeze, in the Town Hall Plaza, with hundreds of people grouped about . . . over one hundred members . . . of the camp bade farewell . . . . They were on their way . . . to fight with a reverence second to none of the allies now fighting desperately to keep the murdering Hun from reaching the gateway to Paris.[7]

172

It was an awe-inspiring spectacle as these men, brown as a berry and with muscles of steel, stood in the most prominent spot in the city . . . listening to the cheering and plaudits of those about them . . . . Gutzon Borglum, on whose property the . . . camp is located addressed the men with stirring emphasis. . . . He said he would work even harder than ever for the volunteers . . . the vibrant . . . "Nazdar" was proclaimed to him and Mrs. Borglum for their hearty cooperation.[8]

But the story that made the biggest news was the Saturday visit of Thomas Masaryk. For the troops and the others attached to the camp it was an unforgettable time. Marie Vokalek was the nurse in the camp hospital. The memory of Masaryk's visit was so vivid that she was able to describe it sixty years later at the age of ninety-two:

Masaryk did not talk much. His manner was marked by a quiet determination and patience. He smiled frequently . . . in such a way that one realized there was a world of will-power behind that smile and one understood better why the Central Powers had placed $30,000 on the head of the man . . . the camp cook prepared a special goulash for the day. Masaryk stood in line with the soldiers waiting his meal portion to be ladled from the cauldron. Later in the day they all gathered to sing to the music of an accordion . . . . He addressed the soldiers "Braskove," an untranslatable, intimate identification of brotherhood.[9]

Sometime during the day Gutzon managed to air his complaints about the alliance and the callous treatment of the men to the Czech leader. He was promised that something would be done. When weeks passed and nothing was done, Gutzon wrote an angry letter to Masaryk:

Your brief note of goodbye to Mrs. Borglum and myself was received . . . . Your passing reference to the camp clearly indicates you are only informed through misrepresentation . . . . Last spring . . . your people came to my place and sought quarters for 150 men. It was through and due to my friendship . . . that I entertained at all a proposition to allow an encampment of technically enemy aliens to gather here . . . . Above all they were utterly without anyone to care for them . . . who met any of their needs. They were without discipline, indulged in drunkenness and fighting, and finally revolted . . . . I brought these matters to your attention — I believe with courtesy . . . . You promised that a proper person, intelligent and with authority would be put in charge . . . my interest in this entire matter was purely a human one . . . had I not suppressed and overlooked and remedied conditions . . . a scandal certainly would have outgrown the camp and reached the National Government in a manner that would have discredited your entire movement . . . my interest in the Middle Europe is closed and I am very glad to forget it.[10]

But Gutzon could not "forget it." Through the years, the feeling that he had been slighted by the Czechoslovaks grew. In 1940, when Masaryk's son, Jan, fled from the Nazis and set up another Czechoslovak government-in-exile, he sought help from those who had helped his father. He did not include Gutzon in this group, but Gutzon felt compelled to contact him:

> I gave the Czechoslovaks their only camping ground in America in that late world war . . . and with the greatest possible sympathy for your father carried through until the very last . . . . The greatest disappointment of my life is . . . the crude, raw indifference that the political mechanism . . . showed towards the services rendered them . . . . You may not know it, but I was probably more responsible than any other individual for securing political recognition by our country of belligerent rights for your soldiers . . . . It is distasteful and painful to refer to these matters, but not having received as much as a postcard of recognition for these services . . . I am writing this to explain why I have declined flatly to give any more help to the Czechoslovaks . . . . I am finally compelled to drop a note to explain my absence from the list of men who want the land of your father built, assembled, and given to the government.[11]

19
Armistice and Peace

On November 18, 1918, the German army collapsed, and the German government surrendered unconditionally. The war was over and the fight for peace began. Governments changed overnight. Old nations disappeared and new nations emerged. The Bolsheviks took over Russia, and the Western nations suddenly felt threatened by a new force. Many changed their previous way of thinking and rewrote some of the demands they had promised to place on the peace table.

Of all the emerging nations, Poland was the most profoundly affected by the new Russia because of its geographical location. Western Europe needed a buffer zone between itself and the Marxists, and Poland was chosen for that role. Poland became a political battleground. The Allies felt that a democratic Poland would provide the security the Allies needed against the threat of a Communist government. The fate of Poland was perceived as a central issue, and all Europe prepared to take a stand.

To the world, Paderewski was the soul of Poland, and because he was a long-time friend Gutzon involved himself as deeply as possible in Polish affairs. He corresponded with Paderewski regularly and often filled his letters with advice:

> I wish I could have a talk with you about the situation in Europe. It is developing much the way I feared . . . . You have apparently united the antagonistic forces of your country and you can not possibly allow anything to interfere with carrying that union to such a point of perfection that it will stand alone for a generation . . . . You have established . . . the political course of Poland during a period of 10 to 25 years . . . . Whenever you retire, I beg you — try if you can, to return to the great work of artist once again.[1]

In essence, Gutzon became an unpaid lobbyist for the cause of a free Poland. He had learned from his defeat at the 1916 convention and the bitter experience of the aircraft investigation. By the time it was all behind him, he knew most of the members of Congress and had a unique understanding of the inner workings of Washington.

Gutzon had been a part of the Washington society scene for more than twenty years. He had friends in Congress from the early days of the Roosevelt administration, but after he became involved in national politics the friendships and feuds were on a different level. His controversial role in uncovering the aircraft scandal and his appearances before committees had forced senators and congressmen to choose sides. None could remain aloof in the face of Gutzon's charges. Those who did not believe him or who felt threatened became his enemies, and those who felt he had earned his reputation as a fighter and was worthy of their respect and support became his friends.

His time in Washington and his contact with the leaders of the emerging European nations gave him a confidence in his knowledge of government that few men in private life possessed. He felt himself the equal of any elected official, but when a friend urged him to become even more active he answered:

> I know I could take the Republican Party, muddling and brainless as it is and oozing with the results of money and reaction. I could unite it with the agricultural interests, alien as they seem to each other. I know this as well as I know my art, but the men who control the machine . . . would resist any invasion in their crime-besmeared wallow by . . . a man who palliates irregularities . . . condones the crimes of his aides in politics, will neither act in time to save himself, nor do I quite believe he wants to be saved . . . . I have helped where I could and when it was needed . . . . I cannot do more . . . .[2]

And when he was asked to run for public office, he replied:

> If I wasn't such a good artist and my work so much needed to make at least a record of what was intended to be our republic . . . I'd run for the presidency. I'd make a better president than 99% of the . . . incompetents who serve . . . . I would probably be elected and if I was I would effect such changes that would result in my getting shot. I would . . . dissolve 70% of the bureaus. I'd get rid of 95% of the professors and Drs. and replace them with practical executives. I'd destroy or coordinate 80% of the laws . . . .[3]

Politics and the fate of governments had become a passion, but Gutzon was also concerned with practical matters of a more personal nature. While he played the role of advisor to many of the world's leaders, he was trying to straighten out his own desperate affairs. Because of the cost of the aircraft investigation, which had not been paid for by the government, the expense of the Czechoslovak camp and the drop in his artistic output, Gutzon's finances were in a shambles. Mary, as usual, did the best she could with the money that trickled in, but she was hard pressed to keep their creditors away from Gutzon.

Paul Warburg, no longer a close friend because of an earlier argument over money, was one of those who grew impatient. When he threatened to sue, Mary wrote to placate him:

> Gutzon has been having a terribly trying time. Practically all art stopped during the war . . . . I know, and Gutzon knows, we are at fault in not having written and stated what we expect to do, but things have been on the point of being settled week by week for the past five years and Gutzon just cannot bear to keep on making promises and excuses . . . . He risked more . . . than many men on the firing line . . . .[4]

As her daughter said, Mary seldom raised her voice, but she always got what she wanted. Warburg stopped threatening and waited with the others.

The massive Sheridan statue that filled the Borgland studio during the war was finished shortly after the fighting stopped. Then Gutzon was asked to create a monument honoring James R. McConnell, the first American airman killed in Europe, and he also spent several weeks in Cuba working on a memorial to General Maximo Gomez, hero of the Cuban revolution.

The commissions were coming in, but collecting for them was something more difficult than creating the work. Gutzon created a statue honoring General Butterfield that had been bequeathed by the general's widow, but Mrs. Butterfield died before the work was completed. Three executors took over the estate and demanded that Gutzon make changes in the statue that Mrs. Butterfield had already approved. When he finally had a statue that satisfied them, two of the executors suddenly died and the third refused to honor Gutzon's contract.

Gutzon was forced to go to court to get the $32,000 that was due him. After the matter was settled and the statue installed in Albany, New York, Gutzon received a phone call from a resident who wanted to know why he had not signed the work. "But I did," Gutzon said, "Right on top of the head. That is the only part of the original statue they didn't make me change."[5]

The Butterfield court battle would have been much more serious, given the state of the Borglum finances, had other commissions not been coming in at such a rapid pace. The coveted contract for Newark's *Wars of America* was finally signed, which was a tremendous satisfaction for the Borglums. The commission had been pending for several years. It promised to be one of Gutzon's most lucrative undertakings, but in his desire to finalize the contract, Gutzon inadvertently based his estimates on old prices. He had not taken into account the sharp rise in prices that followed the war. When no American foundry would consider the work for less than $125,000, Gutzon was forced to turn to an Italian foundry. This delayed the work for several years and would have caused a tremendous problem if Ralph Lum, head of the Newark committee, had not remained a loyal friend. Despite pressure from members of the committee, city officials and the press, Lum forced the groups to remain patient.

It was never a question of whether Gutzon would be the sculptor. The Newark committee had been so pleased with his *Seated Lincoln* that they had awarded Gutzon the contract for the *Wars of America* without seeing a sketch or model. They were talking about details in the contract before Gutzon settled on a concept. At first he had thought about using an upright column surrounded by figures in action, but then decided that would not allow him to express the emotions of war strongly enough. After he discarded the column concept, he settled on his theme:

> My first sketch, following the abandonment of the shaft idea, represented a confused group of men who were attempting to organize themselves and move toward leadership, with Washington and Lincoln symbolically present . . . . I introduced two horses because the horse is not only a companion to man but the closest companion in time of danger . . . artistically and sculpturally, equine excitement and nervous tension can be used realistically or symbolically . . . . The composition indicates such organization . . . and such confusion as extends behind the battle line in the recruiting source and the home . . . the root of our whole political existence is in the home . . . . America's battles are all in defense of her homes.[6]

The result of Gutzon's effort is a heroic-sized grouping of forty-two figures and two horses, all in motion. For two of the models he used himself and his son, Lincoln, and likenesses of many of his friends can be found in other figures.

When Gutzon announced his plan, several other sculptors, mainly from the group he called the establishment, were upset. They believed a project as ambitious as the *Wars* should provide work for several artists. They publicly doubted that one sculptor, certainly one as busy as Gutzon, could complete the project. Arguing that each figure would require six months of work, they calculated that it would take Gutzon more than twenty years to deliver.

Wars of America under construction in the temporary studio at Borgland.

The argument was good for some headlines, but little else. Gutzon had the contract and would execute the commission his way. He started the monument on a makeshift platform built under a tent because there was too much other work in the studio. During the spring and summer the tent was a fine place to work. It was light and airy with the canvas cutting down the breeze, but with the approach of winter it became a bitter workroom. Millard Malin, the Mormon sculptor who was a studio assistant at Borgland, gave a vivid description of the studio:

> Wind was blowing a gale when I arrived. *Wars of America* group . . . was housed in a large circus tent for a studio while Italian stonelayers were building walls of a studio around it. Wind was trying to blow the . . . tent away. I helped save the day by climbing poles inside . . . and lashing down eyelets which fit over pins in the top of the poles. When the sudden gale died down, Mr. Borglum approached me, laughing . . . and asked me to help with the *Wars* . . . .[7]

That was one of the few opportunities Gutzon had to laugh in the makeshift studio. In winter the cold was unbearable. Fires kept burning in fifty-gallon drums helped very little. Looking back on that winter, Gutzon called the attempt to work outdoors one of his hardest, most painful experiences. Most of the time his hands were raw and cracked, but Malin claimed that despite the discomfort Gutzon managed to keep control:

> Mr. Borglum, being a natural showman and having an eye to future commissions, took full advantage of times when movies were being taken for news purposes, and threw on right and left large loaves of clay which we all tossed to him . . . no other sculptor of his own or any other day would have attempted such a freehand performance. My memory of him is of a Titan stamping about in oceans of clay, bringing order out of chaos with hands, feet and a big mallet . . . .[8]

Malin's days with the Borglums were happy ones for him, as he recalled in this passage from his memoirs:

> There were halcyon days in summer when we all stopped work and swam in Mill River where it entered the pond and was quite deep. The Borglums often had distinguished house-guests, and some swam with us . . . . I made a raft for little Mary Ellis . . . by roping slabs of cork . . . and she rode in the midst of the swimmers like a little queen. Mary Ellis was an elfin child . . . .[9]

But like all the men who worked for Gutzon, Malin was aware of the financial problems and sympathetic:

Mr. Borglum was usually "strapped" for money, though his income . . . must have been large . . . when a payment on the place was coming due, Mr. Borglum was sometimes quite hard to live with, from worry, though sunny-tempered as a rule, under his usual difficulties . . . .[10]

Malin remained with Gutzon for several years. On their travels to Washington and Atlanta, they discussed many topics, but they never spoke of the fact that both had been born Mormon. Gutzon had put that part of his life far behind him.

When Theodore Roosevelt died in 1919, there was a scramble for the contracts for Roosevelt memorials. There was much talk about a Roosevelt fountain to be built under the direction of the Audubon Society. In her diary, Mary wrote that the chairman of the society had called at the studio several times to see Gutzon. He did not meet with him, she noted, because the man wanted Gutzon not only to create the statue, but also to organize the committee and raise the funds.

Mary also wrote that Gutzon did meet with Roosevelt's son, Captain Roosevelt, who wanted Gutzon to make a portrait of his father while his likeness was still fresh in his mind. Roosevelt also told Gutzon he did not like most equestrain statues and hated standing figures with baggy trousers.

Gutzon went to work on the portrait, and the result was a vigorous character study that captured the force and humor of his friend. The first Roosevelt bust was bought by a private collector. Before it was cast, Gutzon had an order for a second Roosevelt portrait. In both of these works Gutzon's respect for Roosevelt's forceful nature is obvious. Of all the men he had fought with, Roosevelt was one of the few with whom he could not remain angry. Gutzon was working on the second Roosevelt bust when a reporter from the *New York Evening Telegram* visited the studio:

. . . While working on the bust, frequently surrounded by a gallery of friends, Mr. Borglum told many incidents of his acquaintance with "Teddy" . . . . Mr. Borglum nearly had completed his head when . . . he chopped out a part of the face through the brow. "I've got to put the soul there!", he exclaimed. "His soldier soul!" Then as he remodeled, he said, "In Roosevelt our national spirit lived and grew to world dimensions. His was America's most affirmative voice. In his passing I think of Heine's words: "Place before my bier a sword, for I have been a soldier in the eternal struggle for human rights."[11]

With the war over, committees were again awarding commissions, but not the way they had been. Priorities had changed. The economy was experiencing major difficulties trying to revert to peacetime production. Charles Moore, Chairman of the National Fine Arts Commission, explained how this affected the community:

> The memorial problem at present is . . . the large cities are showing a becoming reticence . . . the victim to the necessity of counting cost . . . . Memorial civic art thrives most in New England. Almost every village green shows a monument which, by reason of design, suggests it has escaped from the sun-drenched burying ground . . . in order to get under the trees . . . . Occasionally the rich man of the town, tricked out in his long forgotten Civil War uniform and mounted on a noble charger, has been set up by the connivance between a doting widow and a sculptor not afraid of his reputation . . . . We have abstractions — particularly the airman, who has already begun to attract the . . . sculptors . . . Borglum's aviator at the University of Virginia, Fraser's sketch from life . . . these are the forerunners . . . .[12]

The statue at the University of Virginia was Gutzon's tribute to James McConnell. It was a work of which Gutzon was particularly proud. It allowed him to express his love for aviation, something he had longed to do for many years. He had lost one opportunity in 1913, when plans for a Wright brothers tribute were washed away in a flood that forced Dayton, Ohio, to abandon the project.

Postwar America was a nation in flux. Although America had been gearing up for the war for three years prior to entering the fighting, it was not prepared physically and emotionally and had to rise to the challenge. New demands were made on factories. The assembly line concept was tested under pressure. The need for factory workers increased at the same time that two million men were being inducted into the armed services. This created opportunities for women, who quickly met the need. Prior to the war, working women were, for the most part, domestics or retail clerks. With the men gone, they became bookkeepers, teachers and workers trained for heavy industry.

When the fighting ended, armament production was stopped as quickly as possible. Some factories closed while those that were well established began slowly to convert to peacetime production. It was a long and tedious process, and as a result there were too many workers and not enough jobs.

The problems were further compounded by the fact that many of the workers had been farm laborers before they moved to the cities, and most did not want to return to their old way of life. In addition, the army had to demobilize almost two million troops who expected to come home to jobs. The Wilson administration recognized the problem, but with no easy answer it did what seemed best. The government delayed bringing the troops home in the hope that, given time, the labor market and the schools would find a way to absorb them.

The troops did not like waiting, and with huge concentrations of idle men in French ports the situation was potentially dangerous. The men wanted to go home, and they were in no mood to listen to the excuses of politicians. Faced with the possibility of riots, the army tried to divert the men by keeping them busy. Men like Solon were asked to remain in Europe to teach. He agreed and spent six months in Paris holding classes in sculpture and drawing.

Sports tournaments became a favorite diversion. Boxing was the cornerstone of the program. It has been estimated that as many as 500,000 soldiers participated. When the doughboys were finally brought home, many decided to make boxing their career.

Recalling the beginning of his involvement, Gutzon wrote, ". . . in 1919 there came to my studio in the woods near Stamford a man named Gavin . . . ."[13] Bill Gavin was a colorful character. He was a short and stocky Englishman, a glib talker and a flashy dresser. His wife was a professional golfer, and he was a fight promoter and matchmaker who was in America to organize a sporting club. He had sought out Gutzon at the suggestion of a mutual friend, and Gutzon had agreed to help him.

Boxing was not a legal professional sport in New York State at that time. The state had tried to allow fights in 1904 and 1912, but each time scandals caused the legislature to repeal the laws. Gavin hoped to force legalization of boxing once again. To start, he wanted to build a power base by forming a private club to promote exhibition bouts. Under the existing statutes, that was legal as long as the shows were for members only and no winners were declared.

Gavin and his ideas appealed to Gutzon. He agreed to introduce the promoter to some of his friends, to recruit members and to serve on a number of committees. He convinced influential men — General Leonard Wood, Coleman Du Pont, Fiorello La Guardia and others — to join Gavin's International Sporting Club. Then he led the campaign that successfully convinced the New York State Legislature to legalize boxing.

Executing commissions and lobbying for boxing did not prevent Gutzon from keeping informed about developments in Europe. He was still particularly concerned with Poland and her efforts to establish a stable government. Paderewski had become the first premier, but after a short time in office he was deposed and forcefully retired to his estate, where he waited, hoping to return to office.

Many Polish groups were fighting for control. One, led by Prince Casimir Lubomirsk, a Paderewski supporter, hoped to seize power by force. When Gutzon learned about the prince's plans, he offered him the use of the abandoned Czech camp at Borgland, but the coup never went beyond the talking stage. Paderewski did not regain the premiership until 1940, when he set up a Polish government in exile, though he did go in and out of favor with the changing governments.

At the beginning of the war, Paderewski had told Gutzon: I shall not play again until Poland is free. I can't play piano while men, women and children are suffering and the world is aflame.[14]

Later, Paderewski expressed doubts about being able to accept giving up his country's highest office and returning to the concert circuit. Gutzon answered "For God's sake, do you not realize that when you abandoned your music to do political housekeeping you stepped down?"

Gutzon deeply believed that, in the hierarchy of a proper society, the artist was on a higher plane than the politician, the banker, the educator or the professional. In a conversation with Franklin Lane, Wilson's millionaire Secretary of the Interior, Gutzon mentioned the fact that Paderewski was the only artist playing a major role in re-shaping Europe. Gutzon thought this odd, but Lane disagreed. When he told Gutzon, more to see his reaction than as an expression of a firm belief, that he felt artists were not practical enough to lead, he knew he was starting an argument. Lane conceded that artists do think on a grand scale, but when he added that he did not think that was enough, Gutzon told him:

> One of these days you people will realize that the imagination . . . of the artist is a powerful factor in the building of a state . . . the trouble with men . . . in politics is that they are recruited almost wholly from the legal or commercial ranks and are mainly occupied with material values . . . not 1% of our statesmen in public life determine in their careers to effect happiness and the mental or social development of their community when they take up the duties of the state.[15]

For Gutzon, political wars never seemed to end. By 1920, he was tired of trying to fight the system from within the ranks of the Republican Party. He was fifty-three years old, vigorous and ready for a new challenge. His confrontation with Wilson and the politicians in his own party had left him angry, frustrated and determined to find another way.

His friend Warren Harding had replaced Wilson in the White House, and Gutzon quickly had a falling out with yet another president. Shortly after Harding took office, Gutzon presented the expense vouchers from the aircraft investigation that Wilson had refused to honor. It seemed only fair that the government should reimburse Gutzon, at least for his out-of-pocket expenses, but Harding was too politically astute not to recognize a "no-win" situation and refused to become involved. There was little Gutzon could do to force the president to act. This added to his frustration, which boiled over when a party fundraiser came to him seeking a contribution. Gutzon told him:

> I got interested in politics when Roosevelt broke loose in 1912 . . . . I found . . . America is being run by small groups of unscrupulous men . . . from the Republican or the Democratic parties . . . . I have found that these men are practically identical . . . . You must recognize in me a negative attitude toward your movement. I think it is a waste of splendid energy, of honest, necessary enthusiasm . . . . I have nothing but contempt for the whole of the Wilson Administration, and I have worse than contempt . . . for Harding's . . . .[16]

Gutzon's passionate personality did not permit him to remain indifferent to any situation. He always reacted to art, politics and his relationships with others on an emotional level. As a result, he often ended up feeling slighted or wronged by former colleagues and associates. He continually said "never again" and then was drawn into another campaign by the issues.

During the 1916 convention, he had made many frineds among the supporters of Bob La Follette. La Follette himself did not appeal to Gutzon because the senator was far too liberal, but Gutzon identified with the farmers and land reformers who rallied to the La Follette cause.

Starting as a grass roots concept in the farm states of the West, the movement quickly crossed party lines because of the issues. In both North and South Dakota, farmers were virtually in revolt. There was talk about seizing or opening state-owned banks and other businesses that were taking a disproportionate share of the farmer's income. The idea appealed to Gutzon because he believed the bankers were the cause of the nation's economic ills.

When the North Dakota farmers formed the Non-Partisan League, Gutzon and Mary travelled west to campaign for their slate of candidates. Accustomed, as they were, to Eastern politics, they were barely prepared for the fight they were getting into. As Mary explained, it was the first time they were backing the side "opposed by the socially elect."[17] They did not expect the anger and vehemence of the other side.

Gutzon and Mary were accused of advocating "free love" when they were met by an angry mob expecting Bill Lemke, a controversial candidate for state office. Mary said it was "fortunate Gutzon could think on his feet," and was able to calm the crowd and capture their interest before they were attacked.

Gutzon remained a member of the league for many years. He became discouraged at times, but he never completely gave up on the North Dakota movement. He used his influence with congressmen whenever a farm issue was being debated and often raised money for Western candidates from his Eastern friends, but after his initial enthusiasm he became more realistic. He realized that the league was in the same position as the Progressives after the 1912 campaign. To have any impact, it would have to become a force within the Republican Party, rather than remain an independent group on the fringe.

20
Stone Mountain Resumed

Jesse Tucker returned from the war eager to resume the work at Stone Mountain. After a short visit with his family, he inspected the abandoned site at the mountain and hurried north to see Gutzon. He found the stairs and platforms in such a dilapidated condition that he felt it was imperative that they be repaired or removed at once. Gutzon told him to return to Georgia, put everything back in order and prepare to start carving.

As soon as Tucker left, Gutzon wrote the women of the United Daughters of the Confederacy to tell them it was time to re-activate the dormant Stone Mountain Memorial Association:

> I am wondering what is being done . . . . It seems that when people have money, they remember less than when they are poor . . . . I have been questioned more in the last year about the great monument in the South than ever before . . . . I hardly meet a man of importance who does not ask me if the monument is progressing . . . . I always tell them it *is*, and we are just waiting for reorganization of the work "after the war.". . . Please let me hear from you.[1]

But Mrs. Plane was in her nineties, and though she still felt committed to the carving, she no longer possessed the energy needed to keep the association active. Gutzon realized that, if he were to have a chance, he would have to find more vigorous leadership than that which was being provided by the local chapter of the UDC. To find such an organization, he once again began commuting between Borgland and Stone Mountain. After several meetings with Sam Venable, Mrs. Plane and a group of Atlanta businessmen, it was agreed that the men would take control of the organization. Their first order of business was to explore ways to finance the carving and to consider a fund-raising offer made by E. Y. Clarke of the KKK.

Gutzon was pleased that action was finally being taken, but he was not altogether happy with the make-up of the new association. He felt many of the members had joined only for the prestige, and until they proved they were sincere and could get results he continued with his own independent efforts. Early in 1920 he wrote to Governor Dorsey of Georgia:

> You were one of the first to recognize the value to Atlanta and the country of this great memorial. I want to ask you to help me go on with the work now . . . . There are many rich men in Virginia and North Carolina who would contribute heavily to this work if they get some expression of definite activity from your city and state . . . . I receive inquiries about it from all over the country. It would not require much money to carve . . . .[2]

It was one of the many times in his life that Gutzon would claim he could raise vast sums for an art project. He simply could not imagine that wealthy patrons would not fight for the opportunity to finance his great carvings. This belief often caused him to make rash statements and promises to committees, which believed him and then were disappointed. Still, no matter how many times the wealthy proved him wrong, he continued to believe there were patrons waiting in the wings.

Governor Dorsey was not convinced. A week after receiving Gutzon's appeal he wrote:

> I wish the circumstances were such that I could lend my aid to the consummation of that project . . . . I think it is a great idea. Undoubtedly some day it will catch the imagination of our people and be put over. I am very dubious now, however, as to your meeting with success.[3]

After the governor's refusal to join in the effort, Gutzon's possibilities were narrowed. He was still not confident that the association would do its share, so he sent Sam Venable to see E. Y. Clarke while he returned to Borgland to attend to pressing business. A few days later Venable sent a telegram:

> . . . Clarke and Forrest made written proposition regarding raising funds for monument submitted to Black and Adair [association members] today . . . . You should come here immediately.[4]

Venable's message had a sense of urgency. He was a member of both the Klan and the association board. Several members of the board balked at using KKK money and he needed Gutzon to help overcome their objections. Gutzon did convince the reluctant members to accept Clarke's offer to help, but not without making several concessions. In order to win their approval, he had to agree that Clarke would have no official connection with the project and would work only through Gutzon.

Gutzon had been involved in the Stone Mountain project for six years, and during that time he had been working without pay. He had a contract that entitled him to a percentage based on over-all cost, but until the actual carving started the association did not feel it was proper for him to take even out-of-pocket expenses. He shared this point of view until he ran into opposition to using Klan money. Then he became angry. In a letter to Clarke, he expressed his feelings about Atlanta's ingratitude and the fact that he was spending so much of his time and his own money on the project. He then mentioned a friend in Washington who was starting a weekly newspaper:

> . . . my friend Lynn Haines . . . is a blue lodge Mason and I want to prepare him for the Klan. He is head and heart of our kind.[5]

While Clarke worked with Venable to raise funds, Gutzon switched his own emphasis to the technical problems that had to be solved before the actual carving could begin. The General Electric Company, after many attempts, had designed a stereopticon projector, which worked in theory, but not in practice, at least at the start. Gutzon etched his composition on glass plates in the thinnest lines possible and tried to project them on bedsheets hung in the trees behind the Stamford studio, but he could not get a visible image. Time and again he adjusted the lens, the light source and the angles, but nothing seemed to help. Discouraged, he was about to give up on the idea of using a projector, when, giving it one last try, he heard Mary Ellis shout, "Look, Daddy! Look! The soldiers are marching through the woods."[6] Darkness had fallen, and the image was passing through the bed sheets, which were evidently too close to the lens, and projecting onto the trees in sharp focus. Gutzon now had a way to project his images onto the side of the cliff.

Despite his apparent preoccupation with Stone Mountain, Gutzon was concerned with many other matters. The studio had become a busy workshop filled with an ever-increasing number of commissions. The *Wars of America* was taking form in the makeshift studio, and he was devoting as much time as possible to finishing the model so that it could be shipped to the Italian foundry.

The International Sporting Club was growing faster than either Gutzon or Bill Gavin had hoped. The exhibitions staged at New York's Commodore Hotel were well attended. Memberships in the club were

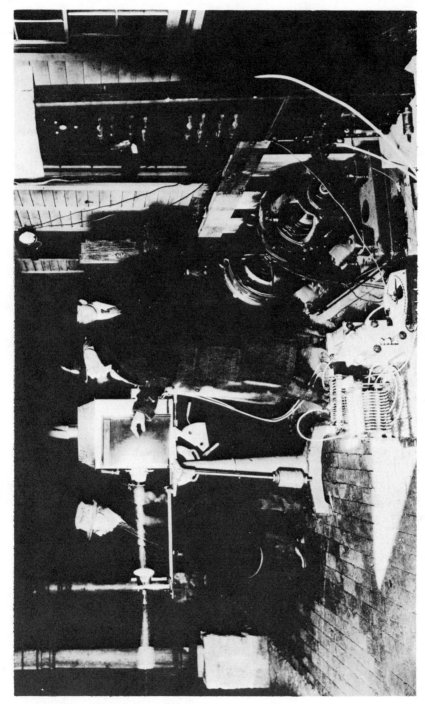

Gutzon Borglum with stereopticon camera used to project Borglum's design onto Stone Mountain.

selling well, and their lobbying effort had resulted in passage of the Walker Law, which legalized boxing in New York State.

To celebrate the signing of the bill by Governor Al Smith, the club scheduled a big night of boxing at Ebbets Field in Brooklyn. On the night of the fights, the much larger-than-expected crowd was filing into the narrow corridors leading to the seats, when those in front discovered that the gates at the end of the passages were locked. With others pushing in behind and threatening to crush them, there was near panic. Suddenly the lights went out, and there was almost a riot before the lights came on and the crowd quieted. Then it was discovered that in the darkness a gunman had held up the cashier and made off with the receipts.

The next day the newly-appointed State Boxing Commission suspended the club's license. Upset by the fiasco, some members resigned while others complained about Gavin and his ability to manage. He countered by announcing plans to build a Manhattan fight arena.

While the site was being prepared, Gutzon planned the interior decor, the frieze and pediments for the outside of the structure and made models of the statues he planned to create for the lobby. Everything seemed to be going as scheduled until the foundation contractor presented his bill. When he was put off, he went to some of the members. Gavin disappeared. An audit was ordered by the club's executive committee. While the accountants were still going through the books, a telegram arrived from Gavin, who was aboard a ship heading home to England:

> I have singlehandedly lifted boxing from the mire to the level of Grand Opera . . . . There are no widows or orphans . . . . I had in the bank $40,000 . . . today I have in the bank barely as many cents . . . . I will return . . . .[7]

But Gavin never returned. The auditors found less than thirteen dollars in the bank and no way to account for the thousands that were missing. Most of the members wrote off their five-hundred dollar memberships as a bad investment and walked away, but Gutzon could not. He felt an obligation to save the club because he had talked so many of his friends into joining. He took over management of the bankrupt organization and announced to the membership and press that he had a friend who was willing to put up the $250,000 the club needed to get started again. That friend turned out to be Coleman Du Pont, but his offer was only to guarantee a loan for ninety days. A lender could not be found who was willing to take the risk beyond that time.

With its last hope gone, the club officially filed for bankruptcy, and the property was put up for auction. It was bought by the group establishing Madison Square Garden, and with the competing International Sporting Club out of business, Tex Richards was able to turn New York City into the boxing capital of the world.

Although several members of the Borglum family had passed away in Gutzon's previous fifty-four years, nothing prepared him for the death of Solon on January 30, 1922. Gutzon, of course, was aware of death as a part of life from early childhood, when he had tried to help his father save lives on the frontier. But with Solon, it was as much the circumstances of his passing as the death itself that created such a traumatic reaction.

Solon, quiet and self-contained, suffered from migraines most of his life. When he had a headache, he wanted only to be left alone. Those around him had learned to respect his wishes. His wife, therefore, saw nothing unusual in his behavior in the days just before his death. Only after several days had elapsed and the pain refused to subside did she become concerned and forced him to see his doctor. The problem was not chronic migraine but an acute appendicitis. The doctor hurriedly operated, but it was too late. The appendix had burst and Solon had peritonitis. There was nothing that could be done. Emma stayed at his bedside, hoping and praying, while Solon slowly slipped into a coma.

Gutzon knew Solon was ill but did not know how seriously. According to Mervyn Davies, Solon's son-in-law and biographer, Gutzon had been asked not to visit because he might alarm his brother, so he stayed away.

On Monday morning, January 30, Solon's condition was so grave that his children were summoned to his bedside. His son came from Dartmouth and his daughter from the family home at Rocky Ranch. Davies describes the scene at the hospital:

It was in the middle of the afternoon when Emma and Monica had . . . left Solon's room for a moment. Solon was in a very deep sleep. Gutzon arrived in time for his brother's last sleep. A replay of familiar words sounded from the room where Solon lay: "We shall do great work together! Wake up, Solon! Wake up!" The distraught man's words could be heard down the corridor. But it was too late for that old dream of "two brothers." Much too late . . . . Death came a few hours later . . . .[8]

When she heard her uncle's voice, Monica lost control of herself. She ran to her father's room and ordered Gutzon out. "It's too late,"

Funeral services for Solon Borglum being conducted in his Silvermine, Connecticut, studio.

she said. "You should have told father that when he could hear you." Gutzon stared at his niece and then fled from the hospital.[9]

Gutzon returned to the hospital late in the afternoon or evening. Solon had been dead for many hours, but Gutzon did not know that. When he did not find his brother in his room, he went searching for him and found his body in a shed, wrapped in a sheet and unattended. That was the final straw. He created such a commotion that Emma could never forgive him. On the day of the funeral, which was held in Solon's studio, Gutzon drove Mary to Rocky Ranch, but either he would not or could not go inside.

For months, Gutzon brooded over Solon's death, until he finally found a way to purge himself. He wrote an open letter to the *New York Times*, which was printed in early March. In his rambling eulogy to his brother he wrote:

The untimely passing . . . of Solon Borglum is a loss to the permanent values in America's cultural development, in the spirit and truth and quality of his interpretation of life in art, that cannot be replaced . . . .[10]

The letter went on to touch on the art issues that bothered Gutzon and those which involved Solon that pleased him. Gutzon proudly referred to Solon's military service:

He was the only one of six brothers . . . in the war, and against every handicap he forced his way to the front and to service in any capacity that lay before him . . . .[11]

Gutzon touched on personal memories, expressed his own philosophy, and then ended with a simple statement:

. . . Solon could and did explain the hard road, when and how he reproduced the mysteries of life — incidentally beauty — and will be remembered by all who were fortunate in knowing him, a brother to all he found here . . . .[12]

KKK — Glory Days and Quick Demise

The people involved with Stone Mountain seemed determined to use the memorial for their own purposes, and the project was being affected, though they refused to believe that it could be. As one committee member wrote, ". . . it may safely be said that there is no difficulty which may be imagined to hinder the work which has not already been overcome . . . ."[1] It was this distorted view of the situation that eventually destroyed the project.

Mountain carving, at its best, is a dangerous endeavor. Failure may be caused by hidden faults in the rock, improper use of dynamite, poor planning and management, or insufficient funds. But those problems were easier to solve than were the political situations that interjected themselves at Stone Mountain, where the monument developed a political life separate from the original intent of the memorial. At the root of the trouble lay the fact that in too many ways Stone Mountain was a Ku Klux Klan project. The fate of the monument was tied to an organization that had a meteoric rise following the war and then became a laughing stock by the middle of the 1920's. If Gutzon had been able to see the danger in time to get out of the fight, the mountain carving might have survived.

Gutzon was essentially a politician who passionately believed he had the answers to the nation's problems and that he was a mover of men who should command a strong national voice. He had tried several times, but he could not seem to find a way to fit into the political mainstream, and that kept him in a state of discontent. He needed not only a cause but an organization to work with.

He was no longer angry with the president in 1921. Once again he thought of Harding as a friend, but he still had little respect for his intellect. When he wrote to government officials, and particularly the president, he did not mince words. In one of his many letters to Harding Gutzon complained:

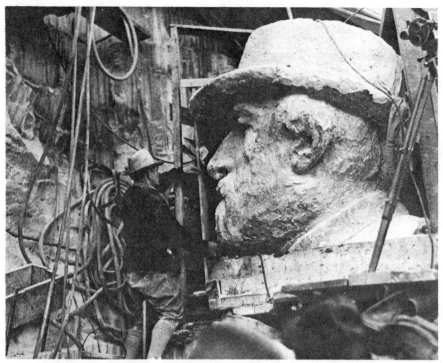

Gutzon Borglum working on his Stone Mountain General Lee.

I am interested in my country because I am a family man. Unless my government is . . . honorable and efficient, my home is not safe . . . and everybody I deal with begins to reflect the immoral, incompetent condition of the national administration . . . . The Wilson administration, the latter two years of it, filled me with horror and fear for the nation . . . but I was more horrified when I found the leaders in the opposing party, yours and my party, were . . . hand in glove with the miscreants.[2]

In another letter to Harding, he expressed his sense of impending doom for the nation:

In the next six or eight months we will be fortunate if we have a nation . . . with conditions that prevail in Europe sharply acting against them, mortgages falling due . . . and the whole country angered and outraged with debts to pay, homes to save, grainaries and cribs and cattleyards gorged with supplies and without markets. Europe helpless, disintergrating, America loaded with debts, loaded with supplies . . . without the ability to function — these conditions are of our making . . . . The general disaster is coming faster than I believed.[3]

196

Gutzon saw the state of the world from his own, unique perspective. He believed that the farmer was the heart of the nation. That was why he supported any agrarian cause that even appeared to have a chance to succeed. With his friends in North Dakota, he had managed to elect a few officials to state office and Congress and to defeat a few who opposed them, but he had no illusions about their being able to become a potent political force without some strong outside influence. For a time he hoped that influence might come from within the Republican Party, though he had no real illusion that that would happen. Yet he tried his best to bring that about while continuing his search for a better way because he had no other viable choice.

That was one of the reasons the Ku Klux Klan was so appealing to him. Originally, he saw the Klan's willingness to finance the most ambitious monument ever attempted by man as an indication of its power and judgment. These were attributes, Gutzon felt, that could be molded into a power base. With the KKK primarily rural in nature, Gutzon reasoned, it would be beyond the control of the big city bankers and would be sympathetic to the agrarian movement.

By joining and trying to mold the Klan, Gutzon was not seeking personal power. He did not want to wear a hood and robe, stand before a burning cross or preach a morality based on fear and floggings. Gutzon was a Klansman, but not for the reasons held by most of the other Klansmen.

The Klan was composed of many factions held together by uniform, leaders and common ideals. Gutzon studied those ideals, the racial and religious prejudice, the flag-waving, parading patriotism and the feeling of justifying moral standards with threats, whips or coats of tar and feathers. There was much about the KKK that appealed to him and much he did not like, but above all he saw a malleable organization that could be turned into a powerful political force strong enough to make national policy.

At first, Gutzon joined the Klan probably to avoid losing the support of Sam Venable and others at Stone Mountain. Then he allowed his imagination to take over, as he had done so often in the past, and he became a member of the organization at the highest level. Believing he would be able to work behind the scenes, he planned to lead the Klan to the White House, where a KKK president would take the power from the bankers and brokers and put it in the hands of the producers. But of more immediate concern was the mountain he had to carve. The project needed several million dollars, and the KKK was offering to help raise the money.

Had the Klan the grassroots support it claimed to have, accepting its offer would have created no problem, but the majority of Southerners were not Klansmen and did not agree with what was said or done in the name of the Klan. The Masons were the strongest fraternal order in the South. At the height of Klan power, which was 1921 to 1923, when the Masonic lodges were being raided by Klan recruiters, Masonic leaders were among the most outspoken Klan critics. They joined the politicians and the press in denouncing the KKK as lawless, violent and dangerous to the American way of life.

This opposition surfaced among the Masons on the Stone Mountain executive board when several members objected to the suggestion that E. Y. Clarke take over the fund-raising. Clarke was a professional fund-raiser who had been hired by Colonel Simmons right after the war to recruit members for the KKK. He was phenomenally successful and is generally credited with being the one man responsible for the growth of the organization.

Gutzon saw Clarke's offer to help the mountain fund-raising as crucial to their success, and he tried to make the reluctant board members understand how important Klan support would be, at the same time agreeing that it would be detrimental if the connection became public knowledge. In a letter to Forrest Adair, a member of the Stone Mountain board, Gutzon wrote:

> Neither you nor I can afford to be involved in any question concerning the Klan . . . political interests in the country are fighting the Klan . . . all organizations of this kind, the Masons being no exception, have had to pass through this period of abuse and misrepresentation . . . in proportion as they have been feared . . . and last summer when the Klan offered $10,000 or the amount needed to cover the work, I put the matter before you and you advised me not to receive the money . . . .[4]

Gutzon wanted the board to allow Clarke to raise the needed funds through his own Southern Advertising Association, rather than directly through the Klan. Under this plan, which would have fooled no one, Clarke would have turned all receipts over to the Stone Mountain Memorial Association, and his fee and expenses would have been returned to him. That way the Klan would not have been officially associated with the mountain carving. It was only a cosmetic solution, but it was enough for Gutzon to win permission to put Clarke to work. But when Clarke did not produce quickly, Gutzon became annoyed with him, as indicated in this letter to Clarke:

198

> It is now several weeks . . . since "definite plans" . . . were agreed
> upon . . . unless you have determined on a hard and fixed plan on which
> I can bank, I shall recommend . . . some other plan . . . .[5]

Clarke was too involved with other matters to be much concerned about
Gutzon's threats. Clarke's rivals for KKK control had caught him drunk
and disorderly, and he was facing criminal charges. Given the choice
of resigning or going to jail, he prudently chose to resign.

While the Klan's position at Stone Mountain became muddled, the
work on the site continued. The big projector had been set up one-half
mile from the mountain, and at night Gutzon was able to project a
perfect image on the face of the mountain. As soon as he transferred
the drawing to the rock, the actual carving could begin. Gutzon and
Tucker planned to paint the outline directly onto the stone at night and
work on the carving during the day. In theory this seemed simple, but
once again a simple task turned out to be far more difficult than imagined. The thinnest line on a glass plate widened to over six feet, and
the sharp edges became diffused when projected half a mile. A worker
would have seemed to have been more in a spotlight than following
a clearly defined outline.

Choosing a particularly dark night to enhance the projection, Gutzon sent Tucker down the cliff in a bosun's seat until he was in one of
the illuminated areas. Discovering that the problem of filling the area
with paint was not as difficult as they had anticipated, Tucker continued
on down through an unlit area. When Gutzon lost sight of his superintendent he became alarmed. He shouted to Tucker through a bullhorn,
ordering him to return to the top, but Tucker was as determined and
stubborn as his boss, and he continued on. He did so despite the fact
that in the darkness the bosun's seat had moved away from the cliff and
was rotating dizzyingly. Fortunately, before he reached the next illuminated area, he was once again close enough to the stone to brace
his feet and stop the spinning before Gutzon became aware of the danger.

The next day Gutzon and Tucker devised a system of guide ropes
to keep the men from rotating, and the painting of the image began
in earnest. When that was completed, jackhammer operators were sent
over the cliff to begin cutting away the unwanted stone. Jackhammers
and wedges seemed the only viable way to do this work, even though
it was a staggering task, considering the amount of stone that had to
be removed. Jean Vanophem, a Belgian engineer in the United States
on vacation, heard about the mountain carving and went south to see
what was being done. He told Gutzon how he had used dynamite to

Lester Barlow, Jesse Tucker and Gutzon Borglum inspecting the vertical surface of Stone Mountain.

cut a tunnel through solid rock and showed him with what precision the explosive could be used. From a practical standpoint, Vanophem's suggestion removed the last barrier, and the mountain carving became completely feasible.

Early in 1923, Hollins Randolph, an Atlanta businessman and a strong Klan supporter, took over for Forrest Adair as head of the Stone Mountain Memorial Association. A short time later the State of Georgia officially recognized the memorial. The state legislature authorized $100,000 for the project, payable at $20,000 per year, and the county matched that figure. This income, along with a few contributions that continued to filter in, gave them enough money to keep working while the association sought more substantial funding.

Gutzon was still convinced that, once the project really got off the ground, wealthy patrons would be eager to finance the work, and with his ability to influence he made others believe as he did. When he asked Lester Barlow to head the fund-raising drive in the North, Barlow was enthusiastic:

> It all takes money, big round cold dollars. I don't like to say dollars and Stone Mountain in the same sentence, but we must. The North will, I believe, if the South dares us, put $2,500,000 right alongside theirs for the completion of the memorial . . . .[6]

Gutzon went north to help Barlow start his drive and met a strange character who became a close friend. D. C. Stephenson was an energetic man in his early thirties. He was a brilliant organizer and a glib talker who expected to become president of the United States. Stephenson was the Grand Dragon of the Northern Realm of the Ku Klux Klan. He was the czar of twenty-two northern states, controlled a huge organization and had amassed a large personal fortune, which permitted him to live on a grand scale.

In 1922, when he was officially installed in office, 200,000 robed Klansmen had gathered in Kokomo, Indiana, to honor him. It was the largest gathering ever held by the Klan and aroused such jealousy in the Southern hierarchy that Stephenson's triumph sowed the seeds of his eventual fall from power.

When Gutzon and Stephenson realized that their political beliefs were similar, they began working together within the Klan, which, unfortunately, tied Gutzon to Stephenson's fate. By 1923, events within the KKK were moving rapidly. Clarke was gone. Colonel Simmons was locked in a battle for control with one of his former aides, Dr. Hiram Evans, a Texas dentist with illusions of grandeur. The fight was taking them in and out of court and onto the front pages of all the anti-Klan newspapers. Evans was winning, but the Klan was paying a terrible price. The charges and countercharges held the KKK up to public ridicule, and many Klansmen were becoming disenchanted. Meanwhile, sensing an opportunity, Evans was trying to solidify his Northern position while trying to win enough Southern support to enable him to take over the entire organization.

When it was almost too late, the leaders realized that their public squabbles were destroying them, and they arranged a peacemaking meeting in Atlanta. Stephenson arrived in a private train. In the early hours of the morning he led a delegation to Simmons' home, woke him and offered him a deal backed by threats. The next day Simmons was pensioned and Evans appointed Imperial Wizard. For his part, Stephenson was offered peace. Evans agreed to forget their differences and to work with him, but they were so suspicious of each other that they could not do so for long. Gutzon, thinking himself a friend of both, tried to intercede.

He attended a Klan strategy meeting in Washington, D.C., and other meetings elsewhere, but he was unable to help ease the tension. As time went on, Evans gained the support he needed within the ranks and he moved to rid himself of Stephenson. After a particularly difficult meeting with Evans, arranged so Gutzon could plead his friend's case, Gutzon reported to Stephenson:

> Regarding the "Dr." I put to him my proposal for a National Conference . . . to stimulate and clarify the mentality of the Klan, and especially its leadership . . . of course I got nowhere . . . there is no ability to see . . . as a result the Klan . . . which numbers . . . five to one of the farmers of the northwest, has so little power . . . it . . . can not affect a single vote in the house or senate . . . . I would not write this way or about this matter at all, had we, you and I, not entered into a common understanding to organize the power within the Klan into an effective body of voters . . . .[7]

Evans went north, convinced the officers of the local klaverns that Stephenson was stealing from them and stripped him of his offices and power. Stephenson made threats, but there was very little he could do. Most of the charges against him were true, and Evans had the proof. He was also intimidated by threats backed by the mysterious sinking of his yacht and burning of one of his mansions.

As the situation became desperate, Gutzon became more involved. Evans had won, but he still was willing to talk with Gutzon, who was acting on Stephenson's behalf. After a series of discussions, Gutzon wired Stephenson:

> Dr. . . . phoned last night at 2 from Cincinnati. I told him . . . that I have full authority to speak . . . . Sit tight and see no one from him . . . . Patience and a perfectly clear program with unfaltering resolution will win this fight . . . .[8]

As usual Gutzon was being overly optimistic. Evans and Stephenson were not reconcilable, and Evans had too many other problems to worry about a beaten Stephenson. Within the local klaverns, a bitterness was surfacing that threatened his leadership. This was especially true in Atlanta, where the opposition was led by Sam Venable and Nathan Forrest. Both had remained loyál to Colonel Simmons, and when Evans became preoccupied with Northern matters they declared open war on Evans and his followers.

The newspapers, especially the anti-Klan *New York World*, had a field day, and Gutzon began receiving some unwanted publicity. He knew he could not afford to have his name linked with the Klan, and whenever it was he issued vehement denials. When the *Atlanta Constitution* reported that he had been named in a lawsuit aimed at the Klan leadership, Gutzon wired:

> Restraining injunction lodged against Atlanta Klan . . . . My name included as defendant . . . no right to involve my name . . . . I am not a member of the Kloncilium, not a Knight of the KKK . . . .[9]

But that was for public consumption. What he had to say within the Klan told a different story, as in this wire to Stephenson:

> I have not sought to be the intermediary between the warring factions, but when I found one Klansman in a bitter personal war against another — each destroying the Klan . . . I did what I was asked to do . . . . I believed the results would justify the personal risks . . . .[10]

22

The Stone Mountain Tragedy

The sky on June 19, 1924, was gray and overcast. Despite the chill, Gutzon, Mary and Lincoln, who had just turned eleven, led a group of frightened dignitaries up the back slope of the mountain, down the steps set on the sheer face of the cliff to the platform just above the carving. From there they went down ladders to the picnic table that had been placed fifty stories up in the air over General Lee's shoulder. Most looked as if they would have preferred to have been less "honored," but they put on brave faces for the photographers and breathed a great sigh of relief when, after a fried-chicken dinner, Gutzon led them from the carving to the speaker's platform on the ground.

The crowd had been gathering all through the morning. A steady stream of automobiles had started from Atlanta before dawn, and they were still coming long after the ceremony had ended.

Mrs. Plane, who was ninety-four years old, arrived shortly after the luncheon had ended. When she had first met Gutzon, she would not shake his hand, but on this special day she allowed him to carry her to her place of honor. It was the one hundredth anniversary of the birth of General Lee and the finest day the South had enjoyed in many years.

There was silence as Mrs. Plane gave the signal and the huge Confederate flag covering Lee's portrait was slowly lowered. The crowd gazed at the portrait in awe as the cracked, hushed voice of an elderly veteran carried over their heads. "My God," he exclaimed, "It's the General!"

The Jackson head was to be carved next, and it quickly began to take shape. A crack was discovered, and Gutzon had to alter its position by blocking out the stone and starting over while he cleared an area for Jefferson Davis. Most of the day-to-day supervision was left to Jesse Tucker, though Gutzon was responsible for the work and the decisions.

He was away much of the time — working on other commissions, raising funds for the memorial, involving himself in politics and trying

Gutzon Borglum with ninety-four year old Helen Plane and Civil War veterans at dedication of Borglum's General Lee at Stone Mountain.

to find a way out of his personal financial difficulties. Once again Gutzon was under tremendous pressure from his creditors. Eugene Meyer, for one, had started suit. He had received no payment since the money for Borgland was borrowed in 1912, and the accrued interest had almost doubled the original debt of $40,000. Meyer finally accepted new notes, but for a long while he resisted attempts to settle the matter. His feeling were hurt by Gutzon's charges that he was one of the financiers who bought an artist's soul with money.

Probably concerned more about his desperate situation than his not being paid, Gutzon suddenly demanded that the Stone Mountain Association give him a formal contract in place of the original agreement. Negotiations were started, but they began to drag, and Gutzon decided he had to take a stand. He ordered Tucker to stop the work, and the association secretary reacted with an angry letter:

> Captain Tucker has informed the executive committee . . . work has been stopped on the steep side and the work would not be resumed until the contract is entered into between the association and yourself . . . after more than seven years of work . . . you have been willing to carry on . . . just as there is to begin a drive in the city . . . the committee has desired a contract for over four months . . . it is not the fault of the committee . . . .[1]

More harsh words were exchanged before the contract was signed and the work resumed. Then everyone shook hands, but the relationship between Gutzon and the association was never quite the same again.

By March 1924 they were forced to re-assess their financial condition. Despite the money from the state and county and a few contributors, the association was having difficulty. The KKK was not able to raise the funds it had promised, and unless another major source was found to finance the carving, the work would never be completed.

After much discussion, someone suggested a commemorative coin. If the association could convince the federal government to mint a Stone Mountain coin, it could raise the millions it needed by selling the coin for at least twice its value.

The executive committee approved the idea, and Gutzon, because of his Washington connections, was asked to seek approval from the government. First he approached Senator Henry Cabot Lodge. The senator thought it was a fine idea, and he took him to Senator Smoot of Utah, head of the Senate Finance Committee. Smoot sent Gutzon to the newly-installed President Calvin Coolidge.

All three Northerners gave the coin idea their blessing, and in a surprisingly short time the necessary legislation was passed by Congress. The only demand that the congressmen made was that Jefferson Davis not be on the coin. They had no qualms about honoring military men, even if they were rebels, but they could not do the same for a politician.

After the legislation was signed by Coolidge, Gutzon was assigned the task of making the model for the coin. He had created many bas-reliefs in his career. He assumed preparing one for a coin would not be difficult, but he had never worked to the exacting standards of the Treasury Department. Before he had an acceptable model, he had created nine different reliefs and had made innumerable trips to Washington.

Meanwhile, on the national scene, the parties were preparing for the upcoming conventions and the November presidential elections. Coolidge, as a new incumbent, was certain to be the Republican candidate, while the large Democratic field seemed headed for a convention battle. Woodrow Wilson's son-in-law, former cabinet member Bill

McAdoo, was seeking support for the Democratic nomination. He was, however, perceived by the press, the public and most of the Democrats as a Klan candidate, an image that was creating problems. The Georgia delegation, with Hollins Randolph and other members of the Stone Mountain Executive Committee, was composed of men loyal to Dr. Evans and was strongly backing McAdoo. D. C. Stephenson wanted to join in the effort, but he was not welcome.

Gutzon seemed willing to join the McAdoo forces, perhaps because he thought it might help bring Evans and Stephenson together, or because he was being pressured by members of the executive committee despite the fact that he was a Republican. It was no secret that Gutzon did not think much of Coolidge, and the candidate he had expected to support, Senator La Follette, was no longer acceptable. In reply to a letter from Stephenson he wrote:

> Your note regarding La Follette is very right and pertinent. La Follette's action in the first instance was a dignified protest . . . . Now it has become a roundup of the socialistic, anarchist and bolshevik elements that have drifted into this country from Europe . . . . It has the appearance of being entirely selfish . . . .[2]

Actually, Stephenson would not have been an asset to any candidate. He was so deeply involved with his own sordid troubles that few wanted to associate with him. Gutzon was an exception. As an old friend, he tried to help Stephenson create an appearance of strength.

Gutzon supported him out of a sense of loyalty, but knowing at the same time that he could not back McAdoo no matter what the consequences, he tried to find a candidate he could back with enthusiasm. He loved the rough and tumble of the campaigns, but not enough to back a Wilson Democrat. He might have been able to rationalize enough to overcome that aversion — until McAdoo announced that, if he could not win, he would back Homer Cummings.

Cummings was Gutzon's Stamford attorney. As far as Gutzon was concerned, the lawyer was responsible for all the trouble he was having with the notes on Borgland. Gutzon believed he had lost the bus company and had been hurt in a dozen other situations because of Cummings' inefficiency. To Gutzon, Cummings was a "Colonel Mouse who would end up with a 'Wilson type cabinet filled with New England reactionaries.' "

To complicate the situation further, at least from Gutzon's standpoint, McAdoo was the candidate of Evans and the Klan, and Evans was refusing all attempts by D. C. Stephenson at reconciliation. That made the issue more than just a choosing of a candidate as far as Gutzon was concerned.

Evans was claiming, in a last-ditch effort to recover the Klan's lost prestige, that he would "serve up the South for McAdoo and bring in the North as well." It was a hollow promise. By labeling him the Klan's candidate, Evans destroyed McAdoo's chances, because his other supporters would not work with the Klan.

When Hollins Randolph had succeeded Forrest Adair as chairman of the Stone Mountain Memorial Association in 1923, he had been elected to serve the one-year term allowed in the by-laws. When it came time to elect his successor, he had forced a rule change and had himself re-elected because he felt the prestige of the office would add to his stature at the Democratic convention, which he was attending as the head of the Georgia delegation.

Sam Venable had bitterly opposed the rule change, but he was voted down after a bitter argument. When the fight was over, Randolph had control of the association and Venable no longer had his seat on the executive committee. For some reason Venable blamed Gutzon, and for a short time the two were not on speaking terms.

At the convention, McAdoo could not overcome his image as the Klan candidate, and he lost his bid to the chant of "Ku Ku McAdoo." The delegates nominated John Davis, and with that nomination the Klan was finished as a political force. As the leader of the Evans forces, Hollins Randolph was particularly bitter. He returned to Atlanta and sat out the campaign.

Gutzon did not want to do the same. He realized he could not back the third-party effort of La Follette and that backing the Democrat Davis was out of the question, but that left only Coolidge and he had a great many misgivings about him. Just a few months before the Republican convention, Gutzon had written a friend, Missy Meloney, to ask:

> What do you know about Coolidge? What is he — what are his dimensions? What are his goals? His life, his official acts and his sophistic essays do not seem to enlighten me. My mind tried to close around his personality and when I seem to succeed I find nothing within. I hope I am entirely wrong because he has a great opportunity . . . .[4]

Gutzon finally decided to support Coolidge. He even tried to recruit Stephenson, though it is doubtful that Coolidge would have been grateful had he known:

> I beg of you to align yourself with the soundest, steadiest forces behind the country today . . . . Have come to know Coolidge personally and am

giving him every help I can. Conspiracies in other two groups are likely to throw this country into chaos . . . .[5]

The situation at Stone Mountain worsened in the heat of the campaign battle. Venable, still very much on the outside, was trying to carry on his fight with Randolph and was still blaming Gutzon for his situation. Randolph was also blaming Gutzon for not supporting McAdoo, and as a result Gutzon was becoming isolated. Despite this, the work on the carving and on the models for the coin progressed. Gutzon was devoting himself to both and trying to ignore the situation around him. Gutzon had weathered so many storms in his life that he could not believe he was in any real difficulty.

In the spring of 1924, Gutzon had received a letter from Doane Robinson, State Historian of South Dakota, asking:

. . . would it be possible for you to design and supervise a massive sculpture . . . the proposal has not passed beyond the mere suggestion, but if it be possible . . . I feel . . . we could arrange to finance such an enterprise . . . .[6]

Robinson had written first to Lorado Taft, but Taft declined because of age and failing health, so Robinson turned to Gutzon. His letter arrived at Stone Mountain while Gutzon was in Connecticut working on yet another model for the coin. Tucker opened it, wrote across the top "Here it is, Borglum. Let's go!" and sent it on. Gutzon reacted with the same enthusiasm. Stone Mountain was the most important project he had ever attempted, but he saw no reason why he would not be able to plan and supervise two mountain carvings at the same time. He wrote Robinson and told him he would make the trip west as soon as possible.

The association's attempts to raise funds had failed; its hopes were centered on the sale of the commemorative coin, but after months of effort it had not yet become a reality. Gutzon was still trying to make a model that all the government committees that were involved would approve, and the delay had given the Grand Army of the Republic, the veterans of the Union Army, a chance to mount a campaign against the minting of a coin honoring "traitors." They had little chance of succeeding, but their action made Randolph and his group nervous and provided them with another excuse to be angry at Gutzon.

Randolph went to Washington twice to testify at hearings held by the Art Commission. He expected Gutzon to be at both hearings, but when he found that Gutzon was not, Randolph felt personally insulted. He began to press Gutzon to finish the model for the coin. Gutzon reacted

Lincoln Borglum, Gutzon Borglum and their guide on the camping trip on which Borglum chose the site for the Mount Rushmore carving.

angrily. He saw their pressure as the work of his KKK enemies and complained to Stephenson that ". . . Texas friend [Evans] organizing attacks on me. It would be impossible for me to give you an understanding of the difficulties . . . and how that has crippled my finances . . . ."[7]

Stephenson's troubles had multiplied. He was under indictment and heading for trial. He was dunning Gutzon. He knew Gutzon could not repay the money he had loaned him, but he wanted the debt secured by a mortgage on Borgland, which could be used as collateral at a bank. Gutzon promised to comply, but he could not because there were already too many liens and mortgages on the property.

Stephenson filed suit, but then became so involved with his other problems that the matter was never pursued. After a sensational trial, he was convicted of kidnapping, raping and causing the death of Marge Oberholtzer and sentenced to thirty years to life in the Indiana State Penitentiary.

In September 1924, Gutzon wired Doane Robinson to tell him he was ready to make the trip west. He travelled by train to Rapid City, accompanied by his twelve-year-old son, Lincoln. They were met by the members of the Rapid City Commercial Club and a number of South

Dakota officials, including Senator Peter Norbeck. After touring the hills on horseback to get the feel of the land, they were the honored guests at a dinner in the A & F Cafe in Rapid City. Before they departed, they agreed to return after everyone had time to think about the project.

Originally, the South Dakotans had been thinking about Wild West figures carved on the spires of the Needles Highway, but Gutzon had other ideas, as the letter to Lester Barlow, written after he returned indicates:

> My own big plan . . . which I have had for years for a great Northern Memorial in the center of the nation is finally materializing . . . it will be located . . . within easy . . . distance of the center of the nation, and the conditions offered me . . . make me believe that a Memorial equal . . . to the Southern Memorial can be secured for the principle of the Union . . . . I have promised to inspect the location, examine the granite . . . .[8]

His mind filled with possibilities, Gutzon returned to Stone Mountain to face the growing problems with the association and to try to get on with the carving. When reporters asked him about his plans for the Northern memorial, he referred them to Lester Barlow, who was acting as his spokesman. Using the story Barlow released to them, the Connecticut papers reported:

> With the Confederal Memorial at Stone Mountain an assured success . . . Gutzon Borglum is planning . . . a National Memorial . . . on a large scale . . . . The Confederate Memorial will not be completed for ten years . . . and by that time it will have cost millions . . . the National Memorial will take 50 years to complete . . . .[9]

Barlow was becoming increasingly important to Gutzon, as well as his good friend. He had left his position in Ohio and had moved to Connecticut, where he built a home on a parcel of Borgland he bought from Mary and Gutzon. Both the Southern Memorial and the Northern Memorial excited Barlow. A man of action, he wanted to do something tangible for both projects and for Gutzon because he believed in him.

His opportunity, or at least what appeared to be his opportunity, came about in a strange way. During the First World War his invention, the Barlow depth charge, had been used by the Allies. After the war, the War Indemnities Board suggested Barlow seek $600,000 as fair compensation. Barlow refused to file a claim because he did not think private citizens should benefit from war. When the government insisted, Barlow relented, but only in his own way. He called a press conference in Atlanta on February 14, 1925, to announce that he would apply for

$300,000. He told reporters that $100,000 would be donated to the Stone Mountain project, another $100,000 would be divided by a number of Cleveland charities, and the balance would go to the National Memorial in South Dakota.

To pursue Barlow's claim, Barlow and Gutzon boarded a Washington-bound train right after the press conference. Even though the government was urging him to apply for the money, there was no guarantee the claim would be approved. They had scheduled meetings with senators, military leaders and attorneys, and both felt confident they would succeed. Senator Norbeck of South Dakota had pledged his support, and Hollins Randolph had promised to join them to give the claim the official backing of the Stone Mountain Memorial Association. That Gutzon believed Randolph would keep his promise indicated that Gutzon, while aware that the situation at Stone Mountain was bad, misjudged the depth of feelings against himself.

Barlow's offer evidently meant little to the association. For them it was all "coin diplomacy." They were counting on the commemorative coin to solve all their problems. The models had been approved, the coin was being minted and delivery was only weeks away. With the prospect of clearing $500,000 before them, their only thoughts were of making sure nothing happened before the coin was delivered. With only $100,000 to gain from the Barlow claim, Randolph had second thoughts about becoming involved and decided not to join Barlow and Gutzon in Washington. He thought he was doing what was safest, but he created the very situation he was trying to avoid. Gutzon interpreted Randolph's absence as a betrayal, and he reacted by sending telegrams to the Treasury Department and President Coolidge demanding that the coins not be released without his approval. He anticipated the association's reaction to his stopping the delivery, but misjudged the depth of their anger and their blind desire to get back at him. He was counting on the fact that in a showdown they knew they needed him to carve the mountain.

According to Mary's notes, Gutzon was forced to act because he was certain Randolph and his friends were planning to divert the proceeds from the coin sales to their own accounts. She said that Gutzon had arranged, with Bernard Baruch and several others, to underwrite the sale of the coin at a minimal cost to the association. It was a deal that she claimed Randolph was to ratify when he met Gutzon in Washington. Mary also charged that before Gutzon left for Washington he was offered a $200,000 bribe if he would not interfere with the coin sale. She said he did not take the offer seriously until Randolph failed to show up; then he realized he was being double-crossed and moved to stop delivery of the coin.

Unable to reach Gutzon in Washington because he would not return his phone calls, Randolph offered Gutzon's position to Tucker. Tucker immediately wired Gutzon and Gutzon took the next train to Atlanta. Tucker met him at the station and they hurried to the mountain where Sam Venable, once more on Gutzon's side, waited. Sam had forgiven Gutzon for whatever he thought he had done because they both were being hounded by the Evans faction of the Klan, under Randolph's direction, and they needed each other.

With Venable no longer on the executive committee of the association, his friendship could not affect Gutzon's immediate future, but his ownership of the mountain meant he would eventually have the final say. When Sam and his sisters agreed to allow their mountain to be carved, they stipulated that if the carving was not completed in twelve years the site would revert to the family.

Only three years were left. Randolph realized that if he were going to fire Gutzon he had to do so early enough to allow another sculptor time to complete the work. Gutzon felt that if it came to a confrontation the association would realize that he was the only one capable of carving. If it did not, he could wait three years and then, with Venable's support, form his own association.

Gutzon was at the carving when word came that the executive committee had met in secret session and had voted to fire him. The press had already run the story as headline news. The resolution issued by Randolph charged that Gutzon had been fired because he ". . . neglected his work . . . found time to deliver a series of lectures . . . and to launch a movement for a great Union Memorial . . . in South Dakota."[10]

Everyone at the mountain at the time agreed on what happened next, but they could not agree on why. Gutzon ordered his crew to break up his model and drop it over the cliff. Later Gutzon claimed he had destroyed the model because it was no longer accurate and would have confused another sculptor. He said he had been forced by the contour of the rock to make so many adjustments that the model had no meaning to anyone but himself. Besides, Gutzon claimed, he could not understand the furor. He believed the models were his to do with as he pleased. Long before there was any trouble he had told the association:

The models, designs and their copyright are under law and contract the property of Gutzon Borglum, their creator and sole owner, and I shall immediately withdraw and enjoin any use of my creations, designs and plans . . . .[11]

That threat was made during a heated debate over another issue, but it clearly expressed Gutzon's belief in ownership. Unfortunately, Randolph did not share his point of view. As far as the association was concerned, the monument, the models and anything pertaining to the project were their property. When they discovered the models had been destroyed, they were outraged and reacted accordingly.

Gutzon was at the Venable home, planning to go north to wait for the public outcry that would return him to the work. Suddenly, Tucker burst into the house and almost bodily forced Gutzon out into his automobile. They were barely out of the driveway when the sheriff and a posse arrived with a warrant for Gutzon's arrest charging him with "willful destruction of association property." When they discovered he was gone, they took off in pursuit.

The chase went on for several hours as Tucker took the backroads heading north with the sheriff right behind them. At times their pursuers came so close that Tucker ordered "the Chief" to get down on the floor in case there was shooting. Finally, in the early morning, they crossed the border to safety in North Carolina. Gutzon was safe, but he was a fugitive from Georgia justice.

23
The Aftermath

Gutzon was beyond the reach of his Georgia enemies, but the fight had just begun. At the invitation of his friend North Carolina Governor Angus McLean, he set up a makeshift studio on the state fairgrounds outside Raleigh and remade his Stone Mountain models. Gutzon was well known and popular in North Carolina as he was throughout the South. His Aycock Memorial in Raleigh and his Zebulon Vance in Statuary Hall in Washington were familiar to most North Carolinians who had sympathetically followed the affair at Stone Mountain.

With a warrant out for his arrest and Georgia seeking extradition, Gutzon was in a difficult position. Georgia demanded that McLean turn him over, but the governor, who had a wry sense of humor, tried to defuse the situation by turning it into a farce. He threatened to ring the fairgrounds with state militiamen if the Georgians tried to take Gutzon by force. He did have Gutzon arrested, however, as the law demanded, and then released him on his own recognizance pending an extradition hearing.

Gutzon was sick at heart. He could not believe that Randolph and the association would willingly sacrifice the carving just to settle a personal grievance with him. He assumed they would attempt to reconcile, but as the extradition hearing approached, the Georgians seemed more determined and angrier. It became obvious that they were serious and would jail him if they could. Faced with that possibility, Gutzon, on the advice of his attorneys, put everything he owned into Mary's name and then prepared to fight to stay out of Georgia.

Gutzon had earned his reputation as a tough fighter. It would have been more in character for him to demand a trial in Atlanta than to fight extradition. His supporters were puzzled by his actions. In one of the many letters he wrote over the next several years, he tried to explain to a friend why he had not voluntarily returned to Georgia:

> I agree with you . . . there is only one way to crush that crowd . . . meet them on their own threshold and destroy them . . . . I should have gone

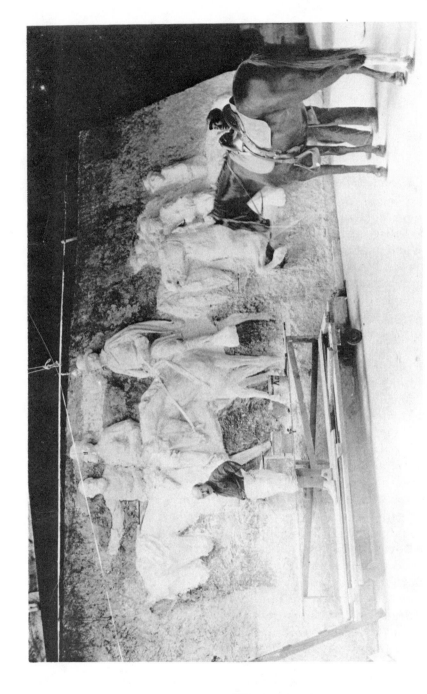

Gutzon Borglum with model of Stone Mountain he remade in Raleigh, North Carolina, studio after he destroyed model and fled Georgia.

back to Atlanta within a week's time . . . . But the governor had information that I was to be killed, accidently or otherwise, that . . . as many as
15 men were lying in wait around my place to destroy me . . . had I been
a single man . . . I would have plunged headlong into it . . . but I had
a wife and children to think of . . . . If I had gone to Atlanta and met
with any kind of violence I should certainly have killed somebody . . . and
I don't want to hurt anybody or destroy anybody . . . . Is it better I destroy
what usefulness there is left in me . . . or go there and battle in that muck?[1]

Gutzon's informant may have been exaggerating. There is no way
to prove that, however, because no charges were ever made beyond those
mentioned in letters, but there is no question that Gutzon believed them.
His claiming he might have killed someone was not an idle boast, but
a real fear and his way of saying he was afraid that if he had confronted
his enemies the situation might have gotten out of hand.

On the day of the extradition hearings, Georgia withdrew its request. Gutzon fought to have the matter concluded one way or the other,
but to no avail. The North Carolina court could not force the Georgians
to proceed. As a result Gutzon was in limbo. He was no longer in immediate danger, but there was still a warrant outstanding, and he could
not return to Georgia without risking arrest. He expressed his sense of
frustration in a letter to Venable:

When they backed out of court in Greensboro they tried to get me to sign
a paper confessing justice in their issuing a warrant against me. This I flatly
refused to do, and challenged them to proceed. This resulted in a long
distance call to your "honorable" district attorney in Atlanta, in which he
said . . . unless I signed, I could sue . . . . I have not cared for any of this
stuff . . . . I shall leave the indictment against me until it rots on the
records.[2]

Gutzon stayed on at the fairgrounds and continued the battle in
the newspapers. He announced that the new model for the Southern
Memorial would be given to Governor McLean for safekeeping. "I shall
do this before I leave the South," he told reporters, "to fulfill to the
Southern people any possible implied promise on my part."[3]

Meanwhile, his supporters in Georgia, of which there were many,
led by Sam Venable, his sisters, the women of the UDC and most of
the private citizens who were anti-Klan or anti-Evans, were trying to
force the association to drop the charges and bring him back. The
Southern press was, for the most part, sympathetic. Randolph was being deluged with letters and telegrams urging him to change his position. The general sentiment among Gutzon's Southern supporters is
perhaps best summed up by Rupert Hughes:

If there are any living sculptors great enough to finish Gutzon Borglum's idea they have too much self-respect and artistic conscience to attempt it . . . . For any minor sculptor to undertake it would be an impertinence inviting disaster. Whatever the merits of the controversy it is a sacrilege to interfere with Borglum's immortal masterpiece. The only honest course is to make peace and let the work go on.[4]

But Randolph would not relent:

There is no doubt whatsoever that the association can get a sculptor . . . of the highest rank to carry on the memorial, and steps to that end are in progress. Re-employment of Borglum is out of the question . . . under any circumstances.[5]

Actually, Randolph could not alter his stand. His personal attacks on Gutzon were so vicious that cooperation would have been impossible. In any case, the decision was not his, or the association's alone. The Klan was involved and it was adamant. In 1927, Petite Mason, Venable's sister, wrote Mary about the Klan's involvement:

I think nothing but a court outside of Georgia . . . or the Klan lifting the ban — will help us now . . . . I wrote Mr. Evans how it was hurting the Klan . . . all around us people were saying, "is it a Klan fight?"[6]

Defending Gutzon made Venable the Klan's enemy. The list of Klan grievances against Gutzon included his refusal to support the effort to nominate McAdoo and his friendship with Stephenson. Evans felt Gutzon's attempts to intercede on Colonel Simmons' behalf were traitorous, but above all Evans could not forgive Gutzon for interfering with the plan to sell the Stone Mountain coins and diverting the proceeds from the KKK. To Evans the coin had meant more than just a profit. It was to be the means by which the KKK would regain its former glory. By wrecking that plan, Gutzon had become a Judas and a pariah to the KKK.

The association tried to interest Lorado Taft in continuing the mountain carving, but he refused. He told the association that no self-respecting artist would take over another man's work. Such was the opinion of most of the art world. Augustus Lukeman, of New York City, however, was an exception.

After corresponding to Lukeman, the association called a meeting in April 1925, and awarded him a contract. Gutzon followed the events closely through reports from friends and newspapers. He was hurt by the association's action, but he was trying not to become bitter. In a confidential letter to Venable, Gutzon expressed his thoughts about the memorial:

> There is but one thing to do — wait. This project has to die in Randolph's hands . . . . I can't read the frightful slander they are publishing against me. I know there is no other man in America who can find his way in that wilderness of granite, nor one who has the courage, training and experience I have had with that particular job . . . this letter is not for publication — I am making no statements.[7]

The Venables did their best in a losing cause. Sam's sister tried to attend the meeting in which Lukeman signed his contract but she was barred. Later, she reported to Mary:

> It was just as predicted — a policeman at the door — what would we do in the sculpture business without the strong arm of the law? . . . Mrs. Saint-Gaudens has sent literature and a letter to a friend of Mr. Lukeman's in California . . . . She asks him to . . . warn him about what he is getting into in accepting the commission . . . .[8]

Criticism by fellow artists angered Lukeman and made him feel he had to justify his position. He did so, ironically, by attacking Gutzon who, perhaps for the first time, was being supported by the establishment.

But despite all the arguments, Lukeman was the sculptor. Backed by the association, he announced that a new concept would have to be created. Gutzon's design, he claimed, was flawed because no "self respecting Southerner would keep his hat on in the presence of a lady," and Gutzon's Lee wore a hat. To military men the statement seemed ludicrous. They said no military commander would review his troops bareheaded. The newspapers treated the debate lightly, but Mary saw the real danger. If Lukeman won, Gutzon's Lee would not survive. The argument became so serious to the Borglums that Mary wrote to sculptor George Barnard to ask if:

> . . . you think it possible to remove General Lee's hat without ruining the head as carved by my husband, in order to conform to Mr. Lukemann's design . . . . Personally I believe the object in trying to remove the hat is just a prelude to destroying the whole thing, and I can easily contemplate murder when I think of such unheard of vandalism . . . .[9]

Everyone, it seemed, except those with the authority, wanted Gutzon returned to Stone Mountain. The public and the majority of the press listened to the arguments until they grew tired of them and still felt that Gutzon should complete the carving. To counter his sentiment, Randolph began a letter-writing campaign. He thought that if he could discredit Gutzon the furor would die, but he only succeeded in bringing more people to Gutzon's defense.

Senator Norbeck, one of Randolph's chief targets because of his strong connection to the South Dakota memorial, summed up the feelings of most in his letter to Randolph:

> I failed to see your point . . . . It would be just as easy to prove that a good artist was not even an average business man, as it would be to prove that a good businessman was not even an average artist. I am not interested in the row . . . . I do sincerely regret that your great undertaking has suffered a serious setback in the minds of the American public.[10]

Lukeman was proceeding with the work on Stone Mountain. Gutzon had to face the reality of the situation and get on with other work. His finances were still in shambles. His attorney in Stamford summed up Gutzon's predicament in a letter to a pressing creditor. "Mr. Borglum," he wrote, "is a great artist, but a poor businessman and I suppose there have been fifty suits of attachment in the last few years."[11]

With the public sympathetic to his plight, Gutzon was in demand. There were hopes that a new Southern memorial could be carved in North Carolina. Gutzon spent several days searching for a site and finally chose a place called Chimney Rock, but the project never went beyond the talking stage. *Wars of America*, for Newark, New Jersey, had finally been cast in Italy and dedication scheduled, much to the relief of everyone concerned. Offers came from many places, but the most important came from San Antonio, Texas, when the Trail Drivers' Association asked him to create a memorial as large as the *Wars*. The contract was so important that Gutzon decided to move his family to Texas.

Characteristically, Gutzon gave little thought to uprooting his family. When he felt it was time to move on, he considered it a perfectly natural thing to do. He learned that at an early age from his father. Before he was five he had lived in Utah, Idaho, Nebraska and Missouri. Raleigh had served the family well, but he had no qualms about taking the children out of school in North Carolina and moving them to San Antonio.

The family was a vital part of Gutzon's existence. Once, when he was explaining why he had not remained in Georgia to face his accusers, he wrote, "I had a wife and two children to think of; and all three of them are more like intimate personal friends than the ordinary relationships of family life allows."[12] Gutzon wanted his family with him wherever he travelled. Mary went along as an understanding wife, but she had some misgivings as a mother:

> When our son Lincoln was born (1912) the father's happiness was touching to behold, as if he alone had created a miracle . . . he talked about his son, telephoned about him, wrote about him to all his friends . . . when hardly a year old he was taken on an overnight visit to friends in Washington, just picked up from his crib, wrapped in a blanket and transferred to a sleeping coach on the train. In sum, the most wonderful baby had suddenly become the sculptor's alter ego, as inseparable from him as his shadow. Once he departed with the child saying he would be back in two days. After a week of anxious waiting on my part, a wire from Georgia announced that both "boys were down there."[13]

Mary's observation that "the most wonderful baby had suddenly become the sculptor's alter ego" seems to have expressed a deep hurt. Much of what she had been to Gutzon was now being fulfilled by the boy. She seldom expressed this kind of feeling because she loved Gutzon and always saw a greater purpose in what he did. Very quickly in their relationship she learned to adjust to the changes in his temperament and tried to smooth his way. She may or may not have agreed to their moving to San Antonio, but she raised no strong objection.

Gutzon enjoyed the people of Texas because they welcomed him as a celebrity and did not take the stories coming out of Stone Mountain seriously. Randolph and the association never stopped trying to ruin his reputation, so it was good for Gutzon to be with people who believed in him.

When the family was settled in a hotel apartment, Gutzon sent for Hugo Villa, his assistant at Stamford. Villa helped set up a studio in an old warehouse that was used periodically by the city to build floats for festivals. The makeshift studio was far from satisfactory, but no other space was available.

He spent a great deal of money to fix up the warehouse, where he began to work on the Trail Drivers' Monument, but a few months later he lost his lease and had to move. It might have been a serious setback if he had not managed to locate and obtain the rights to a charming old building in San Antonio's Brackenridge Park. The new studio suited Gutzon's personality. Set in a lovely wooded area and straddling a stream, it had thick stone walls, a high-beamed ceiling, and room for expansion. There was much about the studio that reminded Gutzon of Borgland. Feeling very much at home, he spent a great deal of money renovating the old structure before he was ready to go back to work.

24

The Northern Memorial

Although Stone Mountain was never far from his thoughts, Gutzon had become reconciled to the fact that he would not be returning to the carving, at least not in the foreseeable future. It was becoming increasingly obvious that his vindication lay in South Dakota. He was corresponding with the two men who were the moving forces behind the project. Doane Robinson and Senator Peter Norbeck.

As a South Dakota senator, Norbeck had witnessed some of Gutzon's Washington presentations, and he was aware of the Stone Mountain fiasco. He believed in the idea of a South Dakota carving and liked Gutzon personally, but he wanted tangible proof of Gutzon's commitment to the project before he involved his constituency.

That commitment, he felt, would come when Gutzon returned to choose a site for the carving. Gutzon understood Norbeck's feelings. He too was anxious to get on with the site selection, but he needed Jesse Tucker to help in the search, and Tucker was ill. While they waited, Gutzon, Norbeck and Robinson discussed, by letter, the two most important aspects of the project, the subject matter to be carved and the method of financing.

Norbeck, astute as well as practical, made it clear at the outset that while a few wealthy South Dakotans might contribute, and he stressed the word *might*, the bulk of the money would have to come from outside the state. Farm income, the mainstay of South Dakota's economy, had been sagging since the war ended. No farmer or rancher struggling to keep his land could be expected to finance a mountain carving, no matter how many tourist dollars the carving would generate.

The senator felt that, with Congress talking about authorizing two Theodore Roosevelt memorials, one in Washington and the other in the West, he and Gutzon should concentrate on a Roosevelt theme and seek federal funding. This was the first concrete suggestion, and it assured Roosevelt his place on the mountain. Gutzon was not convinced, however, that Norbeck's plan was the best approach. He was thinking about how easy it had been to talk Coolidge and the Congress into backing the Stone Mountain coin and felt certain he could get their backing a second time. Gutzon had written to Robinson in January 1925, just two weeks before he was fired at Stone Mountain, to tell him he had suggested to Norbeck that he prepare legislation for the minting of a new commemorative silver dollar.

Norbeck knew that after the trouble at Stone Mountain Congress would never consider a coin for another mountain carving, and he refused to consider Gutzon's idea. It was hard to argue with Norbeck. He was a tough, practical man who had started his career by drilling water wells for his neighbors. He knew his business and his people. Because he was willing to take chances with homesteaders, his business prospered. When he outgrew the need to make money and wanted a deeper involvement with government, he ran for public office. He was elected to a term as governor of South Dakota and then was elected to the United States Senate.

Both Gutzon and Norbeck took part in Teddy Roosevelt's Bull Moose campaign, though they did not know each other them. They met for the first time at the 1916 Republican Convention and again during Gutzon's investigation of the aircraft industry. They remained in contact as the years passed because they shared common interests and views, primarily concerning agriculture and the plight of farmers. As governor, Norbeck had been a progressive leader instituting many of the reforms Gutzon and his North Dakota friends advocated. Norbeck was a social pioneer. In many ways he was idealistic, but his idealism was tempered by his pragmatism. His backing of the carving was vital.

Robinson was an entirely different kind of person. He was an intellectual and the poet laureate of South Dakota. He was the founder of the State Historical Society, a public speaker and a contributor to many publications. He too was respected for his service to the people of South Dakota, but not in the same way as Norbeck.

Robinson knew his people and worked within the system. He studied South Dakota's two-industry economy, its feast or famine mining booms dependent on markets thousands of miles away and its even more dependent farm and ranch community. He wanted to broaden the state's economic base, and he saw in tourism an opportunity to do so. Robinson reasoned that people would travel any distance to see something unusual. In his article "Inception and Development of the Rushmore Idea," he wrote:

> I was invited to address the annual meeting of the Black Hills and Yellowstone Trail Association . . . on January 22, 1924 . . . . While upon

my feet, delivering that address it occurred to me that a colossal monument might be created in the granite uplift of the Black Hills . . . and without consideration projected it up on my audience . . . . It did not however get into the news until January 31 . . . . I had no other plan of action than to continue the agitation until the suggestion sunk into the public consciousness and some person of artistic sense and financial ability should take it up and carry it to success; but about the first of August I received an anonymous letter . . . filled with ridicule and abuse and I concluded to act at once.[1]

Robinson's contribution to the project ended almost with its inception. The idea was his, but he was wise enough to know that others would have to turn it into a reality. When Senator Norbeck agreed to take the lead and Gutzon agreed to be the sculptor, Robinson's work was done. He remained with the project, mostly handling local publicity, but he did not play an important rule in the decision-making process.

In April 1925, while he was still debating with Norbeck over the advisability of turning the project into a federally-funded Roosevelt memorial, Gutzon announced he would return to the Black Hills. In August he arrived with Tucker, Lester Barlow and Lincoln. They were met again by the members of the Rapid City Commercial Club and taken to a camp deep in the Black Hills.

Locals believe that Gutzon's chief guide, park ranger Ted Shoemaker, knew there was only one suitable site for a carving in the Black Hills. Yet he led the party, by horseback, and allowed Gutzon to inspect numerous cliffs and outcroppings before he took him to Rushmore. Gutzon was suitably impressed, but said little as they returned to camp. As soon as he could, he went off by himself to fish, which was one of his ways of being alone with his thoughts. The next ten days they continued to inspect stone formations, more to confirm that Rushmore was the very best site than to find another. When he was finally satisfied, Gutzon called for a team of geologists and asked for a full report on the stone. He was told that the mountain was composed of dozens of minerals, but was primarily a hard granite pegmatite. Dr. O'Harra, Dean of the South Dakota School of Mines and leader of the group, made this observation on the age of the rock:

The years that have passed since Rushmore first disclosed its bold outlines to the blue of the sky no one knows, but of this we are sure, that at the time the Alps had not taken shape, not the Apennines, the Pyrenees . . . the region now occupied by the unmatched Himalayas was little more than a brackish swamp.[2]

227

Gutzon Borglum, Senator Peter Norbeck and actors on top of Mount Rushmore during first dedication in 1925.

Gutzon appreciated the history, but what he really wanted to know was whether the surface cracks went so deep that the rock was unable to be carved. This had to be known before a commitment was made to carve on Mount Rushmore. Dr. O'Harra agreed to make a more extensive survey, while Gutzon took measurements and photographs back to Texas and began working on a concept that would fit the contour of the stone.

When Dr. O'Harra reported favorably, the last technical hurdle was cleared. After much discussion with Senator Norbeck, Gutzon settled on his theme, which he explained in a letter to the senator:

> The portraits should be of Washington and Lincoln, the founder and savior . . . portraits of Jefferson, who is the first great expansionist and Roosevelt who completed commercial control by securing the Panama Canal . . . .[3]

On October 1, 1925, the mountain was dedicated in a colorful ceremony arranged by Gutzon. He announced to the crowd that the first portrait,

228

that of Washington, would be completed in the next twelve months and extended to them the following invitation:

> Meet me here a year from today. As I look back over the incidents that halted the completion of the Confederate Memorial at Stone Mountain, it seems to me that the hand of providence is decreeing that a National Monument like this shall be erected before a monument shall be built to any one section.[4]

The furor over Stone Mountain had faded. Lukeman was carving, but the Stone Mountain Association's attempts to force delivery of the coins or to raise funds through other means had failed so miserably that the association no longer wished to continue the fight publicly. It was also failing in its attempt to force the Venables to give the association more time. Gutzon was following the events closely. He stopped talking to reporters as the twelve-year deadline approached because he thought his chances of returning to the work were improving, and he did not want to alienate the Georgians any further. He knew the monument was doomed unless Randolph allowed him back, because that was the only way the Venables would grant an extension.

Gutzon was pleased, however, to tell the newspapers about the Northern Memorial. Unfortunately, they had been covering Borglum stories and Borglum wars for so long that they automatically began looking for controversies. As a result, every difference of opinion with the South Dakotans was blown out of proportion by the press. There were some arguments between Gutzon and the South Dakotans, but despite the reports none, at least in the early stages, was serious.

The complaints and charges in the letters exchanged by Gutzon, Robinson, Norbeck and members of the Rapid City Commercial Club stemmed from the fact that South Dakotans could not understand a man of Gutzon's temperament, any more than he could understand why they did not fully grasp the significance of his vision. The South Dakotans, with the exception of Senator Norbeck, did not realize how badly Gutzon had been hurt at Stone Mountain and how that affected his outlook. As a result, they overreacted to his demands and took him too much at his word.

Gutzon was wary. Bitter experience had taught him that he could get hurt whenever he sought understanding from businessmen. Stone Mountain had tested him severely. Utterly helpless, he had been forced to watch the shattering of his dream. He did not recognize his own part in the failure and could not admit, not even to himself, that he shared the blame.

The immensity of the Rushmore project also caused Gutzon some uneasiness. Wray Sanders, the self-styled "horse and dude wrangler" who was in charge of the camp when Gutzon chose Rushmore, was surprised when Gutzon awoke in the middle of the night and began talking about his fears and doubts. "He was talking more to himself," Sanders said, "and he was scared about what he was telling folks he was going to do . . . ." Occasionally Gutzon expressed his fears publicly. Speaking at the first Rushmore dedication, Gutzon told the audience:

> I confess I have never been free of fear and anxiety over the outcome of every phase of the undertaking, and quite apart from the enormous physical and nervous strain applied to the craftsmanship and the mechanism, there is the desire, the belief or the hope that so great a mass can be made a tremendous emotional creation, which desire haunts and urges one on continually.[5]

As Gutzon neared his sixtieth birthday he was in total command of his artistic powers. He was still healthy despite some chronic complaints and still looking for worlds to conquer. He could climb mountains and scale cliffs with younger men. He felt he knew more about sculpture, and certainly mountain sculpture, than any man alive. His confidence was seen by his enemies as arrogance, and he had no patience with anyone who attempted to tell him his business.

Factors other than Gutzon's apparent arrogance affected his relationship with the South Dakotans. When Gutzon spoke about the rich patrons waiting to underwrite the carving, he believed they existed. He never could separate a hope from a promise, but the South Dakotans could not understand this. To them a promise was a binding contract. A man like Gutzon, functioning on a level so far removed from theirs, automatically became suspect. Because they shared a common goal with him they tried to keep the peace, but in all the years Gutzon was in South Dakota the locals remained as perplexed by him as they were the day he arrived. As a result, a lonely man was made even lonelier.

Despite Gutzon's promise to the crowd gathered for the dedication that the Washington carving would be completed in 1926, the stone was not even touched that year. As Robinson remarked, this angered some, but not all, South Dakotans:

> During the succeeding year no progress was made and the hostility to the enterprise was even more pronounced than in the first instance, but the people of Rapid City and the Black Hills generally were quite "sold" to the idea and gave it at all times, after the first visit of Mr. Borglum, loyal support.[4]

Gutzon Borglum climbing the back of Mount Rushmore to determine if it is fit for carving. The young man on top is a photographer's assistant. The third man is the self-styled "hoss and dude wrangler" who acted as guide and cook for the scouting party.

231

The "hostility" Robinson referred to came from people who felt mountain carving was a desecration of nature and from those who did not feel a tourist industry would enhance their way of life. Norbeck did not want Gutzon to fight with these critics. As a native South Dakotan, Norbeck felt that he was in a better position to cope with local opposition. He wanted Gutzon to limit himself to speeches that would encourage, not antagonize, their supporters. In his letter to Norbeck from San Antonio, Gutzon acknowledged that Norbeck was right:

> Good luck to your fight. You are right; fleas are in certain quantity good for those they stimulate. I'm sure half the good things I've done have been in resentment of some stupid misunderstanding.[7]

1926

San Antonio was delighted with Gutzon. Soon after the family arrived, many Texans were referring to him as one of their own. They were extremely proud of his model of the Trail Drivers' Association monument, which went on display in January 1926.

Creating the statue had been therapeutic for Gutzon because he had to return to his boyhood days on the frontier. To capture the sense of the cattle drives, he spent hours talking to old-timers and studying Texas longhorns he had brought to the studio. It was also a return to the days when he ran a busy studio and his only concern was creating a monument that would make him proud. The *Trail Drivers* did that for him and went a long way toward easing the pain of Stone Mountain.

The model went on tour to Dallas, Ft. Worth and Houston, and at each stop Gutzon spoke to enthusiastic crowds. The purpose of the tour was to raise money to cast the statue on an herioc scale. If enough funds were contributed, the association planned to create a monument thirty-three feet long.

Touring with the model made Gutzon a Texas celebrity. Texans understood his work and enjoyed listening to him speak. Reporters were assigned to him, and much of what he said made the front pages. The *Trail Drivers* was the topic, but what brought the crowds was curiosity about Stone Mountain, a curiosity which Gutzon claimed was worldwide. In a letter to a friend he had known from his early days in Los Angeles, Mrs. Sidney Smith, he wrote:

> . . . am leaving for a lecture tour Saturday from the eastern coast to California. I received an offer of $50,000 to give a nine month lecture tour on the "truth about the Confederate Memorial". . . .[1]

Whether this offer was in fact made or was simply Gutzon's way of saying everyone was interested is not known, but Gutzon could not spare nine months to talk about the Southern Memorial, not even for $50,000. He was most often asked why he was not suing Randolph and

Model of the Trail Driver's Memorial in San Antonio studio.

the association. In the letter to Mrs. Smith, he said there had already been enough damage and that his enemies were right when they boasted, "Borglum is like a mother before Solomon. He will submit to anything rather than have harm come to his memorial."[2] Gutzon had also written, "The only thing I fear is the damage done on the mountain itself . . . ."[3] He had good reason for that fear, for a new Lee was taking shape several feet below Gutzon's carving.

The Venables and the women of the UDC were still supporting Gutzon and trying to force the association to discuss the situation, but they were having little success. The Georgia Legislature, caught in the middle of a politically unpopular fight, tried to relieve the pressure by arranging for Gutzon to receive one of his most satisfying commissions. The lawmakers were hoping that the commission might ease the tension and possibly provide a way to bring the two sides together.

Following the decision to honor Alexander Stephens, vice-president of the Confederacy, with a place in Statuary Hall, the Georgia legislators turned the project over to the women of the UDC. They authorized them to choose a sculptor and award a contract. The women clearly favored Gutzon, as did the legislators, who could not deal directly with Gutzon because he was still a fugitive from Georgia justice.

The legislators' reasoning is difficult to understand. From the time Gutzon was fired the lawmakers had remained, as a deliberative body, aloof. Yet the final word on the monument would eventually have to come from them. The Venables had notified the association that when the deadline arrived they would take back their mountain. The only chance for the association was a slim hope that the courts or the legislature would rescue them.

Favorable court action seemed unlikely. The terms in the contract were clear, and there was little basis for a legal challenge. Having the legislature annex the property for a state park was the only way the association could hope to retain control. Since most of the lawmakers refused to declare themselves whenever the issue was raised, awarding the Stephens commission made it appear that they were choosing sides.

Gutzon asked no questions. He began at once to make a model of the Stephens statue. When it was time to take it to Georgia for final approval before the final marble was cut in San Antonio, he had to send Mary in his place because of the arrest warrant. A year later, when the finished statue was dedicated in Washington, Gutzon was there and so were many of his Georgia enemies. They shook hands, smiled for the cameras and acted as if they were friends, while the drama at Stone Mountain was playing itself out in a race against the clock.

As the deadline neared, Lukeman was becoming desperate. Clearly, he could not complete the work or get the deadline extended, but he would not give up easily. He destroyed Gutzon's Lee and Jackson in a final attempt to end the hope of Gutzon's return. The expectation was that the Venables would then face reality and allow him to finish rather than see the hope for a Southern Memorial destroyed forever, but the plan did not work. Meanwhile, Gutzon's San Antonio studio filled with statues: the *Trail Drivers*, the Alexander Stephens, models

Wars of America in Veterans Park, Newark, New Jersey. Borglum used his son, Lincoln, and himself as models for the two figures on left, directly behind second horse.

of the Rushmore portraits and dozens of smaller commissions, which Gutzon called "the bill payers."

The long-delayed dedication of the *Wars of America* was set for Memorial Day. The final steps in the installation required Gutzon's presence. Because it was one of the times that he was going to be in one place several weeks, he brought Mary and the children with him. He spent hours on the final details and on planning the dedication ceremony with Newark officials and representatives of the Grand Army of the Republic, the same organization of Union veterans that had fought so hard against the minting of the Stone Mountain coin.

The tremendous critical and public acclaim with which the *Wars* was received was heartwarming vindication for Gutzon. They had waited many years beyond the promised date, but the citizens of Newark agreed that the statue made the waiting worthwhile. Even the Italian foundry that cast the statue tried to toast him. They put cases of champagne in the hollow castings of the two horses, but the sections were welded together without anyone's realizing the champagne was there.

The Newark dedication was a typical Borglum ceremony. Despite a steady rain, 4,000 people filled the bleacher seats and another 10,000 lined the sidewalks and took places on all the surrounding rooftops. The mammoth statue was covered with a giant canvas tethered to balloons, which were supposed to lift the cover. The steady rain, however, caused the cover to become too heavy to rise, but even that could not spoil the day.

When it was Gutzon's turn to speak he could not control his emotions. The newspapers, in fact, featured a photograph of him standing in the rain with is bare head bowed and, according to the caption, "tears trickling down his cheeks." Looking out at the crowd he told them:

> Probably for the first time in the history of this country an artist was permitted to work without interference in the creation of a great public memorial . . . . It is my opinion that the absence of bickering that attended the creation of this work provided a new standard for public monuments . . . .[4]

Although the work at Mount Rushmore had stalled, it remained a major project. After the 1925 dedication and the high hopes of starting the actual work had dissipated, the reality of the situation became painfully clear: there was no money and nothing could be done until there was.

The South Dakota legislature had passed a bill authorizing the carving, but it had struck all portions that would have provided funding.

The Rapid City Commercial Club had paid some of the cost of Gutzon's visits, but it had no experience in fund-raising and did not seem in a hurry to learn. In fact, until the club stopped believing Gutzon could raise large sums, it would not make any real effort to raise funds. Some members of the club were beginning to face the reality of their situation, and they started asking questions. In July, J. B. Green, secretary of the club, wrote Norbeck:

> Borglum is a darned better sculptor than he is a salesman and you are a better salesman than you are a sculptor . . . there are people, however, as you well know, who are suspicious of any progressive step . . . if there is anything you care to suggest . . . which might obtain a better understanding and more rapid progress I will indeed be glad to hear from you . . . .[5]

When Gutzon was questioned about why his friends had not put up the money, he claimed he could not approach his wealthy patrons until South Dakota raised $50,000 as a show of faith. It was one of those statements he often made for effect, but it caused near panic with the South Dakotans. The editor of the influential Sioux Falls *Argus Leader* wired Gutzon to ask if the story was true. Gutzon responded with a denial and then tried to change the subject by claiming that the coin idea was still alive.

A Mount Rushmore commemorative coin still seemed the best hope to Gutzon, despite Norbeck's feeling that their best chance was to seek a direct government appropriation. After some lengthy debates, the senator did introduce a commemorative coin bill, as Gutzon urged, but he admitted later that it was only a political smokescreen designed to fool those who would oppose an appropriation.

What no one involved wanted to admit was that Mount Rushmore's real problems were coming from South Dakota Governor Gunderson. He had opposed the mountain carving as a concept and was doing all he could to prevent it from becoming a reality. With Norbeck and so many other influential people backing the project, Gunderson was putting himself in an unpopular position, which led to his defeat when he ran for reelection. He remained in office until mid 1927, however, and never stopped opposing the carving.

Norbeck, Gutzon and their friends understood the nature of the governor's opposition, but there was little they could do to counter it until Gunderson was gone. While they waited, Gutzon fretted. He could not rid himself of the specter of Stone Mountain and did not feel secure at Mount Rushmore. He expressed the fears in a letter to Norbeck:

. . . designating me as sculptor . . . in such an affirmative manner that it would constitute a binding act . . . and done in such a manner that no future board or group of men could take this plan and do as Stone Mountain politicians did, I can't go through another such abuse of confidence . . . . I have no standing, recognition, nor any official appointment . . . . I was warned by my own men "I was facing another Stone Mountain". . . .[6]

Gutzon was troubled. He had promised a completed Washington in 1926, yet there was no way he could keep that promise. He had promised that his friends would donate millions and had been unable to make good on his pledge. The best he could do was to convince himself, and try to convince others, that the money was not forthcoming because South Dakotans were apathetic.

Gutzon was also tired. He was traveling to promote Rushmore while attempting to keep up with the huge volume of work in the San Antonio studio. He was doing more and making more money than he had ever made, but he still could not meet the demands of his creditors.

One of the millionaire friends to whom Gutzon frequently referred was Herbert Myrick, publisher of a chain of magazines. Myrick was interested in the Rushmore project and had given the idea much publicity. In 1926 he had made the first major contribution. When Myrick realized the extent of Gutzon's financial problems, he attempted to intercede. With the collapse at Stone Mountain, Gutzon's many creditors had become uneasy, and Borgland, even though it was practically judgment-proof because of liens already outstanding, became their target. Suddenly, every note was being called. Gutzon had managed to buy some time by putting everything in Mary's name, but this did not help for long because she had co-signed most of the loans.

The unrelenting pressure was affecting him. Gutzon was earning large fees, but his expenses were staggering. Maintaining Borgland and studios in Raleigh and San Antonio, paying most of his own way as he travelled to promote Rushmore, seeking commissions and trying to meet the demands of the creditors who pressed the most were overwhelming Gutzon.

Myrick tried to relieve the burden, and like so many others before him, he went first to Eugene Meyer:

I think that owing to Mr. Borglum having devoted much of his time for several years to the work on Stone Mountain, to which he advanced over $100,000 of his own . . . and the project owing him in addition a large amount . . . none of which he may ever be able to recover, his finances have become somewhat involved . . . . My plan for a blanket mortgage upon all this property, of say $150,000, to secure an issue of bonds . . . .[7]

Meyer answered:

> The Stone Mountain project to which you refer may have something to do with Mr. Borglum's finances, but it is . . . a fact that he ceased to pay the interest on the mortgage several years before he undertook any work at Stone Mountain.[8]

Before anything could be arranged, Myrick died and Gutzon was forced to struggle on as before. Gutzon and Robinson were still clinging to the hope that a large contributor would ease the burden at Mount Rushmore. Returning from a long trip on which he made stops in Pittsburgh, Detroit, Chicago, Minneapolis and Kansas City, Gutzon wrote an enthusiastic letter to Robinson:

> . . . In Pittsburgh . . . we talked of my plan and all agreed Pennsylvania must handle Washington . . . . In Chicago I called at Dawe's bank . . . . I told him I wanted Illinois to build the Lincoln and I did not want anyone else or any other state to have anything to do with it . . . .[9]

Although he had been encouraged by what he felt had been an enthusiastic reception in most of the cities, Gutzon was tired by the time he reached San Antonio and convinced that no one was helping him. He sent a copy of his letter to Robinson to Norbeck in an attempt to press him into getting more affirmative action from South Dakota, but Norbeck was in no mood to be pressured. "I was delighted upon my return to find your telegram and letter. I was just in the frame of mind to smile,"[10] Norbeck wrote to Gutzon, then went on to present the facts of their situation as he saw them:

> The Atlanta propaganda hurts. Our people are financially distressed and skeptical and say where will the money come from? . . . A great work of art makes its appeal but it is not strong enough to satisfy a hungry man, who agrees with Herbert Spencer, that "eats" must come first.[11]

The year 1926 was almost gone and no work had been done on the mountain.

26
1927

With the possibility of President Coolidge's setting up the summer White House in the Game Lodge in Custer State Park, hopes were running high. The president's presence would create the sort of favorable publicity that attracts contributors. Norbeck had invited Coolidge, and others who were friendly to Rushmore were urging him to accept.

Governor-elect Bill Bulow, the successor to Governor Gunderson and a supporter of the mountain carving, was about to take office. That meant Rushmore would finally have a friend in the governor's mansion. The carving received still another boost when John Boland, a Rapid City businessman, took charge of the Commercial Club's efforts on behalf of Mount Rushmore. Boland was an energetic and enthusiastic man who knew how to get things done. Through his efforts, a number of local merchants contributed to the carving. That, along with the arrival in the Black Hills of Gutzon's model for the mountain, convinced some skeptics and encouraged the project's supporters.

In the beginning Gutzon and Boland worked well together, though they were very different in outlook and temperament. Both wrote long letters to Norbeck praising each other. The cordial relationship did not last, but it was extremely important to Rushmore's well-being while it did.

Everyone concerned with Rushmore saw a Coolidge visit as the key to their chances, but none pretended that the president could be convinced that the mountain carving was important enough to warrant his visit. They knew they needed a better argument and settled on the farm issue, which was too important to ignore. They told the president that it was imperative he spend time in the Midwest and that the lodge in Custer State Park would be about as beautiful a headquarters as he could find.

The campaign was pressed on as many fronts as possible. Doing his share, Gutzon mentioned in a report to Robinson, ". . . I asked Humphrey to get Mellon to tell "Cal" the farmer's women in South Dakota had votes and they would be pleased to know him better."[1]

Coolidge was sensitive to the farm argument because he was in trouble with farmers. He had vetoed the McNary-Haugen Bill, a price-support bill backed by most farmers. In the face of stronger-than-anticipated protests, he had not yet declared himself a candidate for re-election. His aides said the president wanted to give the matter serious thought during the summer and indicated that the reaction to his farm policies would be the determining factor.

In March, while waiting for Coolidge to announce his choice of a summer White House, Norbeck decided to change his strategy. Norbeck, Gutzon, and South Dakota Congressman William Williamson met and agreed to abandon the coin idea in favor of a direct appropriation of $500,000. They also agreed that, before Norbeck and Williamson introduced the necessary legislation, Gutzon would seek the support of his friend Treasury Secretary Andrew Mellon.

At the meeting, Mellon agreed to support a measure that would provide $250,000 in government funds to match an equal amount to be raised through private donations. Norbeck was upset with the plan. It was a totally different arrangement than he had in mind when he sent Gutzon to Mellon, but there was little he could do at that point other than express his displeasure to Gutzon. Norbeck felt Gutzon had introduced the idea of matching funds to put South Dakota on the spot. Fortunately, despite his anger, Norbeck believed in the project strongly enough to submit the altered legislation. Even with Mellon's support, the appropriation bill faced stiff opposition.

Toward the end of March, the president announced that he was giving serious thought to spending the summer in South Dakota. This greatly encouraged South Dakotans and enabled Boland to solicit contributions of $5,000 from each of the four railroads serving the state and from the Hearst-owned Homestake Gold Mine. The money was used to buy and install equipment, to prepare the mountain for carving and to plan the gala celebration they hoped to stage in Coolidge's honor. The money also enabled the Mt. Harney Memorial Association, the organization authorized by the South Dakota State Legislature in 1925 to oversee the project, to enter into formal contracts with Jesse Tucker and Gutzon. Tucker was hired at a yearly salary of $10,000, while Gutzon agreed to work for a percentage of the money spent on the carving. It was a complicated arrangement geared to progress on the carving, and it stipulated that the total could not exceed $87,000.

In May, following Coolidge's announcement that he would be arriving in June, preparations at the mountain began in earnest. Boland and the association started a fund drive in South Dakota schools, and the children responded with pennies and nickels. The campaign was designed to illustrate to the world how much Rushmore meant to South Dakota. It was a fine gesture that earned much favorable publicity and added a few thousand dollars to the treasury.

A surprise donation came from New York attorney Charles Rushmore, who sent $5,000. Rushmore said he was embarrassed by reporters wanting to know what he had done to deserve having the mountain named for him. As a young lawyer at the turn of the century, he was sent west by English clients to determine if their tin mines were worth retaining.

Going west was a great adventure for a city boy, and Rushmore enjoyed himself immensely. He spent days on horseback riding on old Indian trails, inspecting his client's property and taking in the wonders of the Black Hills. His companions were local men used to hard work, a rugged life and a good joke. Rushmore and his guides were passing a cliff called Slaughterhouse Peak by some because an occasional cattle had been butchered there and Cougar Mountain by others because a large cat had once been killed near the top. Rushmore was struck by the awesome beauty of the prominence, and he asked one of his companions what it was called. "Oh," the man answered with a wink to the others, "that's Mount Rushmore." It was a good joke, and somewhere in the re-telling the name stuck. Rushmore barely remembered the incident when reporters first started calling, but he had retained his sense of humor, and with the donation he eased his embarrassment.

Grace and Calvin Coolidge arrived on June 15, 1927, with a large party of aides, secret service men and reporters. For the backers of the mountain carving, it was a tremendous opportunity, and they were determined to make the most of their good fortune. Hanging Squaw Creek, the beautiful, clear stream running past the lodge, for example, was renamed Grace Coolidge Creek and stocked with prize trout, which were confined by nets placed half a mile up and down stream. The first thing the president did was to unpack his fly rod and test the creek. He cast and pulled in a trout, cast again and had another strike. After a few more successful attempts, he tossed his rod away and told the newsmen gathered on the bank that he was "either the best fisherman alive or the luckiest." Call had not been fooled and did not fish again that summer.

Gutzon and his family arrived from San Antonio about a week after the president and began immediately to prepare for the dedication. The ceremony was scheduled for August 10, and he had much to do before then. By August 9 everything was set. The compressors were in place at the foot of the mountain. Stairs to the top had been built, the speaker's platform was ready and the winch and bosun's seat Gutzon planned to use during the ceremony had been tested. In the afternoon the citizens of Keystone pitched in to finish grading the road the presidential limousine would use, and in the evening the town came alive with a buffalo roast and dance financed by the local moonshiners.

For weeks the presidential press corp had been giving Rushmore national publicity while they waited for Coolidge to give them some real news. On the afternoon before the dedication, they got their wish. After a walk with Mrs. Coolidge, the president had his lunch and then, as he walked across the lobby and started up the stairs, he paused dramatically to announce, "I do not choose to run for president in 1928." The reporters pushed forward shouting questions, but Coolidge had said all he was going to say. He continued on to his room with Mrs. Coolidge and retired for his afternoon nap.

Many political observers believed that Coolidge was expressing a sincere desire to bow out, while others were certain he was hoping for a draft. If that was his plan, it did not work. A draft movement never developed, and by the time the convention convened it was too late. Herbert Hoover had the nomination.

Gutzon was no happier about Hoover's nomination than was Coolidge. But on August 10 politics were put aside. Early on this clear, crisp day Gutzon gathered wildflowers into a bouquet. He hired Clyde Ice, a local barnstorming pilot, to fly him over the Game Lodge in an open cockpit biplane. When Grace Coolidge came out on the lawn to wave, Gutzon gallantly tossed the flowers to her. Gutzon was enjoying the flight, but he might not have been had he realized the danger he was in. They had come in so low that Ice could not bank the plane in the narrow canyon and was afraid he could not gain altitude. He was forced to head up the gulch and, fortunately, came out on a meadow where he could turn and climb.[2]

Late in the morning the presidential party started for the mountain. Along the way Coolidge waved to the friendly crowd heading up the slopes with sack lunches and picnic hampers. A team of horses from the Hazeltine Stables in Keystone waited to pull the limousines up a steep embankment about a mile from where the road ended. There the automobiles were parked, and the president rode the rest of the way on horseback.

As Coolidge approached the speaker's platform, the crowd began to cheer. The president was wearing his traditional New England suit

President Calvin Coolidge (with cowboy hat), Gutzon Borglum and South Dakota officials at 1927 dedication.

and vest, but for the occasion he had added cowboy boots and an over-sized cowboy hat. While he waited for the festivities to begin, "Silent Cal" ignored reporters and politicians who were trying to catch his attention and ask him about his future plans. Instead, he stood in front of the platform and gravely shook hands with the children who were lined up waiting to greet him. In his short speech Coolidge told the crowd:

> We have come here to dedicate a cornerstone that was laid by the hand of the Almighty. On this towering wall of Rushmore, in the heart of the Black Hills, is to be inscribed a memorial which will represent some of the outstanding events of American history . . . laid on by the hand of a great artist in sculpture . . . .[3]

The president then handed Gutzon four jackhammer bits. With the eyes of the crowd focused on him, Gutzon made his way to the top of the mountain, where Jesse Tucker waited with a crew. Gutzon strapped himself into the bosun's seat, took his drill bits and jack hammer and, with Tucker operating the winch, was slowly lowered down the sheer cliff to marks painted on the rock. He braced himself, pressed the trigger and leaned on the jack hammer to drill the first hole. He moved on to the next mark, drilled again and, when he had the four master holes for the portrait of George Washington set in the rock, he signalled to Tucker and was hoisted to the top. The carving of Mount Rushmore had begun.

Gutzon returned to the speaker's platform and gave Coolidge one of the drill bits. He gave one to Robinson and the third to Norbeck. The fourth he kept for himself. He took his place at the podium, looked out at the audience and, in a story he enjoyed telling groups that gathered at the mountain in later years, he forgot what he planned to say. Instead, he told the crowd that the work that was to be done on the mountain would outlive our civilization. Then, feeling that the president might have misunderstood because ". . . I was thinking in terms of mankind and they were thinking in political terms," he turned to the men on the speaker's platform and said to Coolidge, "That was an awful thing for me to say, Mr. President . . . ."[4]

When the ceremony ended, Coolidge asked Gutzon how the mountain carving was going to be financed. He suggested that Gutzon visit him in Washington so they could discuss the matter and devise a way. The backers of Rushmore were delighted. The president's suggestion was exactly what they were hoping for when they had invited him to the Hills.

27

1928

Gutzon never stopped believing that he would eventually return to complete the work at Stone Mountain, even after what seemed like the final curtain in 1928. Lukeman and Randolph, running out of time, were becoming desperate. Hearing rumors that they planned to destroy Gutzon's portrait of Lee, Venable went to court seeking a restraining order. At the same time, the UDC started an action to have the indictments against Gutzon dropped.

The women failed in their effort. After Randolph defeated Venable's attempt to stop him, Gutzon's work was blown off the mountain. The women tried again, this time before a grand jury, and even its refusal to take action did not stop Gutzon from trying to return. In April he assured Venable that he could raise the money necessary to restore his carving:

> And you may say further that there was three million pledged for the work thirty days before I left it, and you may also add that I could get underwritten five million in ninety days to restore it, and you may publish this statement in Atlanta.[1]

Even the destruction of his work did not crush Gutzon's spirit; he reacted with almost philosophical detachment. In a letter to his friend Dr. Plato Durham, president of Emory University in Atlanta, he wrote:

> I began many years ago . . . understanding that the spirit of reprisal and vandalism that has prevailed shall cease completely. I . . . shall insist that the partially carved figures now on the mountain, although they replaced my own figures of Lee and Jackson, shall be finished, as begun, by the sculptor responsible for the design.[2]

Gutzon meant that even after the Venables took back their mountain and returned him to the work he would insist that Lukeman finish his own concept. Gutzon had evidently returned, in his own mind, to the grandiose plan of five major groups and felt confident enough to make a magnanimous gesture to Lukeman.

Randolph, in a last, desperate effort, tried to force a bill through the state legislature that would have made the mountain public property, and for a time it appeared he might have a chance. During the hearings, Venable explained his side of the controversy:

Mr. Lukeman's head of General Lee few people recognize. The nose is crooked, the left arm looked withered . . . . The hilt of the sword is gone and the stirrup of the saddle is broken off. The money is all gone and the Lukeman carving of General Lee is a mutilated imperfection that cannot be rectified.[3]

The Randolph bill was defeated, and the Venables took back their mountain. Lukeman returned to New York, and the Stone Mountain Memorial Association declared bankruptcy. Unable to join in the fight in Atlanta because of the indictments, Gutzon had to be content with giving interviews and making speeches while carrying on with his other work. For a time there was talk about forming a new organization and getting on with the carving. Venable and Gutzon were more than willing, but it was impossible to create any serious interest.

Gutzon was still deeply involved in Texas, where he had made many new friends. One, Mrs. Lorine Jones Spoonts, was head of the Corpus Christi Chamber of Commerce. She was enthusiastic, wealthy and, like so many women in his life, completely captivated by Gutzon. She became a good family friend, especially with Mary, and she encouraged Gutzon in all his Texas projects. She was particularly excited about his plan to revitalize the waterfront of Corpus Christi. Gutzon hoped to build a breakwater two miles into the gulf to create a stable harbor and stop the periodic flooding that threatened the downtown area. His plan called for beautiful esplanades, tourist facilities with small shops and restaurants and a huge statue of Christ stilling the waters at the end of the breakwater. The statue was to be Gutzon's gift to the city after construction was completed, but Corpus Christi voters defeated the bond issue that would have financed the project, and the plan was dropped. Other plans for Texas included an outdoor theater for San Antonio, a highway from San Antonio to Brownsville, which would have been lined with palm trees and rose bushes planted by the citizens, and a way to divert the floodwaters of the Missouri to the desert of the Southwest.

All of Gutzon's plans received a great deal of publicity, as did his promise to raise millions for a revitalized Stone Mountain. None of it was lost on the puzzled South Dakotans. They questioned both privately and in their newspapers why their project was stalled for lack of funds if Gutzon could raise money for other works as easily as he claimed.

Gutzon Borglum working on North Carolina memorial for Gettysburg. Bill Tallman (behind and to Borglum's left) posed for the front figure with the gun. Tallman was superintendent at Mount Rushmore for five years.

Norbeck and Williamson were still trying to push an appropriation bill through a reluctant Congress, and Gutzon's boasts were not helping. With no work being done on the mountain and no contributions coming in, Norbeck knew it was only a matter of time before all

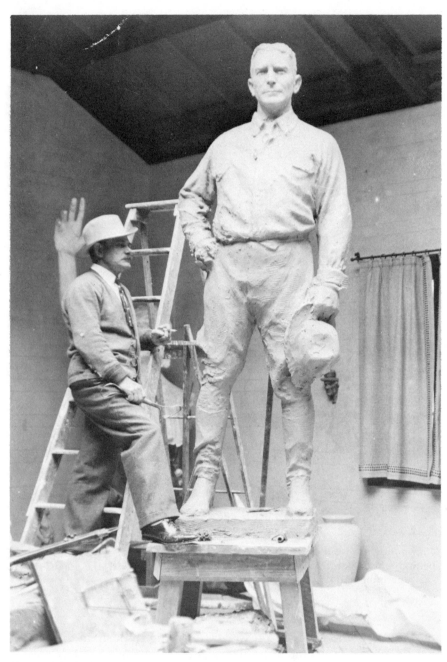

Gutzon Borglum putting finishing touches on General John Greenway for Statuary Hall in the Capitol Building, Washington, D.C.

interest would evaporate. He wrote to John Boland complaining about the lack of effort by the Mt. Harney Memorial Association and expressed his disappointment in Gutzon's efforts.

Gutzon was busy with other matters. Shortly after the Stephens monument was completed, the Georgia legislature awarded him another commission: to create a bust of Sidney Lanier, the South's beloved Civil War poet. At the same time, two new commissions came from North Carolina. One was for two bas-reliefs to flank Gutzon's statue of Governor Aycock in Raleigh; the other was a major commission to create a heroic-sized North Carolina Memorial for the battlefield at Gettysburg.

It seemed the busier he was the more he was in demand. Isabella Greenway of Arizona, seeking a sculptor to create a statue of her husband, General John Greenway, for Statuary Hall and a bust of the general for the state capitol, asked Gutzon to visit her to discuss the projects. His other work delayed him, and before he could make the trip she awarded him both contracts. In writing to thank her, he explained his hectic schedule:

> I had planned, as I promised you, to be in Arizona by the middle of July. When I reached Richmond I was deluged with details for a couple of large groups in sculpture to be made for the Edgar Allan Poe shrine . . . am leaving on the morning of the 14th for Oregon to sign a contract for a monument to Scott . . . .[4]

Old friends were suddenly seeking him out. Ignace Paderewski, the pianist who had become Premier of Poland, commissioned him by mail to create a Woodrow Wilson Memorial. He sent Mary and Lincoln to Europe to discuss the project. Felix Frankfurter, who had been involved in the defense of the anarchists Sacco and Vanzetti, called. The two had been tried for murder and convicted on evidence that seemed contrived. Frankfurter and a defense team worked for seven years on appeals, but in 1927 they lost and the two men were put to death.

Those who believed Sacco and Vanzetti had been victims of those who held different political views were outraged. They vowed to keep the memory of the pair alive by opening a Freedom House in Boston. Gardner Jackson, one of the leaders of the group, suggested that a commemorative bas-relief be created and dedicated at the house on the first anniversary of the executions.

Jackson asked Frankfurter if he thought Gutzon would consider creating the bas-relief, but Frankfurter laughed at the idea of even approaching him. Jackson took Frankfurter's reaction as a challenge and decided to give his idea a try. Gutzon was at Borgland when Jackson's letter reached him. As far as Gutzon was concerned, Reds, Bolsheviks and anarchists were enemies of America, and he had no sympathy for their causes. He had not involved himself in the Sacco and Vanzetti case because of these feelings, but Jackson's letter struck a responsive chord. He phoned and made arrangements to drive up to the Jackson cottage on Cape Cod.

Frankfurter, who lived next door to the Jacksons, was thrilled when he heard his friend was coming. After a discussion that lasted several hours Jackson agreed to put all the details in a letter, and Gutzon assured him he would give the matter serious thought. Then they relaxed while Gutzon and Frankfurter reminisced about their early days in Washington. In the morning Gutzon said goodbye to the Jacksons and commented, "Felix must be mellowing. This was the first time I've been able to get a word in when he was around." Gutzon had hardly pulled away when Frankfurter came to the Jackson cottage and said, "Gutzon must be mellowing. This was the first . . . ."[5]

When Gutzon returned to San Antonio a month later, he found Jackson's letter waiting. During his travels, the project had formed in his mind, and he had decided to take up the cause. He answered Jackson at once:

> Felix knows . . . what side to find me on when a decision must be taken as to whether I will be with Tom Paine, Jefferson and their kind, or with their opponents . . . . Fear not, I will take up the cause of these men if they have been wronged. If two innocent men have been electrocuted under order of the American courts, much as I love my country and always shall, above any and all things, not because it is the most just or best, but . . . because the greatest opportunities for freedom . . . are offered here . . . I will do anything I can to make the martyrdom of these men a burning, living protest against the injustice practiced in the name of modern jurisprudence![6]

Gutzon had his bas-relief ready for the July dedication, but the city had refused to issue the permits Freedom House needed, and it was never able to open. The plaster Gutzon had sent to Boston was put in storage. The bronze was left in the studio at Borgland where it remained until long after his death.

The Rushmore bill, pushed by Senator Norbeck, was slowly making its way through Congress when it ran into a major stumbling block in Senator Louis Cramton of Michigan. President Coolidge finally convinced Cramton to withdraw his opposition, but not before the senator had imposed several conditions. One of these has been mistakenly attributed to Gutzon because it had been one of the conditions he demanded at Stone Mountain. Cramton insisted that no charge ever be made for public admission to the memorial. Gutzon, Norbeck and Robinson had had several discussions about charging a small fee to help offset the cost of carving, and would have, if Cramton had not stopped them.

As the Congressional battle dragged on, the chances of carving in the spring of 1928 faded, and many supporters of the project became disheartened. Norbeck had managed to win Senate approval, but the bill was stalled in the House. Norbeck was already under tremendous pressure when he received a telegram from Gutzon saying that he preferred private financing and that he was "not inclined to stay involved if the federal government took control."[7] He repeated his belief that millions could be raised by private subscription and said he saw no reason why that chance should be destroyed for an appropriation of only $250,000. Gutzon's unwillingness to compromise exasperated Norbeck, as his letter to Robinson indicates:

> He does not want the quarter of a million from Congress now. He wants to go to New York, London, Jerusalem or Heaven to get millions . . . . He is quite certain that a million is more than a quarter of a million, but that is the only thing he is sure about.[8]

When Norbeck finally calmed down, he wrote Gutzon to try to restore Gutzon's perspective:

> Robinson agrees with you and he wants us to go to New York for the big box of free gold . . . . You are wholly uninformed of actual conditions . . . . Our only chance to avoid absolute failure seems to be government appropriation . . . we do not want to fizzle . . . I know you are busy and those telegrams are written under strain . . . .[9]

Gutzon realized that Norbeck was right, and he agreed that he had been "uninformed of actual conditions," until he had had a chance to speak to Jesse Tucker by phone. Then Gutzon interjected an entirely new idea:

> We would extend the development around the memorial into possibly very fine buildings . . . for the purpose of the historical records bearing directly upon the matters the memorial commemorates . . . .[10]

A new idea from Gutzon did not surprise Norbeck, which was one of the reasons they got along so well. Gutzon's mind functioned on a grand, evolving scale. Thinking out loud, as he was with this thought, which became the Hall of Records, was his way of life. It often caused him trouble with "practical" people, who could not keep up with his developing thoughts.

Aware that he had needlessly upset Norbeck, Gutzon tried to explain why he had sent the offending wire:

> I got an indication over the phone that if the government was going to appropriate this money we might lose the Rockefeller interests. This explains my suggestion to "soft-pedal" the bill . . . until we could conclude the Rockefeller matter . . . . I believe I can get quite a sum from Du Pont . . . now, however . . . my optimism is back where it was . . . .[11]

There was another disturbing note in Gutzon's lengthy letter. Jesse Tucker was in the Black Hills putting things in order just in case the money was appropriated and they would be able to start work. Gutzon told Senator Norbeck that he was unhappy because after twelve years of working together he felt Tucker was ignoring his orders.

Norbeck answered with complaints of his own. "I must admit," he wrote, "I am not as stuck on Tucker as I thought,"[12] but he added that he felt they should try to get along with him for the time being. Neither Gutzon nor Norbeck mentioned their real concern, which was how Tucker would be paid from an empty treasury.

Gutzon was on the road so much of the time that much of his contact with Mary and the children came through the mail. They fully supported his efforts, though they missed him. Mary, knowing his schedule, tried to have letters waiting for him at each stop to relieve his loneliness. She sent notes from the children and letters from friends, but tried to shield him from the financial difficulties she was facing. There were times, however, when she was forced to share the burden. She wrote telling him how she had arranged a mortgage so she could send him a thousand dollars and how she was trying to stretch the balance to cover interest payments on the Borgland mortgage, make some badly needed repairs and still "arrange to pay off the brotherhood claim."[13] The "brotherhood claim" was the balance of the note held by D. C. Stephenson, who needed the money to continue to appeal his conviction.

With the Republican nomination going to Herbert Hoover, the outlook for Rushmore dimmed. Reflecting on Coolidge's support of the project, Gutzon wrote:

> He was interested; he knew about as much about art as I do about the late Lama of Tibet, but he knew history . . . .[14]

254

Gutzon's estimation of Coolidge may not have been very high, but it certainly was better than what he had to say about Hoover:

> Hoover was indifferent and dead from the top down. His heart seemed to have stopped beating to the call of laughter, to music, the charm of letters, the color and mystery of Inness and Millet — the power of Angelo or the burning words of Tom Paine . . . . I believe if a rose was put into his hand it would wilt. [15]

When the Democrats nominated Governor Al Smith, the issue of the campaign became Smith's Catholicism. Voters gave all sorts of reasons but prejudice to explain their choice, but no one was fooled by what the vote said about America's fears.

Gutzon knew he had to take a side. He felt he could not sit out a presidential election without losing the right to have his say in Washington. His problem was not knowing which candidate he could honestly support. Always a Republican in one form or another, Gutzon found switching difficult, even though he felt alienated from the party and considered Hoover a most unattractive candidate.

Gutzon often attacked the Republican Party in his speeches without reprisal because the old guard knew that he could be counted on when needed. Gutzon believed he was a policy maker who could arouse the public and assume a leadership role anytime he desired. He felt he functioned best as a visionary thinker.

His plan for diverting the waters of the Missouri was one of the basic issues that separated him from Hoover. As Secretary of Commerce, Hoover also had a plan, about which Gutzon expressed his opinion in a letter to a friend:

> Hoover has a plan for raising the levees and building lakes. He might as well, and I should suggest this as a cartoon . . . he might as well telephone for the plumber for more bathtubs if he found his bathtub was getting flooded . . . . [16]

Gutzon, hiding behind the excuse of being busy, could not make up his mind and was remaining uncharacteristically silent. Many of his friends became concerned when it appeared that he was going to sit out the election. Missy Meloney, publisher of the *New York Herald Tribune*, was one of them. She tried her best to convince him he should back Hoover:

> What are you doing down there in Texas? Hoover is going to be president and that is a new stand for art in the world. With Al Smith in the White

House you would have gold donkeys in all the parks and they would be modelled by Tammany bricklayers . . . . Anyway, Hoover is going to be the next president. Some day you are going to do a great statue of him. He is homely, but so was Lincoln.[17]

Supporting Hoover still was difficult for Gutzon. He disliked Hoover and did not believe he could win. Their relationship had always been formal, but it turned almost hostile early in the campaign, when Hoover rejected Gutzon's suggestion that he be allowed to create a campaign button. In his response to Missy Meloney, he wrote:

Hoover is not going to be elected, and I know you are scared stiff over it . . . . I have no love for Tammany, neither do I for the Republican machine that looted our country of its millions during the war . . . . There is one thing . . . that is certain — God is here, and America will roll on . . . until the next election, and then we may put Coolidge back in office . . . your friend Hoover . . . is not homely. He is just not good looking.[18]

Smith's people hired Gutzon to make a campaign button. When it was finished, Gutzon wrote to Isabella Greenway, a staunch Democrat, telling her about the work and suggesting a way for Smith to win the support of the farmers:

If Governor Smith will issue a statement . . . informing the farmers . . . that he has given their interests considerable thought of late . . . that if he was elected he should call Congress into session for the sole purpose of securing for them . . . such remedial legislation as that great body of our citizenry deserved, I am certain such a message . . . would place Mr. Smith before them in his true light.[19]

Gutzon never did declare himself. In the final analysis, the image of a Vatican-controlled White House proved to be too much for the frightened voters. Smith did not carry even his home state of New York, despite having Governor Franklin Delano Roosevelt as his running mate.

Hoover was elected, and business went on as usual. For Gutzon and the South Dakotans nothing had changed. They were still waiting for Congress to act on the appropriation bill. Toward the end of May the bill finally passed in the House. Because of the Cramton amendments added in the Senate, it was forced into a joint committee to have the differences reconciled. That meant the bill was dead until at least the fall session.

With that disappointing news, everyone connected with the Rushmore project became discouraged. Tucker was particularly distressed. He had been waiting over a year to be paid and had advanced over $2,000 from his own funds. When the news came, he threatened to sue, and it took all Gutzon could do to calm his superintendent:

> My position is no better than yours and the responsibility and burdens exceed it ten fold . . . . I will personally see that you are protected . . . .[20]

Gutzon then borrowed money to pay Tucker some of his back wages.

28
1929

The rock of Rushmore remained exactly as it had been when Gutzon had shut down the operation in the winter of 1927. Most Rushmore backers were discouraged, but Gutzon was still optimistic. He met with President Coolidge, who was serving his last few months in office, and then wired Norbeck to say he had met with Coolidge and briefed him. For Norbeck, Gutzon's wire was further evidence of Gutzon's impracticality:

I have no doubts the clouds furnish a wonderful location for a residence. I appreciate that you have kept in touch with the matter and the president knows even less about it than you do . . . everything is flat in South Dakota as a result of the year's idleness . . . the fact that neither you nor I were able to scare up a few dollars for work during the summer of 1928 has led people to believe that we are just talking hot air . . . most people in South Dakota figure that Stone Mountain is dead and Rushmore is in the same class. . . . I shall be pleased indeed to consider your wishes and your judgement, but I prefer to talk about facts instead of fiction when we get down to business.[1]

Gutzon reacted to Norbeck's black mood with good humor. He sensed that they were at a crossroads, and he answered Norbeck with a six-page letter:

My Dear Senator . . . If I didn't love you so much . . . I would get cross. But no one can respect you as much as I do, know you half as well as I do, agree with you as much as I agree with you . . . . I have a feeling from your letter . . . that you feel I have not raised the money that should be raised . . . . I took every step to get the money from five millionaires . . . but Mr. Du Pont will not let us have the money when we want it . . . get that bill passed in the next two weeks and give me a good commission . . . . I will personally undertake to get $100,000 in pledges . . . . If I don't . . . I promise you to do my work remaining on the mountain without any charges . . . .[2]

259

Because Norbeck had raised the specter of Stone Mountain, whose shadow Gutzon sensed on everything he said and did, he brought Norbeck up to date on the situation there, at least from his perspective:

> Referring to Stone Moiuntain again. I have been there three times this summer upon the urgent request of the old . . . association, begging me to take up the work again. I have made one stipulation . . . I shall have no dealings with the men who betrayed their trust. I shall go back to Stone Mountain if I live long enough, but there will be no work done there for probably two years . . . the work is definitely offered to me and I have definitely agreed to take it up . . . now let us finish the Black Hills first.[3]

Gutzon truly believed he was going to finish the Southern Memorial. He made similar assertions almost to the day he died, and he continued to go to Georgia to meet with his enemies at every opportunity. He was able to go because a complicated arrangement had been worked out, in which a cease-fire was declared for a few days and he was assured he would not be arrested or harmed.

In February Congress passed Public Law #805, and President Coolidge signed the bill as one of his last official acts. The law authorized the president to appoint a twelve-member Mount Rushmore National Commission to take over from the Mt. Harney Memorial Association and take charge of the work at the mountain. It also authorized Coolidge to write a brief history of the United States, which Gutzon would carve on a giant entablature as part of the monument. In addition, it provided $250,000 in federal funds, which were to be matched by private donations.

Funds in the amount of $73,000 had been donated, and the government immediately matched that amount. This meant the work could begin as soon as the president appointed the commission. Gutzon asked Coolidge to appoint eleven members at once. He wanted the last seat left vacant so President Hoover could appoint Coolidge, but Coolidge did not feel that would be proper, even though he knew his refusal would cause further delay, which could have serious consequences. It was obvious that Hoover would not consider the appointing of the Rushmore Commissioners urgent business.

There was no telling when they would be able to begin, and Gutzon tried to use the time to good advantage. The San Antonio studio was filling with work that had to be finished. The North Carolina Memorial for Gettysburg was almost completed, the Wilson statue was taking form and the deadlines for the two Greenways and several lesser works were approaching. Gutzon went to work while he continued to pressure Coolidge hoping he would relent. On March 2 the president did relent and appointed the twelve-member commission. Hoover was sworn in as president March 4, and it appeared that the wait for Rushmore was almost over. Hoover had only to call the Rushmore Commission into session. After a week had passed, Gutzon wrote to Hoover:

> I take it for granted you have been too much absorbed in the initial work of what I expect to be one of the most productive administrations America has enjoyed in her existence to have come in contact with the new federal commission to take over the national memorial in South Dakota.[4]

He suggested that the president call a meeting of the commission in the White House for April 10. Hoover considered Gutzon's suggestion presumptuous. He did not enter into a debate, but showed his annoyance by putting the matter off until June 6. Gutzon took the delay as a personal affront, as it was meant to be, and further coolness developed between the two.

For Gutzon it was the first time in almost thirty years that he did not have easy access to the White House. Even Wilson, a Democrat and a political enemy, had made Gutzon welcome. He could not believe that his White House influence had evaporated, or that his many friends in Congress could not reach the president in his behalf. He had so much faith in these friends, the congressmen and senators from the Midwest states, that he convinced himself they would do more for him than they would do for Norbeck, Williamson or any other South Dakotan. Gutzon believed this so strongly that he often went to Washington without contacting Norbeck. Increasingly annoyed by this, Norbeck wrote to Robinson:

> My own opinion is that the new commission will have to be more firm with Borglum than we have been. His enthusiasm knows no bounds and his originality is marvelous. His enthusiasm is something that is needed in the undertaking, but his unwillingness to cooperate with anyone else is astonishing.[5]

Still smoldering, Norbeck complained to John Boland:

> Borglum will not consult with anyone . . . . I will have to take the matter entirely out of Borglum's hands . . . if he had let us alone we would have had a meeting of the new commission before this time . . . it is plain as day that Borglum is not satisfied to let anyone but himself handle it . . . . There will never be a Rushmore Memorial completed if Borglum is permitted to handle the business end of it. If he can be kept away from the

business management and be kept good-natured 50% of the time, you will get along all right . . . . Borglum does not mean to make trouble . . . .[6]

Finally, toward the end of May, Hoover summoned the Rushmore Commission to the White House. After the commissioners were sworn in, an executive committee was formed and John Boland was elected chairman, which made him the business manager of the project. In the evening a gala banquet was held, and Gutzon shared his dreams with the friends who had gathered to honor him. At such times Gutzon was at his best. Always charming, he could hold an audience spellbound with his unique visions of a new world.

The next day the crew was at the mountain carving on the rock, and John Boland was hard at work setting up a business system. He started by going over all the old bills that had accumulated and discovered that Tucker was owed over $20,000. The only money he had received was the funds Gutzon had personally advanced him; he had not been paid his salary in 1928 or 1929.

Tucker would have accepted partial payment and worked out a suitable arrangement for the balance, but the new commissioners decided instead to challenge his claim because no work had been done on the mountain in 1928. Tucker was shocked. He had proven his loyalty so many times in the years he had been with Gutzon that he felt betrayed. He threatened to sue if he were not paid in full and at once, and again Gutzon had to intercede.

At that time Tucker was important to Gutzon and he did not want to lose him. With Tucker on the job he could attend to his other business and know the work would proceed properly. Gutzon's other commissions required a great deal of travelling. Norbeck said that Gutzon logged over 50,000 miles in 1929. That was quite a feat, considering that commercial aviation was still in its infancy and the network of interstate highways was still a dream of visionaries like Gutzon.

Tucker was mollified for only a short time. When he began to demand his money again, Gutzon knew they would have to part. He also knew he would have to change his way of thinking and start planning to spend more time in South Dakota and on the mountain.

In early August he brought Mary and the children to South Dakota. They still owned their Connecticut estate, but it was in disrepair, and they used it only when business took them east. They also retained their quarters in San Antonio and continued to think of Texas as home. They spent their winters there, whenever possible, and remained involved in civic affairs, but with his most trusted assistants, Hugo Villa, Bill

Tallman, Bob Baillie and others, involved with the mountain, South Dakota seemed the most practical place to work. After the Greenway and Wilson statues were finished and shipped to the foundry, Gutzon did most of his major work in South Dakota.

The Wilson statue had been, personally, one of his most difficult commissions. He had known Wilson for many years, but after the aircraft investigation he had lost respect for the man. Gutzon did not want his personal feelings to be reflected in the statue but knew they would be difficult to mask. In describing the work to Mrs. Greenway, he wrote:

> The big Wilson is done . . . . He is a cold figure, static . . . a symbol of reserve and what we might call an artifical dignity; that is, the dignity that comes from leading the life of the pedagogue . . . . I have made a very sympathetic interpretation, or rather, tried to interpret him as sympathetic and as interested in the world he tried to save.[7]

Despite the many commissions and the large sums involved, the Borglums continued to be plagued by financial problems. Their style of living kept them in debt, and their situation was not helped by the way Gutzon so often put more into a commission than he received. For many years Mary kept them going by mortgaging or selling small parcels of Borgland, but the land was becoming so encumbered it could no longer serve that purpose.

Gutzon decided, in one of his characteristic bursts of enthusiasm, that South Dakota would be the place to redeem their fortune. He purchased a ranch and a large herd of cattle and became a rancher. His reasoning was sound, but his timing was horrendous. The ranch was bought just weeks before the stock market crash, which virtually wiped out the already depressed cattle and grain market.

Like so many others who had invested in properties or a business when prices were relatively high, Gutzon found himself with a new debt, with no market and the country heading for a depression. He was in deeper trouble than ever, but somehow he managed not to allow his financial situation to interfere with his ability to function.

Tucker was so unhappy that the relationship between him and Gutzon was becoming intolerable, as this letter to Norbeck indicates:

> Since writing . . . Tucker demanded all money at once . . . threatens to foul the nest we had lined with silk for him! So goes the world — today will determine or terminate him, I hope.[8]

In the same letter Gutzon expressed his pleasure with the progress that was being made on the mountain and told Norbeck how helpful he was finding John Boland. As head of the executive committee, Boland had broad authority, which he seemed to be using wisely. Gutzon was still trying to take charge of every facet of the work and still making demands for more men and equipment, but Boland was handling his requests without angering him. Gutzon praised Boland in a letter to Norbeck:

> John Boland could not be replaced — he is efficient always. More than fair — human and a loveable friend. I really do not know what I should do without him. We discuss and agree on everything.[9]

Later, Gutzon had a complete change of heart and complained that "this Boland sticks his bottlenose into everything," but in 1929 everything was fine. Part of the reason was that they were having their first good year on the carving. With the government involved, there was a new confidence in the future. The worst problems seemed to be behind them. The portrait of Washington was emerging from the stone, and the space for Jefferson was being cleared to Washington's right. At the rate they were progressing, Gutzon's estimate of five years of carving seemed conservative. The work continued until cold weather drove Gutzon and his men off the mountain. They shut down, but left everything ready so they could resume in the spring. Critics no longer doubted that the project would succeed if they managed to get enough financing.

Boland assured everyone that there was enough money left from the federal appropriation to start up again in the spring and carry through to the Washington dedication, scheduled for July 1930, but he was concerned about what would happen beyond that time. Both he and Gutzon expressed confidence that there would be enough donations to meet their need, but Boland's optimism was based on Gutzon's assurance that his wealthy friends would honor their pledges. Norbeck saw this as just more unwarranted optimism. If private contributors were going to put up the money, he reasoned, they would have done so before the federal funds were advanced. He could not believe that anyone would step forward after the work was underway, especially if that person had not been appointed to the commission. Gutzon had practically hand picked the members on the basis of their wealth, and Norbeck had gone along with his choices. With the exception of John Boland, who had been appointed to oversee the work, it was assumed that the members would be so swept up in the work that they would take it upon themselves to underwrite the project.

When the commission members showed no inclination to back the project financially, the South Dakotans felt they had been misled, but Gutzon remained optimistic. He was certain they would come through, and he was satisfied that there was enough money on hand to assure them of resuming the work in the spring.

Portrait of George Washington emerging from the rock of Mount Rushmore.

29
1930

When word spread through the Black Hills that the "Old Man," as some called Gutzon, or "the Chief," as he was known to others, was returning to Mount Rushmore, the crew headed for the mountain. To some it was just a job, and a job in 1930 was not something to take lightly, but to most it was a challenge they could not resist. They seemed to sense the special purpose of the work and were proud to be involved.

There are as many Borglum stories in the Black Hills as there are old-timers to tell them. Many have become local legends and are considered as much a part of the mountain as the carving itself. The workmen who built the studio buildings at the mountain and the ranch talk about Borglum's ability to sight a fifty-foot beam and tell whether it was off by an inch. Others talked about how many times they were fired by "the Chief" and how many times Lincoln was sent to bring them back. Everyone in the hills had an uncle, father, brother, or grandfather who supplied the Borglums, or did something for them, and never was paid. No one mentions Mary without respect or Gutzon without shaking his head.

The exploits of the Rushmore baseball team were a source of tremendous pride. They were one of the finest outfits in the state, and many of the players, especially in later years when Lincoln was doing the hiring, owed their job to their ability to play. The men talk about Monday mornings when the steps to the top seemed endless because the Saturday night dance, fueled by the local moonshiners, had not ended until Sunday.

They talked about being sent to drill above their heads, such as inside a nostril, where the rock dust fell into their eyes, whenever the "Old Man" was displeased. The legends claim that whenever a tourist asked Gutzon to pose for a photograph he would call Lincoln to his side. As he grew older Lincoln became more and more important to his father. In some ways, he was Gutzon's alter ego, just as his mother had been in the early years of her marriage.

Gutzon took every aspect of Mount Rushmore seriously. He was particularly proud of the crew's safety record. In a report to the Rushmore Commission, he said:

> . . . it may interest you to know I've never lost or injured a man in twenty years of mountain sculpture. Muscle Shoals killed 34; the Oakland Bridge to date has killed 16; Boulder Dam I don't know how many.[1]

It was not literally the truth. There were a few accidents and injuries, but Gutzon's concern for the health and safety of his men was genuine, both on a personal level and in his desire to keep his mountain free of any stigma. He tried to make the jackhammer operators wear masks to protect them from the rock dust and enforced as many safety rules as he could. He was deeply affected by the tram accident that injured five of his men, and he spent several days at the bedside of Red Sanders, the man most severely injured, until the danger was past.

Gutzon cared for his men, but he could never forget that he was "the Chief," and he seldom fraternized with them. In the bunkhouse, where the bachelors slept and ate, a table was reserved for him. He ate there alone, unless Lincoln was with him or he wanted company and asked one of the men to join him.

It was from stories like these that the legends grew, though he did not come to the Hills as a stranger. Few people had not read about him and his exploits at Stone Mountain and elsewhere, and few had not formed an opinion of the man who was coming to carve their mountain. Both Gutzon and Mary were greeted as celebrities and welcomed into the homes of the wealthy Hills residents.

Although they stayed in Keystone and then out at the ranch, the Borglums were familiar figures in Rapid City, the nearest large town. Gutzon's love for the movies brought them to town often, and they were regulars at the A & F Cafe and the dining room of the Alex Johnson Hotel, where the hot buttered rum that Gutzon favored on cold evenings was served.

Despite all the friends and acquaintances and the appearance of being popular, the Borglums felt like outsiders. This feeling was due in part to their having lived in so many places and having been uprooted so often, but it was also due to Gutzon's view of himself as a unique individual. He was a living legend with a self-created image. He had a restless need to look and think beyond the project or concept at hand and to involve himself in the world as a whole. This was true even when the project was as large and important as his mountain carving. He often expressed this in letters to friends: "I wish I had time and did not have to be an artist so much of my time. I would love nothing better than giving this nation three or four big things . . . ."[2]

His eloquence and controversial views made him popular as a public speaker. His skills as a writer gave him an open forum in major magazines and newspapers. He always had something to say, and as he entered his sixties he began to see himself as an elder statesman. He believed age and experience had sharpened his wit and tempered his judgment. His speeches became philosophical and reflective:

> There is one motive in my mind in building this super-memorial and that is the supreme accomplishments of man should be built into, cut into, the crust of this earth, so that these records would have to melt or by wind be worn to dust and blown away before the record . . . as Lincoln said, "shall perish from the earth" . . . . So much for my apology for lifting our accomplishments into the heavens and engraving there in the sun our record away from the meddling fingers of ignorance and avarice.[3]

He was speaking about Rushmore, but Gutzon was really telling his audience how he felt about his purpose in living. In this speech he also spoke about America's forefathers:

> I often wonder what these lone blazers of the trail, these giants of the earth would do now in America . . . . If they would approve of our materialism, our tradesman standards of value and consider the worth and would they approve our memorial to the founding of this nation or question if we have gone far enough to merit the record we are carving . . . .[4]

Work at the mountain resumed early in the spring. Everyone was looking forward to the July 4 dedication ceremony and the unveiling of the portrait of George Washington. Coolidge was writing the history of the United States for the entablature. He hoped to have the beginning ready for the dedication. Gutzon had chosen eight historic dates. When the first ones were ready, Coolidge sent them to Gutzon. A few weeks later Coolidge was shocked to discover that his words had been edited and then released to the papers. Coolidge was offended, probably more that he had not been consulted before the edited version was released than by the editing itself. For the first inscription, Coolidge had written:

THE DECLARATION OF INDEPENDENCE — The eternal right to seek happiness through self-government and the divine duty to defend that right at any sacrifice.

Gutzon had some philosophical problems with the concept of happiness coming "through" government, whether it was "self" or not. The altered text he passed on to reporters read:

> In the year of our Lord 1776 the people declared the eternal right to seek happiness, self-government and the divine duty to defend that right at any sacrifice.

After an argument fought in the press, Coolidge disclaimed all responsibility for the inscription and refused to submit another word. Gutzon tried, at first, to make light of the incident, but when the issue would not die he became annoyed. In a letter to his friend Senator Coleman Du Pont, he expressed his exasperation:

> I have just been having a very interesting tete-a-tete with our friend, Mr. Coolidge. First, he seeks me to write the inscription or tell him what to say; then he seeks me to improve on what he finally says. Then I remind him that HAPPINESS is a HUMAN ambition and not a political matter so obviously, that Coolidge gets peevish and tells the world I have meddled with his text. Gracious, I have written for three different presidents, which they have signed and published . . . . I am telling you this because you must get some amusement out of it . . . .[5]

Coolidge's refusal to write the balance of the history ended, for all intents and purposes, that part of the project, though it was talked about and remained a part of the master plan for several years. The final word on the incident came from Ralph Bellamy, a Rapid City lawyer. In a story Bellamy enjoyed telling, he said he was visiting Coolidge in his Northampton, Massachusetts, home when he was asked how far they were from South Dakota. When he answered, "Two thousand miles," Coolidge is supposed to have sighed and said, "Fine, that is as close as I want to be to Mr. Borglum."[6]

As the years passed, Gutzon's brothers and sisters became closer, even though they were scattered across the country. All were proud of Gutzon's accomplishments and enjoyed following his exploits in the newspapers. They kept scrapbooks and spoke often about their brother to civic clubs and fraternal orders.

Time had eased the pain of Gutzon's youth. His bad feelings had faded and his memories had become exciting adventures, except when he sat down to write his autobiography and made a conscious effort to recall the bad times. That may have been why he never finished the autobiography. He tried to remember James and Ida as loving parents, and when they passed away he had tried to take their place with his brothers and sisters.

No one appointed him head of the family, but when there was trouble or something was needed, the family turned to him, knowing he would respond. When his sister Anna was widowed, he became one of the executors of her husband's estate. When his sister Harriet's marriage failed, Gutzon travelled from Rapid City to Chicago to help her. Whether the crisis was large or small, Gutzon was there when his family needed him.

As the giant portrait of Washington emerged from the rock, Gutzon became excited over his own creation. Speaking to a national audience on the Collier's Radio Hour, he seemed almost in awe of his own achievement:

> A monument's dimensions should be determined by the importance to civilization of the events memorialized . . . . It is the greatness of the western world's adventure that gives us the subject matter for our colossal undertaking . . . . You ask how big these sculptures are? What does that matter? They are as big as the mountains and yet they are small compared to the great contribution to civilization they commemorate . . . . If they should sit in the falls [Niagara] this mighty river would only splash about their ears. If they should walk down the Hudson, they could barely creep under the great bridges . . . and when they reached the Statue of Liberty, they would have to stoop to read her dimming light . . . .[7]

July 4, 1930, was a crisp, clear, sunlit day. The crowd arrived to find a huge American flag draped over the Washington portrait. The seventy-two-foot by forty-foot flag had been sewn by Mary with the help of local women. The effect was similar to the one Gutzon had created at Stone Mountain for the dedication of General Lee and was just as impressive.

The ceremony started with a flourish. There were a twenty-one gun salute, martial music by the army band from Ft. Meade and a series of speeches. Doane Robinson, Dr. O'Harra and Joseph Cullinan, chairman of the Mt. Rushmore Commission, took their turns and were greeted warmly by the crowd, which was waiting patiently for Gutzon.

When it was his turn to speak, he seemed to sense their mood, and he did not disappoint them. Gutzon could hold an audience with any subject, but never quite the way he could when he spoke about his mountain. After he told the crowd what he hoped to accomplish and promised to have the Jefferson ready for the next dedication, he repeated what he said at the 1927 ceremony:

271

Upon Mt. Rushmore we are trying to give to the portrait of Washington all the vigor and power that direct modelling permits and produce a head in sculpture as vital as one can produce at arm's length . . . .[8]

On July 5 the work resumed, but funds were so low that after three weeks they were forced to shut down for almost a month while contributions were solicited. When enough were raised, and the government matched the amount, the crew went back to work and continued until they were forced to stop by the cold.

Gutzon felt the year on the mountain had been productive. His Washington was recognizable and, as he told the commission in his annual report, he felt the Jefferson was taking shape. It did not seem possible that a portrait would be ready for the 1931 dedication, as he promised, but that was of little consequence. It was only important that the portraits be finished.

30
1931

Early in the year, word came that the Polish government was finally ready to allow the Wilson statue to be unveiled, and the Borglums began planning their trip to Europe. Ironically, Paderewski would not be present at the dedication, nor would Gutzon be allowed to visit him. The ex-premier was under virtual house arrest on his estate and would have had to ask permission to travel or receive foreign visitors. To do either would be seen as giving tacit approval to the government in power. Paderewski could not bring himself to do that, not even for the Wilson dedication or to see Gutzon again.

The monument had been Paderewski's idea from the start. He had hired Gutzon and paid him from his own funds, but the government had made it clear that he could not participate in any way. Gutzon did not like the situation any more than he liked the decision that had forced him to alter his original design. He had made the statue with two figures: Wilson with his arm stretched protectively over a kneeling figure representing Poland. The Polish government decided the composition put Poland in a subservient position and insisted the female figure be removed. Without the kneeling figure the statue lost much of its purpose because Gutzon had modelled it as a unit and the two figures were designed compatibly. He would have protested more vehemently than he did, but he could not be certain that the government of Poland would not use his objection to bring further charges against Paderewski. So he felt compelled to comply.

The Borglums were in San Antonio for the winter. In the early spring they returned to South Dakota just long enough for Gutzon to give instructions to his crew. Then they left for Europe. There were nine in the Borglum party: Mary, Lincoln, Mary Ellis, Anna, Gutzon's sister, and four friends. They sailed from New York to Bremen, Germany, where they boarded a train for Poland. After three days in Poland, where Gutzon went over the plans for erecting the statue, they returned to Berlin for several days of touring and then went by boat to Copenhagen.

Gutzon Borglum in his San Antonio, Texas, studio working on Woodrow Wilson statue for Poznan, Poland. Statue was destroyed by Nazis after Poland was invaded.

The trip to Denmark was a wonderful, emotional journey for Gutzon. He had been thinking about the home of his ancestors all his life. He saw the visit to his homeland as a way of re-affirming his heritage and introducing his children to their roots. He often told Lincoln, Mary

Ellis, audiences and friends about the Borglum ancestry and proudly claimed he could trace his family back to ". . . 900 A.D., to Eric the Red and we probably haven't changed much . . . ."[1]

Gutzon greeted the Danes in their own language, but not in the Danish of 1931. He had learned Danish from his mother, Christina, and from James and Ida while he was growing up. He had not spoken the language for many years; as a result his phrasing was from the 1870's. The Danes were delighted with him and his way of speaking, and he became an instant celebrity.

A high point of the visit was an audience with King Christian. Anna, Mary and Gutzon were carefully briefed on what to wear, when to bow and curtsy and what to say in the presence of royalty, but when the king entered the room he acted as if he were the one who was meeting royalty. He welcomed them warmly and told Gutzon he was honored to meet the man who had created the bust of his father, which had been placed in a prominent niche in the throne room. Gutzon had produced the portrait from photographs several years before.

Anna wrote to their brother Frank to share the visit. She enclosed clippings from Danish papers and told him about their visit with the king. She expressed her pride in Gutzon for being awarded a gold cross by the king and called the whole experience "a great moment for us, one that happens once in a lifetime."[2] Everywhere they went people greeted them and invited them to celebrations and banquets planned in their honor. There were so many, she said, they almost could not stand any more, but they did enjoy the way everyone deferred to Gutzon. Then she closed her letter by telling Frank how she now understood why "Poppa and Mama used to say so many lovely things about Copenhagen."[3]

After their audience with King Christian, the Borglums took a journey into the past. They drove up the northern coast to the Borglum Kloister, a former monastery that had been the family home in the eighteenth century. The drive took them along the same roads that Gutzon's father had walked as a Mormon missionary in the 1860's. It brought back a flood of memories and made him remember the long nights on the prairie, sitting in the buggy with his father, allowing the horses to take them safely through the darkness to wherever they were going, and listening to James's stories about the Danish Borglums.

They spent a week in Denmark and then returned to Poland for the dedication. Mrs. Wilson was there along with General Pershing, Bernard Baruch and dignitaries from all over the world who had come to pay their respects. Gutzon had fought with many of the Americans present as a critic of Wilson's policies and during the aircraft investigation, but that was all in the past, at least for that one day when they were gathered to honor Wilson. Everyone present was pleased with the statue, and Wilson's admirers had nothing but praise for Gutzon and his work.

In describing the ceremony to the Omaha Press Club shortly after her return, Anna spoke about the choir singing Polish and American songs, the parade of three hundred delegates and the general air of festivity. She described the hundreds of wreaths from all over the world and the many from America that had red, white and blue flowers. A huge press corps with photographers had gathered to report on the dedication, and they were duly impressed by the finale, in which the flag was removed from the statue and five hundred pigeons released to fly to all the provinces of Poland.

The ceremony should have ended the story of the Wilson Memorial, but it did not. When Hitler came to power and began to exterminate the Jews, many people ignored the situation, but not Gutzon. Despite his anti-Semitic writings and arguments about the world's need for a solution to the "Jewish problem," he could not allow a people to be exterminated without trying to do something. It was as if somewhere deep inside himself he was hearing his old friend Dr. Isidor Singer saying: "Dear Gutzon . . . Anyone reading what you write would think you were an anti-Semite, when you are really a philo-Semite . . . ."[4]

With the first of Hitler's repressive measures, Gutzon became an outspoken, public critic of Nazi policies. He told reporters that "no civilized person could condone barbaric laws," and he vowed to fight such laws at every opportunity.[5] All through the thirties he challenged and attacked the Nazis but they did not respond. Then, just weeks after the Nazis conquered Poland in 1939, Hitler ordered the Wilson statue destroyed because ". . . The Third Reich can not tolerate such art. The artist made the legs too short, the head too large, the arms too . . . ."[6]

With the dedication over, the Borglums returned to South Dakota and the work at Rushmore. Work had progressed well in Gutzon's absence and, in his opinion, almost too well in some instances. With Gutzon away, the men were free to use as much dynamite as they wanted, which was always more than Gutzon allowed. Hardrock miners deal in tonnage. Gutzon's crew did not understand mountain carving, and they were annoyed by his caution and insistence that only small amounts of explosives be used. His concern was that enough stone would be left for carving. He was willing to use three charges where one might do. Gutzon had to be certain that when a charge was required the necessary rock would still be there.

The Jefferson, for example, had been started to the right of Washington, in an area where there was some question as to whether there was sufficient rock. Eventually, the Jefferson had to be destroyed and started again on the left side of Washington. Whether the blasting had destroyed too much of the rock or whether there had never been enough rock initially was never resolved.

This was a constant concern to Gutzon and governed every move he made on the mountain. The Roosevelt portrait was planned from the beginning, but it was not until the middle thirties that Gutzon was able to determine its location. Until the entablature was abandoned and the Lincoln was moved far to Washington's left, Gutzon worked from his three-figure model and kept the Roosevelt separate. The technicalities not only confused the public and the press, but were never fully grasped by most of his crew. As Gutzon explained:

> I put him [Lincoln] where he is to hold the men back and preserve for me by that process stone that I would need. I am not criticizing my men because I know I have the finest lot of assistants and good workmen, but they all think they are geniuses. There are at least half a dozen on the mountain that know more than I can ever hope to know about stone, the use of powder, drilling . . . . I assure you that I can not open my mouth . . . that they do not tell me precisely how each separate part of the work should be done . . . .[7]

The criticism became so intense that Senator Norbeck felt compelled to comment, to which Gutzon answered:

> Your friend [John Boland] has already . . . made the criticism . . . . I agree with you both, the closeness of composition . . . will disappear as the work develops . . . . The head of Lincoln will be set back so far behind Washington that the sun will pass back of the head and light up the face of Lincoln down as far as his upper lip. I can't tell these things to people because they wouldn't know what in the hell I meant, but I can tell it to you . . . .[8]

Mary claimed that too much dynamite had been used on the Jefferson while Gutzon was in Poland and that when he returned he discovered that not enough rock remained to finish the portrait as planned. This story is vehemently denied by many of the men involved. Bill Tallman, Gutzon's superintendent on the project for many years and a long-time studio assistant, is one of those who felt from the beginning that there was a question about whether there was sufficient rock for the Jefferson. In either case, there was an argument over the work that had been done while the Borglums were in Europe, and Hugo Villa was fired.

Tucker was gone, Villa was fired, and superintendent Denison, feeling himself as responsible as Villa, had resigned. Gutzon realized that his original plan of being at the project a few weeks at a time was not realistic. He began to build a real studio at the ranch and to think about turning it into a family home.

With the 200th anniversary of Washington's birth just a year away, Gutzon was planning a celebration that would capture national attention. Hoover and Coolidge had barely spoken to each other since Hoover secured the nomination, but Gutzon hoped to talk both of them into attending the ceremony. It was an ambitious scheme that never materialized, but even the speculation helped keep Rushmore in the news.

While the celebration was still in the planning stage, Gutzon tried to convince several Southern states to sponsor the Jefferson. He offered to make the theme a Southern show honoring the roles Washington and Jefferson had played in founding the nation, if the Southern states would raise the money to complete the Jefferson.

At the same time, Gutzon and Norbeck tried to come up with a way to force the wealthy members of the Rushmore Commission to put up the money, start a fund-raising drive or resign. When they did not respond, work on the Jefferson was stopped in the hope that they would be embarrassed enough to take action, but that did not work either.

With his salary dependent on the amount being spent on the carving, and with the ranch draining their resources, the Borglums were in more trouble than usual. The trip to Europe had put a tremendous strain on their already difficult financial situation. As usual, Gutzon had spent as if he had unlimited funds. It was not that he was extravagant, but they were meeting socialites and royalty. Even under less pretentious circumstances, he had never been able to count pennies. On their once-in-a-lifetime vacation, he wanted his family to have the best.

Gutzon's commissions involved such large sums of money that it was difficult for him to maintain a proper perspective. With each contract came the hope that they were on the verge of settling their vexing financial problems. His busts of Senator Reed of Missouri and John Bovard were ready for delivery. He was expecting a contract to create a monument to Robert Ingersoll, founder of the Free-Thinkers of

Gutzon Borglum finishing the clay model of statue of Robert Ingersoll.

America and the inventor of the dollar pocket watch, and a federal contract to install the statue in Washington, D.C., but that depended on his friends in Congress. Several thousand dollars were due him for his William Jennings Bryan. It was difficult for Gutzon to understand why he was having so much trouble.

Part of his financial problem stemmed from the fact that his original Rushmore contract was predicated on the assumption that the carving would cost $500,000 and would be completed in five years. As it turned out, he was not getting anywhere near the amount he had counted on, and much of what he did receive was put back into the project in a number of ways. He had not anticipated the need to put up money at critical times, such as when Tucker threatened to sue, or for the dozens of trips to seek backers, but he did what had to be done and that made his situation desperate.

In October he discussed his finances with John Boland. The ranch, bought with such high hopes just before the crash and then stocked with comparatively high-priced cattle, was becoming a critical problem. The former owners had a contract on the land and they were threatening to foreclose. Gutzon knew how low the Rushmore treasury was and that he could not collect what was due him, but he saw no reason why he could not be given a note to use as collateral at a bank. Boland would have liked to accommodate him, but he did not think the commission had the authority to issue notes. Some harsh words were exchanged, but Boland held his ground.

The Borglums managed to weather the storm and even find the means to help a group of desperate neighbors. The Sioux living on the nearby reservations were starving. Gutzon visited them, saw their condition and reacted. He wired President Hoover about the situation:

> I have just visited the reservation, and have become disturbed over the existing conditions . . . I feel I must communicate directly with you . . . 75% of the tribe is starving. They are marooned . . . on a vast barren area, timberless and practically gameless as considered for food, even their streams have dried up . . . .[9]

Then, afraid his plea would be ignored or lost in a bureaucratic maze, he tried to shame the president into acting by adding:

> I have, of course, been long familiar with our historic record of locating and destroying, followed by prayer, thanking God for what we had stole from the unarmed Indian, but somehow I had come to think that in our evolution, something like contentment had been developed in those we had not killed off . . . .[10]

But the situation was so critical that Gutzon could not wait for the government. He organized a local relief effort and donated his own cattle. He asked Norbeck to send six buffalo from the Custer State Park herd and obtained blankets and medical supplies from Ft. Meade. His efforts saved many lives and relieved much suffering. The Indians were so grateful that they wanted to make him a blood brother and an honorary chief.

On the day of the ceremony, the Borglums were driven to the Rosebud Reservation by their chauffeur and handyman, Charlie Johnson, in the family's twelve-cylinder touring car. A ceremonial dance and buffalo roast were to be followed by the installation of Gutzon as Chief Inyan Wanblee, Chief Stone Eagle. Gutzon was given the honor of shooting the buffalo. His first shot wounded the animal, and he bolted before Gutzon could shoot again. Charlie Johnson jumped behind the wheel of the black limousine, while Gutzon and the children scrambled into the back. They took off in pursuit, and after hours of bouncing over the dunes of the prairie caught up with their prey.

Shortly after the ceremony, Gutzon received a letter from Henry Standing Bear, leader of the Great Council of American Indians, who shared an Indian dream with him:

> I have started . . . a memorial association among my people to further the project of having an Indian head carved on the rock in the Black Hills . . . . The propriety of this idea coming from the Indians is what I am careful about in this matter . . . . I would ask all white men to be kept out of this idea and the details of the same . . . but prefer to have a conference with you on the whole project before it gets before the public. I have great things planned for this project I want to explain to you . . . .[11]

Gutzon met with Henry Standing Bear to discuss the project, but in the harsh reality of the Depression, and with Rushmore struggling for funds, both realized they could not think in terms of the present. Fortunately, Standing Bear was not a man who gave up easily. Sixteen years later he saw his dream begin to materialize when sculptor Korczak Ziolkowski went to the Black Hills and began carving a monument to Chief Crazy Horse.

The Sioux trusted Gutzon and turned to him often. In November he received a letter from Chief James H. Red Cloud:

> My Dear Brother Chief Inyan Wanblee: My people have always had a lot of faith in the Great Spirit . . . . Our hearts are made happy that you have reached out your long arm and beckoned the White Father to issue

us blankets and clothing . . . . When I told my people that we had a new friend in the Black Hills and that he was going to give us beef, they at first thought that a man with two tongues had fooled me . . . . We believe the Great Spirit has brought you to the Hills to be our friend . . . . We are a vanishing race and our bows and arrows are no longer useful. Our eyesight is dim, our muscles are stiff and we are like women . . . . This land belongs to us, and if the treaty of '68 is carried out, we will be happy and content . . . . My brother, Inyan Wanblee, if you can not get permission for us to visit Washington, won't you plead with the Great White Father to fulfill the treaty of '68?[12]

The treaty of 1868 ceded the Black Hills to the Sioux for "as long as the grass shall grow," but lasted only until 1874, when Custer discovered gold. The Indians repeatedly petitioned the "Great White Father" in Washington, asking for the return of their sacred Paha Sapa, the Black Hills, but to no avail. Whenever possible they made the journey to Washington to plead in person. They were usually welcomed by the White House, given trinkets, posed with the president and then sent home as empty-handed as they had arrived, but somehow they retained their hope and faith. They had to; it was all that sustained them.

When Chief Red Cloud wrote to Gutzon, he was desperate. His people had been suffering for too long and something had to be done. Gutzon was aware of the situation, but he knew there was no chance, under the circumstances, of getting President Hoover to listen to arguments concerning the broken treaty of 1868. The plight of the Indians was not a priority at the best of times, but especially when the country was in the grips of a depression and veterans were marching on Washington. All Gutzon could do was take the story of the Indians to his friends in Congress and quietly work with them to do everything within their power to relieve the Indians' burden.

31
1932

On February 6 Gutzon wired Senator Norbeck:

> The financial situation here with the memorial is such that I am obliged
> utterly against my personal wish or in consideration of the great injury to
> the great memorial itself to shut down the work indefinitely and take up
> the work awaiting me elsewhere . . . . Boland has done everything possi-
> ble to avoid this . . . . I have risked all I have but I must be financed at
> once or I shall have to go away.[1]

Gutzon was not angry at Norbeck. The wire was the start of another
campaign to force the Rushmore commissioners to act. Despite Gutzon's high hopes when they were appointed, they had quickly made
it clear that they felt that backing the carving financially was not their
responsibility. Gutzon was upset because he had argued for the appointment of Cullinan, Sargent, Lowden and the others primarily because
they were wealthy. He assumed they would be swept up in the concept
and see to it that enough money was available to carry on the work.
Norbeck had disagreed from the start. He argued that if the wealthy
commissioners had planned to contribute they would have done so long
before they were appointed. Gutzon countered by saying they were
waiting so they could control the use of their money. He pointed to Stone
Mountain as a valid basis for the commissioners' caution. Norbeck was
not convinced, but he conceded because he did not want the argument
to get out of hand and because he realized a commission of almost all
millionaires would lend substance in the eyes of the public.

Norbeck believed, from the very beginning, that financing would
have to come from the government. He also realized that the burden
of obtaining the financing would be his. He was well aware that with
the nation in the grips of a crippling depression, farmers suffering from
a stubborn drought and depressed markets, unemployment higher than
it had ever been, foreclosures a part of daily life and suicides a common occurrence, the financing of a mountain carving would not be a
priority for everyone.

The senator had a strong affection for Gutzon despite their heated arguments. He usually reacted to Gutzon's tirades as if he were dealing with a wayward son. He argued, chastised and then encouraged. He accepted Gutzon's criticism of South Dakotans, including himself, sent back witty or damning replies and then followed with a show of affection. No matter what the situation, he seemed capable of rising to the occasion and usually managed to restore Gutzon's perspective.

Early in 1932, when Gutzon felt compelled to threaten to walk away, Rushmore's future appeared particularly bleak. There was no money in the treasury. Gutzon, usually the last to give in, was discouraged and again demanded his pay or a note to use as bank collateral. When the demands reached Norbeck, he wired Gutzon at the ranch:

> We will get some money and do work on Rushmore this year. We have good rock and a good sculptor and a few good men in the organization so there is nothing to be discouraged about so far as the undertaking itself goes . . . . I well recognize the necessity of adjusting your personal matters to meet the situation . . . . I think you should have additional income, but you should continue to live at the ranch . . . .[2]

Gutzon reacted the way Norbeck knew he would. The next day he wired the senator:

> Hell! . . . I'm the only one who must go on. I'm chained like Prometheus to the mountain. I've got to spend my last dollar no matter where I have gotten it to see that Rushmore is finished and a great success . . . .[3]

Norbeck's advice that he "continue to live at the ranch" was his way of acknowledging that he realized Gutzon was desperate. Gutzon accepted what Norbeck said, even though he was being refused, because he knew there was little he could do to force the issue. In August, when he repeated his plea for relief and was again turned down, he became philosophical:

> There will be money for the shovel but none for the engineer . . . . It has always been so. I invented the idea of mountain sculpture; I dreamed Stone Mountain . . . I had paid out of my own pocket $130,000, borrowed some of it, which I still owe . . . . They gave my successor $150,000 simply for the models, wrecked my work and buildings, wore out my machinery and wasted all the money and failed — and now ask me to come back without a dollar in the bank. I have obligations in South Dakota I must meet or fail and I'll never do that, even if I've got to let Rushmore go and stay east, where I can get work . . . . What a joke it all is! I'm not blaming a soul on earth for this and that makes it sadder, for it is one of the fundamental

wrongs of civilization that individuals cannot correct and the mob won't understand, because they can't.[4]

Gutzon's depression frequently resulted from his belief that he was misunderstood. The wealthy thought only about their money and making more money. They could not understand the scope of his thinking or what he was offering them in terms of being remembered by posterity. But the mood never lasted long. It would pass with the next thought because there was always hope and the next day's battle. With the public it was different. The "mob" did not or could not appreciate what he was doing. Unless he could talk to them, they greeted most of his efforts with indifference, and for Gutzon indifference was the most difficult, distressing, debilitating emotion of them all.

The Rushmore commissioners' refusal to provide funds continued to embarrass Gutzon. When all his efforts to force them to act failed, he started his campaign to get rid of them so the president could appoint a new commission that would be more cooperative. He made his plans known to Senator Norbeck and then explained his feelings in a letter to John Boland:

> Because of the disastrous and humiliating prospect of shutting down the work this year . . . through failure to provide funds, I am giving you a brief report of my major efforts . . . . I know Mr. Baruch . . . he declined because we have placed Roosevelt instead of Wilson . . . . I got in touch with Mr. Eastman . . . his available funds were all committed. I know Henry Ford, but he is utterly indifferent to matters of this sort . . . this is a national project . . . it deserves the dignity of being handled as a national matter by an all-commission plan . . . . I am, my dear Mr. Boland, making this report because . . . I shall not attend the meeting [of the Rushmore Commission] in Chicago . . . I cannot help you in Chicago; the commission must solve the matter.[5]

Gutzon was increasing the pressure, trying to force them to act or resign. The members were serving at the pleasure of the president. Gutzon assumed that if the commissioners resigned he would be allowed to pick their successors. He had written to Boland, instead of Cullinan or one of the others, because Boland was the head of the executive committee and one of the few members he hoped to retain.

As the 1932 presidential conventions approached, everyone's attention turned to politics and the upcoming race. Roosevelt went into the 1932 convention with little opposition and won the nomination on an early ballot when John Garner of Texas traded his block of Southern votes for the vice-presidential nomination. In his acceptance speech,

Roosevelt told his fellow Democrats that they were about to get a "New Deal" in government. Then he launched a campaign that was carefully planned to avoid controversy.

He realized that Hoover could not defend policies that were obviously not working or propose radical new solutions without explaining why he had not instituted them sooner. All the president could do was to ask for more time and hope Roosevelt would blunder. Roosevelt was too astute a politician, however, to do so. He had watched Hoover defeat Smith in 1928 by ignoring him and had learned his lesson well. He confined himself to telling voters, in the most general terms, what he would do after he was elected. Furthermore, he projected a sense of confidence that lifted the spirit of the nation.

It was not a good time to be a loyal Republican, who had to defend the aimless policies of the Hoover administration. For less than totally committed Republicans, such as Gutzon, the situation was particularly distressing. Besides being a maverick from his days with Teddy Roosevelt, he personally disliked Hoover. In a letter to Senator Howell of Nebraska, he wrote:

> I have been trying to swallow Hoover and I got him down until he reached my soul and then he got crosswise and could go no further . . . .[6]

Gutzon delayed as long as he could to announce his support of Roosevelt:

> I have received a number of earnest messages from friends and enemies, questioning . . . why I . . . will support a Democrat . . . a Republican or Democrat, if he has any mind or conviction . . . and not because some party boss holds the club of party interest over him . . . a man who thinks the trouble in Sioux City, Iowa, or the naked unemployment in Washington needs help and consideration not tanks, sabers and bayonets, who thinks the whole nation and not only Wall Street interests needs his unprejudiced care. I believe FDR has that kind of mind, that kind of character . . . . Never in the republic's history has it been so completely abandoned to its fate with the financial leaders and an entrenched political machine as the past 13 years of Republican mis-rule . . . . I am 100% for this man. He is openly, vigorously for the small home owner, for the farmer, for the forgotten man . . . . We have in FDR a man who I believe will help the forgotten citizen . . . .[7]

Once he declared himself, Gutzon became an active campaigner. He made several speeches supporting Democratic candidates and created a campaign button for Roosevelt and Garner.

From Rushmore's standpoint, the election was crucial. With Hoover's never being a strong supporter of the project and Gutzon's backing of FDR, a Hoover victory very likely would have ended the work. As it was, the carving on the mountain stopped during the campaign for lack of funds and the inability of the commission to change the situation.

Hoover had given the voters a glimpse of what the government might be able to do to ease the impact of the Depression. With his backing Congress had passed a bill forming the Reconstruction Finance Corporation (RFC). The RFC's purpose was to make funds available to the states for various work projects. After four years of adamantly refusing to authorize any programs that would create jobs, Hoover changed his position, but it turned out to be too little and too late. In view of the magnitude of the problem, the RFC was little more than a token gesture. Unemployment had reached a staggering 12,000,000 people. It would have required several times the $300,000,000 in the RFC treasury to have any impact.

Most South Dakotans were wary of the RFC. It was not a grant program, but borrowing against future tax payments went against the grain of most South Dakotans. Only after they realized that they would have to pay the taxes whether they used RFC money or not did the people agree to accept their share.

Norbeck and Gutzon took a different view of the RFC. They saw it as a chance to get the work on the mountain started again. If they could convince RFC officials that the mountain carving and the roads leading to the project qualified, work could resume. They also hoped that the government might feel they had so much invested that it would be better to make the project a national work that should be federally funded. They started a campaign to convince first the South Dakotans and then the RFC officials. They were successful, and in September the work resumed.

The voters rejected Hoover by a wider margin than they had elected him in 1928, but Roosevelt would not be sworn in until March 1933. Little could be expected from a defeated and bitter president. Hoover remained in the White House while newspapers filled with stories of how the nation would change under Roosevelt. But in the interim the Depression deepened, and the plight of the people became more desperate.

The work at Rushmore continued into the late fall and then was halted by the Rushmore commissioners, despite Gutzon's vehement objections. They argued that it would be better to stop while there was still money in the treasury to resume in 1933, while Gutzon felt the money should be used and more found for the following year. Unhappy about the situation, Gutzon wrote Norbeck in December:

> I am leaving here indefinitely, the work is shut down . . . entirely against my wishes, but my wishes are not of much consequence in the direction of the work.[8]

Norbeck, however, was in good spirits. He felt they had turned a corner and quickly wrote Gutzon:

> Cheer up about Rushmore! Remember we have money . . . to work through every good day . . . in 1933. We never were so fortunate . . . . A little delay will not hurt . . . the undertaking . . . . I hope that with the coming of . . . spring it will be convenient for you to go ahead with the work . . . .[9]

32

1933

It was a pleasant walk from the Brackenridge Park studio in San Antonio to the Menger Hotel downtown. The Borglums walked between the two often, usually at a brisk pace set by Gutzon. As with almost everything else about him, his walk had vigor and purpose, but that presented no problem to the family. They all learned to adjust to his stride. They had to or risk being left behind.

Life was changing rapidly for all the Borglums. Mary Ellis was growing up and preparing to leave for a New York boarding school, while twenty-year-old Lincoln was trying to decide about his future. He had his dreams, but he was not certain he could actually make a life for himself away from his father and his father's interests.

Gutzon made it very plain that he not only wanted him nearby, but needed him and wanted him to be a part of all his projects. Mary recognized the closeness as a potential problem. She did not want to influence her son, but in a letter to Mary Ellis she expressed her concern: ". . . Dad hopes he will become his assistant. It would be nice if he wants to . . . ."[1] But she knew the decision would be based primarily on how Lincoln perceived his father's need. Lincoln deferred to Gutzon in all things and seldom revealed his own feelings. In another letter to her daughter, Mary mentioned a party Lincoln wanted to attend, but might not be able to because he was driving his father somewhere that day. "Of course," she wrote, "he would never mention to his father he wanted to. The other day he sprained his arm in the studio and never said a word about it until I noticed he was holding it queerly."[2]

Mary was worried about more than just her son's future. At times she felt the need to be all things to the family. The burden of keeping their finances in a manageable state while helping her children realize their ambitions as they began to go their separate ways would have been difficult under any circumstances. It was especially so, however, in light of her absolute belief that Gutzon was one of the world's truly gifted men and her total devotion to him. She travelled with him whenever possible, she fought his battles, dealt with their creditors and tried to balance Gutzon's needs and their children's needs whenever there was a conflict. When Mary Ellis complained about being in a boarding school and said she would rather go to a public school and live at home the following year, Mary had answered:

> And unless I definitely gave up trying to fit my plans to Dad's (which I will do if it means you not going to school) it will be hard for us to be in one place long enough to follow any line of study in a day school . . . .[3]

What was worrying Mary most were the changes in Gutzon, who was nearing sixty six years of age. While he still looked as vigorous as ever and seemed more than willing to take on the world, his health was beginning to fail. Walking with Mary Ellis from the studio to the hotel one evening, he stopped to catch his breath and told his daughter, "I can't walk that fast anymore."[4] His heart, he said, was not what it had been, and the doctor had ordered him to slow down.

But, despite the doctor's orders, there was no sign of any slowdown in his activities. In February he wrote Francis Case to report on his numerous involvements:

> I am up to my ears in new work and after three or four years of urging and much public speaking Texas has adopted my plan for her great highways . . . . I am working on the road . . . plan together with a memorial at the Alamo and one at San Jacinto . . . . I have been hammering at the Department of the Interior to get some clothing for our squaws who are very badly in need of it in the Sioux reservations . . . .[5]

Gutzon was putting the finishing touches on his statue of William Jennings Bryan, which was to be dedicated in Washington, D.C., in August. He was also working on the statue of Robert Ingersoll, commissioned by the Free-Thinkers of America and authorized by Congress, a memorial honoring General Pershing for Nebraska, and models of Rushmore and his new design for Stone Mountain, which was to be displayed at the Chicago World's Fair.

The Stone Mountain model was particularly important from Gutzon's standpoint. With the work on the Southern memorial stopped and everyone concerned embarrassed by the disfigured stone that remained, there was a genuine, if unrealistic, effort being made to re-activate the project. Under the plan, Gutzon was to be the sculptor, but with his work blown off the mountain and Lukeman's design poorly conceived, the problems were too difficult to overcome.

That, of course, did not prevent Gutzon from dreaming. He devised a scheme whereby he would re-carve on a different part of the stone while Lukeman, or another sculptor, completed the Lukeman design. He hoped his model in Chicago would stimulate enough interest to force the federal government to back the Southern project. With government support, Gutzon planned to have Lincoln supervise the Stone Mountain work while he completed the project at Mount Rushmore by his target date of 1935. In 1933 and 1934 he expected to complete the figures of Washington and Jefferson, rough out the Lincoln, find the space for Roosevelt, prepare the rock for the entablature and carve the first inscription.

It was an ambitious schedule, considering that in the previous five years Jefferson had been blocked in, but only the portrait of Washington was showing real progress. The delays were not his fault. With enough money, he could easily have met his schedule, but without ample funds he could not, and he had no basis for believing money would suddenly be available.

As he waited for the Rushmore season to begin in the spring, Gutzon thought more and more about Texas. He was proud to chair the State Highway Commission and assumed his appointment meant he was finally going to get the recognition he needed to turn some of his Texas dreams into realities. The Corpus Christi waterfront project had been defeated by the voters, and all his other projects had been side-tracked, rejected outright or awarded to others. A lesser man might have given up, but with the Texas centennial only a few years away and new plans for San Antonio on his drawing board, Gutzon's hopes were running high again. He did not realize that his appointment to the highway commission had been made only because the Texans recognized his ability to work with Washington bureaucrats and that they were not obligated to him in any other way.

In late March work started at Mount Rushmore. In April John Boland reported to Senator Norbeck:

> We have been working at Rushmore about one month and we have been making splendid progress . . . . Mr. Borglum is still in San Antonio . . . I am sure the same progress is being made as if he were here, (maybe more) . . . .[6]

The friendship between Boland and Gutzon was deteriorating rapidly. At the beginning they had been very close. Gutzon had called Boland "the one indispensible man," but with Boland's keeping a tight grip on the purse strings, it was inevitable that they would clash.

There seemed no way Gutzon could escape from his money problems and no way he could prevent them from affecting his relationship
with others. When the Rhoades brothers tried to call their note on Gutzon's ranch, he went to Boland for the $3,200 necessary to save the pro-
perty, and then unhappily went elsewhere. As Boland explained to
Norbeck:

> When Mr. Borglum called me . . . I explained . . . that it was impossible
> for the Commission to make him the $3,200 advance . . . he endeavored
> to say all the mean things he could, but I made no reply . . . . I suggested
> I could let him have $500, he stated that was a "peanut" arrangement . . . .
> I offered to intercede with Rhoades . . . but he did not seem to want me
> to . . . . I think I will talk to Rhoades anyway.[7]

Evidently, the Rhoades' threat of foreclosure was an attempt to
increase the pressure on Gutzon, but not a serious attempt to take back
the land. With the nation in the grip of a depression, it would have
been foolish to repossess land being paid for, no matter how slowly.
Bank foreclosures were common occurrences because banks were
restricted by rules and regulations and too ponderous to react quickly
to unusual situations. Individuals, however, could be pressured. Unless
the creditors were foolish, they usually threatened and then backed off
and held their notes until they felt it was time to pressure again. Gutzon's creditors threatened, and it affected his relationship with both
Boland and Norbeck. Gutzon was being hounded and not helped by
the South Dakotans. Feeling a growing sense of isolation, he began to
imagine a plot against himself involving Norbeck. In the notes he was
keeping for his autobiography, he wrote that the reason he had fired
Hugo Villa was Villa's "growing, confidential intimacy with Boland."
He recalled that, after he had fired his assistant, Boland visited Villa
in San Antonio to offer him "the sculpture work on the mountain — and
assured they would get rid of me — the plot was hatched between
Bellamy, Boland, Williamson and Norbeck."[8]
There seemed no basis for such a charge, and Gutzon could not
have seriously believed there was unless he was re-living the events of
Stone Mountain and thinking of how Tucker had been offered the work
there. As with so many other situations that disconcerted him, Gutzon
had a tendency to over-dramatize. In this case, he must have been allowing himself a moment of self-indulgence, for if he did believe what he
had written he could not have continued with the work.
Gutzon, Boland and Norbeck needed each other if Rushmore was
to succeed. When their tempers flared, as they so often did, they had

to talk out their differences. This did not always work, as Gutzon indicated when he wrote to Norbeck in September, but they had to try:

> I wish there was some way the hour you spent in my studio yesterday with Williamson and Boland could be rubbed out and your unjust attack and expressed misunderstanding and unappreciation of actual conditions, actual accomplishments and real responsibility had never been expressed . . . . You have hurt unjustly a friendship this work will fail without . . . . This letter is written for one reason. I am sick over the chronic incompetence that has settled over this great work, while I struggle on unsupported . . . . There is no real trouble here. We have, in spite of stupid penurious practices, non-feasance of a political commission produced something excelling all other monuments, Egyptian or Greek. The sculptor has done this in spite of conditions . . . .[9]

Norbeck sensed from Gutzon's letter that Gutzon was being pushed too far:

> You are right in one thing. I should not get tempery when I speak to people . . . I will apologize when I see you. I have committed many of these sins since my nervous breakdown . . . there is only one important difference in the viewpoint between you and me. I have never believed and I do not believe now, that you can do everything at Rushmore — both be board and sculptor. It has been drifting that way. There is room for difference of opinion . . . but I think one of the causes has been a feeling . . ."Let Borglum do it." I am trying to put a stop to that . . . . The sculptor cannot do it all . . . .[10]

That was the crux of the argument. No one understood the work the way Gutzon did, and he could not remain silent on anything that concerned even the smalled detail. With a weakened heart, with other chronic problems causing physical discomfort and requiring periodic visits to Hot Springs for the mineral baths, with the constant need to travel and his continual financial difficulties, it was hard for him to maintain his perspective.

He felt used and unappreciated, as he remarked in this letter to Norbeck:

> There isn't anything in all this, Senator, but local failure for me; utter indifference as far as appreciation or living compensation is concerned, as coming from the work or those responsible here are concerned. If I need a dollar I may get a quarter, but I mustn't forget, it is a personal favor, a loan. I'm in great need this moment. Up here, nowhere to turn, not a soul. I've no business as business to remain an hour. Why don't I go? I'm certainly not staying because of any help, appreciation or support . . . .[11]

293

Again Norbeck offered his sympathy. "I do recognize," he wrote, "that you cannot have a lot of business worries . . . and be at your best in your art work."[12]

In August Gutzon travelled east for the dedication of his statue honoring William Jennings Bryan. President Roosevelt and Secretary of the Interior Harold Ickes were the main speakers on this festive occasion. When Gutzon left Washington, he went on a lecture tour that kept him away from Rushmore until late fall. The lectures were lucrative, and he needed the money desperately enough to convince himself that his team at the mountain was good enough not to need him on a daily basis. Despite his personal feelings about plots and intrigues, he knew that Boland and Norbeck were a part of that team.

With Roosevelt and the New Dealers altering the concepts of government, Gutzon understood the difficulty of Norbeck's position as the Rushmore representative in Washington. Nothing was sacred, least of all a mountain carving in South Dakota. When an executive order placed the Rushmore Commission under the jurisdiction of the Department of the Interior, Norbeck questioned the order, fought hard and won the right to set the guidelines. When the carving was about to run out of funds, Norbeck went back into battle and pressured the House Appropriations Committee into matching the RFC funds under the provisions of the original Rushmore legislation. Then he laid the groundwork for a direct appropriation. Norbeck knew that he had no chance of gaining approval for his plan in 1933, but he was astute enough to realize that not winning in 1933 would help his chances in 1934.

The year ended on a comparatively high note. Closing down the work at the end of the season, Gutzon wrote Norbeck:

> We should begin on schedule April first. We may not be able to on account of the weather, but plan for April first and be ready . . . . Seven months, with my driller force and carvers doubled, will, in 1934, finish Jefferson and Lincoln, leaving 1935 to finish Roosevelt and cleaning up, besides preparing the panel for the inscription . . . in 1936 . . . .[13]

33
1934

Senator Norbeck was ill. He was in a hospital in Rochester, Minnesota, undergoing a series of operations to stop the throat cancer that was threatening his life. It was a painful, difficult time for him. A brave man, he tried to remain actively involved but he could not escape the reality of his situation. "The sore in my mouth hurts so it is hard to dictate," he wrote John Boland, his closest friend.[1]

As his condition worsened, Norbeck lost his sense of humor and the perspective that had enabled him to keep Rushmore going during the project's most difficult times. He became particularly impatient with Gutzon, who was trying to avoid a fight with the senator while increasing his attacks on Boland.

The problem, as always, was money. The 1933 season had ended with a few thousand dollars left in the treasury. There was enough to start the 1934 season but not enough to finance the full year, and Gutzon did not relish the thought of starting and stopping, as he had been forced to do so often.

The model of Rushmore, exhibited at the Chicago World's Fair, had received a great deal of attention, and Gutzon thought that the publicity could be used to good advantage. He spent the early part of the year travelling between Washington and Chicago, where the Hearst papers were helping him launch a publicity campaign. Norbeck and Boland felt little would come of the effort, and they complained to each other while conceding that they knew of no better alternative. Writing to Norbeck, Boland commented, "He wants flattery and no action and I fear that is all he or Rushmore will receive from the Hearst publicity."[2]

The entablature was another source of controversy. Gutzon still wanted to include it in the monument. When he announced that it would be worked on in 1934, Norbeck became upset and complained to Boland:

> . . . the federal law provides that the inscription shall be written by Calvin Coolidge — instead of his helping Borglum . . . . I wired Borglum at Washington once last fall to please read the federal law on Rushmore so

Lincoln is beginning to emerge from rock while crew is still trying to locate enough solid stone for Roosevelt portrait.

I can't wire the same thing again . . . . Above all things I wish to play fair with Coolidge, who made the memorial possible. I don't want to betray him just because he is dead . . . .[3]

Gutzon had assumed that, with Coolidge's death in 1933, the stipulation that Coolidge write the inscription no longer applied, but Norbeck

296

felt the law was the law until it was changed. The argument continued until the idea of the historical entablature was dropped.

The only matter they all seemed to be able to agree on was their desperate need for money. The matching funds bill was still in effect. There was more than $100,000 that could be drawn against, but only if they could find a way to raise an equal amount privately. Everyone concerned, with the possible exception of Gutzon, felt anyone who wanted to contribute had done so already and that any new drive would be doomed to failure. It was finally decided that Norbeck would attempt to get Congress to release the $100,000 against future contributions. The plan seemed valid because the Black Hills-based Homestake Gold Mine seemed willing to make a substantial contribution if enough progress were made on the carving. There was hope of securing their pledge for $100,000 if they could be assured that that amount would finish the project.

Boland and Norbeck discussed their strategy often. Norbeck felt guardedly optimistic about the government's going along with the advance, but it was not shared by Boland. In late January Boland wrote the senator:

> Since you left I have been thinking a great deal about our $100,000 application. I feel quite confident that you can secure this money if it were not for one thing and that thing is *Borglum* . . . as you know he has many enemies and if some person connected with the Public Works Administration who dislikes Borglum should learn that he receives 25% . . . I fear that he would oppose the granting of our application.[4]

Gutzon was not privy to the Boland-Norbeck exchanges, but they would not have deterred him. Most important, he was feeling confident about his mountain carving. He continued to make the same complaints he had been making from the beginning. He felt he was not being supported properly, not being paid as he should and that Boland and some of the other commissioners were interfering in matters they did not understand.

Gutzon would voice his complaints, but his next letter would be filled with conciliatory remarks and good humor. It was a pattern Gutzon had developed to see them through — and probably it would have if Senator Norbeck's illness had not changed him. He wrote to Gutzon, in a most uncharacteristic way, complaining about a long list of perceived affronts and grievances and threatening to quit the commission. Gutzon reacted quickly:

Now, you can read this, Senator, in any way you like . . . . I don't intend to promise . . . to always agree with you . . . . I know my business, and I know it better than anyone else knows it. I know what I should do out here for the nation, for history, for the particular job itself in spite of the indifferent, uninformed men that are blocking the way and hindering us . . . . If you and I can't be frank with each other without being angry or quitting, the whole thing will have to be carried out in struggles when it should be carried out in friendship . . . . One more word. You and I were chiefly responsible for this mountain child, and you have as much right to desert it as I have, and not a particle more.[5]

But Norbeck was too deeply disturbed and too ill to be easily placated:

Being you are not satisfied with my decision to withdraw from the commission I might give you the further reason that I have lately come to feel that you will do something that will prevent the completion of Rushmore. I would not be surprised any morning to find a statement in the papers that Rushmore has become impossible because of interference from the politicians. The public will enjoy such a statement from you. You will enjoy the public's reaction to your statement . . . . I have made over seven years of effort in this work. It has been a heavy drain on my strength and purse. It keeps getting worse. Your letter made me sick and I am trying to get well . . . . You have to change your ways or Rushmore will never be completed . . . .[6]

Then, in April, while they were still working to obtain the balance of the appropriation from Congress, Norbeck and Boland felt they had reason for a new concern. Stone Mountain talk had started again and they believed it was serious. In a note to Boland, Norbeck said, ". . . I believe Mr. Borglum will spend three-quarters of the time at Stone Mountain this summer . . . ,"[7] but a week later, after the threat disappeared, he wrote with obvious relief, "I think the Stone Mountain deal is a flop. I think Borglum realized he is out of a job unless he can do something on Rushmore this year . . . ."[8]

On June 26 the government released the $100,000, and funding for the monument was assured for 1934 and 1935. Pleased with the victory, Norbeck gave much of the credit for successfully pushing the legislation to Isabella Greenway, Gutzon's good friend and the widow of General John Greenway. She was serving her first term in the House as the Representative from Arizona, and President Roosevelt had appointed her to fill a vacancy on the Rushmore Commission.

Norbeck wrote to another close friend of Gutzon's, Lorine Spoonts of Corpus Christi, who was also a Roosevelt appointee to the commission, reiterating his concerns about Gutzon: "You have knowledge of

my admiration for Mr. Borglum so there is no use arguing about that."
Then he listed all his complaints and told her unless they were firm with
Gutzon they would have a "Stone Mountain blow-up."[9] Norbeck add-
ed that he had warned Gutzon that unless he began to work with the
commission harmoniously he was going to resign, which seemed to please
Gutzon.

It is difficult to understand Norbeck's fears, unless one assumes that
his illness was affecting his judgment. Despite the rhetoric, Gutzon had
proven time and time again that he would do anything to make sure
the carving was completed. No one with any knowledge of the project
should have doubted that.

With the money for the season assured, the war of words stopped,
at least for the time being, and Gutzon was able to concentrate on the
carving. He had his men blow off the Jefferson that had been abandoned and start a new Jefferson on Washington's right. That immediately
changed the appearance of the Washington portrait, which seemed to
move forward and take on a new prominence.

The work proceeded swiftly. Gutzon had Lincoln working with
him, which eased his burden considerably. He began giving serious
thought, once again, to writing his autobiography; he started the book,
but he could never find enough time to give it the thought it required.
Plans for the Texas centennial celebration were moving swiftly, and
Gutzon was lobbying in Washington for funding for several Texas projects. His lecture series was more popular than ever, and he had as many
bookings as he was willing to accept.

Gutzon was concerned with all facets of life. Politically, Gutzon
was still a strong supporter of FDR, but he had deep concerns about
the "Brain Trust" that was guiding the administration and making policy.
He saw a tremendous opportunity to teach values to America's youth,
but thought it was being lost because of improper guidance. To make
his point, he wrote to Aubrey Williams, Director of the Youth
Administration:

> I am not religiously orthodox, but all there is of God in creation is what
> man has in lonely martyrdom wrung from nowhere and everywhere, and
> it has been his consciousness of that that makes him master of the world,
> and not business or money . . . . Have we in gold — the worship of Aaron's
> calf — made our final bow in the hall of world fame, to be remembered with
> Rome for our abuse of wealth? . . . . Have we reached the life line's end
> of the little republic they shaped for us, have we wholly forgotten that what
> we are is something quite outside our business and our bellies, and that

Gutzon Borglum

Sculptor-Orator-Statesman

Poster used to promote speaking engagements.

something in our minds and what there is in our hearts is of real importance? . . . you . . . have it in your hands to give young Americans a chance for heart and soul growth which she has never had . . . .[10]

Aviation remained a passionate interest, as he kept abreast of the latest developments. He was an outspoken critic of the industry and was particularly critical of the seeming lack of interest in developing a safer airplane. He wrote to the president of the United Air Lines:

> I think you must admit the airplane today is not as safe as it was when Orville Wright flew it, and that we have done nothing . . . that can be called constructive common sense development of the plane that could make it something besides a high-powered glider . . . . Nothing will keep the human out of the air . . . there are two things that are killing people — one is the utter stupidity of aeronautical engineers to be satisfied with what Mr. Wright gave us, and the gas engine . . . .[11]

Gutzon wanted to contribute. When he heard that the Roosevelt Administration planned to create a Federal Aviation Commission, he tried to get himself appointed as a commissioner. He wrote to Jim Farley, an aide of FDR's, to say, "I should, of course, prize very highly an opportunity to aid in the development of this branch of our national life . . . ."[12] In a letter to the chairman of the Democratic Party, he predicted, "America and Russia are certain eventually to become the dominating factors in the air in the world, both because of their vast resources . . . ."[13]

But the role Gutzon enjoyed most was sharing his big dreams with the public. Every time he stepped off a train he found a reporter or two waiting on the platform, and the next day local papers would announce, "Borglum in Our City," or "Creator of Mount Rushmore to Speak." The stories were usually accompanied by a photograph of Gutzon, one chosen for dramatic effect. His scraggly mustache and his piercing eyes looking directly into the camera became well known and made the public fill the lecture halls knowing he would not disappoint them.

In Chicago he became a strong advocate for a proposed lakefront airport. Speaking before the Chicago Association of Commerce, he told his audience:

> You men of Chicago can do anything you want here. Why do you let somebody stop you from building a great airport out here by the lake? I came in from New York and it took me as long to get in from the outskirts of Chicago as it did to fly in from Detroit . . . Make it beautiful, and every man that lands there will say, "Have you seen the airport in Chicago? It is wonderful."[14]

The effect of Gutzon's enthusiastic support for the idea was apparent six months later when Chicago's Board of Aldermen voted for the project by a forty-to-two majority.

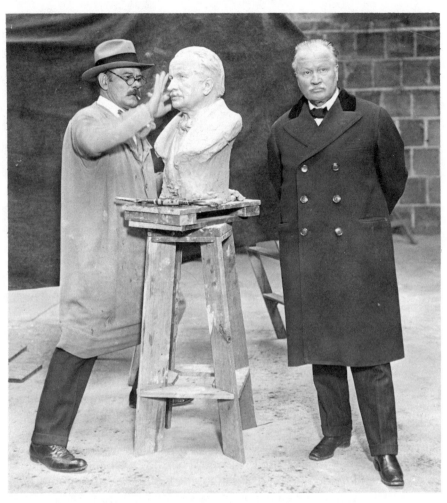

Gutzon Borglum modeling portrait of Pawnee Bill.

Despite the big thoughts and national projects, the Borglums were
struggling to keep themselves together as a unit. The family thrived on
closeness. When they were unable to be with each other, they felt the
separation keenly. Mary Ellis was staying in Stamford while the rest
of the family were in South Dakota because she was attending an Eastern
school. To keep in touch with her, Gutzon would write frequently. He
always shared a special relationship with his daughter. She was his little princess, and he always had a story to cheer her up.

Mary's letter to her daughter portrayed the harsher side of home life. Mary described, for example, a range war with a neighbor and said their foreman had been run off at gunpoint. She often discussed the scarcity of funds and mentioned that part of their income was coming from the sale of small busts of the Rushmore presidents. "I have almost filled all the orders by dint of a great deal of nagging of your father. He gets so mad at me," she wrote.[15] Yet Mary Ellis was very close to her mother. She loved her dearly and described her as a woman who "never raised her voice, but never failed to get anything she went after."[16]

Lincoln had his dreams, but they were not strong enough to counter his father's wishes or needs. At times Lincoln rebelled. He enrolled in college and then announced he would be attending in the fall. When the beginning of the semester passed and he remained on the mountain, Mary became puzzled and concerned. She wrote to Mary Ellis to ask, "has your brother said anything about not going to college?"[17] For some reason Mary felt that she could not ask him herself, perhaps because she had taught both her children by example, if not with words, that their father's needs were paramount to everything else. Gutzon was aware of his son's plans, but he believed Lincoln had a brighter future with him. As far as he was concerned, they were a team.

Gutzon worried more about Mary Ellis and what she would do with her life. He saw her as a young woman with a world of choices, but not necessarily with the ability to choose the right one. Unable to influence her on a day-to-day basis, he sought other ways. When he learned that she had a boyfriend, he offered some fatherly advice, laced with his personal view of women:

My dear Baby, seventeen or less and well launched on the field of romance . . . . Personally my dear and ever dearer girl I don't think you know anything about real love . . . . I have seen no man courting you I thought measured up to my Mary Ellis in mind — energy — charm — or the qualities that go to make great womanhood . . . . I wish some ways you'd been a boy. You have the courage, the surprise and charm that makes way in the world for a man. These qualities belong as naturally to a great woman but women have cultivated the role of following and somewhat like it, but there is a bigger, greater place and service for women when they have greatness, and you have . . . .[18]

All through the season of 1934, work on Rushmore continued at a steady pace. The crew was still carving as Thanksgiving approached, and Gutzon was pleased with his crew and the progress that was being made. He had learned how to get the best out of his hardrock miners.

He would sometimes lose his temper and fire a man, then cool down quickly and send Lincoln to bring the man back. Gutzon made it his business to learn about each man and his family, showed a genuine concern for their problems and helped when they needed a hand. Gutzon was always trying to find a way to do something special for his workers. He wrote to Senator Norbeck early in November to ask for permission to shoot three Custer State Park elks to divide among his men on Thanksgiving. In the same letter, Gutzon expressed his pride in the work his men were accomplishing:

> Mr. Boland visits about once every week . . . he is the only commissioner who keeps in touch with the actual mechanics of creating the great memorial . . . . I am very proud of what we have done with a group of about forty men, utterly unfamiliar with this work, and what can be accomplished with the right kind of guidance . . . .[19]

Despite Gutzon's kind words for Boland, Norbeck felt he was attacking the commission. In his reply to Gutzon, Norbeck defended the commission:

> As to Rushmore . . . the law imposes certain duties and obligations on the board, but you have always attempted to take these over and left nothing for the board, which I believe is the reason you have no active board today. Why should they hang around if there is nothing for them to do except praise the sculptor? This I am willing to do, but I can do it by mail. Now as to the elk . . . I have no authority to do it.[20]

Norbeck's comments reflected, in part, his frustration at being a Republican in a Democratic Senate and his frustration over his failing health. Rushmore affairs were becoming too much for him. Gutzon had kind words for Boland, but he refused to attend the year-end meeting of the commission in Chicago. Norbeck was convinced his failure to appear would hurt the carving. They still had $55,000 due them from the matching fund legislation, but the attempt to match the $100,000 advanced early in the year had failed when Homestake changed its mind about contributing. Norbeck was also concerned about the legality of paying Gutzon's percentage out of the last government appropriation. By the terms of the original agreement, he was to be paid his percentage in direct proportion to the amount of work completed until he received the full $87,000 or the work was finished. The figure was based on the estimate of a $500,000 cost and five years of carving. When the project exceeded both the cost and time estimates, Norbeck became concerned about a Senate challenge. He wanted Gutzon to attend the Chicago meeting so they could discuss the situation.

Norbeck had a plan, but he seemed hesitant to proceed because he had strong reservations about a number of things. He did not like the Lincoln model that Gutzon had proposed:

> I have been trying to get used to your re-modeled Lincoln, but I just can not. I am thinking that maybe it reflects your state of mind, and the problems and annoyances you have had this last year . . . .[21]

Norbeck was preparing to suggest that perhaps they should settle for less of a monument than originally planned:

> I do believe, however, that the completed figures of Washington and Jefferson will make a most impressive memorial, even though it is going to be a great disappointment . . . if the work cannot be continued . . . .[22]

The senator then made his final point: that without a strong commission receiving the full cooperation of the sculptor he was concerned that the work would not be finished. Gutzon took only half a page to answer the senator's five-page letter:

> I am in receipt of your letter . . . . I am glad to have it because it contains nothing but uninformed, or should I say unfounded . . . annoyance . . . . I'm leaving for other work — long waiting. Of course we'll meet again but life is dammed uncertain . . . . The commission will be reorganized, that is inescapable. You are one man who must stay until the memorial is given finished to the world . . . . This commission has not the mind, knowledge, nor interest that actuates service to life. . . . God bless you. Take care of yourself . . . .[23]

34
1935

Mary made the drive from their Hermosa ranch to Rapid City so many times a day — to shop, pick up visitors or run an errand for Gutzon — that is was just another part of her daily routine, but for him it was a treat. After a day on the mountain, they would go to town to have a quiet dinner at the Alex Johnson Hotel, to visit friends or walk the streets and window shop. Sometimes Gutzon went alone and sat in a rear booth at the A & F Cafe to drink hot buttered rum with Bob Dean, owner of the local radio station, or Phil Potter, city desk man at the Rapid City *Journal*. Either way, he usually ended up at the picture show.

The movies were an obsession with Gutzon. Two shows a day, three or four times a week, were a common practice, and it never seemed to matter if he had already seen the film half a dozen times. It was not the plot that drew Gutzon. He enjoyed seeing the stars perform; he had a few favorites and knew many of the actors personally, but what he went to see were horses. He wanted to watch their movements, study the play of muscles under the flesh and the way they carried their riders. Sitting in the dark, he could go back to his childhood on the prairie and remember the Indian ponies he had bought for fifty cents or a dollar.

When he felt the urge to see a show, and that could happen at any time, he insisted that whoever was on hand should go with him to the nearest theater. His children recall that going to the movies was a cross they had to bear, and Mary's letters to friends are filled with such remarks as ". . . and, of course, after dinner we had to go to the movies."[1]

Any movie would do, but Westerns were Gutzon's favorite. The Western theme was such a deeply entrenched part of his psyche that he never wanted to be far from it, and then when he could not get to a theater he accepted Western novels as a substitute. When the Borglums travelled long distances by car, and could arrange for a chauffeur, Mary would sit between Gutzon and the driver reading Zane Grey novels to them, while Gutzon gazed out of the window.

Edwald Hayes, hoist operator, taking sharpened jackhammer bits to top of monument.

As he approached seventy, Gutzon began to understand the need to conserve his strength. He recognized his physical shortcomings and appreciated those friends who could relax, as indicated in this letter to one of those friends:

As we were driving from the mountain last night, I said, "It would be rather fine to take a few days off and go down into Mexico with you only you are such a consummate man of leisure." By God! You make an art of it! And you pride yourself on seeking the cushions that are the softest, the days that are the shortest . . . and . . . the land that boasts a perpetual kind of heaven. I am not making fun of you, Martin. I envy you all these things.[2]

Gutzon's keen sense of humor ran through all his letters, except those he wrote to his political enemies. He was deeply concerned about the state of the nation and the world and felt the moral fiber of America was weakening. He kept up a running correspondence with many members of Congress, attacked those he did not agree with and gave strong support to those who shared his views. To one friendly congressman he wrote, "You don't know how sick I am, as I see America's — civilization's — chance slip and slide along half-heartedly."[3]

His high hopes for the Roosevelt administration were fading, though he had not lost faith in FDR. His argument was with the academicians who were formulating policy. He wired Roosevelt, when the president was vacationing at his Warm Springs, Georgia, retreat: "May I urge your raison d'etre is to recreate a new, better America . . . . When dreams are through you need terribly a few high-powered doers . . . . Still we seem to be muddling along goose-stepping . . . ."[4]

It was the goose-stepping that really bothered Gutzon. It reminded him of the menace of Hitler. He was concerned because he did not feel that FDR had advisors who would react in a crisis. He wrote Mary Ellis predicting a Roosevelt defeat in 1936 because he was certain the voters would not re-elect him "with the baggage he insists on carrying." He added, "They are not bad men, but weak men given the steering wheel may easily become bad — and lose their courage — what little they had."[5]

For Gutzon, *courage* was a key word. He believed that the leaders of the world had to find the courage to present a united front against German aggression or face another world war. It was a belief that caused him no end of trouble and made him many enemies, but which he repeated in conversation, interviews, speeches and letters.

Politics and world affairs, Mount Rushmore, roads for Texas, lectures and thoughts about his autobiography filled his mind, but Gutzon still attempted to win any commission he heard about. His Ingersoll Monument, the model of which had been completed in 1933, was waiting, but until Congress passed the necessary legislation it could not be cast and paid for as a finished work. When the bill became tied up in committee, Gutzon appealed to his friend Congressman Roy Woodruff of Michigan:

> I suppose you are already loaded for bear and your briefcase charged with bills and errands. I have only another request; get on Kent Keller's neck, bridle him and with spurs head him for the jump. Tell him you know that Ingersoll Bill passed next summer won't do Gutzon any good . . . . It can and should be passed this month . . . .[6]

Dynamite blast at Mount Rushmore.

The financial pressure never eased. The brothers holding the note on the South Dakota ranch were constantly threatening foreclosure, and there was an endless number of suits from other creditors. Mary asked a banker friend in Rapid City to go to the Farm Bureau to get "as large a loan as possible on the ranch, divide the sum between the Rhoades brothers and hold everything until we can pay the balance . . . ." Then she added, almost plaintively, ". . . after all, he has done a great deal for South Dakota . . . by the middle of the summer when Rushmore is going again, I feel confident we can meet our obligations. . . ."[7] They put their hopes in the money due on the mountain carving, but the Borglums were remaining afloat because of Mary's ability to sell off small parcels of their property in Connecticut. From the early days of Stone

310

Mountain through 1935, she managed to sell almost $200,000 worth of land. Much of the money went to banks in the form of interest, penalties and the buying back of notes. Another portion went to attorneys, their own and those of the creditors who sued. Eugene Meyer, still holding the original mortgage, received some money, but enough was left to keep the Borglums going and that was all that really counted.

Mary's faith in Gutzon never wavered. He did what he thought best with her backing. If it meant travelling for Rushmore or spending time in Washington at his own expense, she found a way to manage. She spent much of her time trying to find a way to ease their burden. Between them, they developed a scheme to divide Borgland into homsites. Gutzon wrote Meyer seeking a loan of $10,000 to finance the venture: "I have things well in hand and want to act quickly . . . . I doubt if you have made many investments that are as sure of paying you out 100% as this one . . . ," but Meyer refused and the Borglums dropped the idea.[8]

Every facet of the Borglums' existence was involved with the work on the mountain. Keeping promises to creditors hinged on their being paid the money due them on the Rushmore contract. In June 1935 Gutzon appealed to Fred Sargent, Chairman of the Rushmore Commission:

> I have spent over ten years educating the world, getting money for the Memorial, struggling with the government and carving the mountain . . . . There is $14,000 due me right now . . . I said something about my place being foreclosed . . . I need $5,000 to save the property . . . . You . . . have full authority to pay these arrears . . . . If you will . . . we can take the necessary time to adjust the balances and come to a clean, friendly understanding about completing the big job . . . .[9]

Gutzon's appeal was made to Sargent, rather than to Boland, because the two were becoming more and more alienated. Norbeck was strongly backing Boland, yet Gutzon retained his sense of affection for the senator. He became angry when Norbeck would not support him, and he accused the senator of being responsible for insults and betrayals by others, but he invariably softened. Gutzon explained his attitude toward Norbeck in a letter to Mary Ellis:

> Norbeck is a fine man. Don't confuse him with Boland. Every dog has to have a flea. That is fleas like to be carried around — and Norbeck has a swarm of fleas feeding on him. I get angry with him but I never lose my regard for him . . . .[10]

Had Gutzon been aware of Norbeck's changing feelings, he might not have been so charitable. Boland and Norbeck were beginning to feel that the project had progressed far enough so that Gutzon was expendable. In the spring of 1935, with the project in limbo waiting for release of funds that had been made a part of the previous year's appropriation through the Department of the Interior budget, Norbeck and Boland had several private meetings. No one could be certain that the money would not be deleted until it was actually received from the treasury. Both Norbeck and Gutzon were trying to prod the committee that would make the final decision. Norbeck felt he should be handling the situation and was annoyed by Gutzon's presence in Washington. In his letter to Boland, he wrote, "I know you do not need him at Rushmore, but this is the worst place for him to be. He doesn't only want to run the commission, but . . . also the White House . . . ."[11] The next day, in another letter to Boland, he suggested:

> Borglum might do like Tucker. He might "resign," which would clarify the situation, because if we had two heads completed — Washington and Jefferson — we could put a new artist to work on the next head — that is if Borglum left us . . . . Borglum is not satisfied being the sculptor . . . . He has recently suggested whom the president should appoint on the Commission, if and when Congress makes a change in the law. It has already been decided who should be appointed.[12]

The reason for Norbeck's bitterness is hard to understand. He was complaining about Gutzon's interference and at the same time reluctantly admitting that Gutzon had considerable influence. "Believe it or not," he wrote Boland, "Borglum has done more to sell the National Memorial to Congress and the people of the U.S."[13]

Norbeck was frustrated and disappointed. What had started out as a five-year project, which would cost a few hundred thousand dollars of privately contributed funds, had become a consuming project. His efforts on behalf of Rushmore had seriously compromised his position on several matters that came before Congress. He had been forced to trade favors in order to force needed legislation through a reluctant Congress and to make deals with the White House. He knew that that was all part of the political process and believed the result would be worth the effort, but he had not counted on it becoming a career commitment. Each time that he was forced to return to his colleagues with a new scheme for financing the work, his frustration grew.

The $55,000 they were expecting in 1935 was all the government could give them by law. They needed another bill authorizing a direct appropriation, and their only hope of getting that was to win FDR's support. When the president agreed to back them, Congress passed a $200,000 appropriation and sent the bill to a committee. Getting that bill passed by Congress, obsessed with the problems of the Great Depression on the eve of an election year, was a tribute to Norbeck's political skill and Gutzon's charismatic effect on the nation's lawmakers. Gutzon wrote to Mary Ellis as soon as he heard the news: "This will be a great year for us — it is now — and the stupid world thinks I'm a wonder. The damm fools, I always have been whatever I am."[14]

As soon as the money was assured, work on the mountain was resumed, and the clashes between Gutzon and Boland became more severe. Because the funding had been included in the Department of the Interior budget, the National Park Service (NPS) was given jurisdiction, and it began taking an interest in the project. Gutzon welcomed the NPS because he assumed its presence would lessen the influence of the Rushmore Commission. He felt that with his strong Washington ties he could obtain anything he wanted from NPS management and still retain control.

Much had been accomplished by the time the season ended in November. Gutzon had a definite idea about the placement of all four portraits and was no longer concerned about there not being enough rock for the Roosevelt. He set out for the West with Mary to inspect Boulder Dam, a project that intrigued him from an engineering standpoint. From there they drove to San Antonio, stopping along the way to visit friends, and then went on to Mexico for the holidays.

313

35
1936

En route to Boulder Dam, Mary wrote Mary Ellis to tell her that Gutzon was planning to attend the year-end meeting of the Rushmore Commission in Chicago, but added that she was not sure he would. He was becoming excited about plans for the Texas centennial and, she thought, was losing some of his enthusiasm for Rushmore.

As soon as they were back in San Antonio, Gutzon began seeking authorization to start the Texas projects he had been planning for the past ten years. Despite the constant disappointment of proposing projects and then watching helplessly as the voters refused to back him, or having to walk away when the contract was given to a political crony, Gutzon remained optimistic and assumed he would be given his chance.

He was, by nature, an optimist. It was this aspect of his character, more than any other, that gave him the absolute assurance that he could always find a solution to any problem. He was strengthened by Mary, who was described by her daughter as "a strong-willed woman — small in stature, very feminine — appeared to be a pushover for any out-stretched hand — in our home she was ten feet tall and made of iron at the core."[1]

During his years in Texas, Gutzon had learned enough about the people and the state to believe he could influence their decisions. At one time he had felt he was one of them, and had often referred to himself as a Texan, but in 1936 his attitude was more paternal. When he was seeking a commission to honor the heroes of the Alamo, for example, he took his case directly to the White House:

Mr. President . . . Texas has been in the throes of indecision over the proper commemoration of the incomparable sacrifices of the small band of Americans who perished in the Alamo . . . . I understand the great human qualities expressed and that must be commemorated . . . . I believe — yes I know — Texas needs help now in directing the conception and in a lofty rendering of this particular memorial. I want to do it. I understand this decision may be made tomorrow . . . .[2]

315

His wire to FDR contained no direct appeal. He was not asking the president to intervene, but was simply expressing his frustration and trying, as he did in the letters and wires he sent to other influential people all across the country, to create an atmosphere that would embarrass the Texans into making the right decision.

Being appointed Chairman of the Texas Highway Commission and being put in charge of a group in Arizona planning a pageant to celebrate the 400th anniversary of Coronado's travels through the Southwest caused Gutzon to believe his influence was growing. It turned out to be more illusion than substance, but his deep desire to make Texas more beautiful made it difficult for him to see the truth.

Gutzon's imagination made it impossible for him to think small. He saw Arizona's Coronado pageant as a grand celebration that should include Texas and New Mexico. When he brought delegates from the three states together, he was dismayed to find they did not share his thinking. Gutzon had envisioned a grand plan: not a staged Hollywood production, but an authentic recreation with residents from all three states joining in the pageant. After the first meeting, Gutzon realized that the others were not in agreement with him and that many minds would have to be changed before there would be a Coronado pageant.

When he did not receive the Alamo commission, Gutzon was disheartened. When his concept for San Antonio's outdoor theater was awarded to a local architect, he was forced finally to accept reality. He could hope and plan until he died, but he had little chance of receiving a Texas commission.

The Borglums maintained their ranch in South Dakota, kept an apartment in San Antonio and, when they went east, stayed at Borgland. But Gutzon could just as easily have called the Blackstone Hotel in Chicago, or the Metropolitan Club in Washington, home.

Fred Sargent, Chairman of the Rushmore Commission, conducted much of the commission's business from his Chicago office. Gutzon had to be with him on many occasions, which he enjoyed because the city had a strange fascination for him. This he described in a letter to Mary Ellis:

> Chicago is a terrible town — full of terrors — full of liquor — full of people who like terror and liquor — and it is money mad. And yet it is splendid and wonderful like a great sea serpent . . . .[3]

There were many times when Gutzon must have wondered if it was all worth the effort. He was living out of a suitcase, keeping in touch with his family by mail and fighting endless battles. As the method of financing Rushmore evolved from private contributions to matching funds to a fully financed government project, Gutzon's contract lost its validity. Everyone agreed it had to be rewritten, but no one could agree on what the new contract should contain.

Gutzon knew what he wanted. Control was much more important to him than money at that point, and he was not willing to compromise. Boland felt the same way. As business manager, he wanted as much authority as he could get. The decision should have been made by Sargent and the other commissioners, but they tried to stay out of the argument in the hope that the two would reconcile their differences and not force a confrontation.

The original $200,000 appropriation in the Department of the Interior budget had been whittled down to $50,000 in committee and was being held up by technicalities. Norbeck was trying to get the original amount restored while he fought to get the money released, but Boland was urging him to seek only $100,000 because ". . . the sculptor would spend the entire amount . . . ."[4]

Gutzon also was fighting for the money and becoming angry. He felt that the delay was politically motivated and that his art was being compromised. He blamed the commission members and accused them of being shortsighted, politically naive and unfair in their dealings with him. In February 1936 he wrote a long letter to Norbeck, which summed up his feelings:

> You are too old in the game of politics not to understand its meaning or to forget that the nation is overwhelmingly Democratic . . . not to have taken into the council of the commission four or five Democrats . . . the Memorial is not Republican, it is not Democrat, it is a memorial to what this nation's founders aspired to make this nation . . . . I've labored for years under a contract that was conceived in bad faith, dishonest, and has been administered dishonestly. It has long been the intention to correct this and over a year ago the details were agreed upon between the commission and myself, it is still an unfinished piece of business.[5]

Gutzon then wrote Sargent to tell him the reduction in the appropriation was a "distinct slap at Norbeck and his local political machine."[6] He warned that the entire appropriation would be lost if the commission did not take a stand. Although it seemed that Mount Rushmore was heading for the same fate as Stone Mountain, the people involved managed to put their differences aside. The contract issue was allowed to remain in limbo while they joined to fight for the appropriation.

In March Mary Ellis wrote to tell her parents she wanted to get married. With mixed emotions, Gutzon accepted her decision:

> Everybody that is worth anything to themselves falls in love . . . be loyal
> to yourself, by that I mean to the woman you cannot escape being. A great
> love is given to few people, few even are capable of it and still fewer respect
> it . . . nothing is sadder than unrequited love, nothing more enobling than
> fulfilling love . . . there is another thought I want to put in your
> mind . . . no state of mind, love or otherwise, will destroy the soul hunger
> to be what you know you can be . . . .[7]

Gutzon loved his daughter and wanted to say what was in his heart and yet say just the right thing. He went back to his first marriage and allowed some of the bitterness in that relationship to surface. He rarely spoke about the past, primarily because his life with Mary made the past seem unreal. When he did mention "old days" to his children, he did so to remind them that the blood of Eric the Red flowed in their veins. But with his princess, his Mary Ellis, planning to marry, he had to say more:

> . . . be careful you don't get hitched to a freight train when you should
> be in an airplane — and also be careful you don't prove the freight train
> to a high speed engine. My father died of a broken heart. A prince among
> men loved by all — he was chained to the ground . . . do whatever you do
> with all your heart . . . .[8]

The year 1936 was an election year, and FDR was obviously going to seek a second term. There was talk among some of the Republican die-hards of running Hoover against him. The Republican National Committee sent letters to party faithfuls to see if there was any support for a Hoover candidacy, but no one took the idea seriously. The committee also organized a panel of college professors and asked them to make a "complete analysis of what the New Deal has done to the country in three years."[9]

Gutzon thought both moves so stupid that he practically wrote himself out of the party in a letter to Chairman Henry Fletcher:

> I am a Republican . . . but I do not belong to the mossback element . . . do
> not support the professorial group that is chiefly responsible for Roosevelt's
> departure from the platform that the Republicans could do no better than
> adopting . . . . I am going to support Roosevelt — that doesn't mean I have
> sympathy at all for the brain trust crowd . . . . I am going to support Mr.
> Roosevelt because there has not been an able . . . candidate advocating

a program that will deal with the nationwide problems that this country demands to be handled and handled by men, and not "Herr Doktors."[10]

Gutzon's endorsement of FDR and rejection of his own party did not mean that he endorsed New Deal policy. He considered the plans of Secretary of Agriculture Henry Wallace a disaster, he disagreed with almost everything Secretary of the Interior Harold Ickes advocated, and was particularly upset with Work Projects Administrator Harry Hopkins. In a letter to the President of the University of Wisconsin, Gutzon wrote:

I am concerned about how we are going to make decent men and women out of the great herd of overfed, over-idle, untrained, useless human beings that are now lying in the lap of Uncle Sam and forming a new collective lazy leisure class. Wealth has done this; collectiveness does it; Fordism does it . . . millions were swept out of gutters of Europe into bathtubs and palaces . . . and run through our colleges, as we dip cattle for ticks, to give them what we conceive an education . . . . Our CCC camps are rendezvous for idleness . . . the boys are worse when they leave the camps than when they went in. They have received protection, food and clothing and a bed, idleness for nothing . . . . There is not a voice raised today in America against the destruction of ideals among our well-to-do and our middle class . . . .[11]

The Civilian Conservation Corps (CCC) camps bothered Gutzon tremendously. He could easily have obtained permission to use the CCC laborers, but did not feel they were disciplined enough to be trusted. In most communities the CCC camps were viewed with suspicion. In the Black Hills there was constant trouble between the camp boys and the locals, especially on Saturday nights in the Pactola Valley dance hall.

Gutzon waged his political battles on one front and his battle for control of Mount Rushmore on another. Within the bounds of knowing that the monument must not be damaged, Boland, Norbeck and Gutzon fought on while the commissioners ignored the situation. They accepted temperamental outbursts from both sides as a fact of life that had nothing to do with the monument, and to a degree they were correct. In the course of the years, the carving had developed a character and life of its own.

Gutzon saw himself as a long-suffering Prometheus bound to his rock and felt his rock was being attacked. He had given up on Norbeck. Instead, he brought his complaints to Fred Sargent. That put the chairman in a difficult position because Boland was also looking for him to intercede. When Sargent received a proposal from Boland, he wrote

319

Gutzon to ask if he could work under the rules Boland proposed. Boland was suggesting, in effect, that Gutzon limit himself to removing stone and stay out of everything else. Gutzon replied to Sargent:

> Boland and Norbeck have itched for years to lift me and direct every detail of that highly specialized, dangerous and all but impossible task and now in the middle of the stream stripped of my strength, robbed of funds, not a single intelligent assistant allowed, short of power, defaulting or utterly ignorant assistance, I holler to the government for a little friendly rope — you holler back, let your horse go . . . .[12]

They seemed at an impasse, but when the appropriation was finally approved, work resumed at the mountain as if nothing were wrong. In July Gutzon warned Sargent that all the sculptural work had to be completed in 1936 because he had contracted for another work in 1937. He said he would not longer be able to be a physical presence at the mountain, but could only provide general sculptural instructions. "It might interest you to know," he wrote, "that my successor at the Southern memorial was at Stone Mountain only once . . . ."[13]

The 1937 commitment was the old dream of returning to Stone Mountain. Mary had written Mary Ellis to tell her that the Stone Mountain people were reviving interest and that "Dad has an appointment to meet the President and Secretary of the Chamber of Commerce of Atlanta in Chicago . . . ."[14]

Gutzon's warning to Sargent was sincere, but it was also an attempt to increase the pressure because changes were taking place at Rushmore that Gutzon did not like. The National Park Service had assigned an engineer to the project. Julian C. Spotts was a likeable and competent civil engineer. He arrived prepared to survey the work, make recommendations, install purchasing and reporting systems required by the government and to do whatever else was needed to make the project more efficient. He had no idea that an emotional struggle was taking place, but he quickly found out.

When Spotts first showed up, Gutzon was delighted. As he wrote to Sargent, "Getting the national administration to assign me a resident engineer, I have opened one door in Washington and shut another in Rapid City."[15] But when things did not work out that way, Gutzon was even more upset than he had been before.

He disagreed with Spotts on many technical issues. The systems Gutzon and Lincoln used to remove rock came from trial and error methods that were, at best, adaptations of accepted norms. Spotts saw much of what they did as inefficient, and Gutzon saw him as a "going

Gutzon Borglum in hoist car. Because of the difficulty in finding a good location to study perspective Borglum often took a hoist car part way to the top and studied his work from that vantage point.

by the book" engineer. There was no question that Spotts knew his business, but he had no experience with carving mountains. Some of his suggestions were valid. He improved the air lines and the lift to the top of Roosevelt and changed some of the equipment in the foundry, but none of that was fundamentally important.

The real problems, at least at the beginning, were more procedural than substantive. Spotts wanted daily reports, which Gutzon felt were unnecessary. He wanted all requests for material on proper forms, and he wanted to enforce a number of government rules that had been patently ignored by Gutzon as bureacratic nonsense. Gutzon had never worked that way. He did much of his planning in his head and on location. Lincoln, knowing how his father thought and reacted, worked much the same way, as he assumed responsibility for the daily operation.

Spotts' responsibility for preparing reports and approving all purchases put him in almost constant contact with Boland. This made him appear to be in the enemy camp, at least to Gutzon. After a short while, Gutzon and Spotts got in the habit of exchanging long letters of complaint even though they had offices less than a hundred feet apart, and Gutzon began taking his complaints to Spotts' superiors in the NPS. Eventually Spotts grew tired of the conflict. When he felt he was no longer being productive, he requested a transfer, and when he left, the wife of one of the mountain workers went with him.

It was time to dedicate the Jefferson, but no firm date had been set because Norbeck and Gutzon were trying to persuade FDR to visit Mount Rushmore. When the president agreed to be there at the end of August, the date was set for the ceremony. Gutzon wrote to Emil Hurja, Democratic Party Chairman, to make sure he understood the political importance of the president's visit:

> I "guessed" about as you figured on the last election. I wired Mr. Roosevelt he would sweep everything from the Hudson to the Pacific except Pennsylvania . . . . If the President does not come out here, you'd better cut the *doubtful* off South Dakota and write sure for Landon. Pooh Pooh this as most Democrats, if you like . . . .[16]

The president arrived in Rapid City by special train on a Saturday night. The Jefferson ceremony was scheduled for 11 a.m. Sunday, but no one told the presidential party. On Sunday morning, after breakfast, FDR asked his host, Dr. Guy March of the School of Mines, if they could attend a worship service. Dr. March proudly escorted the president to his church in Rapid City.

Gutzon Borglum greeting President Franklin Delano Roosevelt at dedication of Jefferson portrait in 1936.

When FDR had not arrived at the monument by 11:30 and had not sent word that he would be delayed, Gutzon went ahead and held the dedication. He put on a good show, but it was not nearly as good as the one which he put on two hours later when FDR showed up. Gutzon had accepted the fact that the president did not plan to speak to the audience, but he did not give up the hope that FDR might change his mind. In his own speech he tried to make the president understand how he felt about the mountain:

> Mr. President, there have been two moments in history strangely comparable to this — when the hearts of men reached deliberately into the tomorrow of the centuries and called to heaven with the same prayer — the same pride — the same faith. The first was when the artist-sculptor-builders of the first great pyramids turned to Cheops, ruler of Egypt and said: The work is complete . . . . The other great moment in the soul struggle of enlightened humanity was when Phidias, standing under the portico of the Parthenon on the Acropolis, said to Pericles, then Governor of Athens: "The dream of Greece and her message to civilization is complete." . . . I want you, Mr. President, to dedicate this memorial as a shrine

to democracy . . . with the prayer that it shall not perish from the earth. I would ask the vast audience here, the people everywhere to join in such a prayer . . . .[17]

Sensing that Roosevelt had understood, Gutzon looked at FDR, took a deep breath and stepped toward him with a portable microphone. Roosevelt's aides moved quickly to intercept him, but the president waved them aside with his famous grin and took the microphone from Gutzon. Then, sitting in his open-top limousine, with Gutzon alongside, his foot on the running board, the president told the crowd how thrilled he was to see the magnificent "Shrine of Democracy." Listening to the president praise his work was a thrilling, tearful moment for Gutzon, a moment that made the struggle worthwhile.

In September Mary Ellis was married. A few weeks later, Mary and Gutzon went to Arizona for the funeral of his brother Frank. Then, on December 20, Senator Norbeck lost his long, brave fight and died of the throat cancer that had plagued him his last four years.

1937

In January, Gutzon signed a $15,000 contract with the Northwest Territory Commission for a memorial to be placed in Marietta, Ohio. Then he left New York and sailed on a German liner to Cherbourg. His statue of Tom Paine, commissioned by the Free-Thinkers of America, had been finished and shipped to M. Rudier, the Parisian foundry master who cast for Rodin.

The finished work, cast in bronze and coated with gold leaf, was to be placed in a park across from the American Embassy in Paris. Gutzon had planned to arrive in time to supervise the finishing touches and to arrange for the installation, but when he reached Paris he discovered that the foundry had been delayed and the statue would not be ready.

Gutzon was of course disappointed, but since he was already in Europe, he decided to make the best of the situation. Many of his friends had gathered for the celebration. The Free-Thinkers were there in force, and the embassy had invited many dignitaries. With so many guests on hand, a party was scheduled, and Helen Keller, who was in Paris, where she had come on her world tour to recover from the loss of her teacher, Annie Sullivan, agreed to be one of the honored guests.

At the party, Gutzon and Helen reacted as kindred spirits. She told Gutzon that she admired him because he thought greatly through his art. "When skill and daring meet," she said, "a masterpiece is born."[1] During dinner, she expressed a desire to "see" the sculpture of Rodin, and Gutzon promised to make that possible.

The next morning he drove her to the Rodin Museum, where he had arranged for a private showing. The public had been excluded. All the ropes and barriers had been removed. Using a folding chair as a stepstool, she went from statue to statue and explored them with her fingers. When she touched *The Thinker*, she said, "In every limb I feel the throes of an emerging mind . . . . Rodin might have named him 'trying to think'. . . . It reminds me of the force that shook me when teacher spelled water."[2] As they went from statue to statue, Gutzon told her, "Few people have understood the elemental meaning of Rodin's symbols as you do," and he concluded that the reason was that she was seeing with the mind's eye, as well as the soul's, and that gave her a unique perspective.[3] Later, in an article he wrote for the *New York Herald Tribune*, Gutzon called the visit the most memorable hour of his life. In the article he said, "From it I learned that the soul, over and above the body, has eyes."[4]

The delay in casting the Paine proved to be a blessing in disguise. When the Nazis captured Paris, in 1940, they systematically searched for and destroyed most of the statues in the city. Without question, Gutzon's Paine would have suffered the same fate as his Woodrow Wilson if it had fallen into Nazi hands. Fortunately, the statue had been hidden behind a false wall, and when the foundry was searched it was not discovered. The casting was completed after the war, and in 1948 it was installed in the park across from the American Embassy in Paris.

When he returned from Paris in February, he joined Mary in San Antonio and began working on his concept for the Marietta memorial and the arrangments for the Coronado pageant. He was having difficulty generating support for the pageant. Those who were in favor of holding the celebration could not agree on a concrete plan, so the project was abandoned.

Gutzon remained politically active. He had supported FDR in his successful bid for re-election, despite his grave reservations about the New Deal "Brain Trust." He remained optimistic about the future though he was worried about the direction the world was going and had deep concerns about how the New Dealers would handle a crisis. When he was asked how he felt about the nation's spiritual outlook, he answered:

> I'm an optimist through and through and, as I understand human growth and compare the past with present conditions, I cannot see anything but the profoundest revolution of history here is necessary to cleanse the forefront of liberal thought, which America represents.[5]

Gutzon believed that the world was heading for a catastrophic war, and he could not believe that the signs were not clear to others. He was upset by the New Deal's new direction and policies, which were being adopted because the New Dealers were upset with the Supreme Court. Having been re-elected with a clear mandate, the administration was frustrated by the way the Supreme Court was striking down so many of its new concepts. Led by Chief Justice Charles Evans Hughes, the Republican candidate in 1916 when Wilson was re-elected, and composed of old justices who had been appointed by Hoover, Coolidge, Harding, Wilson and Taft, the court was philosophically opposed to the administration. When they struck down the National Recovery Act, after it had been declared the bulwark of Roosevelt's plan for economic recovery, the battlelines were clearly drawn.

In his second term, FDR decided it was time to do something about the court. In his famous court-packing plan, he had a bill introduced that called for sweeping reforms in the court system. Gutzon was outraged. He believed the scheme could destroy American democracy, as he indicated in his letter to Senator Austin:

> I don't know who has led the President into the position history will inevitably give him of having moved, rather taken, the most destructive step ever taken by any President of the United States against the principles and practices of democracy . . . .[6]

He would have liked to have gone public with his opposition, but felt he had to stay in the background because, as he told another close friend, Senator Burt Wheeler, his work on Mount Rushmore restrained him from involvement in political confrontations.

Since Rushmore was being funded by the government, Gutzon could not afford to antagonize the administration, but, as he told Wheeler, "If the need comes, I will sacrifice everything . . . ."[7] He watched the battle from the sidelines and then wrote to Chief Justice Hughes, whom he had known for thirty years. Although never friends, Gutzon and Hughes respected each other and had worked together on several occasions. Gutzon had supported Hughes' presidential bid in 1916 and Hughes' attempt to unravel the story Gutzon had uncovered in his aircraft-scandal investigation. After Gutzon's effort forced Wilson to act, he had appointed Hughes to head a special board of inquiry. Gutzon had cooperated fully until he realized that Hughes was not going to seek indictments against any of the real culprits. Gutzon was afraid that, as chief justice, Hughes might react to the court-packing scheme with the same timidity. He expressed this concern in a letter to Hughes:

> The world knows you are especially marked for this attack upon the independence of the Supreme Court, and I am not alone in wondering if you will, and why you have not already made answer to the nation camouflaged plan to subvert the only remaining independent department of our triangle government to the will and whim of politics . . . . Again you, more than any other living American, can warn the nation, yes, the world that civilization in its upward struggle must perish if our courts are not held sacred and above the heat . . . of political ambition . . . . Don't allow yourself, or the great office that you preside over to be degraded without protest.[8]

The opposition to the president's plan was so widespread that he could not force it through Congress. Finally, as the furor mounted, Roosevelt accepted a compromise that was little more than a face-saving gesture to allow him to withdraw the legislation graciously.

But from that point on, Gutzon grew increasingly disenchanted with the administration. He saw other trends developing that alarmed him. He was particularly concerned by the way the unions were trying to organize the heavy industries. Labor leader John L. Lewis was making headway in the coal fields, and the auto workers had struck some of the major manufacturers.

FDR had been re-elected with strong support from labor, but many of his supporters, and particularly those like Gutzon who had crossed over from the Republicans, expected the president to reject the demands of the unions. For FDR it was a matter of priorities, and as it turned out the unions had more influence than ex-Republicans. When the administration backed the unions, Gutzon became an outspoken critic. In another letter to Senator Wheeler, Gutzon wrote, "The spectacle of Lewis and his juggernaut threat marching through the country . . . a partner of the political machine in Washington fills me with a kind of horror . . . ."[9] While to his old friend Congressman Roy Woodruff, he wrote:

> I hope Chrysler will sit tight and that they will tackle Ford and that Ford and Chrysler and General Motors will lock their doors on the whole damn crowd. I think the time has come for the automobile industry to retaliate . . . . It's hard for me to believe the President has not made some kind of an agreement . . . that puts him in Lewis' power.[10]

Work resumed at Mount Rushmore in April. The Appropriations Committee had held a hearing before making the final authorization and had asked A. E. Demaray, of the National Park Service, how much he thought would be needed to complete the memorial. How he could even attempt to answer such a question is difficult to imagine, but he told the committee that, because of the temperamental nature of the sculptor, it was difficult to estimate how much work could be done or how much it would cost.

Gutzon was justifiably upset by the unwarranted attack and would have challenged the NPS if Boland had not intervened. He convinced Gutzon that a fight with Demaray could hurt the monument. Gutzon accepted Boland's advice because he really did not want to get in an argument with the NPS. He recognized the validity of Boland's argument and realized it presented an opportunity to ease the tensions that had been building between himself and Boland.

He was also concerned about the impact that world events could have on the future of Rushmore. With the death of Senator Norbeck, the monument had lost its best congressional voice and much of its influence. Gutzon tried to pick up the slack, but his growing unhappiness with the administration was threatening his friendship with FDR. Under the circumstances, he could not afford to antagonize the NPS.

The tranquillity of the 1937 season was disturbed by only minor incidents, such as the one that precipitated Demaray's attack. Gutzon's reply, which was first cleared with Boland, was published in the Rapid City *Journal*:

> If America wants a product of art; if America wants an interpretation of Washington's character, of Jefferson's intelligence, of Lincoln's vision and soul, of Theodore Roosevelt's force and modernness — then she must trust to the judgement, insight and understanding of an artist.[11]

A much stronger reply would have been justified. The public interest in the affair was a good indication that the American people thought Mount Rushmore belonged to them, but this had some drawbacks. Since Congress funded the project, senators and representatives were constantly trying to influence the work. The debate about who should be portrayed on the mountain went on long after the issue had been decided. There was Southern opposition to Lincoln and pressure from the Democrats for the inclusion of Woodrow Wilson. When an effort was made to include Susan B. Anthony, Gutzon himself was forced to deal with the issue, which he tried to do diplomatically. Gutzon favored equal rights for women, but he did not feel that Anthony's portrait corresponded with his conception of the monument's purpose.

Gutzon turned seventy in March and began to think about his own mortality. As he assessed his situation, he realized neither he nor Mary considered Borgland their home and that they did not want to spend their winters in South Dakota. He could see that the monument was nearing completion and felt a need to have a home to go to after Mount Rushmore was finished.

After much searching, Gutzon and Mary located a lovely estate in Montecito, California, just up the coast from Santa Barbara. The moment Gutzon saw the property he thought of it as his own, though no deal had been consummated. He wrote to Frank Lloyd Wright:

I have bought a home in California. I traded some of my acreage in the East and I am planning a couple of studios there. There will be no chance of your building them for me. I am going to do that myself, but I would value very highly suggestions and designs made by Frank Lloyd Wright. This will be my last home—the only home I have ever had, as a matter of fact.[12]

Gutzon and Wright enjoyed a tempestuous friendship. They disagreed on almost everything, from Wright's political sympathies to Gutzon's contempt for modern architecture. They were friends because they respected each other and found arguing a great sport. When the Sylvan Lake Lodge in Custer State Park burned, Gutzon enlisted Wright's help in its rebuilding. He often wrote to Wright to check on the progress and to complain that petty local politics prevented him from taking a more active role:

My father was a philosopher, and he said to me one day, "Gutzon, make friends. If a man will not be your friend see to it that he is your enemy. No one is more useful than a friend, but next to him is your enemy. For real usefulness he will advertise you. He will keep you alert and in good fighting condition, and there are many things in this world we must fight for." In that respect, Frank, you and I are two peas in a pod.[13]

In July the last of the Texas contracts Gutzon still hoped to receive, the Alamo Centotaph, was awarded to a local artist. A few weeks later, *Time* Magazine, in a barbed filler, reported:

Out of San Antonio, Texas, last week rumbled one of the last vans full of plaster and clay models of sculpture by mountain-carver Gutzon Borglum, who closed up his studio and left Texas for good . . . . During the twelve years he called San Antonio his home, big-eared, irascible sculptor Borglum never finished a Texas job . . . .[14]

Mary was extremely upset by the report. It reminded her too much of the attacks that had filled the papers after the argument at St. John the Divine and later at Stone Mountain. The magazine's owners were their neighbors in Connecticut, whom she thought were good friends. In her letter of protest to Mrs. Manfred Gottfried, she wrote:

It's alright to make "good clean fun" of the people who are doing things in the world but plain malice is something else . . . . Some of his best monuments were made there. Even the realistic touch about the van loads of models leaving the studio is pure fabrication . . . .[15]

Mary also wrote to Mary Ellis to tell her they were thinking of suing, but the Borglums decided not to pursue the matter, though they would have had a strong case. The decision to leave Texas had been made months before the Alamo award. Had he received the contract, it would have been gratifying, but would not have changed their decision to settle in California.

Contrary to Gutzon's claim in his letter to Wright, he had not yet purchased the California estate; he had only entered into negotiations. The property was actually in litigation, with some of the heirs of the owner contesting the will. Gutzon assumed that this technicality would only cause some delay. Gutzon was so certain that the property would be his that he obtained permission for Mary Ellis and her husband to spend some time at the estate. In his letter to his daughter, he wrote, "It is very tiring to linger here. My heart and mind are in California."[16]

Knowing that financing the purchase was going to be a problem, Gutzon wrote to Eugene Meyer to invite him to the Lincoln dedication and to tell him he wanted to discuss the possibility of turning Borgland into a housing development. Meyer refused the invitation to attend the Rushmore ceremony because he was still angry at the way he had been treated when he had refused, on several occasions, to re-finance the Borgland mortgage. Because of the way Meyer felt, they never did discuss the Borgland development.

The Lincoln dedication was held in September 1937. It was a typical Borglum show designed to delight the crowd. Gutzon chose September 15, the 150th anniversary of the adoption of the Constitution. The keynote speaker was Senator Edward Burke of Nebraska, a conservative Republican, and he used the opportunity to attack FDR for his court-packing scheme. Following the senator's speech, bands from Ft. Meade and the Homestake Gold Mine entertained the five thousand guests, and then, as usual, Gutzon made a speech. He used the occasion to pay tribute to Senator Norbeck and some of the other individuals who had been connected with the project and had died. He said they were ". . . with the Gods. We must carry on their work."[17]

With the season coming to a close, the year of grace that followed Norbeck's death was also ending. In his letter to Francis Case, Gutzon wrote:

I expect to close the work here as soon as the weather stops me and then I shall go back to Washington and from there to California . . . . I expect to make some very radical proposals regarding the work here. It has been

331

Portrait of President Lincoln as it neared completion.

so badly handled all these years that unless something radical and progressive is done it will drag along another ten years and I shall be getting money from a tired and indifferent Congress, which is distasteful to me . . . .[18]

The Montecito estate was never purchased. A fire destroyed some of the buildings after Mary Ellis and her husband left. The fire so complicated the closing of the estate that the property could not be cleared for sale, but Gutzon never gave up hope and never stopped planning to retire there.

37
1938

California was always in Gutzon's thoughts. To the daughter of one of his earliest patrons, he wrote:

> I shall never cease to regret that I have not been able to spend my life there, but the world, its troubles, my own desire to be in the trenches or in the front ranks fighting the battles, have kept me where the battles are fought.[1]

For Gutzon, those battles were being fought on many fronts. He was now preparing for a fight at Rushmore, to which he referred in a letter to FDR:

> I would rather say anything else on earth to you, Mr. President, and I'll avoid anything that may embarrass you, but no other way . . . is open to me . . . . I shall not return to the work until these matters are corrected . . . .[2]

Although he was still on friendly terms with the president, he had decided to return to the Republican Party by seeking an appointment to the party's national advisory committee. His friends in Congress did not approve of the move, pointing out how much he needed the goodwill of FDR to complete the monument. But Gutzon would not be deterred. When he first wrote Roy Woodruff to ask for the appointment and was refused by his friend, Gutzon replied that it did not matter to him. But obviously it did matter. If it had not, Gutzon would have abandoned his campaign. A few weeks later, he contacted Woodruff again and suggested he was not being considered because they were afraid of him. "You know damn well," he wrote, "that I would release one or two disturbing ideas to your moss-grown, iron-bound Republicans that might require secret and executive sessions to keep away the hungering Republic." Then he expressed the ambivalence that had been with him from the time he had first decided to support FDR: "I have nothing but admiration for a great President, but all his dreams have remained dreams . . . ."[3]

Gutzon saw FDR as a man entrapped by those who advised him, yet he saw the Republicans as weak and afraid. In a letter to Roy Woodruff, Gutzon expressed his dissatisfaction with both parties:

> My private opinion is that the best men in America today are that group of Democrats who saved the Constitution and the Government, and if you and I and other Republicans have not got the integrity to admit that and lick the New Dealers and the Communists with their own weapons, we had better submit to anything the dilettante from Hyde Park may dream . . . .[4]

No one could make a statement like that and expect to influence either party. Gutzon fought hard for the rest of his life, but he never was accepted back into the good graces of the Republican Party because he would not stop criticizing anything he felt was wrong and because his Republican friends in Congress recognized the importance of Mount Rushmore and wished to protect him from himself.

Gutzon's interests went beyond national politics and his art. He built a fine reputation as a lecturer, writer and commentator on the American way of life. He had followed with great interest the emergence of Fiorello La Guardia as New York's mayor. He was pleased when the "Little Flower" defeated Tammany Hall and the corrupt bosses who had controlled the city for decades. When La Guardia was first elected in 1933 he was a candidate on a Fusion ticket, a coalition of independents who joined with disenchanted Democrats and Republicans. When he was re-elected, he was still the Fusion candidate, but his party had became a major factor in the city. Gutzon wired La Guardia to tell him that he wanted to congratulate New York City on making him mayor again. Gutzon then gave La Guardia advice concerning the New York World's Fair, which was due to open in 1939:

> I have been extremely interested in the Fair . . . . They have grown from being honest exhibits . . . into the realm of ballyhoo . . . in Texas . . . the vulgarest that a vulgar tradesmen group could produce to entice and seduce the worst element to patronize . . . . I very much doubt . . . you will escape the cry for quantity, flair and noise to the disadvantage and further degredation of Quality — a mood that is running rampant in America . . . .[5]

The lecture circuit was an important part of Gutzon's life. It presented him with a forum in which he could at least present and discuss his ideas and the issues that troubled him. The circuit did not take the place of a political position, which would have given him an opportunity to affect policy, but it was a medium for his opinions.

One of Gutzon's running feuds was with America's architects. Writing to Frank Lloyd Wright's secretary, he bemoaned the fact that there was not a building in America that he felt would provide a fitting background for the Venus De Milo or any other masterpiece. Then, anticipating the retort, he added, "For the architects to say we can get those figures is nonsense. They have never asked for them and they don't know what to do with them when offered . . . ."[6] In the same letter, he claimed that the Lincoln in the Capital's Lincoln Memorial would have been his if he had been willing to "shoehorn a statue all out of proportion to the place it occupied." He also called Daniel Chester French's Lincoln an abortion.[7]

The battle for control of Mount Rushmore was continuing along the lines that had formed down through the years. It was Gutzon against the forces of the Rapid City politicians, led by John Boland and aided by an indifferent commission. At least that was Gutzon's view. Although Norbeck was no longer there, the National Park Service was a strong presence and it more than made up the difference.

Gutzon was angry and upset, but not defenseless. He felt he could count on FDR despite their political differences, and he was right. He knew that Congress had invested too heavily in the carving to withdraw its support, and most congressmen left no doubt that they understood Gutzon's importance to the carving. With the exception of a few who had opposed the project from the beginning and would have liked to see it fail, if only to embarrass its backers, it was obvious that Congress would do everything possible to see it completed.

The battles were fought in Washington. A new appropriation was needed to continue the work and that meant new legislation. Gutzon demanded that, as part of the bill, they include provisions for sweeping changes in the way the work was administered. He said he would not continue to work under a commission that abrogated its authority to the NPS. Unless he was given a fair contract, adequate power at the mountain and control over the hiring, he did not feel he could continue.

Gutzon wanted the present commission dissolved. That would rid him of Boland. He wanted a new commission appointed, one that would be independent of the NPS and have a stronger say in all matters that concerned the monument. When some of his proposals were opposed, he demanded that the issues be brought before a congressional committee at a public hearing. When the assistant director of the NPS attempted to reconcile their differences to avoid a public fight, Gutzon wrote him:

Gutzon Borglum branding cattle on his Hermosa, South Dakota, ranch.

Thank you for your note and the spirit of it. I have always felt toward our government that it was paternal in the part it played in civilization and I have had too much to do with too many of its administrators to discontinue that feeling, so I know when . . . citizens are dishonestly treated it is due to the actions of petty . . . officials straining and outwilling and misreading what is right and fair . . . .[8]

Gutzon was confident at the hearings. His good friend Kent Keller was chairing the meeting, and Roy Woodruff and other friends had been appointed to serve. As soon as the committee was named, it was clear that Boland and the commission would not survive.

At the hearings, the NPS argued for continuing control, a few members of the panel questioned the need for a new commission, some suggested they retain the old one, and others asked why a commission was needed at all. There was some discussion about the entablature, the Grand Staircase and the Hall of Records, but it was all routine. As Roy Woodruff had told his colleagues, "You can complete Rushmore without anyone you can name — except Borglum. The thing to do is give him what he wants."[9]

When the hearings were over, an appropriation had been approved for $300,000. All the commissioners, including Boland, had resigned, and

336

a smaller commission, made up of members Gutzon had recommended, had been appointed. Jurisdiction remained with the NPS, but with the understanding that Gutzon was in charge. Writing to a friend about his victory, he exclaimed:

> I am here in the Black Hills. I have licked the little political racketeers that have been riding Rushmore almost to death; rescued my Pegasus before his heart was quite broken, and now we are off on the homestretch! All of us happy — except the racketeers. [10]

With the new appropriations there seemed to be enough money to finish the work, and with Lincoln as his superintendent, Gutzon felt he finally had the kind of help he had always wanted. He decided to push the work through the winter. The men draped huge canvases over the scaffolding to cut the bitter wind. They tried to keep warm by building fires in fifty-gallon drums, but they were often forced to stop because their air lines froze.

Gutzon's new contract gave the Borglums a little more peace of mind, but Mary was still trying to straighten out their finances in preparation for the purchase of the estate in Montecito. Their chances of acquiring the estate were becoming more remote, but Gutzon refused to believe that the purchase would not turn out all right in the end.

He was finding it increasingly difficult not to become cynical about the state of the world and the world's leaders. He was able to see beyond daily events to the disastrous future. He could share his views with reporters and the people who packed the lecture halls to hear him speak, but he wanted to affect national policy directly, and that was denied him. He knew the world was heading toward war and he wanted to prevent it before it was too late. To relieve his frustration, he wrote a great many letters to people whom he thought he could force to act. Gutzon summed up his views in a letter to his friend Roy Woodruff:

> We are living in wonderful times. England and France have inflated that Prince of Knaves, Hitler, and it is very tempting to Franklin to think that by bolstering up our navy he will bolster up England and put the world in order again. It can be done, and would be a damm good thing to do, but it will leave us with despotism on our hands, and the Democracy of the Westworld destroyed. [11]

With Rushmore demanding so much of his time, his lecture commitments increasing and his growing concern for the state of the world, Gutzon's interests in what seemed like parochial matters lessened. He would no longer accept meaningless commissions or appointments to committees, such as the Coronado pageant group he had joined in the mid-thirties.

Gutzon was still planning to write his autobiography, but he kept putting it off. Mary had started writing the book, but Gutzon objected. He wanted to tell his story his own way, and for a short time he spent several hours a day dictating to Mary. A week before Christmas, with the men still carving on the mountain, he wrote Missy Meloney:

> Now, about publishing. I am going to publish — and this year — and I am preparing that is, assembling, an autobiography — constructive, sweeping one-man war — accomplishments . . . . Little, Brown wants this but they are kind of flirting . . . . You know I am very much of a now person; tomorrow may be another now — certainly not a hangover![12]

Gutzon had his title. It described the way he lived his life. In a letter to Helen Keller, he had written. "I lead a one-man war pretty nearly all the time and my battlefield is the world and my enemies are mainly fools, and an occasional one-track mentality that just gives me trouble because I like two tracks, and sometimes three or four."[13]

38
1939

Lincoln was coming into his own on the mountain. He had relieved his father of most of his physical duties and, as supervisor, had proven himself to be superbly fitted to carry out his father's orders. Gutzon had become so popular on the lecture circuit that his agent was able to book as many engagements as he would accept. His schedule from November 1938 to March 1939 called for speeches in South Dakota, Virginia, New Jersey, Illinois, Minnesota and Ohio. In the flyer that was sent to the lecture halls, Gutzon gave this description of himself:

> Viking and Crusader . . . Is religious, with no orthodox leanings; . . . utterly opposed to the buccaneer economic tactics that have prevailed in high finance in America since 1866 . . . opposed to John L. Lewis' method of militarizing the untrained and incompetent for purpose of ballot . . .An outdoor man . . . who makes athletics his chiefest delight. Physical efficiency and perfection are a creed . . . .[1]

Gutzon filled the lecture halls at every stop. He spoke on art, politics, labor problems and gave a particularly popular lecture titled "The International Court and Embargo — The Way To World Peace." He was always outspoken, knew how to use humor and never disappointed an audience. He spoke about Rushmore, the art of mountain carving and the dream that he had never let die — Stone Mountain. Speaking to a travel bureau association gathered at Mount Rushmore, he said:

> Mount Rushmore is a logical thing. Stone Mountain should have been something fine. The sweet, pathetic, poetical memory we tried to build there should have been finished as a dream of a group of sincere men. They failed. We are glad they failed . . . but the story was a mighty story and should have been completed . . . .[2]

In a letter to Isabella Greenway he claimed, "They are hammering me, the various congressmen, governors and senators to get quickly through

Hall of Records being carved in rock behind Mount Rushmore. This formation is separated from carving by a narrow valley. Hall was never completed.

my work here and come down to finish Stone Mountain . . . and two books in the writing and a third planned . . . ."[3]

Early in the year, a young artist, who later went on to turn Henry Standing Bear's dream of creating an Indian monument in the Black Hills into a reality, showed up at Gutzon's door. Korczak Ziolkowski was a sculptor, and he wanted to work with the sculptor he admired most. Korczak was a handsome, strong, vigorous artist who had earned a fine reputation in the East. He was hired as sculptor's assistant and given quarters at the ranch. According to Lincoln, he expected to become Gutzon's first assistant, which was the position Lincoln held, and that caused considerable friction from the very beginning.

Gutzon was on the road most of the time, and Korczak resented taking orders from Lincoln. He had not come west to work with the sculptor's son. He was assigned to the model of the Hall of Records, but being indoors made him restless. Whenever he complained too much, Lincoln sent him to the top of the mountain and allowed him to cut stone on the entrance to the Hall. There are still two acorns flanking the rough-cut opening in the wall of the cliff that were carved by Korczak.

He had been working on the model for about three weeks when Korczak told Lincoln he did not want to continue making the model out of plaster because he thought wood was a better medium. Korczak clearly knew what the reaction would be. It was not his place to choose the medium, and even if it had been, plaster was the best material to use for this purpose. When Gutzon heard about the incident, he realized Korczak was not working out and sent a wire to Lincoln ordering him to fire Korczak.

Lincoln delivered the message. Some of the workers had to risk their lives trying to break up the fistfight between the two powerful young men. The next day Korczak went up to the ranch house and apologized. A few days later he packed his belongings and returned to the East.[4] In 1947 he returned to the Black Hills, filing a mining claim on a mountain north of the town of Custer and began the largest sculptural project ever attempted — the Chief Crazy Horse Monument.

Mary caught a cold in April that turned into a near fatal case of influenza. Before she fully recovered, Gutzon became ill and had to spend several weeks in bed. Friends, concerned about their health and the hectic pace they set despite their age, began suggesting they spend their winters in a climate less harsh than South Dakota's. Mrs. Greenway wrote to ask where they would be spending the summer, and Gutzon, evidently feeling better, answered playfully:

341

Where will I be this summer? God alone knows and he is an uncommunicative blessing. I am one of Hugo's dreams. My beloved mother (what a beautiful thing she was! You always remind me of her) said that I was born in Idaho, but Victor Hugo says, "where the soul awakes, there and there only your spirit is born." That happened to me in California when I was twelve or thirteen, more or less. I have loved her ever since. I have dreamed of nestling into her quiet nooks, wander over her vastness, paint and model the things that she alone awakens, but I have just about given that up. A little prayer whispers to me now and then, "may I be buried there?"[5]

In May Gutzon's sister Anna died. That left only Auguste, Harriet and Gutzon, of the nine Borglum children. In June Gutzon's control of the Mount Rushmore operation suddenly seemed threatened when President Roosevelt turned control back to the NPS without giving any explanation. "I feel at this moment utterly alone, and somewhat deserted . . . ," wrote Gutzon. In the final bill funding the carving, Congress had transferred control of the mountain to the Treasury Department, as Gutzon had requested. That meant the NPS had no jurisdiction. But in May the president reversed himself and signed an executive order returning control to the Department of the Interior and the NPS.

The order appeared to be the work of Gutzon's old enemy Harold Ickes, the Secretary of the Interior, but Gutzon could not prove that when he went to Washington. He returned to Rushmore hurt and angry. In a letter to his friend Josephine Logan, Gutzon saw himself as the mother before Solomon:

I hope you have never known what the mother before King Solomon felt when she was fighting for the possession of her own child, and rather than see it cut in two she was willing to give it to her enemy. For over two months I have been fighting like a cornered puma for Mount Rushmore . . . . I think I have succeeded as the real mother succeeded, but I am not crowing; rather, like the boy who whistled when he went through the graveyard.[6]

Gutzon might have won his point if he had been able to stay in Washington longer. He had demonstrated time and time again that he could influence FDR. But he was needed in South Dakota, where they were preparing for the gala celebration to be held on July 2, 1939, to honor the fiftieth anniversary of South Dakota's statehood. Cowboy star William Hart, South Dakota's favorite, was to be one of the attractions, along with fireworks, Indian dances, speeches and the unveiling of the last of the four portraits on Rushmore — Teddy Roosevelt.

342

The festivities began early in the afternoon with the official dedication and a number of political speeches. Then it was Hart's turn to take the microphone. He presented the Sioux Chiefs with buffalo robes and spoke to them in sign language, to the delight of the crowd, before starting his speech. He was halfway through his speech when the radio time ran out and the microphone went dead. Hart was livid. He stepped to the edge of the platform and began screaming at those responsible. He was rapidly losing control when Louella Jones Borglum, Lincoln's wife, saved the day. She jumped onto the stage, threw her arms around Hart and silenced him with a kiss. Then she turned and led the smiling cowboy off the stage.[7]

Louella may have been trying to make up for another incident for which she felt at least partially responsible. NBC had sent a young announcer out from New York to handle the commentary. His name was Lynne Brandt. He was doing a fine job of describing the day and the festivities for the large crowd and the thousands who were listening on the radio. Toward the end of the hour-long program he found that he had more time left than he expected. To fill in the moments, he began to name dramatically the four presidents on the mountain. When he came to the third president, he said, "President Franklin Delano Roose . . . ." Before he could finish, the hushed crowd came to life and shouted, "No! Teddy!" but it was too late. The mistake was on the air.[8]

Brandt, as it turned out, was a victim of his own youth and a desire to impress two very pretty young women. When he had arrived the previous day, he had boasted to Louella and Mary Ellis that he had never made a mistake on the air. He told them he was the son of a minister, and because he always prayed before he broadcast he felt he could not make an error. That was before he tested his theory after a round of Black Hills parties, which lasted until morning. They had started at the barbecue at the Borglum ranch and then had gone on to celebrations in the surrounding towns. They had a great time, but by morning Brandt was a little bit the worse for wear. As soon as the wires were cleared (the radio hook-up had required all the phone lines in the area), Gutzon sent a wire urging NBC not to fire the young announcer, but he was too late. Gutzon's wire crossed the wire that had been sent from New York dismissing Brandt.

The switch from the Treasury Department back to the Department of the Interior and the NPS had bothered Gutzon, but his fears seemed unwarranted. The work on Mount Rushmore proceeded with little change and no interference from the NPS. They may have been playing a waiting game, because a problem of major importance was beginning to worry everyone concerned with the carving.

The last appropriation had been made on the assurance by Gutzon and the South Dakota congressional delegation that it would definitely finish the work and that they would not return to ask for more money. At the time that seemed valid, but it was becoming increasingly obvious that more money would be needed to finish the project. There was no question, given the amount the government had already invested, that it would have to see the work through to completion, but the need was embarrassing. Congressman Case acknowledged this in a letter to the NPS:

> It was promised the work would be completed by June 1940 with the money appropriated. Judging by what has been related to me, the money is not going to do the job and I am interested that at least we shall be able to say that at least the money was used for the purpose for which it was appropriated, if we have to ask for further funds.[9]

They did have to ask, and new hearings were scheduled, primarily to satisfy the opponents of the carving. There was some political maneuvering, in which Gutzon felt he was being mistreated, and he wrote directly to the president:

> Before troubling you with the petty details relating to our Memorial I want to congratulate you on your position on the embargo and your purpose to create a sound neutrality law . . . . My father told me early in life to "be fair-always, as far as you can, but be on the fair side." And your uncle Theodore said, "where there is a moral issue, beware of a heartless neutrality."[10]

FDR was trying desperately to find a way to help America's allies and still appear neutral. He was stopping all arms shipments and then circumventing his own rules by "loaning" ships and aircraft to the British. It was a position Gutzon supported and had been advocating ever since he recognized the threat of the Nazis. The letter also illustrates the relationship between FDR and Gutzon. They were no longer on the same side politically, but unlike so many others he disagreed with, Gutzon could not help admiring Roosevelt, for whom he frequently expressed a fondness as a man. Similarly, FDR seemed capable of forgiving Gutzon in any situation. Somehow he recognized that Gutzon was not opposing his policies for petty or personal reasons, but because of principle, and that could be tolerated and even enjoyed. Knowing how much

Gutzon needed his support at Rushmore, FDR had to admire his courage. The president interceded in the debate over the final appropriation and the money was secured, but only for the actual portraits. All of Gutzon's other plans had to be, at least temporarily, abandoned.

As concerned as he was with Rushmore, Gutzon was even more concerned with the state of the world. The thought of war was intolerable to him, as he remarked to Roosevelt:

> There is only one service you can render greater than what you have . . . accomplished, and that is, stand like a mountain against sending our boys into foreign lands to die in foreign wars . . . .[11]

Gutzon favored neutrality on the side of the Allies. He thought that Roosevelt's "cash and carry" policy on arms would deny the Germans while arming the British and would keep America out of the fighting. He believed this even after the Nazis invaded Poland in September 1939. He felt America's future would depend on the strength of Roosevelt and the man who succeeded him. He saw that the coming battle for the White House was crucial and was trying to find a way to get into the fight.

He was, at least in his own mind, a Republican, and he wanted to address the Republican convention in Chicago. He wrote to Roy Woodruff, "I believe I could do big things on the platform under the inspiration and prod that would mean. As Teddy Roosevelt once said, '. . . I know a man my age should learn to keep his mouth shut, but I can't. I have so damn much to say . . . ."[12]

Addressing the convention was a remote possibility at best. Not only was he not a power in the party, but he was not even a member in good standing, and those in charge would have been afraid of giving Gutzon a forum. He had fought so many times with the Republican National Chairman, John Hamilton, over issues that Hamilton had become an enemy, and Hamilton was in charge of the program. Resigned to his alienation from the party, Gutzon confided his view of Hamilton in a letter to Ed Rumely:

> It is all right to address the Republican Party — God knows they need address, and it shouldn't be ancient platitudes at the Old Stand. I don't dare say too much about Hamilton for fear we will be jumping out of the refrigerator onto a cake of ice. He never set anything on fire, enthused, or awakened anything or anybody.[13]

39
1940

The war in Europe had become a death struggle. Russia and Germany had signed a non-aggression pact and quickly divided Poland. England and France reacted by declaring war, but the real fighting had not begun.

Most Americans were dead set against entering the war, but they were in favor of building up the army and remaining neutral on the side of the Allies. They wanted Washington to do everything possible, except commit American troops.

The parties were heading for their presidential conventions. A Republican free-for-all was developing, but the Democrats were strangely quiet. FDR had refused to declare himself in or out of the race. He appeared ready to break the honored two-term tradition started by George Washington, but only if his party demanded that he do so at the convention. Because he was not a declared candidate it was difficult for other Democrats to enter the race without appearing disloyal.

FDR was certainly acting like a candidate. Just as Wilson had done in 1916, when the war in Europe was heating up and America's war policy was the most important political issue, FDR was promising to keep America neutral. No one believed he would be able to keep that promise, anymore than they had believed Wilson, but until war actually came that was what they wanted to hear from the president.

The Republicans seemed pleased with the Democrats' dilemma. They felt they could not lose. If Roosevelt ran again, they would have the third term issue. If not, their candidate would be running against a less notable Democrat, who would not have time to put together an effective organization. In either case, the Republicans felt their chances were good, and many of them were seeking the nomination.

Early in the race, Gutzon was backing Bill Gannett, founder of the Gannett newspaper chain and a good friend. Gannett stood for much of what Gutzon advocated, and Gutzon tried to bring others to Gannett's cause. In his letter to Ed Rumely, Gutzon summarized Gannett's program:

Mount Rushmore in the final stages.

The program that Mr. Gannett outlines [includes] "restoration of confidence, restoration of farmers' income, restoration of a sound monetary system, restoration of friendly relations between capital and labor, restoration of a wholesale relief relationship between government and the dependents among our people, a restoration of the initiative and security to enterprise that wishes to expand. Of course, the keeping us out of war . . . ."[1]

Gutzon's health problems began to bother him. He checked into a hospital in Colorado Springs for what he called "a very careful and exhaustive build-up," but which was actually an attempt to correct a bladder condition he did not like to talk about. While there he kept up his correspondence. In a letter to Mrs. Gannett, he wrote:

It is with greatest interest that I am watching . . . Frank's [Bill's] battle for the presidency . . . I hope he will treat it as a battle . . . . Dewey has contributed nothing that lies within the realm of reason or philosophy of government . . . . He has attracted attention through his struggle in the gangster world . . . . *Liberty* Magazine is pushing the G-Man, Hoover . . . . America needs some militant leaders but I wouldn't turn to the police force for these . . . .[3]

Gutzon would have liked to have gotten into the struggle through more than a letter-writing campaign, but as the sculptor-engineer of a government-financed project, he could not afford the risk.

The work at Rushmore was proceeding on schedule. Gutzon was satisfied with his crew and took great pride in the job Lincoln was doing, but he was running out of money again. He wrote to his good friends in Congress to see if there was a way funding could be obtained quietly, but it was impossible to by-pass the legislative process. As Roy Woodruff pointed out in the kind of letter that could only be written by one close friend to another:

> I can understand how annoying it is to you to be bothered with things like budget estimates, etc., but we can not forget that after all the budget law *is* the budget law . . . . So if what I suggest you do constitutes an annoyance, forget the annoyance, as everyone must do at certain times in their lives, and keep your eye on the object only . . . . When are you coming to Washington? Somehow things do not seem to go correctly unless you get down here occasionally to straighten them out.[4]

Gutzon's correspondence with his many friends, and particularly those in Congress, reveals much about his relationship with others. Even angry letters reflect the charm, charisma, and spice that Gutzon's friends found so compelling. His genius was undeniable. Even his enemies recognized his ability to do so many things better than others and his ability to think on a scale beyond the imagination of most. The difference between his enemies and his friends was that his friends were willing to overlook his weaknesses, while his enemies magnified them.

Above all Gutzon provoked reactions. No one who came in contact with him remained indifferent, and very few could resist his power of persuasion. The reaction of men like Eugene Meyer, who carried his grievance with him for over twenty years, is a good indication of how much they had valued his friendship when they were friends.

Gutzon wanted to take Woodruff's suggestion and go to Washington to "straighten them out," but he had a more important matter on his mind. In April Mary Ellis gave birth to a son, and Gutzon became a grandfather. It was a wonderful moment for him, but it was also one for reflection. David Borglum Vhay was born into a world heading for war, and Gutzon was greatly concerned about his legacy. The baby was a direct descendant of Eric the Red, and Gutzon wanted him to have his chance in a world of hope, not violence. As his grandfather, he hoped to do all within his power to make that possible.

Gutzon was writing to FDR on a regular basis, but not about Rushmore. Thanking the president's secretary for sending a copy of a speech he had requested, he wrote:

> Of course what Hitler, et al., stands for cannot succeed. This world would never have reached its present position if the spirit that destroyed Czechoslovakia, destroyed Poland, robbed Denmark, lied its way into Norway and is now destroying in hundreds of thousands unoffending people in the Netherlands and Belgium — if that spirit meant success — the world would be a wilderness, robbery and murder the ideals in place of what we care for. Excuse this but I am so wrought up over what is happening.[5]

Gutzon was not just letting off steam. He was trying to share the insights that he believed escaped those who were concerned with power struggles and personal ambition. He attacked many things and often took a cynical view, but he never gave up his basic belief in man's integrity.

A few weeks later, when the White House announced a new program to produce 50,000 aircraft, Gutzon wrote:

> My purpose in this letter is to warn, and again warn, you against any organization that will assure us in any way a repetition of the colossal miscarriage of 1917-18. The control of spending of the money necessary to create your 50,000 planes, the thought of which I think is genius, is a mighty temptation.[6]

In June, as Gutzon was preparing to go to Washington to fight for more money, the first serious accident at Mount Rushmore occurred. The cable car, used to take men and equipment up to the top, was on the way up the mountain when the main shaft in the hoist house snapped. The car came back down the cable at a terrifying rate of speed, but Gus Schramm, one of the men in the car, managed to slow it by squeezing the hand brake that gripped the cable. The brake came apart, however, and the car once again began to pick up speed.

Matt Reilly, the foreman on the project, was in the hoist house with Ed Hayes, the hoist operator. Reilly somehow managed to slide an iron bar between the spokes of the giant wheel and slowed the car down just before it slammed into the bottom platform.

One passenger, Hap Anderson, had tried to jump clear as the car passed over the bunkhouse, but he had missed the roof and landed in a gully, suffering a broken arm and internal injuries. When Gutzon reached the scene, Anderson was being rushed to a Rapid City hospital. With Ed Hayes driving, Gutzon followed the ambulance into town. He stayed there until Anderson was out of danger.

The party conventions were held in July. The Democrats nominated FDR on the first ballor, but the Republicans deadlocked. Finally, after a bitter fight, they settled, on a businessman with a great deal of personal charm, but very little political muscle, Wendell Willkie.

Willkie put up a good fight under difficult circumstances. The convention had split the party, and many Republicans, angry because their candidate had not been nominated, sat out the campaign. When Willkie tried to challenge Roosevelt, the president would not respond. He presented himself as an incumbent too busy with world affairs, too busy keeping the nation out of war, to campaign. He asked the voters not to "change horses in midstream" and said he was willing to accept their decision. On election day the voters gave him, by a wide margin, the vote of confidence he was seeking.

Gutzon felt that Roosevelt had destroyed a valuable part of America's heritage and had harmed the country almost irrevocably by breaking precedent. He wrote to Ed Rumely, who had supported FDR, warning of America's slide toward totalitarianism:

> Now that the dust of battle politically in America has cleared away, I want to compliment you men who care more for politics than character and principle, who have done an admirable job of breaking the third term tradition and opening the way for some form of Hitler totalitarian government . . . for the first time I regretted anything was holding me, for I certainly would have gotten into the big fight anywhere and everywhere . . . .[7]

To Wendell Willkie he wrote, "Tonight, don't forget, you are the leader of a crusade to restore freedom to the liberty hungry of the world gathered in America . . . . Don't forget 23 million . . . gave Wendell Willkie their allegiance."[8]

Meanwhile, in Washington, Congressman Case was quietly working to secure enough money to enable Gutzon to complete the carving. Case was having difficulty because, in 1939, in his testimony before the committee headed by Kent Keller, Gutzon had said for the record:

> I have promised the commission and I have promised the President, and I will promise you, if there is any more money needed I will go out with my hat and get the money.[9]

The difficulty in estimating the cost of a project with as many unknown factors as Rushmore was obvious. Most congressmen knew this and were prepared to make the adjustments necessary to support the work until it was finished, but those who were playing party politics in an election year were making it difficult.

Gutzon was becoming tired of the battles. His letters, particularly those written to old friends like Roy Woodruff, reflect his weariness:

> Neither you nor I will ever live to see this world on an even keel again or civilization restored to a point where it can feel it can safely point its course and be an honor to the great men who have given it what greatness it has, from Socrates to date. But we are facing Europe's complete breakdown through the grossest neglect and incompetence of politicians, military men, and government officials in democracies. It is only because of the Atlantic Ocean . . . that we have escaped Hitler's heel . . . .[10]

Gutzon finally went to Roosevelt to ask for support for the monument. In August $86,000 was appropriated with the stipulation that it be used only to refine the portraits. Gutzon wanted very much to work on the Hall of Records. He felt that without it the monument had no meaning, but he could not press the issue because of the mood of Congress.

In early November, when work had ended for the season, Gutzon, Mary and Lincoln gave a party for the crew in the ballroom of the Alex Johnson Hotel in Rapid City. After dinner, as each man filed past the Borglum table to shake hands with "the Chief" and say a few words, Gutzon reached down and took a *Saturday Evening Post* off the top of the stack alongside his chair. It was the issue with the profile of Mount Rushmore's Washington on the cover. He wrote a short, personal message, signed his name and then passed it on to Lincoln, who added words of his own. For most of the men, this was the most dramatic moment of their lives, and they treasured it as long as they lived.

As 1940 came to a close, Gutzon reflected on his reputation:

> I have been accused of being a brave and courageous man. I have never been as brave or courageous as I feel. I think I have graduated out of my habitual timidity and in the future I intend to assert and fight, fight, fight on.[11]

His friends would have smiled at that bit of self-analysis, and his enemies might have winced. On the surface he certainly did not appear to have lost any of his ability to fight for what he believed in, and he had never shown a lack of bravery or courage.

40
1941

Gutzon was three months from his seventy-fourth birthday. Mount Rushmore had become the center of his artistic existence, and world affairs his major concern. He was against war, but he was also against appeasement. Senator Burt Wheeler, a friend from his days with the agrarian movement when both thought that Bob La Follette had the answers, saw the war coming and began, at least the way Gutzon perceived it, to advocate appeasing Hitler. Gutzon was so upset that he wrote Wheeler to remind him of a similar incident:

> I have been following you in all you have said in your opposition to the course our country is taking against the greatest murder lust ever invented . . . . There is one single human obligation now before all decent fathers, mothers, governments — *Stop Hitler and his cutthroats* . . . . How leave a job that's ours for our children to correct? It reminds me of the slave question when drafting the Constitution they side-stepped an afternoon's task for political convenience, which cost their grandchildren a million lives.[1]

The letter to Wheeler was one of the last Gutzon wrote. In late January he left South Dakota with Mary and their poodle, Bo, for an extended speaking tour. Lincoln and his wife, Louella, drove them to the railroad station in Rapid City, then waited with them until the train pulled out of the station.

For a while Lincoln drove the road that paralleled the track and kept pace with his parent's train. He saw his father in the window and was suddenly overcome with a sense of foreboding. "I'll never see Dad alive again," he thought, and then tried to shake off the feeling as the road turned away from the track and his parents slipped from view.[2]

When the Borglums reached Chicago, the first stop on their journey, they registered, as usual, at the Blackstone Hotel. They were looking forward to their stay in the city, despite the cold and the snow piled high in the streets. After spending a few days seeing the sights and renewing old acquaintances, Gutzon visited his doctor, who was an old family friend. The bladder problem, which had been treated in 1939 had not gone away and was causing a great deal of discomfort. When his friend recommended surgery, Gutzon agreed and checked into Henrotin Hospital.

The February 17 operation was successful, according to the doctors, but Gutzon did not respond to post-operative treatment the way Mary thought he should, and she became alarmed. Later, when she was writing his biography, Mary noted that, after the surgery, Gutzon had told her, "they are killing me," but she had thought he was just hallucinating because of the anesthetic. Then, she added, "and it makes it harder to bear and I blame myself for not taking him out of the hospital."[3]

As the situation became more grave, Mary sent for her children. Lincoln arrived first. When Mary Ellis, coming from her home in Reno, reached the hospital, she found her mother being treated for a broken wrist. Mary had slipped on the ice while taking Bo for a walk.

Mary was Gutzon's reality. When he woke from a nap to find her not at his side, he demanded to know where she was. Mary Ellis tried to reassure him. She told him that the accident was not serious, but he began to panic, and even with the help of the nurses, she was having trouble keeping him in bed. Finally, Mary Ellis and the nurses decided he would have to be sedated. While he slept, an adverse reaction to the sedative set in worsening his condition.

There was little Mary, Lincoln and Mary Ellis could do but wait in a bedside vigil, which lasted almost a week, until, on March 6, 1941, Gutzon died quietly in his sleep.[4] The official cause of death was coronary sclerosis, but with a man as battle-scared as Gutzon Borglum, it is difficult to assign the cause of death to any one factor.

He died much as he had lived: controversial and belligerent to the very end. The world reacted to the news of his death with shock. Just the day before, the widow of Senator William Borah of Idaho had announced that the senator was to be honored in Statuary Hall and, of course, Gutzon Borglum would be her sculptor.

Gutzon's personal acquaintances could not believe he was gone. To them he was as tough as the stone of his beloved mountain. Messages of grief and condolence poured in from people on the street, friends, relatives, government officials and royalty. Every newspaper in the country carried the story on the front page and noted his achievements. Congress, wishing to honor him, pushed through a bill authorizing his burial at Mount Rushmore. In the meantime, the family placed his remains in a vault at Rosehill Cemetery, in Chicago.

When Lincoln returned to Mount Rushmore, he had much to do. If his father's plans were to be followed, he would require eighteen months of work to finish the monument, but with Gutzon gone and the situation in Europe growing more critical, the government decided not to appropriate any more money and to end the carving as soon as possible. When the money ran out in October, Lincoln packed all the equipment as if he were coming back, paid off the crew and stopped work.

The resolution authorizing Gutzon's burial at Mount Rushmore became law, but the family was not certain he would have wanted to have been buried there. No provisions had been made in the bill for Mary's burial at Rushmore, which Gutzon would have wanted, and there was that curious statement of Gutzon's in his letter to Isabella Greenway:

> . . . Hugo says, "where the soul awakes, there and there only your spirit is born." That happened to me in California . . . I have loved her ever since . . . . A little prayer whispers to me now and then "may I be buried there?"[5]

"May I be buried there?" The family decided to accept the request of the Forest Lawn Cemetery in Glendale, California, to honor him by making him the first person to be elected an "Immortal of Memorial Court of Honors, because of his idealistic and timeless contributions to merit and achievement for humanity and the world at large."[6] On November 14, 1944, John Gutzon de la Mothe Borglum was entombed in the Court of Honors.

Mount Rushmore

Abbreviations Used In Notes

AB — Auguste Borglum
GB — Gutzon Borglum
JB — John Boland
LB — Lincoln Borglum
MB — Mary Borglum
SB — Solon Borglum
EYC — E. Y. Clarke
FC — Francis Case
LC — Library of Congress, Manuscript Division, Washington, D.C.
MD — Monica Davies
IG — Isabella Greenway
HH — Herbert Hoover
EUL — Emory University Library, Atlanta, Ga.
PUL — Princeton University Library, Princeton, N.J.
USDL — University of South Dakota Library, Vermillion, S.D.
MM — Missy Meloney
PN — Peter Norbeck
HP — Helen Plane
DR — Doane Robinson
ER — Ed Rumely
FDR — Franklin Delano Roosevelt
HR — Hollins Randolph
LDS — Church of Latter-Day Saints
RBS — Rushmore-Borglum Story, Keystone, S.D.
TR — Teddy Roosevelt
DCS — David C. Stephenson
FS — Fred Sargent
MEV — Mary Ellis Vhay
SV — Sam Venable
BW — Burt Wheeler
PW — Paul Warburg
RW — Roy Woodruff
WW — Woodrow Wilson

Notes

PROLOGUE

[1]Wendell Borglum, "Borglum and Titterton Family History," RBS; [2]Felix Frankfurter, *Felix Frankfurter Reminisces: Recorded in Talks With Dr. Harlan B. Phillips*, (New York: Reynal, 1960), p.55; [3]GB, "The One Man War," GB Papers, LC; [4]*Ibid.*; [5]Letter received from MEV; [6]GB Papers, LC; [7]GB Papers, LC, and Merlo Pusey, *Eugene Meyer* (New York: Knopf, 1974); [8]Eugene Meyer to O. R. McGuire, 24 May 1941, GB Papers, LC; [9]GB to Sam Cott's secretary and executor, Davis, 22 April 1946, GB Papers, LC; [10]GB Papers, LC; [11]Robert Coughlan, "Konklave in Kokomo," in *The Aspirin Age: 1919-1941*, ed. Isabel Leighton (New York: Simon and Schuster, 1949), p. 114; [12]GB and DCS, GB Papers, LC, and David Chalmers, *Hooded Americanism: The History of the Ku Klux Klan* (New York: Watts, 1981); [13]Adolf Hitler, quoted in *Art Digest*, 1 December 1939; [14]GB to SV, 10 April 1928, GB Papers, LC; [15]PN to GB, 25 January 1928, PN Papers, USDL; [16]GB, *Overland Monthly*, 1912, p. 106.

CHAPTER 1: The New Jerusalem

[1]Richard Jensen, "The Borglum Family in the LDS," LDS Historical Department, Salt Lake City, Utah; [2]Christiane Aldous' journal, LDS Historical Department, Salt Lake City, Utah; [3]Mervyn Davies, *The Man Who Stood Alone* (Chester, Conn.: Pequot Press, 1974), p. 18; [4] Stephen Hirshson, *The Lion of the Lord: A Biography of Brigham Young* (New York: Knopf, 1969), p. 273.

CHAPTER 2: Omaha

[1]GB's notes for "The One Man War," GB Papers, LC; [2]Davies, p.77; [3]GB's notes for "The One Man War," GB Papers, LC; [4]*Ibid.*; [5]GB's notes for "The Saga of Johan," GB Papers, LC; [6]GB Papers, LC; [7]*Ibid.*; [8]*Ibid.*; [9]*Ibid.*; [10]*Ibid.*; [11]*Ibid.*; [12]*Ibid.*; [13]*Ibid.*; [14]*Ibid.*; [15]*Ibid.*; [16]AB to Rosemund Frost, MB Papers, LC; [17]AB to Frost, MB Papers, LC; [18]Jensen; [19]Henry W. Casper, *History of the Catholic Church in Nebraska* (Milwaukee: Catholic Life Publications, 1960), p. 202; [20]Letter received from Richard C. Harrington, Creighton University, 30 October 1979.

CHAPTER 3: California

[1]GB's notes, GB Papers, LC; [2]Bob Davis, quoted by MB, GB Papers, LC; [3]Charles Lummis, "Borglum and His Work," *Land of Sunshine*, December 1895, pp. 35-37; [4]*Los Angeles Times*, 17 September 1887; [5]John Hart, Jr. *Annals of Sierra Madre* (Sierra Madre: Sierra Madre Historical Society, 1950); [6]GB's notes, GB Papers, LC; [7]Isobel Field, *This Life I've Loved* (New York: Longmans, Green, 1937), pp. 77-78; [8]Emily Carr, *Growing Pains: The Autobiography of Emily Carr* (Toronto: Clarke, Irwin, 1946), p. 20; [9]Field, p.78; [10]Bob Davis, quoted by MB, GB Papers, LC; [11]*Los Angeles Times*, 28 October 1889.

CHAPTER 4: Paris

[1]AB to Frost; [2]*Los Angeles Times*, 30 June 1890; [3]*Ibid.*; [4]*Los Angeles Times*, 22 March 1891; [5]*Ibid.*; [6]*Los Angeles Times*, 10 June 1891; [7]*Ibid.*; [8]GB Papers, LC; [9]*Ibid.*; [10]AB to Frost, 6 February 1947; [11]*Ibid.*

CHAPTER 5: Sierra Madre

[1]GB to Emily Carr, 29 July 1893, GB Papers, LC; [2]*Los Angeles Times*, 28 October 1889; [3]Lummis; [4]Catherine C. Phillips, *Jessie Benton Frémont: A Woman Who Made History* (San Francisco: J. H. Nash, 1935), p. 239; [5]GB to CL, 3 December 1895, GB Papers, LC; [6]CL to GB, 5 December 1895, GB Papers, LC; [7]GB to CL, 11 December 1895, GB Papers, LC; [8]CL to GB, 15 December 1895, GB Papers, LC; [9]Taylor & Taylor, attorneys for Mrs. Stanford, to GB, GB Papers, LC; [10]Jessie Frémont to GB, GB Papers, LC.

CHAPTER 6: London

[1]Jessie Frémont to GB, 13 January 1897, GB Papers, LC; [2]Hal Dane to GB, 25 April 1897, GB Papers, LC; [3]Conversations with MD, daughter of SB; [4]Rockford, Ill., *Daily Register Gazette*, 22 October 1897, RBS; [5]*Ibid.*; [6]GB's London journal, GB Papers, LC; [7]*Ibid.*; [8]*Ibid.*; [9]*Ibid.*; [10]*Ibid.*; [11]*Ibid.*; [12]*Ibid.*; [13]*Ibid.*; [14]Howard Pierce, "Gutzon Borglum — Father and Sculptor," *Thunderbird*, April 1946, p. 8; [15]GB's London journal; [16]*Ibid.*; [17]*Ibid.*; [18]*Ibid.*; [19]*Ibid.*; [20]*Ibid.*; [21]*Ibid.*; [22]GB to AB, 12 October 1899, GB Papers, LC; [23]GB to AB, GB Papers, LC; [24]AB to Frost, 21 September 1946, GB Papers, LC; [25]GB's London journal.

CHAPTER 7: After London

[1]GB's London journal; [2]Conversation with MD; [3]GB to AB, GB Papers, LC; [4]GB's London journal; [5]*Ibid.*; [6]*Ibid.*; [7]GB's notes, GB Papers, LC; [8]*Ibid.*

CHAPTER 8: Gutzon Borglum

[1]New York *Evening Mail*, 3 February 1912, RBS; [2]Lillian Whiting, *Sunday Inter Ocean*, 15 December 1901, GB Papers, LC; [3]GB's notes, GB Papers, LC; [4]GB to H. A. Vale, 29 February 1912, GB Papers, LC; [5]*Ibid.*; [6]*Ibid.*; [7]Davies, p. 13; [8]AB to MB, 16 February 1947, GB Papers, LC; [9]Ida Borglum's diary, 29 October 1904, GB Papers, LC; [10]Conversations with Francis Borglum Moore, daughter of Frank Borglum.

CHAPTER 9: New York

[1]Izora Chandler, "Gutzon Borglum, a Great American Sculptor," *Epworth Herald*, 7 July 1906, RBS; [2]GB, "How Your Face Betrays You," written for the New York *American-Examiner*, reprinted in *Butte Miner*, 21 June 1914, RBS; [3]MB's notes, GB Papers, LC; [4]*Ibid.*; [5]GB's notes, GB Papers, LC; [6]Davies, p. 119; [7]Frankfurter, p. 55; [8]GB to Drake, 12 March 1904, GB Papers, LC; [9]Davies, p. 129; [10]Cathedral Committee Report, 18 April 1907, Cathedral of St. John the Divine Archives, New York; [11]Rupert Hughes, "The Sculpture of Gutzon Borglum" *Appleton's Magazine*, December 1906, pp 709-17; [12]Robert J. Casey and Mary Borglum, *Give the Man Room: The Story of Gutzon Borglum* (Indianapolis: Bobbs — Merrill, 1952), p. 92; [13]GB to Heins & LaFarge, 24 January 1907, Cathedral of St. John the Divine Archives, New York; [14]GB to W. R. Huntington, 25 February 1907, Cathedral of St. John the Divine Archives, New York; [15]Huntington to HR, GB Papers, LC.

CHAPTER 10: Six Wars At a Time

[1]Ida Borglum to GB, 23 March 1910, GB Papers, LC; [2]GB to G.A. Taylor, 12 September 1914, GB Papers, LC; [3]MB's notes, GB Papers, LC; [4]GB to PW, 23 September 1908, GB Papers, LC; [5]GB to Wallace Collins, 20 October 1905, GB Papers, LC; [6]GB to MB, 2 May 1907, GB Papers, LC; [7]GB to MB, 6 May 1907, GB Papers, LC; [8]GB to MB, 11 May 1907, GB Papers, LC; [9]MB to GB, 5 September 1907, GB Papers, LC; [10]GB to Richard Tyler, 2 September 1904, GB Papers, LC; [11]GB, "Individuality, Sincerity, and Reverence in American Art," *The Craftsman*, October 1908, pp. 3-6; [12]MB's notes, GB Papers, LC.

CHAPTER 11: "The Jewish Problem"

[1]MB's notes, GB Papers, LC; [2]Conversations with MEV; [3]GB, "The Jewish Question," GB Papers, LC; [4]Isidor Singer to GB, 18 August 1922, GB Papers, LC; [5]GB to Isidor Singer, 17 August 1922, GB Papers, LC; [6]GB to leaders of the Jewish community, 9 April 1927, GB Papers, LC; [7]GB to Davis, executor for Sam Colt's estate, 22 April 1926, GB Papers, LC;

[8]GB, "The Jewish Question," GB Papers, LC; [9]GB to Isidor Singer, 4 October 1920, GB Papers, LC; [10]GB to RW, 5 June 1940, GB Papers, LC; [11]Hitler, quoted in *Art Digest*, December 1939, RBS.

CHAPTER 12: After Forty

[1]GB's journal, 24 March 1907, GB Papers, LC; [2]William Gaynor to GB, 12 April 1911, GB Papers, LC; [3]GB to Gaynor, 12 April 1911, GB Papers, LC; [4]Gaynor to GB, 13 April 1911, GB Papers, LC; [5]GB Papers, LC; [6]GB to Associated Press, 6 March 1934, GB Papers, LC; [7]GB to Leon Dabo, GB Papers, LC; [8]GB, in *Everybody's Magazine*, Feburary 1910, p. 220, RBS; [9]Bob Baille to William Bulow, 16 January 1947, GB Papers, LC; [10]John Barret to GB, 20 March 1909, GB Papers, LC; [11]GB to Barret, December 1908, GB Papers, LC; [12]SB to Albert Kelsey, 31 November 1908, GB Papers, LC; [13]GB to Kelsey, GB Papers, LC; [14]MB, GB Papers, LC; [15]Pusey, p. 152; [16]GB, quoted in Philadelphia *Press*, 3 August 1909, RBS; [17]*Ibid.*; [18]GB to K. Takamura, 13 November 1907, GB Papers, LC; [19]MB to Robert J. Casey, 21 February 1952, Robert J. Casey Papers, Newberry Library, Chicago.

CHAPTER 13: Mary and Gutzon

[1]*New York Times*, 21 May 1909; [2]GB to PW, GB Papers, LC; [3]WW or Dean Andrew West, who often answered inquiries for WW, to H. R. Probasco, 20 December 1909, PUL; [4]MB's notes, GB Papers, LC; [5]Ida Borglum to S. Hagsted, 7 September 1909, GB Papers, LC; [6]GB to J. Munnerlyn, 11 March 1914, GB Papers, LC; [7]GB, in Lincoln Dedication Program, Memorial Day, 1911, RBS; [8]*Ibid.*; [9]GB to PW, 18 March 1910, GB Papers, LC; [10]*Ibid.*; [11]GB to PW, 11 October 1910, GB Papers, LC; [12]"A Greater Stamford," *Stamford Advocate*, GB Papers, LC; [13]GB's article, GB Papers, LC; [14]GB, "What I Would Do With $10,000,000," *World Magazine*, 29 March 1914; [15]GB to A. F. Mathew, GB Papers, LC; [16]GB to W. B. Faville, 3 March 1912, GB Papers, LC; [17]GB to Karl Bitter, 22 July 1913, GB Papers, LC; [18]Bitter to GB, 3 July 1913, GB Papers, LC.

CHAPTER 14: James Lincoln Borglum

[1]GB to W. Howland, 13 June 1913, GB Papers, LC; [2]Borglum and Casey, p. 107; [3]*Ibid.*; [4]MB to PW, 11 April 1919, GB Papers, LC; [5]GB to E. Kennedy, 8 July 1911, GB Papers, LC; [6]Borglum and Casey, p. 105; [7]*Stamford Citizen*, 10 May 1912; [8]Borglum and Casey, p. 110; [9]TR to GB, 12 November 1912, GB Papers, LC; [10]GB, "The Revolt in Art," *Lotus*, 1913; [11]Davies, p. 185.

CHAPTER 15: Stone Mountain—Ku Klux Klan

[1]HP to John Graves, 13 January 1915, and HP to the Philadelphia *Public Ledger*, 14 January 1916, HP Papers, EUL; [2]GB to HP, 9 July 1915, GB Papers, LC; [3]*Ibid.*; [4]HP to *Public Ledger*, 14 January 1916, HP Papers, EUL; [5]Conversations with MD; [6]MB's notes, GB Papers, LC; [7]GB to HP, 17 December 1915, HP Papers, EUL; [8]HP to GB, 17 December 1915, HP Papers, EUL.

CHAPTER 16: Roosevelt, the Convention and the Old Guard

[1]GB to TR, 13 January 1916, GB Papers, LC; [2]GB to TR in MB's notes, GB Papers, LC; [3]GB to TR, April 1916, GB Papers, LC; [4]GB to TR, 30 October 1917, GB Papers, LC.

CHAPTER 17: The War to End All Wars

[1]MB's notes, GB Papers, LC; [2]*Aerial Age Weekly*, 9 July 1917, p. 563, RBS; [3]WW to Joseph Tumulty, December 1917, WW Papers, PUL; [4]WW to GB, 2 January 1918, GB Papers, LC; [5]GB to Haviland H. Lund, 20 February 1922, GB Papers, LC; [6]Emile Gauvreau, *The Wild Blue Yonder: Sons of the Prophet Carry On* (New York: Dutton, 1944); [7]GB to WW, 21 January 1918, GB Papers, LC; [8]WW to GB, 15 April 1918, GB Papers, LC; [9]*North American Review*, 15 September 1922, GB Papers, LC; [10]Borglum and Casey, p. 149.

CHAPTER 18: Czechoslovaks

[1]Conversations with MEV; [2]Catherine B. Phillips, *Paderewski: The Story of a Modern Immortal* (New York: Macmillan, 1934), pp. 317-18; [3]Daniel Tanzone, *Slovaks of Yonkers* (New York: privately printed); [4]*Stamford Advocate*, 26 August 1918; [5]*Stamford Advocate*, 19 September 1918; [6]*Stamford Advocate*, 9 September 1918; [7]*Stamford Advocate*, 16 July 1918; [8]*Ibid.*; [9]Miroslav Velek, *Of Granite Carved* (privately printed); [10]GB to Thomas Masaryk, GB Papers, LC; [11]GB to Jan Masaryk, 18 June 1940, GB Papers, LC.

CHAPTER 19: Armistice and Peace

[1]GB to Paderewski, 19 August 1919, GB Papers, LC; [2]GB to H. Lund, 8 April 1922, GB Papers, LC; [3]GB to William Lemke, May 1935, GB Papers, LC; [4]MB to PW, 11 April 1919, GB Papers, LC; [5]Conversation with LB; [6]MB's notes, GB Papers, LC; [7]*Memoirs of Millard Malin* (privately printed), LDS Historical Department; [8]*Ibid.*; [9]*Ibid.*; [10]*Ibid.*; [11]"Second Bust of Roosevelt by Gutzon Borglum Wins Praise from Connoisseurs," New York *Evening Telegram*, 13 November 1919; [12]Charles Moore, "Fallen On the Field of Honor," *The Outlook*, 18 February 1920, p. 275; [13]GB's notes, GB

Papers, LC; [14]Phillips, p. 358; [15]GB, "Liberator of Poland," New York *Herald Tribune*, 13 April 1928; [16]GB to J. A. Hopkins, 25 July 1922, GB Papers, LC; [17]Edward Blackorby, *Prairie Rebel: The Public Life of William Lemke* (Lincoln: University of Nebraska Press, 1963), p. 96n.

CHAPTER 20: Stone Mountain Resumed

[1]GB to HP, 10 December 1919, HP Papers, EUL; [2]GB to Hugh Dorsey, 3 March 1920, GB Papers, LC; [3]Dorsey to GB, 15 March 1920, GB Papers, LC; [4]SV to GB, 21 December 1921, GB Papers, LC; [5]GB to EYC, 21 February 1923, GB Papers, LC; [6]Conversations with MEV; [7]William Gavin to International Sporting Club, 10 December 1920, GB Papers, LC; [8]Davies, p. 232; [9]Conversations with MD; [10]GB's open letter to *New York Times*, 1 March 1923; [11]*Ibid.;* [12]*Ibid.*

CHAPTER 21: KKK – Glory Days and Quick Demise

[1]Roger Winter to GB, 12 May 1924, GB Papers, LC; [2]GB to Warren Harding, 23 August 1922, GB Papers, LC; [3]*Ibid.;* [4]GB to Forrest Adair, 31 January 1923, GB Papers, LC; [5]GB to EYC, 21 February 1923, GB Papers, LC; [6]Lester Barlow to GB, 20 February 1923, RBS; [7]GB to DCS, 20 December 1923, GB Papers, LC; [8]GB to DCS, 1 October 1923, GB Papers, LC; [9]GB to Atlanta *Constitution*, 23 June 1923, GB Papers, LC; [10]GB to DCS, 23 June 1923, GB Papers, LC.

CHAPTER 22: The Stone Mountain Tragedy

[1]George Webb to GB, 20 August 1923, GB Papers, LC; [2]GB to DCS, 28 January 1924, GB Papers, LC; [3]*Ibid.;* [4]GB to Fred Howe, 7 August 1923, GB Papers, LC; [5]GB to DCS, 8 October 1924, GB Papers, LC; [6]DR to GB, 20 August 1924, GB Papers, LC; [7]GB to DCS, 27 August 1924, GB Papers, LC; [8]GB to Barlow, 29 August 1924, GB Papers, LC; [9]*Stamford Advocate*, 6 March 1925; [10]Randolph Resolution, RBS; [11]GB to Stone Mountain Memorial Association, March 1924, GB Papers, LC.

CHAPTER 23: The Aftermath

[1]GB to Mrs. Walter Lamarr, 8 April 1928, GB Papers, LC; [2]GB to SV, 10 April 1928, GB Papers, LC; [3]GB, 14 March 1925, RBS; [4]Rupert Hughes, quoted in letter from Hudson Markin to GB, 7 March 1925, GB Papers, LC; [5]HR, quoted by Associated Press, 7 March 1925; [6]Petite Mason to MB, 10 May 1925, EUL; [7]GB to SV, 31 March 1925, GB Papers, LC; [8]Mason to MB, 23 April 1925, EUL; [9]MB to George Bernard, 18 Nov. 1925, GB Papers, LC; [10]PN to HR, 2 April 1925, USDL; [11] Homer Cummings to creditor, GB Papers, LC; [12]GB to Lamarr, 8 April 1928, GB Papers, LC; [13]MB's notes, GB Papers, LC.

CHAPTER 24: Tue Northern Memorial

[1]DR, "Inception and Development of the Rushmore Idea," *Black Hills Engineer*, November 1930, p. 334; [2]Cleophas C. O'Harra, "The Black Hills, Birthplace of the Americas," *Black Hills Engineer*, November 1930, p. 301; [3]GB to PN, 28 August 1925, USDL; [4]GB, Mount Rushmore Dedication, 1 October 1925; [5]*Ibid.;* [6]DR, "Inception and Development of the Rushmore Idea;" [7]GB to PN, 3 November 1925, USDL.

CHAPTER 25: 1926

[1]GB to Mrs. Sidney Smith, 5 February 1926, GB Papers, LC; [2]*Ibid.;* [3]*Ibid.;* [4]GB, *Wars of America* Dedication, Newark, N.J., 31 May 1926; [5]J. B. Green to PN, 1 July 1926, USDL; [6]GB to PN, 15 January 1927, USDL; [7]Herbert Myrick to Eugene Meyer, 10 January 1927, GB Papers, LC; [8]Meyer to Myrick, January 1927, GB Papers, LC; [9]GB to DR, 16 November 1926, Doane Robinson Papers, South Dakota State Historical Society Archives; [10]PN to GB, 27 September 1926, USDL; [11]*Ibid.*

CHAPTER 26: 1927

[1]GB to DR, 16 November 1926, GB Papers, LC; [2]Conversations with Clyde Ice; [3]Calvin Coolidge, Mount Rushmore Dedication, 10 August 1927; [4]GB to Boy Scouts of America, Mount Rushmore, 19 May 1939.

CHAPTER 27: 1928

[1]GB to SV, 10 April 1928, GB Papers, LC; [2]GB to Plato Durham, 17 July 1928, GB Papers, LC; [3]SV, in Atlanta *Constitution*, 30 September 1928; [4]GB to IG, 11 August 1928, RBS; [5]Conversations with Mrs. Gardner Jackson; [6]GB to Gardner Jackson, 12 June 1928, GB Papers, LC; [7]PN to DR, 18 May 1928, USDL; [8]*Ibid.;* [9]PN to GB, 19 May 1928, USDL; [10]GB to PN, May 1928, USDL; [11]*Ibid.;* [12]PN to GB, 28 May 1928, USDL; [13]MB to MEV, MEV Papers; [14]GB to Aubrey Williams, 20 December 1930, GB Papers, LC; [15]*Ibid.;* [16]GB to George Baer, 28 May 1927, GB Papers, LC; [17]MM to GB, 27 September 1928, GB Papers, LC; [18]GB to MM, 1 October 1928, GB Papers, LC; [19]GB to IG, 18 September 1928, GB Papers, LC; [20]GB to Jesse Tucker, 24 June 1928, GB Papers, LC.

CHAPTER 28: 1929

[1]PN to GB, 25 January 1929, USDL; [2]GB to PN, 1 February 1929, USDL; [3]*Ibid.;* [4]GB to HH, 12 March 1929, RBS; [5]PN to GB, 1 June 1929, USDL; [6]PN to JB, 17 May 1929, USDL; [7]GB to IG, 5 November 1929, GB Papers, LC; [8]GB to PN, 22 September 1929, GB Papers, LC; [9]GB to PN, 17 May 1930, GB Papers, LC.

[1]GB to FS, 27 July 1935, GB Papers, LC; [2]GB to Eric Wood, 1 August 1929, GB Papers, LC; [3]GB "The Political Importance and the Art Character of the National Memorial at Mount Rushmore," *Black Hills Engineer*, November 1930, p. 291; [4]*Ibid.*; [5]GB to Coleman Du Pont, 17 May 1930, GB Papers, LC; [6]Ralph Bellamy, quoted in Warren Morrell's review of Gilbert Fite's *Mount Rushmore*, 16 September 1952, RBS; [7]GB, on Collier Radio Hour, New York, 18 January 1931; [8]GB, Washington Dedication, Mount Rushmore, 4 July 1930.

[1]GB's notes, GB Papers, LC; [2]Anna Darlow to Frank Borglum, 24 June 1931, RBS; [3]*Ibid.*; [4]Isidor Singer to GB, 17 August 1922, GB Papers, LC; [5]GB interviews, 1933-40, and conversations with MEV; [6]Hitler, quoted in *Art Digest*, 1 December 1939; [7]GB to PN, 1 September 1931, GB Papers, LC; [8]*Ibid.*; [9]GB to HH, 10 October 1931, GB Papers, LC; [10]*Ibid.*; [11]Henry Standing Bear to GB, 22 November 1931, GB Papers, LC; [12]James H. Red Cloud to GB, 21 January 1932, GB Papers, LC.

[1]GB to PN, 6 February 1932, GB Papers, LC; [2]PN to GB, 8 February 1932, USDL; [3]GB to PN, 24 February 1932, USDL; [4]GB to PN, 12 August 1932, USDL; [5]GB to JB, 4 April 1932, USDL; [6]GB to Robert Howell, 25 January 1932, GB Papers, LC; [7]GB, 7 September 1932, GB Papers, LC; [8]GB to PN, 10 December 1932, GB Papers, LC; [9]PN to GB, 14 December 1932, USDL.

[1]MB to MEV, MEV Papers; [2]MB to MEV, 22 April 1933, MEV Papers; [3]MB to MEV, 20 December 1933, MEV Papers; [4]Conversation with MEV; [5]GB to FC, 4 February 1933, GB Papers, LC; [6]JB to PN, 26 April 1933, USDL; [7]JB to PN, 11 October 1933, USDL; [8]GB's notes, GB Papers, LC; [9]GB to PN, 14 September 1933, GB Papers, LC; [10]PN to GB, 21 September 1933, USDL; [11]GB to PN, USDL; [12]PN to GB, 24 September 1933, USDL; [13]GB to PN, 4 October 1933, USDL.

[1]PN to JB, 20 February 1934, USDL; [2]JB to PN, 7 April 1934, USDL; [3]PN to JB, 20 February 1934, USDL; [4]JB to PN, 30 January 1934, USDL; [5]GB to PN, 2 July 1934, USDL; [6]PN to GB, 3 July 1934, USDL; [7]PN to JB, 16 April 1934, USDL; [8]PN to JB, 23 April 1934, USDL; [9]PN to Lorine Spoonts, 12 June 1934, USDL; [10]GB to Aubrey Williams, 20 December 1933, GB Papers, LC; [11]GB to A. H. Smith, 20 April 1937, GB Papers, LC; [12]GB

to Jim Farley, 28 May 1934, GB Papers, LC; [13]GB To Emil Hurja, 30 May 1934, GB Papers, LC; [14]GB to Chicago Association of Commerce, 7 November 1934; [15]MB to MEV, 14 December 1934, MEV Papers; [16]Conversations with MEV; [17]MB to MEV, MEV Papers; [18]GB to MEV, MEV Papers; [19]GB to PN, 13 November 1934, GB Papers, LC; [20]PN to GB, 19 November 1934, USDL; [21]PN to GB, 18 December 1934, USDL; [22]*Ibid.*; [23]GB to PN, 17 December 1934, USDL.

CHAPTER 34: 1935

[1]Conversations with MEV and LB, MB's letters, and Lester Barlow's diaries; [2]GB to Martin, 17 November 1934, GB Papers, LC; [3]GB to Lawrence Westbrook, 2 January 1935, GB Papers, LC; [4]GB to FDR, FDR Library, Hyde Park, New York; [5]GB to MEV, 4 April 1935, GB Papers, LC; [6]GB to RW, 3 January 1935, GB Papers, LC; [7]MB to Miser, 25 April 1935, GB Papers, LC; [8]GB to Meyer, 14 March 1935, GB Papers, LC; [9]GB to FS, 5 June 1935, GB Papers, LC; [10]GB to MEV, 1 July 1935, MEV Papers; [11]PN to JB, 5 June 1935, USDL; [12]PN to JB, 6 June 1935, USDL; [13]PN to JB, 9 July 1935, USDL; [14]GB to MEV, 1 July 1935, MEV Papers.

CHAPTER 35: 1936

[1]Conversations with MEV; [2]GB to FDR, 7 January 1936, GB Papers, LC; [3]GB to MEV, MEV Papers; [4]JB to PN, 11 January 1936, USDL; [5]GB to PN, 4 February 1936, GB Papers, LC; [6]GB to FS, 21 February 1936, GB Papers, LC; [7]GB to MEV, 7 March 1936, MEV Papers; [8]*Ibid.*; [9]Henry Fletcher, 9 April 1936; [10]GB to Fletcher, 10 April 1936, GB Papers, LC; [11]GB to Glenn Frank, 10 April 1936, GB Papers, LC; [12]GB to FS, GB Papers, LC; [13]GB to FS, July 1927, GB Papers, LC; [14]GB to MEV, MEV Papers; [15]GB to FS, 8 November 1936, GB Papers, LC; [16]GB to Hurja, 19 August 1936, GB Papers, LC; [17]GB to FDR, 30 August 1936, GB Papers, LC.

CHAPTER 36: 1937

[1]Joseph P. Lash, *Helen and Teacher* (New York: Delacorte/Seymour Lawrence, 1980), p. 638; [2]*Ibid.*; [3]*Ibid.*; [4]GB, "Eyes of the Soul," New York *Herald Tribune*, 27 February 1937; [5]GB to George Vaughn, 18 January 1935, GB Papers, LC; [6]GB to Austin, 24 March 1937, GB Papers, LC; [7]GB to BW, 25 February 1937, GB Papers, LC; [8]GB to Charles E. Hughes, GB Papers, LC; [9]GB to BW, 25 February 1937, GB Papers, LC; [10]GB to RW, 25 March 1937, GB Papers, LC; [11]GB, in Rapid City *Journal*, 12 May 1937; [12]GB to Frank Lloyd Wright, 26 May 1937, GB Papers, LC; [13]GB to Wright, 9 February 1937, GB Papers, LC; [14]"Sculptor Troubles," *Time*, 9 August 1937, p. 52; [15]MB to Mrs. Manfred Gottfried, 9 August 1937, GB Papers,

LC; [16]GB to MEV, 22 August 1937, MEV Papers; [17]GB, Lincoln Dedication, Mount Rushmore, 17 September 1937; [18]GB to FC, 15 October 1937, GB Papers, LC.

CHAPTER 37: 1938

[1]GB to Helen Fentress, 21 December 1938, GB Papers, LC; [2]GB to FDR, 9 May 1938, GB Papers, LC; [3]GB to RW, 13 December 1937, GB Papers, LC; [4]*Ibid.*; [5]GB to Fiorello La Guardia, 27 November 1937, GB Papers, LC; [6]GB to Karl Jensen, 19 April 1937, GB Papers, LC; [7]*Ibid.*; [8]GB to A. E. Demaray, 21 February 1938, GB Papers, LC; [9]RW, Rushmore budget hearings, 1938; [10]GB to MM, 27 August 1938, GB Papers, LC; [11]GB to RW, 28 November 1938, GB Papers, LC; [12]GB to MM, 17 December 1938, GB Papers, LC; [13]GB to Helen Keller, 29 March 1939, GB Papers, LC.

CHAPTER 38: 1939

[1]GB's lecture tour brochure, GB Papers, LC; [2]GB, Address at Mount Rushmore, 24 May 1940; [3]GB to IG, 27 April 1939, GB Papers, LC; [4]Conversations with LB and Jim La Rue, a worker who was present at the fight; [5]GB to IG, 27 April 1939, GB Papers, LC; [6]GB to Josephine Logan, 29 July 1939, GB Papers, LC; [7]Conversations with MEV; [8]Conversations with MEV and Robert Dean; [9]FC to NPS, 12 July 1939, GB Papers, LC; [10]GB to FDR, 29 September 1939, GB Papers, LC; [11]GB to FDR, 30 October 1939, GB Papers, LC; [12]GB to RW, 8 May 1940, GB Papers, LC; [13]GB to ER, 29 August 1939, GB Papers, LC.

CHAPTER 39: 1940

[1]*Ibid.*; [2]*Ibid.*; [3]GB to Mrs. Frank Gannett, 10 March 1940, GB Papers, LC; [4]RW to GB, 26 March 1940, GB Papers, LC; [5]GB to M. A. LeHand, 17 May 1940, GB Papers, LC; [6]GB to FDR, 27 May 1940, GB Papers, LC; [7]GB to ER, 17 November 1940, GB Papers, LC; [8]GB to Wendell Willkie, 11 November 1940, GB Papers, LC; [9]GB to Associated Press, 2 April 1940, RBS; [10]GB to RW, 15 June 1940, GB Papers, LC; [11]GB to ER, 2 December 1940, GB Papers, LC.

CHAPTER 40: 1941

[1]GB to BW, 22 January 1941, GB Papers, LC; [2]Conversations with LB; [3]MB's notes, and MB to Margaret Thornton, GB Papers, LC; [4]Conversations with MEV and LB; [5]GB to IG, 27 April 1939, GB Papers, LC; [6]GB's crypt, Forest Lawn Cemetery, Court of Honors, Glendale, Ca.

Gutzon Borglum's Works

The following is a partial list of Gutzon Borglum's public monuments, paintings and statues. Many other works are in private collections.

The Rushmore-Borglum Story, Keystone, South Dakota, has the largest collection of Borglum paintings, plaster and bronze studies for public monuments, plaster and bronze statues, finished and partially completed marbles, bas-reliefs, sketches and Borglum memorabilia.

Forest Lawn Cemetery, Glendale, California, where Borglum is entombed, has several Borglum bronzes in its collection.

Borglum's *Nero* is part of the collection of Brookgreen Gardens, Murrells Inlet, South Carolina.

One of Borglum's largest and finest paintings. *Staging Over the Sierra Madres*, is owned by the Joslyn Museum in Omaha, Nebraska.

One of Borglum's major bronzes, the *Mares of Diomedes*, is owned by the Metropolitan Museum of Art, New York City. The statue is on exhibit at the Buffalo Bill Historical Center, Cody, Wyoming.

Borglum's marble portrait of Abraham Lincoln is part of the permanent collection in the Capitol Building, Washington, D.C. A bronze of the same portrait is on display in the White House, another is on the Lincoln gravemarker in Springfield, Illinois, another on the campus of CCNY in New York City, a similar portrait is part of the collection of the Detroit Museum of Art, Detroit, Michigan, and the latest casting is part of the Rushmore-Borglum Story collection.

Borglum created more statues for Statuary Hall in the Capitol Building than any other sculptor. These works include his marble of a seated Alexander Stephens, his standing portrait of General John Greenway and his statue of Zebulon Vance. Also in Washington, Rock Creek Cemetery displays his Ffoulke family memorial, *Rabboni*, Sheridan Park has his memorial to General Philip Sheridan, and his William Jennings Bryan is on Potomac Drive.

Several of Borglum's major works can be found in Newark, New Jersey: the majestic *Seated Lincoln*, on the county court house steps, the massive *Wars of America* in Veterans' Park, and the Pilgrims and Indians Memorial across from the Historical Society.

The Cathedral of St. John the Divine, in New York City, has over one hundred Borglum statues on display on the exterior of the building and in the Kings and Belmont Chapels. Other New York works include his Henry Ward Beecher outside the Plymouth Church in Brooklyn, his bas-relief honoring Robert L. Stevenson in Saranac Lake, New York, and his statue of General Butterfield in Albany, New York.

His major Texas work is the Trail Drivers' Memorial, on display outside the Witte Museum in San Antonio.

Borglum's gargoyles decorate the Class of '79 dormitory on the campus of Princeton University, Princeton, New Jersey. Other New Jersey works include his Newark statues, *The Seated Lincoln*, the *Wars of America* and the Pilgrims and Indians Monument.

In Connecticut Borglum's work can be found at the Stamford Museum and Nature Center, on the marquee of the Hartman Theater in Stamford, and in Bridgeport where he created the Wheeler Fountain and the sculpture for St. John's Episcopal Church.

In 1928 Borglum created a bas-relief honoring the memory of Sacco and Vanzetti. The original plaster is on display in the Boston Public Library. An aluminum casting is owned by the Boston Community Church, and the only bronze is a part of the collection of the Rushmore-Borglum Story.

In the West Borglum's works can be found in Portland, Oregon, where he created a monument honoring Harvey Scott, in Prescott, Arizona, where a bust of General John Greenway is on display in the Capitol Building, in Nevada where his statue honoring John Mackay is in front of the School of Mines Building on the Reno campus of the University of Nevada, in Pierre, South Dakota, where his portrait of Senator Peter Norbeck is on display in the lobby of the Capitol Building, and at the Mount Rushmore National Monument, where portraits of various South Dakotans are displayed along with the huge carving on Mount Rushmore.

One of the features of the Gettysburg battlefield in Pennsylvania is Borglum's tribute to the gallant fighters of North Carolina, his five-figure statue, The North Carolina Memorial. In the capitol of North Carolina, Raleigh, stands his bronze and stone Governor Aycock Memorial.

There are two Borglum monuments in Chicago: his Governor Peter Altgeld Memorial and his equestrian General Philip Sheridan.

Across from the American Embassy in Paris, in a small park, stands Borglum's statue of Thomas Paine. Originally scheduled for a 1939 dedication, which was fortunately delayed because the foundry was not ready, the statue remained hidden during World War II and was dedicated in 1948. If not for the delay, it probably would have been destroyed by the Nazis, just as Borglum's Woodrow Wilson, in Poznan, Poland, was destroyed.

Index

Coronado, 316, 326, 338
Cox, Allyn, 99
Cramton, Louis, 252, 253, 256
Creighton University, 25
Crow Creek Reservation, 64
Cullinan, Joseph, 271, 283, 285
Cummings, Homer, 208
Custer, George, 113, 282

D

Dabo, Leon, 113
Dalou, Jules, 39
Dane, Hal, 52
Darlow, Anna Borglum, 271, 273, 275, 276, 342
Davies, Bob, 28, 33, 53
Davies, Mervyn, 87, 90, 192
Davies, Monica Borglum, 147, 192
Davis, Jefferson, 205, 207
Davis, John, 209
Davis, Sam, 118, 119
Dean, Robert, 307
Deeds, Edward, 161
Demaray, A. E., 328, 329
Democratic Party, 138, 207, 208, 209, 255, 256, 261, 286, 301, 304, 322, 329, 334, 347, 351
Dennison, J. C., 278
Dorsey, Hugh, 188
Douglas, Stephen, 14
Duchamp, Marcel, 142
Duncan, Isadora, 61, 63
Duncan, Joseph, 61, 63
Du Pont, Coleman, 183, 191, 270
Durham, Plato, 247

E

Eakin, Thomas, 41
Earheart, W. J., 20, 21
Ellis, James, 150
Eric the Red, 318
Evans, Hiram, 201, 202, 208, 209, 214
Ezekiel, Moses, 145

F

Faidy, Harriet Borglum, 271, 342
Farley, James A., 301
Federal Aviation Administration, 301
Fields, Isobel, 31, 32
Fletcher, Henry, 318

Forest Lawn Cemetery, Glendale, California, 355
Forrest, Nathan B., 149
Forrest, Nathan B. II, 149, 203
Frankfurter, Felix, 2, 3, 88, 103, 251, 252
Free-Thinkers of America, 278, 290, 325
Fremont, Jessie Benton, 33, 34, 40, 45, 49, 51, 52, 54, 72, 76, 87, 119
Fremont, John Charles, 33
French, Daniel Chester, 72, 80, 335

G

Gannett, Frank (Bill), 247, 348
Gannett, (Mrs.) Frank (Bill), 348
Garner, John, 285, 286
Gavin, William, 183, 189, 191
Gavreau, Emile, 163
Gaynor, William, 112
General Electric Company, 189
Gomez, Maximo, 177
Gottfried, (Mrs.) Manfred, 330
Graves, John Temple, 145
Green, J. B., 238
Greenough, Horatio, 99
Greenway, Isabella, 251, 256, 263, 298, 339, 341, 355
Greenway, John, 251
Gunderson, Carl, 238, 241

H

Hamilton, John, 345
Harding, Warren, 185, 195, 196, 326
Hart, John Jr., 30, 43
Hart, William Jr., 342, 343
Havemeyer, (Mrs.) Henry, 172
Hayes, Edward, 350, 351
Hearst Syndicate, 295
Heins, George L., 76, 80, 90, 93
Heins & LaFarge, 91, 93
Hitler, Adolf, 6, 108, 109, 276, 309, 337, 350, 352, 353
Hoffman, Malvina, 117
Homestake Gold Mine, 242, 296, 304, 331
Hoover, Herbert, 244, 254, 255, 256, 260, 261, 262, 263, 278, 280, 282, 286, 287, 288, 318, 326
Hopkins, Harry, 319
Howell, Robert, 286